DATE DUE

Watch the Skies!

A Chronicle of the Flying Saucer Myth

Curtis Peebles

Smithsonian Institution Press

Washington and London

Editor: Nancy P. Dutro

Library of Congress Cataloging-in-Publication Data
Peebles, Curtis.
    Watch the skies! : a chronicle of the flying saucer myth / by
Curtis Peebles.
        p.   cm.
    Includes bibliographical references and index.
    ISBN 1-56098-343-4
    1. Unidentified flying objects–Sightings and encounters–
History. I. Title.
    TL789.3.P44 1994
    001.9'42–dc20   93-26819
                                 CIP
British Library Cataloging-in-Publication Data available
Manufactured in the United States of America
99 98 97 96 95 94   5 4 3 2 1

∞ The paper used in this publication meets the minimum requirements of the American National
Standard for Permanence of Paper for Printed Library Materials Z39.48-1984.

Contents

Introduction

This book is a chronicle of the flying saucer myth—the system of beliefs that have developed around the idea that alien spacecraft are being seen in Earth's skies. These beliefs did not suddenly spring into existence fully formed. Rather, a set of conflicting ideas originated, the myth was defined, then the beliefs evolved over nearly half a century. Moreover, the flying saucer myth is not a single, monolithic set of doctrines. As soon as the flying saucer myth was defined, schisms began to develop among "believers"—those people who accepted the idea that flying saucers were extraordinary objects. Not all believers held the same beliefs, and these schisms soon led to open warfare. This interaction between believers has been a major influence on the myth's history.

The flying saucer myth not only concerns disk-shaped spaceships and the aliens who supposedly pilot them. Because it also involves how the believers view the role and nature of government, and how the government relates to the people, the U.S. government has had to deal with the flying saucer myth. Presidents have denied their existence; they were a twenty-two-year headache for the Air Force, and were investigated by Congress and the CIA. This interaction both fed the flying saucer myth and brought about the very things the government sought to avoid.

A similar interaction has taken place between the flying saucer myth and the larger society. The flying saucer myth is a mirror to the events of postwar America—the paranoia of the 1950s, the social turmoil of the 1960s, the "me generation" of the 1970s and the nihilism of the 1980s, and the early 1990s. As the flying saucer myth entered popular culture, images and ideas were created which, in turn, shaped the flying saucer myth itself.

The flying saucer myth, unlike myths of historical eras, is an ongoing, living, and changing mythology. When the author began this project in 1988, the beliefs which now dominate the flying saucer myth were only just emerging. Since then, they have come to supersede the traditional version, dating from the 1950s and 1960s. Looking ahead, a few predictions are offered for the future of the flying saucer myth.

Because this is a book about beliefs, it is only fair that the author's beliefs are made clear. I am a skeptic. I believe flying saucer reports are misinterpretations of conventional objects, phenomena, and experiences. I do not believe the evidence indicates the Earth is under massive surveillance by disk-shaped alien spaceships. I base this conclusion on several decades of interest in UFOs, along with the source material that went into this book. This includes the Air Force's Project Blue Book files, Air Force, FBI and CIA documents, UFO books, magazines, reports, white papers, lectures, newsletters, and discussions with believers and skeptics alike. This forms a body of source material best described as official, unofficial, and antiofficial. These conclusions are those of the author; readers are encouraged to make up their own minds.

The chapter epigraphs are from the works of A. Conan Doyle, whose fictional detective, Sherlock Holmes, showed the importance of collecting and analyzing small, seemingly unconnected clues. Part of the appeal of the flying saucer myth is that it allows both believers and skeptics to *be* Sherlock Holmes.

Many people, skeptics and believers alike, provided information for this book. Not all, however, wished their names to be connected with the subject. I want to express my thanks to Thornton L. Page, "High Government Official," James E. Oberg, Jim Moseley, Martin Kottmeyer, Dennis Stillings, J. P. Cahn, Robert Sheaffer, Martin Gardner, Philip J. Klass, "C," "D," "G," "M," "Q," "S," and "Dr. X," Eric Herr, Chuck Jines, and the members of the Orion UFO group, "Sigmund," "Dr. Clayton Forrester," the National Archives, the San Diego Aerospace Museum, California Interlibrary Loan, San Diego State University Library, the National Air and Space Museum, Lee Saegesser and the NASA History Office, and Smokey.

Prologue

> ... in order to give you an idea of the facts, I
> must go back to the commencement of the affair.
>
> —*The Five Orange Pips*

In the fourth decade of the twentieth century, there arose a new myth. It was a technological myth for an age that had seen the V-2 rocket and the atomic bomb. It held that extraterrestrial spacecraft were cruising Earth's skies. Because of their shape, they became known as "Flying Saucers."

The prologue to the flying saucer myth went back fifty years. Between November 1896 and the end of April 1897, people from California to the Midwest saw "Mysterious Airships." Most were lights in the sky with the dimly glimpsed shape of a cylindrical gas bag, wings and spinning propellers. A few people described alien visitors. By spring's end, the reports had stopped and the events were forgotten. Then, in 1909–10 and again in 1913, "airships" were seen over England. This time they were German, scouting an invasion. Other sightings were made in Europe, the United States, Canada, Japan, New Zealand and South Africa. The sightings were blamed on war jitters.[1]

From 1906 until his death in 1932, Charles Fort, an ex-reporter, writer, and self-appointed gadfly of orthodox science, collected reports of strange occurrences, including objects in the sky. They were published in four books: *The Book of the Damned, New Lands, Lo!,* and *Wild Talents.* He devoted a chapter to "unknown luminous things" seen in the sky which might be "lights on the vessels of explorers, from somewhere else." Many of the objects were disk-shaped. He speculated, "Perhaps there are inhabitants of Mars, who are secretly sending reports upon the ways of this world to their governments."

Fort's most sensational speculation was that the Earth and its inhabitants were owned by some higher intelligent beings who visit the Earth from time to time to check up on their "property." Fort also suggested "that all this has been known, perhaps for ages, to certain ones upon the Earth, a cult or order, members of which function like bellwethers to the rest of us, or as superior slaves or overseers, directing us in accordance with instructions received—from Somewhere else."[2,3]

Between 1933 and 1937, as war clouds gathered over Europe, sightings were made of "ghost airplanes" and "ghost fliers" over northern Scandinavia. These were, as the name suggested, airplanelike objects.[4]

In 1944–45, Allied pilots over Germany reported "Foo-Fighters." These were glowing objects that paced their aircraft. They were described as "large orange glows" or "a small amber disk." The aircrews thought they were a German secret weapon meant to cause problems with the aircraft's ignition system. Ultimately, the Foo-Fighters were judged to be electrical or optical phenomena or mass hallucinations.[5,6] In the Pacific, B-29 crewmen reported what was thought to be a Japanese fighter equipped with a searchlight. Finally, it was noticed the light was always to the east of the B-29s—it was the planet Venus, in the predawn sky.[7]

All these sightings were "Seven Day Wonders." They appeared, spread, attracted wide attention, then disappeared as if they had never occurred. They made no impact on the public mind nor did they give rise to a new mythology. Next time would be different.

Ghost Rockets

Starting in May 1946, sightings were made in Sweden of spool-, torpedo-, or cigar-shaped rocketlike objects, often with small fins. They were called "ghost rockets." By July 9, about thirty reports had come in.

At 2:30 P.M. on July 9, a bright daylight meteor was seen throughout Sweden and generated some 250 reports. The next day a special committee was set up to investigate the ghost rocket sightings—the first UFO investigation group. The chairman was Col. Bengt Jacobson, head of the Material Department of the Air Administration. The committee also had representatives from the Defense Staff, Air Administration, Research Institute of National Defense (FDA), Defense Radio Institute (FRA), and the Naval Administration. The sighting reports from civilian and military personnel were collected by the Air Defense Department of the Defense Staff. The committee considered the possibility that the ghost rockets were V-1 flying bombs built by the Soviets and flown over Sweden as an act of intimidation.[8]

During the summer, reports began to appear in the European press. One of the first reports was in the French newspaper *Resistance* on July 19:

> During the last few months the population of the southern part of Sweden, and those of the northern part, have been somewhat disturbed; from time to time, especially at night, bright meteors, traveling at fantastic speeds, cross their skies. Within fractions of seconds these bolides appear and disappear, vanishing into the deepness of space with an infernal roaring.

By mid-August, the ghost rockets had captured the popular imagination, and sightings spread throughout Europe—reports came in from Denmark, Norway, Spain, Greece, French Morocco, Portugal and Turkey.[9] At the same time, reports of the Swedish ghost rockets reached U.S. newspapers. Headlines read SWEDEN UNDER ROCKET SHOWER and ROCKETS SAIL OVER SWEDEN. The newspaper reports also included a few U.S. sightings.[10]

As summer turned to fall, the excitement over the ghost rockets died down. Between May and December, 997 sighting reports were made. At least 225 were described as "metallic" and rocket shaped, sometimes with small fins. Some thirty fragments were turned in as having fallen from ghost rockets. Most turned out to be pieces of slag and none resembled part of a rocket.[11] In all, the Swedes were able to explain about eighty percent of the sightings. The remaining twenty percent were, in the vernacular to come, "unidentified."[12]

Yet there was still one element missing. The Swedish investigators had considered the idea of the ghost rockets being an advanced flying bomb built by the Soviets; impressive, but not extraterrestrial. To see how they came to be thought of as alien spacecraft, we must turn to a strange little man named Raymond A. Palmer—the man who invented flying saucers.

The Man Who Invented Flying Saucers

Raymond A. Palmer was born in August 1910 in Milwaukee. As a child, he was severely injured in a street accident, which left him a hunchbacked dwarf only four feet tall. His childhood was difficult and painful.[13] Palmer sought escape in "pulp" magazines. They were printed on cheap pulpwood paper (thus the name) with colorful, often lurid, covers. The stories were ground out by writers paid a penny a word.[14] In the late 1920s, Palmer began writing science fiction for the pulps. His first story, "The Time Ray of Jandra," was published in the June 1930 *Wonder Stories*. Success did not come easily—Palmer later claimed he received 100 rejections before selling his second story.[15] He became a skilled writer of not only science fiction but westerns, adventures, mystery, romance, and even pornography. This brought in a few dollars during the hard years of the depression.

By 1938, Palmer, only 28 years old at the time, was selected to be *Amazing Stories* magazine's new editor. Palmer slanted the magazine toward teenaged boys and expanded it to 200–250 pages.[16,17] Palmer also became aware of an increasing mysticism among his readers. He noted that whenever "Atlantis" or "Lemuria" (two sunken continents) appeared in a title, circulation went up. He began looking for a way to exploit this mysticism to boost sales.[18] Then he received a letter.

The Shaver Mystery

The letter was from Richard S. Shaver, a welder in a war plant in Barto, Pennsylvania. He claimed that words and syllables of the Atlantean language still existed in English. The letter was published in the January 1944 issue under the title "An Ancient Language?". Shaver thanked Palmer and sent him a long, rambling letter entitled "Warning to Future Man."[19] Palmer rewrote Shaver's letter, expanding it to three times its original length and changing the title to "I Remember Lemuria!". He also began advertising it as a *true* story.[20] The decision to portray Shaver's shopworn fantasies as real was a calculated one by Palmer, who sought to beat the other magazines by capturing the occult fringe.

"I Remember Lemuria!" appeared in the March 1945 issue of *Amazing Stories*. The story described Shaver's past life in Lemuria 12,000 years ago. The lost continents of Atlantis and Lemuria had been colonized about 150,000 years ago by space beings called Atlans and Titans. Over time, the Sun began sending out poisonous radiation from heavy metals. Called detrimental energy, this forced the Atlans and Titans to build vast underground cities for protection. Despite this, the harmful radiation began to damage them and they left Earth.[22] The second Shaver story followed in the June 1945 issue. Called "Thought Records of Lemuria," it described how Shaver had begun to hear voices coming from his welding machine. Shaver wrote:

> The voices came from beings I came to realize were not human; not normal modern men at all. They lived in great caves far beneath the surface. These alien minds I listened to seemed to know that they had great power, seemed conscious of the fact they were evil. . . .
>
> Who were these voices? It took me several years to figure it out, but finally I was successful. And when I finally had learned the truth, they knew that I had discovered it, was becoming informed as to them, their place of residence, their mode of living, their evil thoughts. And since fear is one of their mainsprings, they feared me.[23]

"They" were the Deros (detrimental robots), a race of inferior humans who had entered the caverns and begun to operate the machines the Atlans and Titans had left behind. The machines began giving off radiation which turned them into a race of midget idiots. They used the rays to read people's minds and to drive them insane. The Deros were responsible for all the evil and misfortune in the world.[24] Shaver finally went down into a cave seeking help from the Teros (integrative robots). They also lived underground but, unlike the Deros, their minds had not been contaminated by the radioactivity. Shaver found a group of Teros who showed him thought records which allowed him to see his past lives in Lemuria.[25]

So began what became known as the "Shaver Mystery." Shaver claimed all his stories were based on these "thought records."[26] In reality, Shaver had spent time in a mental hospital, possibly as long as eight years. Palmer knew this (and both would admit it years later). The whole Deros story is symptomatic of paranoid schizophrenia. Among the symptoms is the hearing of voices, often while operating some kind of electrical equipment. Victims also claim "thought waves" are being carried through air ducts, pipes, or electrical wiring. They commonly believe a death ray is causing health problems, destroying their brain, or causing them to hear voices.[27]

The Shaver Mystery was able to give an all-encompassing explanation for the state of the world—it was all the Deros's fault. This offered both terror and hope: terror, because evil beings were tormenting humans for their own amusement; hope, because there was a reason behind supposedly irrational events. There was also an "us vs. them" appeal. Many of the more serious science fiction readers objected to the portrayal of Shaver's stories as real and threatened to stop buying the magazine. Some, however, were attracted by the idea of having some "secret knowledge" condemned by authorities.

The response to Shaver's stories was remarkable—by the end of 1945, *Amazing Stories'* circulation had climbed to 250,000 per month.[28] The letters to the editor also soared, going from forty to fifty per month up to 2,500.[29] Many of the letters reported the sighting of strange objects in the sky or meetings with alien beings.[30]

As more Shaver stories were printed, Palmer began dropping hints that alien spacecraft were out there. In the July 1946 issue, Palmer wrote:

> If you don't think space ships visit the Earth regularly, as in this story ["Cult of the Witch Queen"] then the files of Charles Fort and your editor's own files are something you should see. . . . And if you think responsible parties in world governments are ignorant of the fact of space ships visiting the Earth, you just don't think the way we do.

One would be hard pressed to find a more concise summary of the flying saucer myth. Yet this was a year before the first widely publicized sighting. In September 1946, Palmer told a letter writer, "As for space ships . . . personally we believe these ships do visit the Earth."[31]

Meanwhile, back in the real world, relations between the West and the Soviet Union began a slow deterioration. On the home front, this was a time of shortages and double-digit inflation. In the longer term, there were fears of a new depression due to the disruption of the world economy.

A turning point in the Cold War came in the spring and early summer of 1947. In March, the Truman Doctrine was announced—the U.S. would provide aid to countries threatened by Communist expansion, including military force. This was followed, in early June, by the Marshall Plan for economic aid to the battered economies of Europe. Both represented departures from the traditional U.S. policy of avoiding "foreign entanglements." This new role of superpower was one many people found difficult to accept. The isolationist impulse was still strong, and many feared this involvement would lead to atomic war with the Soviet Union.[32,33]

Since the flurry in August 1946 during the ghost rocket flap, scattered U.S. sightings continued to be made. In April 1947, two Weather Bureau employees at Richmond, Virginia, saw metallic-looking disks on three occasions while tracking weather balloons. The disks were like an ellipse with a flat bottom and a round top. The disk was larger than the balloon and moved at a high speed. Another sighting was made the following month by an RCA field engineer. He saw a disk flying near his home in Oklahoma City. It was flying at a high speed and left no trail.[34]

In all, sixteen sightings made before the end of June 1947 would later be reported to the Air Force.[35]

—   —   —

In late June 1947, a private pilot took off in his light plane from Chehalis, Washington, on a flight to Yakima. The flight would pass near Mt. Rainier. The date was June 24, 1947, the pilot's name was Kenneth Arnold, and the Age of Confusion was about to begin.

The Age of Confusion Begins

Come Watson . . . The game is afoot.

—*The Adventure of the Abbey Grange*

On the summer day the flying saucer myth began, Kenneth Arnold was a 32-year-old successful businessman, married with two daughters. He owned the Great Western Fire Control Supply and flew his own light aircraft. Kenneth Arnold was, in the vernacular to come, a reliable witness.

On the afternoon of Tuesday, June 24, 1947, Kenneth Arnold was flying toward Mt. Rainier at an altitude of 9,200 feet. The air was smooth and clear and Arnold sat back to enjoy the ride. After two or three minutes, Arnold noticed a bright flash. He saw, to the left and north of Mt. Rainier, "a chain of nine peculiar looking aircraft flying from north to south at approximately 9,500 feet elevation and going, seemingly, in a definite direction of about 170 degrees." They were in the same part of the sky where he had seen the flash. The objects were approaching Mt. Rainier at a high rate of speed. Every few seconds, two or three of them would dip or change direction and flash in the sunlight.

At first, Arnold could not judge size or shape. As they passed Mt. Rainier, the objects were outlined against the snow. He drew them later as having a curved front third, straight edges, and a rear edge that came to a rounded point. He judged they were about fifty feet long, a little less wide and only three feet thick. When seen edge-on, they were a black line. The finish was mirror bright. Arnold could see no tail.

He decided to time them. As the first object passed the southern edge of Mt. Rainier, Arnold saw the sweep second hand of the clock read exactly 2:59 P.M. He continued to watch the objects as they swerved in and out of the mountain peaks. Arnold estimated the distance to them as twenty to twenty-five miles. Arnold also turned the aircraft to view them out a side window. Using landmarks he found the "chain" was at least five miles long. When the last of the nine objects passed the crest of Mt. Adams, Arnold found 102 seconds had passed. He could still see the reflections from the objects as they continued south. The sighting kept bothering him as he flew on to Yakima, Washington.

Arnold did not measure the distance between the two peaks until he landed at Pendleton, Oregon, later that afternoon. He found it was forty-seven miles which gave a ground speed of 1,700 mph—more than twice the speed of sound. No aircraft had yet flown as fast as the speed of sound. Other pilots suggested the objects might be guided missiles. Several ex-Army pilots told him they had been briefed that they might see similar objects while overseas (a probable reference to "Foo-Fighters"). A former Army Air Force pilot said, "What you observed, I am convinced, is some type of jet or rocket propelled ship that is in the process of being tested by our government or even it could possibly be by some foreign government."[1] Thus, within a few hours of the first sighting, the working hypothesis was U.S. secret weapons or Soviet aircraft.

Arnold took his map and calculations to the local FBI office, but found it closed. He then decided to go to the *East Oregonian* newspaper. Arnold talked with Nolan Skiff, the editor of the "End of the Week" column. He said the objects "flew like a saucer would if you skipped it across the water." A report was sent out on the Associated Press wire. It read:

PENDLETON, Ore. June 25 (AP)—Nine bright saucer-like objects flying at "incredible speed" at 10,000 feet altitude were reported here today by Kenneth Arnold, Boise, Idaho, [a] pilot who said he could not hazard a guess as to what they were.

Arnold, a United States Forest Service employee engaged in searching for a missing plane, said he sighted the mysterious objects yesterday at three p.m. They were flying between Mount Rainier and Mount Adams, in Washington State, he said, and appeared to weave in and out of formation. Arnold said that he clocked and estimated their speed at 1,200 miles an hour.[2,3]

When the report of the Arnold sighting first appeared, local newspaper editors considered it a hoax. When they looked into Arnold's background as a businessman, Deputy Federal Marshal, and pilot, their attitude changed. The most impressive thing to them was the speed estimate.[4] Front page stories appeared on the "flying disks," "flying platters," or, to use the more popular term, "flying saucers."

The 1947 Flap

The AP dispatch went out in the late morning of June 25. Newspapers in the northwestern U.S. carried the report that evening. The following day (June 26), it had spread nationwide. Newspapers not only carried reports of Arnold's sighting, but others which began to be made.[5,6] July 4, 1947, saw a flood of reports from the Portland, Oregon, area. Several policemen, four harbor patrolmen, and people on the street reported seeing disks "shaped like chrome hubcaps." They were moving very fast and oscillated.[7]

The same day, newspapers carried an Army Air Force statement saying they had not developed a new secret weapon that was responsible for the saucer sightings. A study of the reports had "not produced enough facts to warrant further investigation." The Air Materiel Command suggested the sightings might be due to three causes: the Sun reflecting on low clouds; small meteors breaking up and their crystals reflecting the Sun; or large, flat hailstones forming under icing conditions, then gliding through the air.[8] Newspapers carrying the statement quoted several scientists as saying the explanations were nonsense. The first small seed had been planted.

That same evening, the crew of United Airlines Flight 105 saw two formations of disks. At 9:12 P.M., soon after takeoff, Capt. E. J. Smith and his co-pilot saw a loose formation of five disk-shaped objects. They called the stewardess to the cockpit. She looked out the window and said, "Why, there's a formation of those flying disks!" The five disks flew off suddenly, then four more came into view. The sighting lasted for ten minutes. The next day Captain Smith met with Arnold and they became friends.[9]

The July 6 *New York Times* carried a list of the various hypotheses for the saucers. In addition to the natural and man-made possibilities, it also suggested, "They may be visitants from another planet launched from spaceships anchored above the stratosphere."[10]

On July 8, the most sensational report was made. The public relations officer at Roswell Field, Lt. Walter Haut, said a flying disk had been found. The next day this was retracted; the debris was identified as a radar weather balloon. William W. "Mac" Brazel, the New Mexico rancher who found the debris, described it as pieces of paper covered with foil, small sticks, and torn pieces of gray rubber. With the radar balloon explanation, the "Roswell Incident" was quickly forgotten.[11]

The week of July 4 represented the high point of the 1947 flap. Although centered on the Northwest, sightings had been made throughout the U.S., Canada, and overseas. In mid-July, the number of reports started to decline.

The flying saucer myth had begun.

The Army Air Force Becomes Involved

In the days following the Arnold sighting, there had been no coordinated effort by the Army Air Force to collect data. Intelligence officers were reluctant to begin local investigations, as they had no specific orders. The event that first gained the Army Air Force's attention was a series of sightings at Muroc Field on July 8. The first occurred at 10 A.M., when several officers and airmen saw three silver-colored objects heading in a westerly direction. The next occurred ten minutes later when test pilot Maj. J. C. Wise was running up the engine of an XP-84 before a test flight. He happened to look up and to the north, and saw a spherical, yellow-white object. If the object was the size of a normal airplane, he estimated it was at 10,000 to 12,000 feet and flying at 200 to 225 mph.

At 11:50 A.M., Col. Signa A. Gilkey, Maj. Richard R. Shoop, Capt. John Paul Stapp, and two technicians on nearby Rogers Dry Lake were watching a formation of two P-82s and an A-26. The technicians saw a round object: "The color was silver, resembling an aluminum painted fabric, and did not appear as dense as a parachute canopy." They estimated the object was lower than 20,000 feet and descending at three times the rate of a parachute. It drifted slightly against the prevailing wind. In their report, they said, "It presented a distinct oval-shaped outline, with two projections on the upper surface which may have been thick fins or knobs." When the object descended to the level of the mountain tops, it was lost from sight. It had been seen for 90 seconds by four of the five people in the truck.

Exactly four hours later, a P-51 pilot, flying at 20,000 feet, forty miles south of Muroc, saw above him a "flat object of a light reflecting nature" with no vertical fin or wings. The pilot tried to climb after it, but the P-51 could not reach the object.[12,13]

The Muroc sightings, along with others at White Sands and at atomic bomb facilities, convinced the Army Air Force that flying saucers were a very serious problem. Classified orders were issued to investigate all flying saucer sightings. The information was to be sent to the Technical Intelligence Division (TID) of the Air Materiel Command at Wright-Patterson Field.[14] In late July, two intelligence officers, Lt. Frank M. Brown and Capt. William Davidson, met with Arnold. He gave them an account of the incident and drawings. Arnold was asked not to discuss the sighting and to call the two intelligence officers if anything should come up.[15]

At TID, the situation during July 1947 was one of confusion bordering on panic, as each person was off investigating his own theory. There seems little doubt TID considered the flying saucers to be "real" (i.e., not a hoax or misinterpretation). The theories as to their origin could be divided into the earthly and non-earthly. The leading earthly candidate was the Soviets—it was thought that they might have used wartime German research to develop a high-performance aircraft. A distant second earthly source was the U.S. Navy, which had built a disk-shaped aircraft called the XF5U-1. The Navy scrapped the plane before it had ever flown. One memo written in July asked, "Are you positive the Navy junked the XF5U-1 project?" Non-earthly explanations were led by alien spacecraft with space animals a distant second and a mixture of other theories far behind.

By the end of July 1947, TID's confusion had passed and the Soviets emerged as the most probable source. An examination of data on German wartime research and any possible Soviet developments was started. Only a few high-ranking officers knew of TID's speculations or work.[16]

The Maury Island Mystery

Raymond Palmer was quick to both publicly embrace the flying saucers and link them with the Shaver Mystery. In the October 1947 *Amazing Stories* he wrote:

> A part of the now world-famous Shaver Mystery has now been proved! On June 25 (and subsequent confirmation included earlier dates) mysterious supersonic vessels, either space ships or ships from the caves, were sighted in this country! A summation of facts proves that these ships were not, nor can be, attributed to any civilization now on the face of the Earth.[17]

In the meantime, Palmer received a letter from two Tacoma harbor patrolmen—Fred Lee Crisman and Harold A. Dahl. The letter said they had seen a group of flying saucers and had fragments from one of them. Crisman was known to Palmer. A year before, Crisman had written a letter claiming he had had an underground battle with the Deros.[18] Palmer asked Kenneth Arnold, to whom he had written earlier, to investigate the story. Arnold agreed.

Between July 29 and 31, Arnold met several times with Dahl and Crisman. Dahl told him that at about 2 P.M. on June 21, 1947, he was in his boat off Maury Island near Tacoma. With him were two crewmen, Dahl's 15-year-old son, and his dog. Suddenly they saw six very large "doughnut-shaped" objects. Five of them were very slowly circling above the sixth which seemed to be in trouble. The objects were spherical with flattened tops and bottoms, a hole in the center, and large portholes along their rims.

Dahl beached the boat on Maury Island and began taking pictures. One of the objects descended and touched the center one as if to repair it. There was a dull thud and the center object began spewing out sheets of very light metal and black rocklike material. His son's arm was injured, the dog was killed, and the boat's wheelhouse was damaged by the nearly molten rock.

The six objects then rose and headed out to sea. After they had left, Dahl tried to use his radio but found it was being jammed. Dahl and his crew loaded some of the metal sheets and rocklike debris on the boat, then headed back to Tacoma. Dahl's son was treated at the hospital while Dahl reported to his superior—Fred Lee Crisman. Crisman did not believe his story about how the boat was damaged.

On the morning following the sighting, Dahl said he had breakfast with a mysterious stranger wearing a black suit who drove a 1947 Buick sedan. The stranger said Dahl had seen something he should not have and warned "that if he loved his family and didn't want anything to happen to his general welfare, he would not discuss his experience with anyone." Dahl also said the photos were covered with spots as if they had been exposed to radiation.

Crisman's story was that, at first, he was very angry over the damage. Then he became curious and, the morning after the sighting, took a boat to Maury Island. He found about twenty tons of debris scattered on the beach. As Crisman was examining the fragments, another of the objects flew out of a cloud. Arnold and United Airlines Capt. E. J. Smith examined the debris, which looked like lava rock and scrap aircraft aluminum. They did not see the photos, as Crisman had misplaced them.

By this point, the morning of July 31, Arnold and Smith felt the need for help. They decided to call the intelligence officers, Lieutenant Brown and Captain Davidson. Arnold outlined the story and they agreed to fly up.[19] They arrived that same afternoon. They interrogated Crisman and Dahl and examined the debris. They quickly determined it was a hoax. Not wanting to embarrass Arnold and Smith, they did not tell them it was a hoax. Rather, they said the B-25 was needed back at Hamilton Field the next day. Before leaving, Lieutenant Brown and Captain Davidson discussed the case with the intelligence officer at McChord Field. Early on the morning of August 1, they took off.[20]

The next afternoon the *Tacoma Times* carried the headline: SABOTAGE HINTED IN CRASH OF ARMY BOMBER AT KELSO. The article reported that the B-25, "had been sabotaged 'or shot down' to prevent shipment of flying disk fragments." It continued that an intelligence officer had confirmed, "that the ill-fated craft had been carrying 'classified material'." Lieutenant Brown and Captain Davidson were killed in the crash. The B-25's crew chief and a passenger were able to bail out.[21]

The Army Air Force found that a burned exhaust stack had set the left wing on fire. Before the two intelligence officers could bail out, the wing broke free and tore off the tail. There was no sabotage. The "classified material" was only a file of reports they had offered to take back to Hamilton; the reports had nothing to do with flying saucers.

The Army Air Force also checked out Crisman and Dahl. Rather than "harbor patrolmen," they merely operated several barely seaworthy boats to salvage floating lumber. The "debris" was slag. There was no mysterious stranger. As the official report put it:

> Both [Crisman and Dahl] admitted that the rock fragments had nothing to do with flying saucers. The whole thing was a hoax. They had sent the rock fragments to [Palmer] as a joke. One of the patrolmen wrote to [Palmer] stating that the rock could have been part of a flying saucer. He had said the rock came from a flying saucer because that's what [Palmer] wanted him to say.[22]

The August 4 San Francisco *News* also carried a report that "Mr. Dahl went to the *United Press* Bureau at Tacoma and denied he had any parts of a flying disc. He exhibited metallic stones, which he said he picked up on the beach at Maury Island shortly before the flying saucer craze swept the country."[23]

In retrospect, the newspaper publicity about the B-25 crash was the first to give a sinister air to the flying saucer myth. The talk of "sabotage," "mysterious stranger," and "classified material" gave it a "conspiratorial" atmosphere. The Army Air Force knew it was a hoax and why the plane crashed, but the public had only the contradictory newspaper accounts. As yet, however, this feeling of conspiracy and the myth itself remained undefined.

Project Sign

In the late summer of 1947, the commander of the newly independent U.S. Air Force had made a verbal request for a preliminary study of the flying saucer reports. On September 23, Lt. Gen. Nathan F. Twining, the commander of the Air Materiel Command, sent him a preliminary report. The report's conclusions were:

a. The phenomenon reported is something real and not visionary or fictitious.

b. There are objects probably approximating the shape of a disc, of such appreciable size as to appear to be as large as man-made aircraft.

c. There is a possibility that some of the incidents may be caused by natural phenomena, such as meteors.

d. The reported operating characteristics such as extreme rates of climb, maneuverability (particularly in roll), and actions which must be considered evasive when sighted or contacted by friendly aircraft and radar, lend belief to the possibility that some of the objects are controlled either manually, automatically or remotely.

e. The apparent common description of the objects is as follows:

(1) Metallic or light reflecting.

(2) Absence of trail, except in a few instances when the object apparently was operating under high performance conditions.

(3) Circular or elliptical in shape, flat on bottom and domed on top.

(4) Several reports of well kept formation flights varying from three to nine objects.

(5) Normally no associated sound, except in three instances a substantial rumbling roar was noted.

(6) Level flight speeds normally above 300 knots are estimated.

f. It is possible within the present U.S. knowledge—provided extensive detailed development is undertaken—to construct a piloted aircraft which has the general description of the object in subparagraph (e) above which would be capable of an approximate range of 7,000 miles at subsonic speeds.

g. Any development in this country along the lines indicated would be extremely expensive, time consuming and at the considerable expense of current projects and therefore, if directed, should be set up independently of existing projects.

h. Due consideration must be given the following:
  (1) The possibility that these objects are of domestic origin—the prod-
      uct of some high security project not known to AC/AS-2 or this
      Command.
  (2) The lack of physical evidence in the shape of crash recovered
      exhibits which would undeniably prove the existence of these ob-
      jects.
  (3) The possibility that some foreign nation has a form of propulsion
      possibly nuclear, which is outside of our domestic knowledge.

Based on these conclusions, General Twining requested a permanent
project be set up to study the saucer reports. Until it was approved, the
investigation would continue "in order to more closely define the nature of the phenomenon."[24] At the time Twining's report was written,
TID was confident that, in a few months or a year at most, they would
know if the saucers were Soviet or from space.

By the end of 1947, the Air Force had completed its review of
German wartime research. The results raised an awe-inspiring possibility—no known material could withstand the stress of the reported maneuvers and the reported high speeds. The Air Force's Aeromedical
Laboratory added that, even if the aircraft could be built, the human
body could not withstand the G-forces of the reported maneuvers. If the
flying saucers weren't "ours" and they weren't "theirs," could it be they
came from OUT THERE?

Opinion at TID began to shift away from the Soviets toward outer
space. This was not based on any evidence, but on two beliefs: that the
flying saucers were real objects, and that only a technologically advanced, non-earthly civilization could build them.[25] Yet all this rested
on a slender reed: that the *reported* maneuvers and speeds were an *accurate* account of the sightings. If they were in error, then the whole pyra-
mid came crashing down.

On December 30, 1947, Maj. Gen. L. C. Craigie, Director of Research
and Development, issued an order approving a permanent flying saucer
investigation group "to collect, collate, evaluate and distribute to interested government agencies and contractors all information concerning
sightings and phenomena in the atmosphere which can be construed to
be of concern to the national security." It was given the code name
"Project Sign." The security classification was "restricted": the lowest
rating. Project Sign's priority was 2A (1A was the highest national priority).[26] So began the Air Force's twenty-two-year involvement with flying saucers. During 1947, 122 flying saucer reports were received; 12
would remain unidentified.[27]

Thus, by the end of 1947, the Air Force investigators were, in secret, moving toward the Extraterrestrial Hypothesis, while publicly dismissing flying saucers as natural phenomena and hoaxes. To those in the press writing stories on flying saucers, a different picture was emerging. Whenever a reporter went to interview a person who had seen a saucer, he found the Air Force had already been there. It was clear that the Air Force was intensely interested in flying saucers. The implication was that behind all the questions, there was something there.

Edward J. Ruppelt, who headed the Air Force flying saucer investigation in 1951–53, wrote years later that the situation at the end of 1947 was a series of question marks. "Probably none of the people, military or civilian, who made the public statements were at all qualified to do so but they had done it, their comments had been printed, and their comments had been read. Their comments formed the question mark."[28]

The seeds had begun to sprout.

The Flying Saucer Myth 1947

Strange disk-shaped aircraft have been seen.

They are capable of very high speeds and maneuvers that include 90° turns.

They may be U.S. secret weapons, Soviet reconnaissance aircraft, or from outer space.

The Classics

> But we hold several threads in our hands, and the
> odds are that one or other of them guides us to
> the truth.
>
> —*The Hound of the Baskervilles*

Although 1947 saw the beginning of the flying saucer myth, it was during 1948 and 1949 that the beliefs and attitudes surrounding it took a more definite form. The primary reason for this was "The Classics"— three sightings made in 1948. The first of the classics came only eight days after General Craigie approved Project Sign.

The Death of Mantell

Capt. Thomas F. Mantell, Jr. was a pilot with the Kentucky Air National Guard 165th Fighter Squadron. By January of 1948, he had 67 hours of flight time in the F-51D (41 hours in the previous 90 days). Mantell had 2867 hours total flight time, most in transports. On January 7, 1948, Captain Mantell and three other ANG pilots were to make a low-altitude navigation training flight from Marietta AFB at Marietta, Georgia, to Standiford AFB, Kentucky.

The four aircraft were preflighted by the pilots. None of the aircraft was serviced with oxygen as none was available at Marietta AFB. When the pilots checked in, they did not request oxygen from the line chief or operations. As the flight would be at low altitude, it was not considered necessary. The four aircraft took off at about 1:40 P.M. CST. Captain

Mantell, in aircraft NG 3869, was flight leader. The other pilots were 1st Lt. R. K. Hendricks (NG 336), 1st Lt. A. W. Clements (NG 800), and 2d Lt. B. A. Hammond (NG 737).[1]

At about 1:20 P.M. CST, the Kentucky State Police reported to the Fort Knox Military Police that "an unusual aircraft or object . . . circular in appearance approximately 250–300 feet in diameter" had been seen over Mansville, Kentucky. The Fort Knox MPs notified nearby Godman AFB. Soon after, the object was seen over Irvington, then Owensboro, Kentucky, as it slowly moved south.[2] At 1:45 P.M., T/Sgt. Quinton A. Blackwell, the chief operator at the Godman control tower, saw the object in the southwestern sky. He asked PFC Stanley Oliver if he saw it too. PFC Oliver said, "to me it had the resemblance of an ice cream cone topped with red." The object appeared stationary, looking like a parachute with some red light around the lower part. The operations officer, Capt. Gary W. Carter, was called at about 2:07 P.M. Captain Carter wrote later, "Lt. Orner pointed out the object to the southwest, which was easily discernible with the naked eye. The object appeared round and white (whiter than the clouds that passed in front of it) and could be seen through cirrus clouds." He watched it through field glasses for three or four minutes, then called commanding officer Col. Guy F. Hix, who came to the tower at about 2:20 P.M.

At about 2:40 P.M., the four F-51s neared Godman AFB from the south. Mantell was asked if he could investigate the object. He agreed and asked for a bearing.[3] Lieutenant Hendricks received permission to continue on to Standiford AFB. Captain Mantell, Lieutenant Clements and Lieutenant Hammond turned southwest and began a spiral climb. Mantell reported he was at 7,500 feet and climbing. At about 2:45 P.M., Mantell radioed he saw the object at "12 o'clock high." As the three planes reached about 14,000 feet, they began a climb at maximum power. Mantell was out ahead of the others.[4]

As they passed through 15,000 feet, Mantell reported, "The object is directly ahead of and above me now, moving at about half my speed." The tower asked for a description and Mantell responded, "It appears to be a metallic object or possibly reflection of Sun from a metallic object, and it is of tremendous size." He added, "I'm still climbing, the object is above and ahead of me moving at about my speed or faster. I'm trying to close in for a better look." This transmission was made at 3:15 P.M.[5] As the three planes passed 22,000 feet, Clements and Hammond broke off the climb owing to lack of oxygen. When they last saw Mantell, he was at 22,500 feet and still climbing. Mantell radioed he would go to 25,000 feet for ten minutes. Subsequent transmissions were garbled and attempts to contact him went unanswered.

When Mantell reached an altitude of around 25,000 feet, he passed out from lack of oxygen. The F-51 continued to climb, then leveled off at 30,000 feet. The engine torque caused the airplane to begin a gradual left turn. The turn steepened into a high-speed spiral dive. The aircraft began to break up between 20,000 and 10,000 feet.

The wreckage crashed on the William J. Phillips's farm near Franklin, Kentucky. The main part of the fuselage landed on its left side. The right wing was lying alongside. It had impacted only 45 feet from a barn. The left wing was about 60 feet to the west. About 1,000 feet to the northeast were torn bits of the rear fuselage, the tail and glass from the canopy. Still in the plane was the body of Capt. Thomas F. Mantell, Jr. His seat belt was shredded and his watch had stopped at 3:18 P.M.[6]

The two other pilots, unaware Mantell had crashed, flew back to Standiford AFB. As they neared Godman AFB, Lieutenant Clements radioed that "it appears like the reflection of sunlight on an airplane canopy." After landing at Standiford AFB, Clements refueled and serviced with oxygen, then took off to search for the object. He reached an altitude of 32,000 feet but could find nothing.[7] At 3:50 P.M., the Godman tower lost sight of the object. Reports began coming in from areas farther south in Kentucky and in Tennessee. At 4:00 P.M., the object was seen at Madisonville, Kentucky. When seen through a telescope it was identified as a balloon by one observer.[8] Between 4:30 and 4:45 P.M., a Dr. Seyfert, an astronomer at Vanderbilt University, watched an object in the sky south-southeast of Nashville, Tennessee. Viewed through binoculars, he said it was "a pear-shaped balloon with cables and a basket attached."[9]

Several hours later, around sunset, a flaming object was seen just above the southwestern horizon. About a dozen airfield towers in the midwest reported the object was visible for about twenty minutes before it set below the horizon.

The news of the incident spread rapidly. The *Louisville Courier* carried the headline: "F-51 and Capt. Mantell Destroyed Chasing Flying Saucer."[10] With the headlines came wild rumors—the flying saucer was a Soviet missile; it was a spacecraft that knocked down the F-51 when it got too close; Captain Mantell's body was riddled with bullets; the body was missing; the plane had completely disintegrated in the air; the wreckage was radioactive.

The Air Force began two investigations—of the crash and of the sighting. The cause of the crash was clear enough. At 25,000 feet, a person without oxygen will pass out within a few minutes. The emergency canopy lock was still in place; Mantell had made no attempt to bail out. The throttle was set at one-fourth open, mixture at "Idle cut-off" and prop-pitch at "Full increase r.p.m." All these steps would cause the F-51 to slow down. This implied Mantell had revived and tried to slow the aircraft and pull out of the dive. The attempt overstressed the aircraft and it broke up. The wreckage was not radioactive nor were there any bullet holes.[11]

The Project Sign investigators went to Godman AFB and interviewed those involved. The statements, written on January 9, had slight differences in time and specific wording of the transmissions. (They had not been recorded.) On the whole, however, they told the same story. The object had angular size and had drifted across the sky slowly—taking over two hours from when the object was first spotted at Godman AFB until it was lost from sight.[12]

Publicly, Project Sign said the sighting was of the planet Venus. At 3:00 P.M. Venus was south-southwest of Godman AFB and 33° above the horizon. This was similar to the tower crew's description. The object's slow movement across the sky was consistent with a celestial body (15° per hour). The one problem was that Venus was at only half its maximum brightness, making it hard to see against the bright sky. The sightings made across the midwest during the evening of January 7 were definitely Venus. The flaming appearance was due to its light traveling through the thick and turbulent atmosphere near the horizon. Project Sign investigators also checked the possibility that it was a weather balloon but found that none of these small balloons was in the area.

The offhand, nonchalant way the sighting was dismissed as being Venus caused the press to feel the Air Force had a great deal of confidence in its solution. Within Project Sign, however, the picture was far different. They had become convinced flying saucers were extraterrestrial spacecraft and Mantell had died chasing one. Project Sign began assembling a group of consultants in early 1948. They were to weed out the mistaken reports so Project Sign could concentrate on the "real" flying saucers. One consultant was Dr. J. Allen Hynek, an astrophysicist and head of Ohio State University's Astronomy Department. Thus began Hynek's twenty-one-year involvement with the Air Force investigation and a lifetime as a part of the flying saucer myth.[13]

The Chiles-Whitted Sighting

Six months after Mantell's death the second of the three classics occurred. At 2:45 A.M. on July 24, 1948, Eastern Airlines Flight 576 was flying near Montgomery, Alabama, at 5,000 feet, heading for Atlanta, Georgia. The pilot was Capt. Clarence S. Chiles; the co-pilot was First Officer John B. Whitted. The night was clear with the Moon, four days past full, shining through scattered clouds that were about 1,000 feet above the DC-3.

Chiles saw a dull red glow above and ahead of the aircraft. He said to Whitted, "Look, here comes a new Army jet job." In the next few seconds, the glowing object closed on the DC-3 on an apparent collision course. As it streaked past the right side of the aircraft, the two crewmen saw a cylindrical wingless object with two rows of windows along its side. Flames were coming out of its tail. Chiles estimated it missed their plane by only 700 feet; Whitted thought the distance was one-half mile. Only one of the passengers saw anything. C. L. McKelvie reported only a bright streak of light. Chiles estimated the sighting had lasted about ten seconds.[14,15]

After landing in Atlanta, Chiles and Whitted reported the incident to the Air Force. Their descriptions were a close match. Both said it was about 100 feet long and 25 to 30 feet in diameter. The basic shape was like that of a B-29 fuselage. They disagreed on some details. Chiles's drawing of the object showed the nose had a long boom and a lighted cockpit. The entire center section was transparent and brightly lit with small blue lights on the frame. The fuselage was tapered and its underside had a dark blue glow. The flames were coming from a nozzle and were widely flared out. Whitted's drawing was of a cylindrical object with six rectangular windows. The flames came from the entire rear end and did not flare out. He did not see any boom, cockpit, or nozzle. He also thought the flame became a deeper red and lengthened as the object pulled up. Considering they had a close look at the object for only a few second, these discrepancies were not considered significant.[16]

Neither pilot heard any sound. In their report to Project Sign, both agreed "no disturbance was felt from air waves, nor was there any wash or mechanical disturbance when the object passed."[17]

Chiles and Whitted rejected the idea that the object might have been a meteor because it seemed to show what would later be called "intelligent control." Chiles said the object "flashed down and we veered to the left and it veered to its left. . . . Then, as if the pilot had seen us and wanted to avoid us, it pulled up with a tremendous burst of flame out of its rear and zoomed up into the clouds."[18] Project Sign believed it was an alien spacecraft.[19]

Disagreeing with this analysis was Dr. Hynek. He suggested the object was a very bright meteor. Records from amateur astronomers indicated a large number of bright meteors on the night of July 23/24. The flaming tail and sudden disappearance were consistent with the brief passage of a meteor.[20] As for the "windows," Hynek wrote, "It will have to be left to the psychologists to tell us whether the immediate trail of a bright meteor could produce the subjective impression of a ship with lighted windows."[21] The Air Force project officer rejected this: "It is obvious that this object was not a meteor." He concluded that the object "remains unidentified as to origin, construction and power source."[22]

Estimate of the Situation

In the wake of the Chiles-Whitted sighting, TID and Project Sign thought it was time to make a formal "Estimate of the Situation." Their report became the most controversial document in the early history of the flying saucer myth. The Estimate of the Situation had "Top Secret" stamped across its black legal-sized cover. The report noted that flying saucer reports had not started with Arnold's sighting. Previous incidents included the sighting by the weather observer in Richmond, Virginia, a P-47 pilot and three others in his formation who saw a "silver flying wing," and the English "ghost airplanes" that had been picked up on radar in early 1947. All of the sightings in the Estimate of the Situation came from pilots, scientists, or other reliable witnesses and were listed as unidentified. The report's conclusion was that flying saucers were real and they came from outer space.

At the same time, others were preparing their own "Estimate of the Situation." The first of these was the "mainstream" press. Reporters were checking with their "reliable sources." Contacts inside the Pentagon told reporters that flying saucer reports were averaging several per day. Airline pilots said they had had many sightings. Airline personnel from vice presidents to ramp boys were talking freely about these sightings. It was looking more and more like a "big story."[23]

Raymond Palmer was also busy. He started his own pulp magazine, called *Fate*, specializing in "true" stories of the occult.[24] In early 1948, the first issue of *Fate* (Spring 1948) hit the newsstands. It carried an article by Arnold entitled "I *Did* See the Flying Disks!"[25] There were some differences between his account in *Fate* and his official report. Arnold now said the saucers gave him "an eerie feeling." More importantly, the shape of the objects had changed—rather than disks, they now resembled crescents. Arnold also said the lead saucer had been darker with a slightly different form.[26] The next issue (Summer 1948) had another article by Arnold: "Are Space Visitors Here?" It described blue-green-purple globes of light seen by a fisherman in Ontario. Arnold suggested they were extraterrestrial spacecraft. This was apparently the first magazine article to say flying saucers were from outer space. In the Fall 1948 issue, another of his articles, "Phantom Lights in Nevada," described pale red or yellow disks seen close to the ground at night near McDermott, Nevada.[27]

Fate magazine had a major role in the early development of the flying saucer myth. It was the only magazine at this time to regularly feature stories about flying saucers. By saying flying saucers were from some other planet, *Fate* shifted popular beliefs away from the U.S. secret weapon or Soviet reconnaissance aircraft theories. The influence of Palmer and *Fate* could be seen at the first flying saucer convention, held in the fall of 1948 at the Labor Temple on 14th Street in New York City. Most of the thirty people who attended were carrying copies of the latest issue of *Fate*.[28]

By the end of September, Project Sign's Estimate of the Situation was completed and working its way up the Air Force chain of command. A few days later the third of the classics occurred—a North Dakota Air National Guard pilot had a dogfight with a flying saucer.[29]

The Gorman Dogfight

George F. Gorman was a 25-year-old construction manager and a second lieutenant in the North Dakota Air National Guard. On the night of October 1, 1948, he was flying with his squadron on a cross-country mission in their F-51s. After the others had landed at Fargo, North Dakota, at 8:30 P.M., Gorman decided to remain in the air and do some night flying. Conditions were perfect—unlimited visibility and dark, with no Moon. On the northeastern horizon, the northern lights were visible. It was now 9:00 P.M. and his F-51 was flying at 270 mph at about 1,500 feet altitude.

Lieutenant Gorman noticed a Piper Cub light plane below him circling the football field. At almost the same time, he saw a light blinking on and off going from east to west. Gorman looked for the silhouette of wings or a fusclage but could see none. In contrast, the outline of the Piper Cub was clearly visible. At 9:07 P.M., Gorman called the Hector Airport tower and asked if there were any other planes in the air besides his F-51 and the Piper Cub. The tower called the Piper Cub's pilot, Dr. A. D. Cannon. Both Cannon and his passenger, Einar Neilson, saw the light above and to the north of them. It was moving very swiftly toward the west. At first they thought it was the F-51, but then they saw the fighter. The tower radioed to Gorman that no other aircraft were in the area.

Gorman responded that he was peeling off and giving chase. The dogfight was on. After peeling off, Gorman realized the light was going too fast to catch in a straight chase so he tried to cut it off in turns. The F-51 was at full power and was flying between 300 and 400 mph. The light was circling to the left so Gorman cut back to the right for a head-on pass at about 5,000 feet. The light approached head-on and a collision seemed inevitable. Then the object veered and passed 500 feet above Gorman's F-51. He later described the object as a ball of light, six to eight inches in diameter. He also said that when the object began flying at high speed, the light had increased in intensity and was no longer flashing.

After the pass, Gorman lost sight of the object. When he found the light again, it had made a 180° turn and was starting another head-on pass. Gorman watched the object close and as it went into a vertical climb, he also pulled up, trying to ram. The chase continued to 14,000 feet when the F-51 stalled out. The object was 2,000 feet above him and circling to the left.

Gorman recovered and made two more circles to the left with the object. The light pulled away from the F-51 and started another head-on pass. The object broke off while still a considerable distance away from Gorman's plane. It was now over Hector Airport and was heading to the northwest at about 11,000 feet. Gorman circled to the left trying to cut the object off until he was about 25 miles southwest of Fargo. He was at 14,000 feet with the object below him at 11,000 feet. He went to full power, trying to catch it in a diving turn. The light started yet another head-on pass, then went into a vertical climb. Gorman also pulled up and saw the object traveling straight up until he lost sight of it. The time was 9:27 P.M.[30,31] Project Sign investigators arrived at Fargo only a few hours after the dogfight. They interviewed Gorman, Cannon and his passenger, and two Civil Aeronautics Authority (CAA) tower operators. In a sworn statement taken on October 23, Gorman said:

> I am convinced that there was definite thought behind its maneuvers.
>
> I am further convinced that the object was governed by the laws of inertia because its acceleration was rapid but not immediate and although it was able to turn fairly tight at considerable speed, it still followed a natural curve. When I attempted to turn with the object I blacked out temporarily due to excessive speed. I am in fairly good physical condition and I do not believe there are many if any pilots who could withstand the turn and speed effected by the object, and remain conscious.
>
> The object was not only able to out turn and out speed my aircraft . . . but was able to attain a far steeper climb and was able to maintain a constant rate of climb far in excess of my aircraft.[32]

The investigators also checked the F-51 with a Geiger counter. The readings showed Gorman's plane was measurably more radioactive than several other F-51s that had not been flown for several days. The possibility of the light being another aircraft, Canadian Vampire jet fighters, or a weather balloon was investigated and dismissed. When the TID team arrived back at Wright-Patterson AFB, they held a meeting. Their conclusion was that something remarkable had occurred.

And so it seemed—an experienced, technically qualified witness had been able to interact with an unknown object for twenty-seven minutes. The small ball of light, apparently atomic powered, was unlike any earthly aircraft. It was able to reach 600 mph and dogfight a human pilot to a standstill, then break off at will. The slight radioactive reading from Gorman's F-51 was the first objectively measurable evidence from a flying saucer sighting. And then it all fell apart.

Rejection

A few days after the Gorman sighting, Air Force Chief of Staff Gen. Hoyt S. Vandenberg rejected the Estimate of the Situation. He did not believe the report's evidence was sufficient to support its conclusions.[33] At first, the rejection of the Estimate of the Situation did not have an impact on morale at Project Sign. As the months passed, however, their enthusiasm started to ebb. They now had to be prodded to investigate sightings. More work was being passed off to the other investigative groups.

The Gorman sighting also collapsed at the end of 1948. The radioactivity of Gorman's F-51 was natural—an aircraft flying at 20,000 to 30,000 feet will be hit by more cosmic rays compared to one shielded by the full thickness of the Earth's atmosphere. This increased exposure will show up as radioactivity. The Air Weather Service identified the object as a lighted weather balloon that had been released from the weather station at Fargo at 8:50 P.M. The wind carried the balloon first west, then to the northwest. After ten minutes, the balloon was near the Fargo airport where Gorman and the other witnesses in the Piper Cub saw it. The "maneuvers" the balloon performed were illusions caused by its movement, the F-51's maneuvers, and the lack of a reference point in the dark night sky. It was noted that none of the other witnesses saw the light maneuvering as Gorman described.[34] It was later suggested that Jupiter was the object chased to the southwest. Jupiter, at a magnitude of -1.7 was very low in the southwestern sky at the time, and set at 9:27 P.M.—the time the lighted object disappeared.[35,36]

By the end of 1948, several hundred sightings had been reported to the Air Force of which 156 were saved as worth analysis. About 36 were unknown (although by the end of the project in 1969 this was cut to 7).[37]

The Green Fireballs

As 1948 was ending, another series of sightings began. In late November 1948, people around Albuquerque, New Mexico, started reporting "green streaks" or "green flares" in the night sky. The intelligence officers at Kirtland AFB and at Project Sign thought they were just that— green signal flares. The reports continued coming in, however, and the flare solution was reconsidered.

The night of December 5, 1948, marked the real start of the "Green Fireball" flap. At 9:05 P.M., the crew of an Air Force C-47 saw a green fireball. Then at 9:27 P.M., they were startled by another. It appeared low on the horizon, then arched upward and seemed to level out. The object looked like a huge meteor but was a bright green color and did not descend. The crew thought it was larger then any meteor they had ever seen. The pilot radioed Kirtland AFB to report the sighting.

A few minutes later the captain of Pioneer Airlines Flight 63 reported he had seen a similar object and would make a report when they landed at Albuquerque. He told intelligence officers the sighting occurred at 9:35 P.M. The crew saw a "shooting star" ahead and above them. They thought it was too low and on too flat a trajectory to be a meteor. The object approached the airliner head-on, turning from orange-red to green. As the green fireball grew larger, the captain thought it was going to collide with the airliner and he racked the DC-3 into a tight turn. When the green fireball came abreast of the plane, it began to descend and faded out. The object was as big or bigger than the full Moon. By the next morning an investigation was underway.

The military's concern over the green fireballs was due to the location of the sightings. New Mexico was the site for most of U.S. atomic weapons development.[38] The main research center was at Los Alamos, and Kirtland AFB was the site of the "DP Vault"—the atomic bomb storage site.[39] The security implications made it critical to determine if the green fireballs were only meteors, or were Soviet or from outer space.

Because the green fireballs resembled meteors, the intelligence officers at Kirtland AFB called Dr. Lincoln La Paz, director of the University of New Mexico's Institute of Meteoritics. During the 1947 flap, he had also made a flying saucer sighting.[40] La Paz and a team of intelligence officers began interviewing witnesses. It was determined that a total of eight green fireballs had been seen. One of them was more spectacular and caused most of the reports. After several days of nonstop work, La Paz had plotted the object's impact point. The team searched the area repeatedly but no meteorite turned up. At this point, La Paz began to doubt that the green fireballs were meteors.

Throughout December 1948 and January 1949, the green fireball sightings were being made almost every night. The sighting reports sent to Project Sign indicated that the green fireballs were being seen only in the Albuquerque area. A Los Alamos Laboratory staff member saw one while flying his Navion light plane north of Santa Fe. He described it as follows:

> Take a soft ball and paint it with some kind of fluorescent paint that will glow a bright green in the dark, then have someone take the ball out about 100 feet in front of you and about 10 feet above you. Have him throw the ball right at your face, as hard as he can throw it. That's what a green fireball looks like.[41]

In mid-February 1949, a meeting was held at Los Alamos to discuss the green fireballs. Making up the group were military officers, Los Alamos scientists, La Paz, Dr. Joseph Kaplan, an expert on the physics of the upper atmosphere, and Dr. Edward Teller, who was then doing preliminary work on a hydrogen bomb. Most had seen a green fireball.

La Paz led a group who believed the green fireballs were not natural objects. He based this on three points—the trajectory was too flat, the color was too green, and no debris had been found at the estimated impact point. It was suggested that the green fireballs might be test vehicles from the flying saucers, learning more about reentering into the Earth's atmosphere.

Most of the people at the meeting felt the green fireballs were simply unusual meteors. Green meteors, although not common, were known. The "too flat" trajectory was a question of perspective; from some viewpoints, a curved flight path looks flat. Not finding meteor fragments was not that unusual either. The large number of green fireball sightings was due to clear weather over the southwest during December 1948 and January 1949.

After two days, the meeting concluded the green fireballs were a natural phenomenon. La Paz's theories were considered but were felt to lack evidence. It was recommended the Air Force Cambridge Research Laboratory set up a program to photograph the green fireballs and measure their speed, altitude and size. It was called Project Twinkle and initial work began in the summer of 1949.

Factions

The spacecraft vs. natural phenomenon debate had, by this time, also split Project Sign into factions. On one side were those who still believed flying saucers were interplanetary spaceships. This group included generals, high-ranking civilians, and scientists—they were not "crackpots." They were undaunted by the rejection of the Estimate of the Situation and the failure to find proof. On the other side were the skeptics. Many were "ex-believers." When the early sightings were made, they had been convinced flying saucers were spaceships. But, as time passed and no proof was found, they changed their minds. As far as the skeptics were concerned, the green fireballs were the final mystery. The Los Alamos meeting had shown they were meteors and the entire subject could now be dismissed.[42]

The two sides fought over the sightings. Their struggle can be seen in the differing opinions over the Arnold sighting. Dr. J. Allen Hynek found a basic flaw in the account. For Arnold's 1,700 mph timing to be accurate, the objects had to be twenty to twenty-five miles away. Yet at this distance, an object forty-five to fifty feet long would not be visible to the naked eye. If Arnold's size estimate of forty-five to fifty feet was correct, the nine disks had to be less than a mile away. Clearly, either the distance or size estimates had to be wrong. Hynek concluded that the objects were airplanes flying at subsonic speed.[43]

The pro-saucer side argued that Arnold knew where the objects were—he was familiar with the area. Also, he said at one point that the objects passed behind a mountain peak. This would confirm that the disks were twenty to twenty-five miles away rather than nearby objects seen against the more distant mountains. This, in turn, would confirm the 1,700 mph timing.[44]

The believers had a basic weakness—for the past year and a half they had been looking for proof and had failed. General Vandenberg had rejected what they considered their best evidence. The skeptics, in contrast, had been able to show that many of the reports were really of Venus, balloons, or other ordinary objects—why not all of them? This certainly fit the facts and explained the lack of evidence. By early 1949, the skeptics had gained predominance.

Project Grudge

With the change in prevailing opinion came a new name. On February 11, 1949, an order was issued changing it from Project Sign to "Project Grudge."[45,46] Also in February, the Project Sign staff completed their final report. Classified "Secret," it reflected the factions within the project. On one hand it stated:

> The possibility that some of the incidents may represent technical developments far in advance of knowledge available to engineers and scientists of this country has been considered. No facts are available to personnel at this Command that will permit an objective assessment of this possibility. All information so far presented on the possible existence of space ships from another planet or of aircraft propelled by an advanced type of atomic power plant have been largely conjecture.

Yet, the report also included a detailed engineering analysis of a disk-shaped aircraft. It read in part:

> The disk or circular planform has not been used . . . for the reason that the induced drag . . . would apparently be excessively high. . . . the maximum possible lift coefficient to be expected from such low aspect ratio planforms should be poor. In addition, . . . [a disk] would present difficult design problems, to achieve static longitudinal stability. . . .
> Thus, performance in climb, at altitude and for long-range conditions

would be relatively poor, although high speed would be little affected. . . .

At supersonic speeds, where the induced drag is small, the circular plan-form offers the probability of reduced drag.

A similar engineering study of cylindrical objects was based on Chiles and Whitted's ten-second encounter. It read in part:

> While the cigar or torpedo-shaped body represents an efficient form for the fuselage of an airplane or the body of a guided missile, in neither case has it been used as a primary-lift producing surface. However . . . a fuselage of the dimensions reported by Eastern Airlines pilots Whitted and Chiles in the Montgomery, Alabama incident could support a load comparable to the weight of an aircraft of this size at flying speeds in the subsonic range. . . .
>
> While no stabilizing fins were apparent on the "flying fuselage" reported by Whitted and Chiles, it is possible that vanes within the jet, operated by a gyroservo system could have provided static stability, longitudinally, directionally and laterally. . . .
>
> The propulsive system of this type of vehicle would appear to be a jet or rocket engine. The specific fuel consumption of engines of this type would be rather high. . . . If this type of unidentified aerial object has extremely long range, it is probable that the method of propulsion is one which is far in advance of presently known engines.

Based on study of 243 U.S. reports and 30 foreign sightings, Project Sign recommended:

> Future activity on this project should be carried on at the minimum level necessary to record, summarize, and evaluate the data received on future reports and to complete the specialized investigations now in progress. When and if a sufficient number of incidents are solved to indicate that these sightings do not represent a threat to the security of the nation, the assignment of special project status to the activity could be terminated. Future investigations of reports would then be handled on a routine basis like any other intelligence work.[47]

The final report also included two scientific overviews of the subject. The first, by Prof. George E. Valley of the Massachusetts Institute of Technology and the Air Force Scientific Advisory Board, covered a number of areas. He found that "rays" and "beams" were not a practical flying saucer propulsion system as they would require considerably more power than was available worldwide. Magnetic propulsion systems were also not practical. Finally, an antigravity shield seemed to be ruled out by the theory of general relativity.

As for possible causes, Valley looked at natural phenomena and hallucinatory or psychological factors. He suggested comparing the rate of sightings during the 1947 flap to the curve of crank letters. About the Soviet secret weapon theory, he wrote that, if true, "we would have plenty to worry about. It is the author's opinion that only an accidental discovery of a degree of novelty never before achieved could suffice to explain such devices. It is doubtful whether a potential enemy would arouse our curiosity in so idle a fashion."

Concerning alien spacecraft:

> If there is an extraterrestrial civilization which can make such objects as are reported then it is most probable that its development is far in advance of ours. This argument can be supported on probability arguments alone without recourse to astronomical hypotheses.
>
> Such a civilization might observe that on Earth we now have atomic bombs and are fast developing rockets. In view of the past history of mankind, they should be alarmed. We should, therefore, expect at this time above all to behold such visitations.
>
> Since the acts of mankind most easily observed from a distance are A-bomb explosions we should expect some relation to obtain between the time of A-bomb explosions, the time at which space ships are seen and the time required for such ships to arrive and return to home-base.

The possibility of extraterrestrial civilizations and their interest in atomic bomb tests was dealt with more extensively in the second of the overviews. Written by Dr. James E. Lipp of the Rand Corporation, it noted:

> The first flying objects were sighted in the Spring of 1947, after a total of 5 atomic bomb explosions, i.e., Alamogordo, Hiroshima, Nagasaki, Crossroads A and Crossroads B. Of these, the first two were in positions to be seen from Mars, the third was very doubtful (at the edge of the Earth's disc in daylight) and the last two were on the wrong side of Earth.

Lipp also raised the question of why "they" had just flitted about in the skies of Earth without making contact:

> It is hard to believe that any technically accomplished race would come here, flaunt its ability in mysterious ways and then simply go away. To this writer, long-time practice of space travel implies advanced engineering and science, weapons and ways of thinking. It is not plausible (as many fiction writers do) to mix space ships and broadswords. Furthermore, a race which had enough initiative to explore among the planets would hardly be too timid to follow through when the job was accomplished.

He concluded:

> The lack of purpose apparent in the various episodes is also puzzling. Only one motive can be assigned; that the spacemen are "feeling out" our defenses without wanting to be belligerent. If so, they must have been satisfied long ago that we can't catch them. It seems fruitless for them to keep repeating the same experiment.
>
> Although visits from outer space are believed to be possible, they are believed to be very improbable. In particular, the actions attributed to the "fly-

ing objects" reported during 1947 and 1948 seem inconsistent with the requirements for space travel.

Lipp's comments are interesting for a number of reasons. They may be the first U.S. government-sponsored study of life in the universe. Lipp concluded that while civilizations on Mars or Venus were unlikely owing to the harsh conditions, the majority of stars were suitable for the potential development of life.[48]

From the Project Sign final report it is possible to trace "official attitudes" on flying saucers. The scientific community was open to the idea of alien civilizations and the possibility of interstellar travel, but was skeptical about flying saucers. The Air Force was of two minds, reflecting the split within the project. On one hand, there was no proof (such as a crashed disk) that flying saucers were real. Yet on the other, the objects were described in engineering terms that implied they were real.

These events unfolded against a threatening international and domestic situation. By the spring of 1948, disagreements between the West and the Soviets over the occupation of Germany had reached an impasse. On June 24, 1948, all ground traffic between the Western occupation zones and Berlin, deep inside the Soviet zone, was halted. The Berlin Blockade had started. The Berlin Airlift continued until May 12, 1949, when the blockade was lifted.[49]

On the domestic front, the "Age of Suspicion" was beginning. In August 1948, Elizabeth Bentley, a former courier for Soviet intelligence, named thirty-seven former government officials as Soviet spies. Whittaker Chambers named Alger Hiss, former adviser to President Franklin D. Roosevelt and the U.S. delegation to the U.N., as a communist and a Soviet spy. On December 15, 1948, Hiss was indicted.[50] On March 4, 1949, Judith Coplon, a Justice Department employee, was arrested as a Soviet spy.[51] An atmosphere of suspicion had been created. And suspicion of conspiracy and cover-up was about to become central to the flying saucer myth.

Suspicions

As Project Grudge got underway in late February 1949, its staff had different attitudes from the believers of Project Sign. Ruppelt described this period as the "dark ages." He depicted the investigators as determined to solve every case, no matter how lame the explanation. Although this may be an exaggeration, it is clear that Air Force interest in flying saucers had faded.

There was another difference. Project Sign, believing flying saucers were real, had kept its conclusions secret. The Project Grudge staff embarked on a public relations effort to ease public concerns. A number of writers had approached the Air Force seeking information on flying saucers. All of them were seen as believers, however, and it was not until Sidney Shalett, a writer with the *Saturday Evening Post* asked, that the Air Force agreed to help. Shalett spent some two months researching the subject. (Because the code word "Grudge" was classified, Shalett used the term "Project Saucer" to refer to the Air Force investigation.)[52]

The Air Force began its public relations campaign against the flying saucer myth on April 27, 1949. A long press release was issued which detailed the Air Force's investigation. It was based on Hynek's solutions to specific sightings and the Project Sign final report.[53]

The first part of Shalett's two-part article, titled "What You Can Believe About Flying Saucers," came out on April 30. It began by using such terms as "the Great Flying Saucer Scare," "full blown screwiness" and "fearsome freaks." He said that public furor grew to such a point that the Air Force "with considerable and understandable reluctance" set up "Project Saucer" in January 1948. So far, Shalett wrote, they had "some 250 instances of 'unidentified flying objects'." (This was the first public use of the term "UFO".) After talking with the investigators Shalett concluded, "I have found that if there is a scrap of bona fide evidence to support the notion that our inventive geniuses or any potential enemy, on this or any other planet, is spewing saucers over America, the Air Force has been unable to locate it."

Considerable space was devoted to the Mantell crash. Shalett concluded that Mantell had died while chasing either Venus or a Navy Skyhook balloon launched from Minneapolis, Minnesota. Shalett described some of the causes of sightings—some twenty-five percent were astronomical (stars, planets and meteors) while a similar percent were balloons (both small weather balloons and the huge Skyhooks). The Skyhooks were 100 feet tall and 70 feet in diameter. A scientist told Shalett, "At sunset the balloons glow like a huge evening star in the reflected rays of the Sun. . . . Thousands of people in the Minneapolis area have observed this phenomenon with mixed emotions, ranging from mild interest to terror."

Shalett also noted the emotionalism surrounding the saucers: "However, the investigating authorities have learned that all the logic in the world will not convince the witness who wants to believe that the thing he sighted was something sinister or maybe interplanetary."[54]

Part 2 appeared in the May 7, 1949, issue. To explain how experienced pilots could be fooled, Shalett noted the aeromedical effects of high-altitude and high-speed flight. Shalett gave a long account of the Gorman sighting and a similar one that occurred near Washington, D.C., on November 18, 1948. To check that a balloon could seem to become a high-speed maneuvering saucer, Shalett asked a pilot to make several passes at a weather balloon. Shalett reported: "He came down and told me, with some surprise, it definitely appeared to be turning at the same rate as his plane, and at times it even seemed to be turning faster than his aircraft."[55]

Shalett's articles had a critical, but today little-remembered, role in the development of the flying saucer myth. Among the press, it was known that the Air Force was very interested in flying saucer reports but there was little information on its investigation or conclusions. The press release and the Shalett article were the Air Force's first detailed public statement on the subject of flying saucers. As far as the Air Force was concerned, UFOs were not real, the matter was closed, and Project Grudge became largely dormant.

Some in the public and press disagreed. To them the Shalett article seemed contradictory. The description of how reluctantly the Air Force had been dragged into investigating flying saucers did not jibe with their high level of interest in late 1947 and during 1948. Now suddenly, the Air Force was saying there was nothing to them. Yet it was still investigating the sightings. "Reliable sources" in the military told reporters they did not "buy" the article.

The suspicion grew that there might be more, that the article was an attempt by the Air Force to hide what it "really" knew. The Shalett article caused the vague, undefined suspicions that had been growing since the 1947 flap to bloom. Several writers, believing they were on the trail of the story of the millennium, started their own investigations.[56]

So by the spring of 1949, all the elements of the flying saucer myth were in place. Yet it was still undefined. Each person had his own version based on what they had read or heard or thought about the subject. There were common threads but not a set of standardized beliefs.

The Flying Saucer Myth 1948–1949

Basic Beliefs

Strange disk-shaped aircraft have been seen.

The flying saucers have speed and maneuverability far beyond those of conventional aircraft, including 90° turns.

Beliefs Not Fully Accepted

Flying saucers are extraterrestrial space ships.

The Air Force knows more about the saucers than it has admitted.

The Myth Defined

We must define the situation a little more clearly.
It may bear some more innocent interpretation.

—*The Adventure of the Red Circle*

The events which defined the flying saucer myth were set in motion by a telegram addressed to Donald E. Keyhoe, a free-lance writer. It read:

NEW YORK N.Y., MAY 9, 1949

HAVE BEEN INVESTIGATING FLYING SAUCER MYSTERY. FIRST TIP HINTED GIGANTIC HOAX TO COVER UP OFFICIAL SECRET. BELIEVE IT MAY HAVE BEEN PLANTED TO HIDE REAL ANSWER. LOOKS LIKE TERRIFIC STORY. CAN YOU TAKE OVER WASHINGTON END?

KEN W. PURDY, EDITOR, TRUE MAGAZINE[1]

Keyhoe was born in 1897 and graduated from the Naval Academy at Annapolis in 1919. He served in the Marine Corps as a pilot. In 1923 he was injured in a plane crash and retired as a Major. In 1927, as chief of information for the Department of Commerce, Keyhoe had accompanied Charles Lindbergh on his U.S. tour after the trans-Atlantic flight. The following year he wrote a book called *Flying with Lindbergh*. During the 1930s and 1940s, Keyhoe was a free-lance aviation writer.[2,3] Like many others, he also wrote for the pulps.[4] In the 1940s he wrote on Axis espionage and Communist activities. One of these articles was "Hitler's Plan to Seize the United States Merchant Marine" in the January 1941 *Cosmopolitan*. It claimed the FBI had knowledge of the plot. In fact, no such conspiracy existed.[5] Keyhoe continued free-lance writing after World War II, but the pulps were dying.[6] By early 1949, Keyhoe was having problems making ends meet and was looking for ideas. Then the *True* telegram arrived and changed everything.

A Question of Methods

Keyhoe met with Ken Purdy the day after receiving his telegram. Purdy was suspicious that the Air Force was covering up what it knew about flying saucers. His suspicions centered on the *Saturday Evening Post* articles and the Air Force press release:

> For fifteen months Project "Saucer" is buttoned up tight. Top secret. Then suddenly [Defense Secretary John] Forrestal gets the *Saturday Evening Post* to run two articles, brushing the whole thing off. The first piece hits the stands—and what happens?
>
> That same day, the Air Force rushes out this Project "Saucer" report. It admits they haven't identified the disks in any important cases. They say it's still serious enough . . . "to require constant vigilance by Project 'Saucer' personnel and the civilian population."

As for the Air Force press release, Purdy said, "The report contradicts itself. It looks as if they're trying to warn people and yet they're scared to say too much."

As the meeting ended, Purdy gave Keyhoe a summary of the sighting reports *True* had collected. He also warned Keyhoe, "Watch out for fake tips. You'll probably run into some people at the Pentagon who'll talk to you off the record. That handcuffs a writer."

One thing stands out from Keyhoe's meeting with Purdy. From the very start, both were convinced that flying saucers were real, and that the Air Force knew it and was covering it up. The "Big Story," in their eyes, was *what* the flying saucers *were*. Moreover, they assumed any statement or explanation by the Air Force was deception and trickery. Every comment, every action, every rumor was fitted into this preexisting belief.

In his meeting with Purdy, only two possibilities had been discussed—U.S. secret weapons or Soviet missiles. Keyhoe thought both ideas had problems. The secret development of an atomic engine could explain the flying saucer's speed and range, yet, such a secret device would not be tested in so public a manner; thousands of people could see it. On the other hand, if they were Soviet, Keyhoe asked himself, why would they run the risk of testing such a device over the U.S.?

In mid-June 1949, Keyhoe met again with Purdy and John DuBarry,

True's aviation editor. Keyhoe outlined four possibilities: flying saucers do not exist; Soviet guided missiles; U.S. guided missiles; a psychological warfare hoax intended to convince the Soviets the U.S. had a secret weapon. Then Purdy made another suggestion: the flying saucers were interplanetary. He quoted several experts who believed that they were from outer space and that the Air Force knew or suspected it. In discussing the possibility, Keyhoe raised an issue that would become a central part of the flying saucer myth. If the objects truly were extraterrestrial spacecraft, he said, "It could set off a panic that would make that Orson Welles thing look like a picnic."

That evening Keyhoe flew back to Washington, D.C. During the flight, he thought about the early sightings *True* had collected. Clearly, reports from the late 1800s and the early twentieth century could not have been caused by secret guided missiles. As he later put it, "The answer seemed inevitable"—the flying saucers were extraterrestrial spacecraft. He thought about how unbelievable a DC-6 would have been fifty years before. With all that had happened—airplanes, the V-2 rocket, the atomic bomb and plans for space travel—were alien spacecraft really all that remarkable? Keyhoe thought.

This was a turning point in the flying saucer myth. By the time the plane had landed, Keyhoe had accepted the "Extraterrestrial Hypothesis." He decided to concentrate on those cases where the objects were described as "space ships." It was a stunning moment. As Keyhoe later wrote:

> As I waited for a taxi, I looked up at the sky. It was a clear summer night, without a single cloud. Beyond the low hills to the west I could see the stars.
> I can still remember thinking *If it's true, then the stars will never again seem the same.*

During the summer and fall of 1949, Keyhoe criss-crossed the country. Unable to talk with "Project Saucer" personnel, he interviewed witnesses and others with opinions on flying saucers. It was at this point the basic flaws in Keyhoe's investigation became apparent. The following was typical:

> "Charley, there's a rumor that airline pilots have been ordered not to talk," I told Planck. "You know anything about it?"
> "You mean ordered by the Air Force or the companies?" he said.
> "The Air Force *and* the C.A.A."
> "If the C.A.A.'s in on it, it's a top-level deal," said Charley.

Keyhoe's sources were relying on newspaper accounts, rumors and airport gossip to shape their opinions. In Keyhoe's eyes, however, the sources' status transformed their opinions into "proof." Keyhoe used similar questionable methods in analyzing Air Force statements. While rereading the Air Force press release, he ran across the following paragraph: "Preliminary study of the more than 240 domestic and thirty foreign incidents by Astro-Physicist Hynek indicates that an over-all total of about 30% can probably be explained away as astronomical phenomena."

Finding the term "explained away" suspicious, he began going through the report "line by line." Keyhoe began to speculate that the "Project Saucer" teams were both checking out the reports and diverting attention away from the "truth." This was done, he thought, by suggesting plausible (but false) solutions to "explain away" the sightings. He further speculated that terms like "explaining away" "would probably be used in discussions of ways and means; they undoubtedly would be used in secret official papers. And since this published preliminary report had been made up from censored secret files, the use of those familiar words might have been overlooked."

Keyhoe was now sure the Air Force was involved in a cover-up "to explain away the sightings and hide the real answer."[7] All this was based on the words "explained away." In reality, he was twisting the Air Force comments completely out of context and then forcing them to fit his and Purdy's fixed ideas about a cover-up. Yet, to Keyhoe, it was further proof the flying saucers were extraterrestrial spaceships.

While Keyhoe was deciding that "Project Saucer" was hard at work covering up flying saucers, the true situation at Project Grudge was far different. By the summer of 1949, investigation of new sightings had all but stopped. Reports continued to be forwarded to TID at the rate of ten per month, but they were discarded. What little work was being done was on a report on older sightings (prespring 1949).[8]

"The Flying Saucers Are Real"

In early October 1949, Keyhoe met with Purdy to make the final decisions on the story. The three "classics"—the Mantell, Chiles-Whitted, and Gorman cases, along with the early sightings, would be used to support *True's* conclusion that the flying saucers were alien spacecraft. Both Keyhoe and Purdy believed that if a flying saucer made a low pass over a large city, it could trigger a stampede, unless the public was fully prepared. Both believed the Air Force *wanted True* to publish the article.

Keyhoe told Purdy that he had told the Air Force Press Branch officials that *True* intended to say flying saucers were spaceships. The Air Force made no attempt to stop him. Keyhoe was told that "Project Saucer" had found nothing that posed a threat to the United States or involved security. Rather than concluding from this that flying saucers did not exist, Keyhoe said, "I'm absolutely convinced now that there's an official policy to let the thing leak out. . . . It also would explain those Project 'Saucer' hints in the April report." Purdy responded, "I think we're being used as a trial balloon. We've let them know what we're doing. If they'd wanted to stop us, the Air Force could easily have done it."

The January 1950 issue of *True* carried Keyhoe's article. Entitled "The Flying Saucers Are Real," it made the following four claims:

1. For the last 175 years the Earth was being closely watched by intelligent beings from another planet.

2. The intensity of this observation and the number of flying saucers entering the Earth's atmosphere had increased during the previous two years.

3. Three different types of alien spaceships had been seen—a small non-piloted disk equipped with a television transmitter, a very large metallic disk that worked much like a helicopter, and a cylindrical, wingless aircraft.

4. The actions of the flying saucers were identical to U.S. ideas and plans for space exploration.

The issue arrived in subscribers' mailboxes and on the newsstands soon after Christmas. Within hours, radio commentators had broken the story. The wire services picked it up as well and some newspapers carried front-page stories. *True* was flooded with long-distance phone calls and letters.[9] "The Flying Saucers Are Real" was later described as the most widely read and discussed magazine article up to that time.

The Questions Grow

The Air Force moved quickly to counter Keyhoe's article. On December 27, 1949, it was announced that Project Grudge was being closed down and that in a few days a final report would be issued. As it turned out, the "Grudge Report" only caused the questions and doubts to grow. Of the 273 incidents covered, thirty-two percent were astronomical objects, another twelve percent were sightings of weather or Skyhook balloons. Of the remaining fifty-six percent, Project Grudge found thirty-three percent were hoaxes, did not contain enough information, or were possibly misidentified airplanes. This left twenty-three percent as unidentified.

The report's final appendix dealt with these. It was called "Summary of the Evaluation of Remaining Reports." Each sighting was explained. The effect was the opposite of the one hoped for. One reporter thought the Grudge Report was a poor attempt to put out a "fake" report that was meant to cover up the real story. Thus, rather than clearing up the situation, it raised even more questions in the minds of some. An example of this can be seen in the Grudge Report's account of the Mantell incident. After noting the similarities between the location of the object and Venus, Hynek wrote:

> . . . but on January 7, 1948, Venus was less than half as bright as it is when most brilliant. However, under exceptionally good atmospheric conditions and with the eye shielded from the direct rays of the Sun, Venus might be seen as an exceedingly tiny bright point of light. . . . While it is thus physically possible to see Venus at such times, usually its pinpoint character and the large expanse of sky makes its casual detection very unlikely. . . .
>
> It has been unofficially reported that the object was a Navy cosmic ray balloon. If this can be established, it is to be preferred as an explanation. However, if one accepts the assumption that reports from various other locations in the state refer to the same object, any such device must have been a good many miles high—25 to 30—in order to have been seen clearly, almost simultaneously, from places 175 miles apart.
>
> It is entirely possible, of course, that the first sightings were of some sort of balloon or aircraft, but that when these reports came to Godman Field, a careful scrutiny of the sky revealed Venus, and it could be that Lieutenant Mantell did actually give chase to the planet, even though whatever objects had been the source of the excitement elsewhere had disappeared. . . . The one piece of evidence that leads this investigator to believe that at the time of Lieutenant Mantell's death he was actually trying to reach Venus is that the object appeared essentially stationary (or moving steadily away from him) and that he could not seem to gain on it. . . .
>
> Regarding the daylight sighting from Godman Field and other places in Kentucky, there seems so far to be no single explanation that does not rely greatly on coincidence. If all reports were of a single object, in the knowledge of this investigator no man-made object could have been large enough and far enough away for the approximately simultaneous sightings. It is most unlikely, however, that so many separate persons should at that time have [fixed] on Venus in the daylight sky. It seems, therefore, much more probable that more than one object was involved: the sightings might have included two or more balloons (or aircraft); or they might have included both Venus (in the fatal chase) and balloons.

In retrospect, Hynek both confused the issue and overlooked the vital matter of the Skyhook balloon. At the time, however, a more sinister interpretation was put on the account by the believers. To these people, the Grudge Report tended to support Keyhoe's idea of a cover-up.

The Grudge Report concluded:

1. Evaluation of reports of unidentified flying objects constitute no direct threat to the United States.
2. Reports of unidentified flying objects are the result of:
    a. A mild form of mass hysteria or "war nerves".
    b. Individuals who fabricate such reports to perpetrate a hoax or seek publicity.
    c. Psychopathological persons.
    d. Misidentification of various conventional objects.[10]

Keyhoe was, not surprisingly, among those who suspected the Grudge Report.[11] His suspicions grew with the interview of Maj. Jerry Boggs. According to Ruppelt, Boggs's only involvement with flying saucers was to write a short intelligence summary. When an expert was needed for an interview, he was picked.[12] When Keyhoe asked him about the Mantell case, Boggs said Mantell had been chasing Venus. Keyhoe responded that the April press release said Venus was too dim to be seen. Boggs replied, "They rechecked after that report." Keyhoe wrote later, "I was sure now why Major Jerry Boggs had been chosen for his job. . . . No one would ever catch this man off guard, no matter what secret was given him to conceal."[13]

True followed up Keyhoe's article with another in the March 1950 issue. Entitled "How Scientists Tracked Flying Saucers," it was written by Commander R. B. McLaughlin, the former commander of the Navy's development effort at the White Sands Proving Ground. He stated that on several occasions, during 1948 and 1949, he or his group had made flying saucer sightings. The best had occurred on April 24, 1949, when an object was tracked with a telescope. They found the object had been moving at a speed of 25,200 mph at an altitude of 56 miles when the object was first seen. At one point, it passed in front of a range of mountains, giving an estimated size of 40 feet wide and 100 feet long. He concluded—"I am convinced that it was a flying saucer, and further, that these disks are spaceships from another planet, operated by animate, intelligent beings."[14,15] (In fact, a 100-foot object 56 miles away is only 1.2 arc seconds across—too small to see in the daylight sky or for any shape to be seen.)

The twin articles sparked a wave of publicity and sightings during early 1950. Whereas 186 sightings were submitted in 1949 (22 of which were never identified), the total for 1950 was 210 (27 unidentified).[16] The monthly totals peaked in March with 41 and ebbed in late spring.[17]

The most spectacular of the March sightings occurred on St. Patrick's Day above the small town of Farmington, New Mexico. At about 10:15 A.M. on March 17, the Mayor of Farmington, the local newspaper staff, ex-pilots, the highway patrol, and most of the town's inhabitants saw between 500 and "thousands" of flying saucers. They seemed to dart in and out, missing each other by inches. Word of the invasion of Farmington spread around the country. The next day the Air Force dismissed the mass reports with "There's nothing to it," but offered no explanation. Several years later, Ruppelt would disclose that a Skyhook balloon, launched from Holloman AFB, had burst over Farmington as it floated at 60,000 feet. The pieces of thin plastic drifted on the wind and, reflecting the sunlight, looked like saucers.

True struck again with their April issue (mailed in late March 1950). It carried seven photos of flying saucers. As Ruppelt noted, "It didn't take a photo-interpretation expert to tell all seven could be of doubtful lineage." By the end of spring 1950, flying saucers had received several months of steady publicity in the wake of the Keyhoe article. Virtually all of it was on the "pro" side.[18] It was now time for the next step in the development of the flying saucer myth.

"The Flying Saucers Are Real" II

Keyhoe was busy expanding his *True* article into a book. It was published in June 1950, also under the title *The Flying Saucers Are Real*. Because the book was so personal, it gives an insight into the thought processes by which the flying saucer myth was defined. Keyhoe's belief that the public would panic was clearly based on the 1938 Orson Welles "War of the Worlds" Panic. A radio broadcast of the H. G. Wells story (updated to 1938) had been mistaken for an actual news report. A major part, however, was Keyhoe's own attitude. At one point he wrote:

> Like most people, I had grown up believing the Earth was the center of everything—life, intelligence and religion. Now, for the first time in my life, that belief was shaken.
> . . . if these sightings were true, the shoe was on the other foot. We would

be faced with a race of beings at least two hundred years ahead of our civilization, perhaps thousands. In their eyes, we might look like the primitives.

The McLaughlin article was seen by Keyhoe as part of a "carefully thought out plan" to prepare the public "for a dramatic disclosure" about "the secret of the disks." Keyhoe believed this disclosure "may be imminent." (Thus he became the first of many to make such a statement.)

Ironically, the role of Ken Purdy, *True*'s editor, in this belief in a cover-up (and in defining the flying saucer myth) has not been appreciated. It was Purdy who raised the cover-up idea in his telegram to Keyhoe. It was also Purdy who suggested the Extraterrestrial Hypothesis to Keyhoe and decided how the article should be slanted. If Keyhoe defined the flying saucer myth, it was Purdy who had the major influence on Keyhoe.

Keyhoe spent considerable time speculating about "them"—the beings who piloted the saucers. Specifically, why were they here? He suggested that the extraterrestrials were afraid humans would detonate several very large H-bombs and knock the Earth out of its orbit. It would then career around the solar system, endangering Mars or Venus. (At this time it was thought these planets were the home worlds of the saucer pilots.) Keyhoe also speculated on the aliens making "contact": "It might be a long time before they would try to make contact. But I had a conviction that when it came, it would be a peaceful mission, not an ultimatum. It could even be the means of ending wars on Earth." He further speculated that there might be some "block to making contact," but felt it was more likely the "spacemen's plans are not complete." (Keyhoe also suspected "they" would look like "us.") The *True* article and the book made Keyhoe the most important figure in the flying saucer myth. This was a distinction he would hold for the next twenty years.

As with the *True* article, Keyhoe's book was not marked by either scholarship or logical thought. The balloon explanation for the Mantell case was dismissed because the object was seen in towns 175 miles apart. Keyhoe assumed it was seen simultaneously, which meant it was 30 miles high. The meteor explanation for the Chiles-Whitted sighting was dismissed because Major Boggs suggested it. The weather balloon explanation for the Gorman dogfight was rejected by Keyhoe because one of the weather observers said the balloon went in another direction.

Using these arguments, Keyhoe claimed the number of unidentified sightings was nearly 200. In retrospect, it is clear how little real research Keyhoe did. There was no "Deep Throat"; no inside information. He did not know of the internal divisions of Project Sign, the Estimate of the Situation, or any of the events of 1947–49.

Instead, Keyhoe "reconstructed" the events of the previous three years. In his view, the Air Force was "puzzled and badly worried" by the 1947 flap. They had begun "to suspect the truth" soon after Mantell's death, if not before. Then, Keyhoe thought, "Project Saucer" was set up to both investigate and cover up the "truth" about the saucers. This continued until the spring of 1949 when "top-level orders" were issued to let the story "gradually leak out, in order to prepare the American people." This was the reason for the April 27, 1949, press release and the *Saturday Evening Post* article. The *True* article was also considered part of this education program. The public reaction was mistaken by the Air Force for hysteria and they hastily issued the Grudge Report. Keyhoe also thought Major Boggs was sent out to conceal the true explanations for the Mantell, Chiles-Whitted, and Gorman cases. In early 1950, it was decided that the public was better prepared than had originally been thought and a limited number of case summaries was given to Washington newsmen in order to plant the Extraterrestrial Hypothesis.[19] The small seed planted during the 1947 flap, that sprouted amid the vague suspicions of "The Classics," had now become full grown.

While Keyhoe was spinning his elaborate story of an Air Force cover-up, reality was far different. With the completion of the Grudge Report, the project was shut down. The reports, memos, photos and other papers were pulled from the filing cabinets, tied up with string, and thrown into boxes. In the process, many of the records were lost, destroyed, or taken as souvenirs. The investigation team was disbanded. When flying saucer sightings were submitted to the Air Force, they were to be dealt with as any other intelligence report. The lack of official interest, however, meant they got only the most limited of time and effort.[20]

The flying saucer myth was defined against a background of conspiracy, fear, and espionage. The Age of Suspicion continued to grow with the conviction of Judith Coplon and Alger Hiss.[21] In Eastern Europe, the Soviets had gained total control. In China, Communist forces under Mao Tse-tung had pushed Chiang Kai-shek's Nationalist forces off the mainland. On September 21, 1949, Mao proclaimed the founding of the People's Republic of China. Two days later, President Truman issued a brief statement—"We have evidence an atomic explosion occurred in the USSR." On January 31, 1950, he announced development had begun on the H-bomb. Then, on February 2, 1950, Klaus Fuchs was arrested by Scotland Yard for giving A-bomb secrets to the Soviets.

Given the mood of the country, it was inevitable somebody would use the issue of communism to gain national prominence. On February 9, Sen. Joseph R. McCarthy claimed 207 Communist Party members were working at the State Department. For the next four years, McCarthism was a rallying point for all the fears of the early Cold War years.[22]

While McCarthy chased headlines, the FBI closed in on the atomic spy ring. By June 1950, Harry Gold and David Greenglass had confessed to giving the Soviets design information on the A-bomb, and implicated Julius and Ethel Rosenberg as leaders of the network.[23]

On June 25, 1950, 90,000 North Korean troops invaded South Korea. The poorly equipped South Korean army collapsed. Within days, U.S. troops, aircraft and naval forces had been committed. The Korean War had begun. World War III loomed.

"Behind the Flying Saucers"

It all started innocently enough. In 1948, George Bawra was editor of the *Aztec Independent-Review*. He wrote a tongue-in-cheek story about a flying saucer that crashed near Aztec, New Mexico.[24] His harmless prank then got out of hand, becoming one of the more controversial parts of the flying saucer myth. The story was picked up, and within the next year, over a hundred newspapers carried the "little men from Venus" report.

At their October 1949 meeting, Keyhoe and Purdy briefly discussed it. The version they heard involved two saucers that crashed in the southwestern desert. Aboard were the bodies of several crewmen—oddly dressed and only three feet tall. Keyhoe and Purdy decided the story was just a hoax.

In early 1950, Keyhoe went to Denver to talk with George Koehler of radio station KMYR. Koehler claimed to have accidently learned of the two saucer crashes near a radar station on the southwestern border. The *Kansas City Star* carried the following account:

> Each of the two ships seen by Koehler was occupied by a crew of two. In the badly damaged ship, those bodies were charred so badly that little could be learned from them. The occupants of the other ship, while dead when

they were found, were not burned or disfigured, and, when Koehler saw them, they were in a perfect state of preservation. Medical reports, according to Koehler, showed that these men were almost identical with Earth-dwelling humans, except for a few minor differences. They were of a uniform height of three feet, were uniformly blond, beardless and their teeth were completely free of fillings or cavities. They did not wear undergarments, but had their bodies taped.

The ships seemed to be magnetically controlled and powered.

In addition to a piece of metal, Koehler had a clock or automatic calendar taken from one of the crafts.

Koehler said that the best assumption as to the source of the ships was the planet Venus.

Keyhoe asked to see the metal fragment. Koehler said it had been sent to another city, as were the photos of the crashed saucer and the "space clock." Keyhoe decided the story was a hoax. On the flight home, Keyhoe read a newspaper story saying that Koehler had admitted the story was a joke. Keyhoe noted, "But in spite of this, the 'little men' story goes on and on."[25]

The story became part of the flying saucer myth on September 8, 1950, with publication of Frank Scully's book *Behind the Flying Saucers.*[26] Scully was a columnist with *Variety.*[27] According to Scully's book, a lecture was given to 350 students at the University of Denver on March 8, 1950. The speaker was Silas M. Newton, a millionaire oilman who used microwaves to find oil and gold deposits. He said a scientist friend, a "Dr. Gee," had been called in to examine three crashed saucers.

The first went down in a very rocky area twelve miles east of Aztec, New Mexico. It was 99.99 feet in diameter. The cabin was 18 feet across and 72 inches high. (All measurements were divisible by nine; but only when expressed in English units.) The only damage was a small hole in a porthole. Inside were the bodies of sixteen crewmen, all between 36 and 42 inches tall. Their skins were charred a very dark brown. Dr. Gee told Scully later he and his team thought the porthole had broken in space and the crew was burned by air rushing out. The crew was dressed in dark blue clothing, similar in style to that of the 1890s. They were 35 to 40 years old and had no cavities or fillings. The crew ate small wafers and drank water twice as heavy as Earth water. Their home planet was thought to be Venus. Dr. Gee said they also found several booklets with a pictorial-type script.

The second saucer landed near a proving ground in Arizona. It was 72 feet across and followed the "rule of nine." The sixteen crewmen were dead. Dr. Gee said they had been dead only two or three hours when the saucer was found. The door was open and they died when exposed to the Earth's atmosphere. The crew's bodies were not burned; all were short and had fair complexions.

The third ship was much smaller—only 36 feet in diameter. Only two dead crewmen were aboard; one was halfway out the hatch, the other was sitting at the control board. It had landed in Paradise Valley near Phoenix. The saucer was later moved to Wright-Patterson AFB.

The saucers flew by crawling forward from one magnetic line of force to the next. Dr. Gee said there were 1,257 lines to the square centimeter. Newton explained that Mantell's plane was "demagnetized" and it disintegrated.

The Newton/Dr. Gee story was a hoax and the pair were, in fact, con men. Scully was not their only victim. The truth would not be known for another two years, however. Still, it is possible, using internal evidence alone, to show it was a hoax. No scientist would claim magnetic lines of force were real objects. They are only a way to show areas of equal strength of the magnetic field (similar to contour lines on a map showing areas of equal elevation; one could not climb up a mountain by pulling on them). Another indication the story was a hoax was the way the "facts" changed from one telling to the next. Koehler said only two saucers had crashed, each carried only two crewmen, the first saucer was badly damaged, and its crew so charred that little could be learned from the bodies. These inconsistencies are all the more remarkable given it was Koehler who introduced Newton at the University of Denver lecture.

Behind the Flying Saucers heaped abuse on the Air Force, scientists, the University of Denver administration and any other symbol of authority. Scully used such phrases as "double standard of morality," "incompetent time servers," "official censorship," "reign of error," "Prussian Junkers," "disturbed personalities," "secrecy and incompetence," and "brass hats." Scully also claimed Keyhoe (spelled "Kehoe" in the book) and the newspaper had lied when they said Koehler had admitted the story was a joke. Scully's belief in flying saucers was motivated by a contempt for all authority. Scully summed up his own view as follows: "If the Pentagon tells you flying saucers are *here* don't believe them. If they say they are a *myth* don't believe them. Just don't believe them. Believe me."[28]

Any book that claimed to have proof that three flying saucers had been captured was bound to attract attention. *Behind the Flying Saucers* was reviewed by *Time, Saturday Review,* and *Science Digest.*[29] *Time* referred to Scully as an "operator" and said, "Measured for scientific credibility,

Scully's science ranks below the comic books." It noted that two factors behind the public's readiness to believe in the story—"man's incurable yearning for marvels" and "the present-day effectiveness of 'military security'. . . has made the public suspicious of all official denials."[30]

Flying Saucers and Hollywood

In the late 1940s, Hollywood studios saw the possibilities of movies with flying saucer themes. The first of these films was released in 1950 and 1951. The films, in retrospect, had a considerable influence on the emerging flying saucer myth. Taken together, they gave a visual reality to what Keyhoe and Scully described. Anybody seeing the films would "know" what a flying saucer "looked like." The first movie to use the theme was *The Flying Saucer,* released in 1950. Despite the title, the film owed little to the flying saucer myth. The flying saucer in the title was an advanced aircraft used as a plot device for a run-of-the-mill spy story.[31,32]

The most influential flying saucer movie was *The Day the Earth Stood Still.* As this 1951 film starts, a saucer is spotted flying at high speed and altitude. It lands in Washington, D.C., and is surrounded by troops. The crewman, Klaatu (Michael Rennie), is shot. Gort (Lock Martin), his eight-foot tall robot, vaporizes several rifles, a tank and a cannon. Klaatu is taken to Walter Reed hospital where he unsuccessfully asks that a meeting be arranged with world leaders, so he can give them a message.

Klaatu escapes from the hospital, assumes the human identity of "Mr. Carpenter" and takes a room at a boarding house. There he meets several "ordinary" people—Mrs. Helen Benson (Patricia Neal), a war widow, Bobby Benson (Billy Gray), her son, and Tom Stevens (Hugh Marlowe), Helen Benson's fiancé. Klaatu meets with Professor Barnhardt (Sam Jaffe playing an Einstein-like figure) and explains that the Earth, with its advancing technology, poses a threat to the peace of the Galaxy. Barnhardt offers to arrange a meeting of the world's scientists at the saucer. He also suggests Klaatu demonstrate his power. Klaatu agrees, and two days later, all electrical power all over the world is shut off for thirty minutes.

The Earth does "stand still," but by this time, Tom Stevens knows "Mr. Carpenter" is Klaatu and calls the Army. Helen Benson and Klaatu escape in a taxi. As the Army closes in, Klaatu warns Helen Benson that

Gort may destroy the Earth if anything happens to him. The taxi is stopped and Klaatu is killed. Helen Benson escapes in the confusion and arrives at the saucer. Just as Gort is about to fire the beam, she utters the film's most famous line—"Gort! Klaatu barada nikto." Gort recovers Klaatu's body and brings him temporarily back to life so he can deliver his message—other planets live under a peace enforced by robot policemen like Gort. "In matters of aggression, we have given them absolute power over us," Klaatu explains. "This power cannot be revoked. At the first sign of violence, they act automatically against the aggressor. The penalty for provoking their action is too terrible to risk." He gives the Earth an ultimatum—join them and live under this peace, or face destruction. Klaatu boards the saucer, it lifts off and climbs into the night sky.[33]

The Day the Earth Stood Still's impact on the flying saucer myth is due to its religious overtones. Consider the film as allegory—a handsome, intelligent being comes down from the heavens with a message of peace and love. The message is rejected and he must hide, ultimately being betrayed and killed. He is resurrected and gives the world a choice—peace or destruction. He then ascends to heaven. Except for the rather obvious "Mr. Carpenter," the allegory is subtle and works on an unconscious level.[34]

The other flying saucer movie of 1951 was *The Thing from Another World*. Although it is also considered a classic, *The Thing* had little impact on the flying saucer myth. This story of an arctic research base menaced by the Thing (James Arness)—an intelligent plant that drinks blood—is a much more narrow reflection of its time. At the start of the film, there is speculation that the aircraft is Soviet. Dr. Carrington (Robert Cornthwaite), the chief scientist, has a beard and wears a fur hat which makes him look Soviet. The film's most familiar line—"Watch the Skies! Keep Watching the Skies!" can be interpreted as a call for vigilance against the "Red Menace."[35,36]

Given these reflections of Cold War attitudes, it is not surprising *The Thing from Another World* added little to the flying saucer myth. The Thing, like the Soviets, was a "threat from outside," the Cold War dressed up in alien form. In contrast, *The Day the Earth Stood Still* offered an escape from the fears of the Cold War—even if it was a peace enforced by Gort.

The years 1950 and 1951 were a critical period in the development of the flying saucer myth. It was at this time the basic myth was defined. Keyhoe did not create it; some elements went back to Fort, Palmer, and

Shaver. What he did do was to publicize a specific set of beliefs and, as a result, establish them in the public mind. Although, over the following years, other features would be added, these basic patterns have lasted to this day.

The Flying Saucer Myth 1950–1951

Basic Beliefs

Disk-shaped objects have been seen in the Earth's atmosphere for hundreds of years.

These flying saucers are extraterrestrial spacecraft flown by alien beings.

They are capable of maneuvers and speeds beyond those of Earth aircraft.

They are here to observe human activities such as nuclear testing which concerns them and may pose a threat to them.

The United States government knows this to be true, has proof and is covering it up.

The reason for this cover-up is to prevent panic.

Beliefs Not Fully Accepted

One possibility for the proof is the recovery of crashed flying saucers and the bodies of their crews.

The 1952 Flap

> Imagine, then, my thrill of terror . . .
>
> —*The Adventure of the Speckled Band*

Between early 1950 and the late summer of 1951, Air Force involvement with flying saucers had virtually ended. Only one intelligence officer, a lieutenant, handled the incoming reports. The attitude at the Air Technical Intelligence Center (ATIC)—TID's new name—was one of ridicule. One intelligence officer said, "One of these days all of these crazy pilots will kill themselves, the crazy people on the ground will be locked up, and there won't be any more flying saucer reports."[1]

The Fort Monmouth Sightings

Attention from the press began the revival of Air Force interest in flying saucers. In the spring of 1951, Robert Ginna of *Life* magazine came to ATIC to research UFO reports. The power of *Life* sent a wave of fear through the ATIC staff. Ginna asked a long list of questions. Each time, the Project Grudge investigator would have to leave the room to hunt down the file. Several times the response, "I'm sorry, that's classified" got them out of tight spots. Ginna was not impressed.

About two months later, a new officer was assigned as the Project Grudge investigator. He was Lt. Jerry Cummings, an Air Force Reservist recalled to duty following the outbreak of the Korean War. He believed the investigation should be handled on a systematic basis. Whenever a good report came in, Cummings passed it to Capt. Edward J. Ruppelt, who sat at the desk across from him. Ruppelt was also a reservist recalled to active duty. His talks with Cummings were training for his role in events to come.

Throughout the summer of 1951, Lieutenant Cummings tried to increase Project Grudge's respectability within ATIC. It arrived with a two-day series of incidents at the Army Signal Corps radar center at Fort Monmouth, New Jersey. They began at 11:10 A.M. on September 10. A student radar operator picked up a target flying at low altitude. He tried to switch the radar to automatic tracking, in which the radar followed the target without operator assistance. He failed, tried again and failed once more. Embarrassed, he said, "It's going too fast for the set. That means it's going faster than a jet!" He tried for three minutes, but was never able to get an automatic track.

Twenty-five minutes later, the crew of a T-33 jet trainer, flying at 20,000 feet over Point Pleasant, New Jersey, saw a dull silver disk, thirty to fifty feet in diameter, at about 5,000 feet. The pilot went after the disk. As he did, the object stopped its descent, hovered, then made a turn and went out to sea.

Then at 3:15 P.M., the radar group received a frantic call from the Fort Monmouth headquarters asking them to track an object high and to the north. This was the direction in which the first, high-speed object had vanished. They picked up the new target at an altitude of 93,000 feet— far above any aircraft. It was visible as a silver speck moving slowly in the sky.

The wave of sightings continued the next day. During the morning, two radars picked up a target which could not be automatically tracked. It climbed almost straight up, leveled off, then climbed again and went into a dive. The sightings ended that afternoon after another slow-moving target was picked up.

Maj. Gen. C. P. Cabell, director of Air Force intelligence, also received a copy of the report and ordered an investigation. Once this was completed, he wanted a personal report. Lieutenant Cummings and Lt. Col. N. R. Rosengarten (chief of the aircraft and missiles branch of ATIC) were soon headed to Fort Monmouth. For two days straight, they investigated the sightings. Cummings and Rosengarten were ordered to brief General Cabell and his staff.

Cummings and Rosengarten's report lasted about two hours. Near the end, a general asked Cummings to review the activities of Project

Grudge for the past eighteen months. Cummings told them that, in practical terms, the project was dead. All of the generals and three-fourths of the full colonels turned purple with rage. From their anger came orders that a new investigation effort was to be set up. For the moment, it would keep the old Project Grudge code name.

Ironically, having achieved his goal of official support, Lieutenant Cummings would not be leading the new project. Within days of returning from the meeting, Cummings was released from active duty. The next day, Captain Ruppelt was called to Colonel Rosengarten's office and was asked to take over Project Grudge. So began the "Age of Ruppelt."

It took time to sort out the Fort Monmouth sightings. The first radar sighting was due to the student's error. He had not followed the correct procedure for putting the radar on automatic tracking. The target was an ordinary airplane. (The only "proof" the object was flying at high speed was the inability of the radar to automatically track it.) The T-33 sighting was caused by a balloon. The second radar sighting was also a balloon. The frantic phone call from headquarters was to settle a bet on how high it was. The two radar sightings on the second day were caused by another balloon and by weather. A layer of warm, humid air over one of cool, dry air can cause radar signals to bend, strike the ground and be reflected back. The objects also seem to travel at high speed. The illusion was completed by the operator's belief that something strange was going on.[2]

The Fort Monmouth sightings have great historical significance because they generated high-level interest, acceptance, and belief in flying saucers by Air Force command personnel.

The New Project Grudge and Project Blue Book

The new Project Grudge was formally established on October 27, 1951. Captain Ruppelt and Lt. Henry Metscher spent the next month rereading the pre-1951 sighting reports. Ruppelt also sought the means to both collect and analyze new sightings. The first step was to ask for new Air Force regulations to speed reports to ATIC. (In the past, some sighting reports by Air Force personnel had taken up to two months to reach the investigators.) He also saw the need for a standardized questionnaire. The data from past sightings were often imprecise and random. The Air Force issued a contract to Ohio State University to develop such a form.

A statistical study would also be made by the Battelle Memorial Institute.

To gain instrument data, Ruppelt began development of cameras to photograph radarscopes and a diffraction grid to find the spectrum of light from an object. Hynek was named chief scientific consultant. Other scientists were also asked to help. To keep the Air Force aware of the investigation's results, a monthly classified report would be issued.[3]

Another change Ruppelt made would have a longer impact. He did not like the term "flying saucer"—"because," he wrote later, "it seems to represent weird stories, hoaxes, etc, sort of a joke."[4] To replace it, Ruppelt popularized the term "Unidentified Flying Object" (UFO).

By mid-December 1951, Ruppelt was ready. He and Col. Frank Dunn briefed Maj Gen. John A. Samford, the new Director of Intelligence. Dunn outlined the plan—each UFO sighting would be investigated in an unbiased manner. If it could not be identified as a balloon, meteor, or other conventional object, it would be considered "unidentified." It would be filed with other such cases. Later, these would be analyzed. The staff would not speculate on the source of the unknowns.

Ruppelt then reviewed the situation as of the end of 1951. The number of sightings was not directly controlled by the level of newspaper publicity. In the latter part of 1951, the number of reports had gone up even though there had been no publicity. The frequency of reports was seasonal—each July the number of reports went up sharply. This was the peak for the year. There was also a minor peak around Christmas. UFOs were seen more frequently around military sites, ports, and industrial areas.

Ruppelt ended his briefing by noting that there was no proof UFOs were real. All the recommendations for an expanded investigation were based on the existence of reliable reports of strange objects.[5] It was to be an intelligence-gathering effort. If the Soviets were to make overflights of the U.S. using some exotic aircraft, it might be reported as a flying saucer.[6] Ruppelt's plan was approved within a few days, though it still lacked money and staff. Maj. Dewey J. Fournet was assigned to handle liaison with other branches of the government.

The Death of Mantell—Solved

An early result of Ruppelt's efforts was the solution to the Mantell incident. In early 1952, Ruppelt reread the original file, talked with the peo-

ple who had worked on Project Sign, and also went to see Hynek. Ruppelt became convinced the object was not Venus. The tower operators had all described an object with angular size—Venus would have been a point of light.

The only theory left was a Skyhook balloon. The description fit and Ruppelt found the two reports identifying the object as a balloon. Project Sign, believing it was an alien spaceship, never checked out the reports. Later, when no proof was found, the Venus solution became an easy out. The weather charts from January 7 indicated that a balloon would drift over Kentucky and Tennessee. Ruppelt decided Mantell had died trying to reach a Skyhook balloon floating on the edge of space. It was later found that a Skyhook had been launched from Camp Ripley, Minnesota, early that morning.[7,8]

Prelude to the Great Flap

Once the wave of sightings that followed Keyhoe's 1950 article passed, the number of sightings settled down. In all, there were 210 sightings (27 unidentified) reported to the Air Force during 1950. The number of sightings declined in early 1951, but as summer turned to fall, it began going up, triple and quadruple that of the spring. The final total for 1951 was 169 sightings (22 unidentified). This was still below the totals for both 1949 and 1950.[9,10]

There had been no large-scale publicity during this time. In early 1952, this began to change. On January 29 crewmen on two different B-29s over North Korea saw disk-shaped objects pace their plane. One was described as orange with small blue flames around the rim which seemed to revolve as it flew. The press picked up the story and the number of flying saucer stories grew. *Time* carried the story in the March 3, 1952, issue. Although noting the objects might have been the glow from the exhausts of jet night fighters, it added: "The interesting point is that the Air Force, after investigating hundreds of flying saucer stories and pooh-poohing them all, has apparently decided to become less hostile towards mysteries in the sky."[11]

By March 1952, Ruppelt's briefings and reorganization, as well as an upswing in reports (especially from Korea), resulted in an improvement in status. The code name was also changed to Project Blue Book.[12,13]

In April, events gained a momentum of their own. On April 3, the Air Force announced it was still studying UFOs and would continue as long as there were unidentified sightings. The press release cautioned that this action should not be seen as indicating the Air Force had reached any conclusions about UFOs.[14] Two days later, the Air Force issued Air Force Letter 200-5. It ordered the intelligence officers at all Air Force bases to teletype any sighting reports to Blue Book immediately, followed by a more detailed written report. The Blue Book staff was also authorized to bypass the normal chain of command, giving it an almost unique status.[15]

Then came the April 7, 1952, issue of *Life*. It carried H. Bradford Darrach and Robert Ginna's article, "Have We Visitors from Space?" The article opened by saying the Air Force was investigating sightings and that "this policy of positive action has been adopted to find out, as soon as possible what is responsible for observations that have been made." "These disclosures," they wrote, "sharply amending past Air Force policy" were based on a review by *Life*, with the Air Force, of all the facts. *Life* concluded:

> Disks, cylinders and similar objects of geometrical form . . . for several years have been, and may be now . . . present in the atmosphere of Earth.
> Globes of green fire also, of a brightness more intense than the full Moon's, have frequently passed through the skies.
> These objects cannot be explained by present science as natural phenomena—but solely as artificial devices, created and operated by a high intelligence.
> Finally, no power plant known or projected on Earth could account for the performance of these devices.

The article detailed ten sighting reports by technically qualified witnesses. Each summary was followed by an analysis that eliminated any possibility the sightings were mistakes. Many were based on files declassified by the Blue Book staff. This was followed by a list of what flying saucers were not—"psychological phenomena," U.S. or Soviet secret weapons, "distortions of the atmosphere resulting from atomic activity," or "all Skyhook balloons."

After saying what they *were not, Life* began implying what they *might be*. The article quoted Dr. Walther Riedel, a former German rocket scientist, as saying, "I am completely convinced that they have an out-of-world basis." Dr. Maurice A. Boit, a leading aerodynamicist, said, "My opinion for some time has been that they have an extraterrestrial origin." The article concluded: "Answers may come in a generation—or tomorrow. Somewhere in the dark skies there may be those who know."[16]

The article did not say "The Flying Saucers Are Real"; it just said they might be. Or so it seemed. The ten reports and the analyses that followed were written in such a way that the only logical possibility seemed to be the Extraterrestrial Hypothesis. It sought to have the reader convince himself. (Only later would it become clear that the accounts of the sightings were distorted and that the analyses were based on questionable assumptions.)

As with the Shallett article three years before, some read meanings into the *Life* article. Keyhoe had said the Air Force wanted the "truth" to leak out slowly. Might this be "it"? Some believed that the Air Force had inspired the *Life* article. Darrach and Ginna had talked with an Air Force general in the Pentagon who strongly believed flying saucers were interplanetary spaceships. This was also the personal opinion of several very high-ranking officers, and they had unofficially influenced *Life*.[17]

The *Life* article fed the press interest that had been building over the past few months. Between April 3 and 6, about 350 newspapers carried some mention of the *Life* article.[18] This was reflected in Blue Book's clipping service. In March, a letter-sized envelope with a dozen clippings had arrived every few days. These had grown fatter until they were replaced by manila envelopes. By May, the newspaper clippings were coming in shoe boxes. To cope with the flood of news requests, Al Chop, a civilian with the Air Force Press Desk, was picked to be Blue Book's Public Relations Officer.[19]

The number of UFO sightings went up sharply in April. On the day after publication of the *Life* article, nine sighting reports were made. The following day, however, the number fell back to normal. Within days, the number picked up again. By this time, the new reporting procedures had gone into effect. By the end of April, eighty-two reports had been sent to the Air Force.

What may have been occurring was a very complex interrelationship. *Life* said the Air Force was interested in flying saucers. People would then be more likely to report a sighting. The new regulations meant that reports that might have been ignored or thrown away before were now sent to Blue Book. The open press policy meant that questions were not brushed off as before. This, along with the increased number of reports, resulted in more newspaper articles which caused people to watch the skies.

The wave seemed to fade in May. The number of reports dropped slightly, to seventy-nine.[20] Ruppelt planned to clear up the backlog of reports during June. In fact, the Great Flap of 1952 was about to begin.

The Great Flap of 1952

The 1952 flap started in June. The Blue Book situation map, which showed the location of incoming reports, indicated a buildup on the East Coast. In mid-June, Captain Ruppelt went to Washington, D.C., to give a briefing to General Samford, his staff, Naval Intelligence, and the CIA. Ruppelt went over the past few months' reports and unknown cases, which were at a record twenty-two percent. He continued that Blue Book had no proof UFOs were real—the unknown cases could be explained as only misinterpretations of common objects *if* a few assumptions were made. At this point, a colonel on General Samford's staff spoke up: "Isn't it true that if you make a few positive assumptions instead of negative assumptions, you can just as easily prove that UFO's are interplanetary spaceships?"

The colonel concluded by saying, "Why not just simply believe that most people know what they saw?" His statement pointed out a developing trend: there were now many people in high positions within the Air Force who believed UFOs were alien spacecraft. This feeling had been building during the first half of 1952. The split between the believers and skeptics within the Air Force grew over the following days as reports continued to come in. The enthusiasm of the believers took root and grew in the Pentagon, at Air Defense Command Headquarters, on the Research and Development Board, and in other government agencies.[21]

The debate within the Air Force was unknown to the public. The public's beliefs were being shaped by the press coverage, word of mouth, and the flying saucer myth. In June and early July, several national magazines carried flying saucer articles. The June 9 *Life* carried "Saucer Reactions," a selection of letters generated by the earlier "Have We Visitors from Space?" The same day, *Time* carried an interview with Harvard astronomer Dr. Donald H. Menzel. He believed flying saucers were caused by atmospheric mirages, refractions, ice crystals, and temperature inversions. Menzel expanded on this in a June 17 *Look* article entitled "The Truth About Flying Saucers." On July 1, *Look* published "Hunt for the Flying Saucers."[22]

By the end of June, the publicity started to die down. The upcoming political conventions pushed flying saucers off the front page. The 1952 campaign had many issues—the stalemated Korean War, corruption in Washington, and fears about communist infiltration. Relations with the Soviets were frozen in hostile rigidity. Looming over all this was the impending test of the first U.S. H-bomb, and the possibility of human extinction it raised.

After a flurry of reports on July 1, the number of sightings also fell off. During the first few days of July, only two or three good reports came in. Over the next several days, however, the number of reports again began to climb. By mid-July, the Blue Book staff was putting in fourteen-hour days, six days a week. Reports were running at twenty per day, and Air Force intelligence officers all over the country were being swamped with sightings. Blue Book told them to send the best of the reports. Unknowns were running at forty percent.

The center of the Great Flap of 1952 continued to be the East Coast of the U.S. On July 10, a National Airlines crew saw a light "too bright to be a lighted balloon and too slow to be a big meteor" while flying near Quantico, Virginia, just south of Washington, D.C. On July 13, another airline crew flying southwest of Washington saw a light below them. It climbed to the airliner's altitude and followed it for several minutes, went into a steep climb and disappeared. On July 14, a Pan American Airlines crew flying from New York to Miami saw eight UFOs near Newport News, Virginia. This was also south of Washington, D.C.

This pattern of sightings around the Washington area was noted by the Blue Book staff and people in the Pentagon. In mid-July, Ruppelt was discussing it with a scientist who made a prediction. He said, "Within the next few days, they're going to blow up and you're going to have the granddaddy of all UFO sightings. The sighting will occur in Washington or New York, probably Washington."[23]

Within days, his prediction had come true.

The Invasion of Washington

The main event of the 1952 flap began just before midnight on Saturday, July 19, in Washington, D.C. The day had been hot and humid with a high of 93°F. That night, the temperature fell to 76°F.[24] At 11:40 P.M., a controller at Air Route Traffic Control (ARTC) at Washington National Airport noticed several targets on the long-range radar. Eight targets were counted; most of the radar images were fair to weak, and moving at about 100 to 130 mph. The tower's short-range radar confirmed the targets, but no visual targets were seen.

Because the targets were east and south of Andrews AFB, the base was notified.[25] An airman called the Andrews tower and reported seeing objects in the night sky. At 12:05 A.M., he told the tower to look south. A tower operator reported seeing an orange ball of fire with a tail which made a circular movement, then took off "at an unbelievable speed." A few seconds later, he saw a similar object make an arclike pattern and then vanish.[26]

At about the same time, an ARTC controller asked the pilot of a Capital Airlines flight to watch for any unusual lights. Soon after clearing the traffic pattern, the pilot radioed, "There's one—off to the right—and there it goes." As the pilot reported the sighting, the controller noticed that a target that had been to the right of the Capital airliner was now gone. Over the next fourteen minutes, the airliner's crew saw six more lights, some moving very rapidly and some hovering.[27,28] At about 2:00 A.M. EST, ARTC reported tracking a target passing over Andrews AFB which faded out to the southwest. The Andrews AFB radar did not pick up the target, but the tower reported a light to the east that was changing color. An Air Force captain went outside and spotted the light. It was 10° to 15° above the horizon and changed color from red to orange to green and back to red. It seemed to float but would occasionally dip. He compared the light to a star at the same elevation but the star was not moving or changing color.

Around this time, another airliner sighting was made. A pilot flying into National Airport from the south called the tower and reported a light following his plane at "eight o'clock level." The tower checked its radar and found a target following to the left of the airliner. The target followed it until four miles from touchdown.

As the morning wore on, doubts about the nature of the sightings began growing at Andrews AFB. The Air Force captain went outside again at 3:00 A.M., and saw the "light" and the star. The light was still changing color but no longer appeared to move. He concluded that the light was only a star and its "movement" was an illusion. A tower operator felt it was the "power of suggestion" that made a star move or turned meteors into spaceships.[29]

At ARTC, there were no such doubts. The controllers wondered how long this would go on. At 3:00 A.M., ARTC called the Air Force Command Post. The controller wrote later:

> They were doing nothing about it so I asked if it was possible for something like this to happen, even though we gave them all this information, without anything being done about it. The man who was supposed to be in charge and to whom I had been talking, said he guessed so. Then another voice came on who identified himself as the Combat Officer and said that all

the information was being forwarded to higher authority and would not discuss it any further. I insisted I wanted to know if it was being forwarded tonight and he said yes, but would not give me any hint as to what was being done about all these things flying around Washington.

The conversation ended with the Combat Officer saying "that they were not really concerned about it anyway, that somebody else was supposed to handle it." ARTC continued to pick up radar targets after sunrise. As late as 5:40 A.M., there were seven targets in the area.[30]

Ruppelt and Air Force intelligence first learned of the sightings on Monday, July 21, from Washington newspapers. That afternoon, a meeting was held to discuss the night's events. Although there was some discussion of temperature inversions and false radar echoes, the consensus was that these had been real targets. The controllers were viewed as too experienced to be fooled by an echo caused by an inversion. From Ruppelt's account, it appears that the Washington sightings had convinced the Blue Book staff that the Extraterrestrial Hypothesis was at least a possibility.

The sightings seemed impressive. Unknown objects had been picked up by several radars. They had displayed apparent speeds ranging from 100 to 7,000 mph. The objects had been tracked in the prohibited airspace over the White House and the Capitol. They had also been seen, in the positions indicated by the radars, by witnesses on the ground and in the air. In later years, this would be called a "Radar-Visual" case.

Yet there were inconsistencies that would lead to a solution. There were three radar sites—National Airport, Bolling AFB (just east of National across the Potomac River), and Andrews AFB, ten miles east of National. The radar coverage of all three overlapped. During the night of July 19/20, many targets were picked up in this area of overlap. Yet, only *once* was a target in this overlap picked up by all three radars, and it lasted only thirty seconds.[31] A control tower operator at Andrews AFB commented: "All night [ARTC] was reporting objects near or over Andrews, but Andrews Approach Control could see nothing, however they could see the various aircraft reported so their [radar] screen was apparently in good operation."[32]

The meaning of this inconsistency would not be clear for another year. For the moment, UFO sightings continued to come in at the rate of more than forty per day; a third were unknowns. The Air Force was being swamped with reports. One week passed, and the second act of the "Invasion of Washington" was about to begin.

It started on Saturday, July 26. The same ARTC controllers were on duty. At 10:30 P.M. EST, they again picked up slow-moving radar targets. By 10:50 P.M., there were four targets in a rough line abreast. They were 1.5 miles apart and moving at less than 100 mph. At the same time, eight other targets were scattered over the radar scope. The controllers called Andrews AFB at 11:00 P.M. and found that they also had unknown targets. Several commercial pilots also reported seeing lights described as "orange to white" or like a "cigarette glow" (red-orange). At about 11:30 P.M., one of the ARTC controllers directed an Air Force B-25 to intercept the radar targets. For about one hour and twenty minutes the B-25 was vectored to numerous targets. Each time, the vector took the plane over a busy highway or intersection.

At midnight, two F-94 interceptors were scrambled from New Castle County AFB and flew south to defend the capital against the unknown interlopers. When the pair of F-94s arrived in the Washington area, civilian air traffic was cleared and the ARTC controllers began directing the interceptors to the radar targets. The results were anticlimactic. The F-94s flew through "a batch of radar returns" without results. Only one of the pilots saw anything. Lt. William Patterson reported seeing four lights at one point and a single light ahead of him that went out.[33] In an interview with the press early Sunday morning, he said:

> I tried to make contact with the bogies below 1,000 feet, but [the ARTC controllers] vectored us around. I saw several bright lights. I was at my maximum speed, but even then I had no closing speed. I ceased chasing them because I saw no chance of overtaking them. I was vectored into new objects. Later I chased a single bright light which I estimated about 10 miles away. I lost visual contact with it [at] about 2 miles.[34]

While these events were underway, Robert Ginna of *Life* called Ruppelt in Dayton and told him of the sightings. Ruppelt had Maj. Dewey Fournet and a Lieutenant Holcomb, a Navy electronics expert, go to National Airport. When they arrived at 1:15 A.M. EST, they found Al Chop already there. By this time, the F-94s had run low on fuel and returned to base.

Lieutenant Holcomb checked the radar scopes and saw "7 good solid targets." He checked with the airport's weather station and determined there was a slight temperature inversion, but felt the radar targets were not due to it. A second pair of F-94s took off from New Castle County AFB. When they arrived over Washington, however, the strong targets were gone. ARTC controllers directed the F-94s to several dim targets with no results. The F-94s ran low on fuel and headed back. Major Fournet and Lieutenant Holcomb remained until 5:15 A.M. EST but no more strong targets were detected, only dim and unstable echoes caused by the temperature inversion.[35] On this anticlimactic note, the Invasion of Washington ended.

Aftermath

Ruppelt flew into Washington in the late afternoon of Monday, July 28. He found the newspaper headlines were about the weekend sightings: FIERY OBJECTS OUTRUN JETS OVER CAPITAL—INVESTIGATION VEILED IN SECRECY FOLLOWING VAIN CHASE[36]

As the Air Force investigation got underway on Tuesday morning, July 29, the mood was one of confusion. At 10:00 A.M., Brigadier General Landry, the President's air aide, called the Pentagon to request information about the sightings. Ruppelt took the call and said they could have been caused by weather but that he had no proof. (President Truman was listening in on the conversation.) This was not the only call; the Pentagon's telephone circuits were overloaded. All the while, new UFO reports, some of them radar-visual sightings, continued to flood in.

At midmorning, Maj. Gen. John Samford, director of Air Force intelligence, issued word he would have a press conference that afternoon on the UFO sightings. It was the largest press conference held since World War II. General Samford said the Air Force was reasonably convinced the radar echos had been caused by a temperature inversion. Capt. Roy L. James, ATIC's radar expert, provided detail on inversions. General Samford said the Air Force had received a number of reports from "credible observers of relatively incredible things." He concluded by saying the Air Force had no evidence UFOs posed a threat to the U.S.[37,38]

Press reaction was mixed. Most accepted the Air Force explanation of the Washington sightings. Agreement was not uniform, however. There had been little time to conduct a full investigation and General Samford did not have all the facts, so he had to "hedge" on many of his answers. Many in the press and public got the impression that the Air Force was covering up, and this was reflected in some of the press coverage.[39]

During the months that followed, the echoes continued as several magazines published articles on the Washington sightings. The August 4 issue of *Life* carried an article entitled "Washington Blips." It suggested the Air Force had "known more about the blips than it admitted." The year ended with an article in the December *True* by Keyhoe, which rejected the idea that the radar echoes were caused by an inversion.[40]

The Invasion of Washington was the climax of the 1952 flap. The buildup and fade-out of the 1952 flap can be traced in the Blue Book monthly totals. In April (the month the *Life* article was published and the new procedures were established) 82 reports were made; 79 were made in May, 148 in June, and 536 in July. The July total was twice the total for each of the years 1947–1951. In August, the sightings trailed off—326 were made. This fell to 124 in September and only 61 in October. (Each month's total was half the one before.) November and December saw 50 and 42 reports, respectively. The total for 1952 was 1501 sightings; 303 remained unidentified.[41] Never before or after did Blue Book and the Air Force undergo such a tidal wave of reports.

Investigation

At the July 29 press conference, General Samford had said the Air Force would call in outside scientists to look at the Washington sightings. This investigation was made by Richard C. Borden and Tirey K. Vickers of the CAA's Technical Development and Evaluation Center. It had long been known that radar echoes were sometimes picked up from what seemed to be clear skies. These spurious echoes appeared more frequently on calm summer nights and were caused by weather—inversions and areas of air turbulence.

The first step in the CAA's study was to catalog all reports of unknown radar targets at ARTC over a three-month period and compare it to weather data for the Washington area. The report said, "It was then discovered that a temperature inversion had been indicated in almost every instance when the unidentified radar targets or visual objects had been reported."

Borden and Vickers concluded that different air masses moving at different speeds near the inversion's boundary set up eddies. These eddies formed bulges in the inversion which acted like a lens to concentrate and reflect the signal to the ground, where it was then reflected back to the radar. As the bulges drifted on the wind, the object seemed to move—in each case, the targets' movements matched the wind direction. The apparent supersonic speed of some targets was caused by the sudden fading of the inversion bulges. Targets were there on one sweep of the radar and gone the next. If they were assumed to be real objects, the operator also assumed they suddenly accelerated out of range.[42]

Both nights of the Washington sightings (July 19–20 and 26–27) had "rather peculiar" weather conditions. Both had been hot and humid days. After dark, the heat and moisture from the ground radiated away, causing both temperature inversions and a drop in humidity with altitude. At 10:00 P.M. EST on July 19, weather data showed a 3.1°F surface inversion. At 12,575 to 14,400 feet, there was a layer formed by overlying moist air. The humidity went from 84% at the ground to 20% at the layer's base, then climbed to 70% at the top of the layer. (It had rained during the late afternoon of July 19.) Such conditions would cause false radar targets. The 10:00 P.M. weather data for July 26 showed a 2.2°F surface inversion, but it lacked a humidity lapse sufficient to cause false radar echoes. There was, however, a 1.6°F inversion between 3,658 and 4,183 feet that was marked by a sharp humidity drop. This layer was strong enough to produce the false echoes.[43]

While the CAA investigation was under way, Blue Book was also looking into the case. Ruppelt talked to an airline pilot who confirmed that the radar was taking some odd bounces. The pilot said the tower asked if he could help track a UFO ahead of his plane. Several times the plane passed the radar target's position, yet the only object they could see was a Wilson Lines steamship on the Potomac River. The pilot concluded that "the radar was sure as hell picking up the steamboat." He added there were so many lights around Washington it was easy to see a "mysterious light" in any direction.[44]

The Crashed Saucer Con

In the two years since it was published, Frank Scully's *Behind the Flying Saucers* had sold 60,000 copies in hardback, been serialized in a magazine, and been published in a 25-cent paperback. And then, with a single article, the book was totally discredited. The article was written by J. P. Cahn, a journalist with the *San Francisco Chronicle*, and published, surprisingly, in the September 1952 issue of *True*.

Cahn met with Scully and oil man Silas M. Newton. Cahn made Newton a proposal: as a public service, would he and Dr. Gee be willing to tell the whole story, with names and photographs. Newton was reluctant but said he would talk it over with Dr. Gee. If he was agreeable, Cahn might see some of the artifacts from the saucers.

A week later, they met again at San Francisco's Palace Hotel. With Cahn was Scott Newhall, Sunday editor of the *Chronicle*. In the middle of a discussion of magnetics, Newton looked over his shoulder, then pulled out a handkerchief and untied it. Inside it were four objects. Two were disks about the size of a nickel. The metal had a powdery looking finish and was unmarked except for a few small nicks. The other two were gears, fine-toothed and the size of a pocket watch. Both were stained, Newton explained, by acid used in the 150 tests that had been run on them. When tapped, they rang with a clear sharp tone. They "seemed to be touched with star dust."

Later, in Newton's hotel room, he pulled a set of photos from his briefcase and put them face down on his lap. Cahn realized he was being given the buildup. Finally, Newton turned the first photo around. It was a fuzzy shot of the desert. "That's where the first saucer landed," Newton explained. There were several more similar shots. Then, as he was putting the pictures away, Newton stopped, gave them a sly look, slid one print up from behind the others and then put it back. In that brief instant, Cahn saw what looked like a large beach umbrella on its side. The implication was they had just seen one of the crashed saucers.

To find out what Newton was up to, Cahn went to Denver. There he learned Scully had distorted the events surrounding Newton's University of Denver lecture. The day after the lecture, the *Denver Post* quoted the class's instructor, Francis Broman, as saying its scientific value was "absolute zero." Broman told Cahn the lecture was not "a confidential scientific discourse" but the regular 12:40 P.M. basic science class which met every day. Cahn also checked on George T. Koehler who had been with Newton at the lecture. Cahn caught him in several lies, including that he had been a football player with the Chicago Bears.

Cahn decided he had to get one of the disks for analysis and find Dr. Gee. Stanford Research Institute was willing to do the tests, but when Cahn suggested the disks be analyzed, Newton exploded with anger— Cahn had been chasing him for two months, he was a busy man, he had told Scully the saucer story as a favor and all he had gotten for it was abuse and persecution. And then the tone changed. Newton said in a calm voice:

> I've talked with my people and their statement to me was, see, that Scully made $25 or $30,000 out of his book on what little information we've furnished him. They said to me, "Now if we lay all this stuff on the line, it's going to take a lot of time and we want to know what there is in it for us."

After this near-disaster, Cahn decided he would have to pull a switch. Newhall machined several disks of varying sizes. The idea was to have a close match. Cahn then dangled a series of meetings to entice Newton to produce the disks but Newton made excuses and did not produce them.

Stymied in his attempt to steal a disk, Cahn began looking into Newton's background and found that he had been arrested twice during the 1930s for grand larceny and false securities statements. Both times, the charges were dismissed. Clearly, Newton tended to get into trouble but always wormed his way out.

Cahn began checking into Newton's current activities. While reviewing Newton's phone records, Cahn found he was making a lot of calls to Leo A. GeBauer in Phoenix, Arizona. GeBauer ran the Western Radio & Engineering Company—a radio and television parts supply house. Both Scully and Newton had said "Dr. Gee" lived in Phoenix.

Before Cahn could go to Phoenix, Newton called to set up a meeting. At the meeting, Newton pulled out the handkerchief, spread the disks and gears on the table and said, "I suppose you want to see these again." Cahn had the fake disks with him but one look made it clear they were poor copies. Cahn palmed the best fake and asked Newton to see one of the disks. Cahn held it in one hand, then let it drop into his cupped hand—with the fake. He went through the motions of hefting the disk, keeping the two tightly palmed to keep from mixing them up. Then, looking Newton right in the eye, Cahn handed him the fake. Newton did not notice the switch.

Within five minutes, Cahn was heading for the Stanford Research Institute. They chipped off a tiny piece and checked its melting point, ran a gravimetric analysis, examined its structure with a microscope and made a spectrochemical analysis. The disk was grade 2S aluminum, 99.5% pure with a melting point of 657°F, of the type used in pots and pans.

Scully was confused and upset when shown the lab report on the disk. He did identify Dr. Gee as GeBauer. He also promised to help Cahn uncover the reason for the hoax if GeBauer denied being Dr. Gee in writing.

A Better Business Bureau investigation uncovered some inconsistencies in GeBauer's background. Instead of degrees from Armour Institute, Creighton University, and the University of Berlin, he now claimed only an electrical engineering degree from Louis Institute of Technology. In Scully's book, he was described as having led 1,700 scientists doing some 35,000 experiments, costing $1 billion in top secret magnetic research. GeBauer now said he had only been Chief of Laboratories at the AiResearch Company—in fact he had only been a maintenance man.

When Cahn confronted GeBauer, he denied being Dr. Gee. GeBauer finally wrote a letter to this effect.

When Cahn called Scully with the denial, he refused to listen. When he sent a photostat copy of GeBauer's statement, Scully's only response was a violent letter and a phone call "that should have short-circuited the entire Bell System." Cahn concluded Scully had been blinded by his long-standing friendship with Newton, although, as Cahn noted, "that takes some believing about Scully."[45] What Cahn did not know in September 1952 was why Newton and GeBauer had gone to all the trouble of concocting the crashed saucer story. That would soon become clear.

Convictions and Belief

In the days following publication of the article, *True* received a number of letters from people who had been victims of Newton and GeBauer. For twenty-five years, alone or as a team, they had sold worthless stocks and fake machines. Yet, in all the cases, the three-year statute of limitations had expired. There was no chance to prosecute. Then two possibilities appeared.

The first was a Denver millionaire named Herman Flader. In early 1949, Flader paid $4,000 for GeBauer's "doodlebug." This was a secret oil-detecting device that worked, GeBauer said, on the same magnetic principles as flying saucers. Next Flader bought a half interest in three more machines. The cost was $28,552.30. Newton was also getting money out of Flader—$152,000 for drilling on Dutton Creek, Wyoming, $1,500 for an oil lease near Newhall, California, and $49,400 for an oil field outside Mojave, California. In all, Flader lost $231,452.30.

Cahn asked if Flader had any proof of his story. He brought out a stack of canceled checks. Each was signed by Newton or GeBauer. Cahn checked the dates and found some were just within the three-year limit. Flader also showed him two of GeBauer's doodlebugs—they were war surplus U.S. Army radio transmitter tuning units. Flader agreed to press charges and they went to see Denver D.A. Bert Keating.

Cahn also met with Herman Corsun, a Phoenix delicatessen owner who had been taken for $3,350 by GeBauer for an oil lease near Casper, Wyoming. Corsun was mad and wanted to file charges immediately, but reluctantly agreed to hold off until charges could be filed in Denver.

On October 10, 1952, charges were quietly filed. It was not until October 14 that they were arrested by the FBI—Newton in Hollywood and GeBauer in Phoenix. The day after the arrest, eleven civil suits were filed against Newton totaling over $137,700. Newton and GeBauer were soon out on bail and the trial was postponed several times. They used this time to settle as many of the civil suits as possible. Herman Corsun settled for $2,300 and several 17-inch TV sets.

The trial did not begin until November 10, 1953. Newton and GeBauer were charged with conducting a confidence game and conspiracy to commit a confidence game. Herman Flader spent nearly a week on the stand as the state's first witness. He was cross-examined for four days but stuck to his story. The defense received another setback when D.A. Keating brought in a tuner unit identical to the ones for which Flader paid $18,500. He bought it at a local surplus store—for $3.50. The trial was a rout—the jury took less than five hours to find them guilty on both counts.[46]

For his part, Scully never admitted he had been taken by the two con men. In a letter dated April 12, 1954, he wrote, "My chief witnesses as you describe them have not repudiated one sentence of *Behind the Flying Saucers*. Dr. Gee was a composite of 8 different scientists, whose stories were tape recorded and then synthesized by me where they were in substantial agreement."[47]

Cahn's exposé had a long-term effect on the flying saucer myth. The crashed saucer story was destroyed and for the next twenty-five years, any such tale was relegated to the far fringes.

The Flying Saucer Myth 1952

Basic Beliefs

Disk-shaped objects have been seen in the Earth's atmosphere for hundreds of years.

These flying saucers are extraterrestrial spacecraft flown by alien beings.

They are capable of maneuvers and speeds beyond those of Earth aircraft and have been picked up on radar, which proves their existence.

The beings are here to observe human activities, such as nuclear testing, which concern them and may pose a threat.

The U.S. government knows this to be true, has proof and is covering it up.

The reason for this is to prevent panic.

Beliefs Discredited

Crashed flying saucers have been recovered along with their dead crewmen.

The Robertson Panel

> They lay all the evidence before me, and I am
> generally able, by the help of my knowledge . . .
> to set them straight.
>
> —*A Study in Scarlet*

The 1952 flap left the U.S. government divided. Some, including Blue Book staff members, believed the mass of reports was proof UFOs were extraterrestrial spaceships. The other group was not concerned about UFOs but, rather, about the reports themselves. So many UFO inquiries had come into the Air Force that regular intelligence work was affected.[1] It was this second belief—that UFO reports could clog communications channels—which brought the Central Intelligence Agency into the controversy.

CIA Involvement

Until the summer of 1952, the CIA had little interest in flying saucers. With the 1952 flap and the Invasion of Washington, however, this changed. On July 29 (the day of General Samford's press conference), Ralph L. Clark, Acting Assistant Director for Scientific Intelligence, wrote a memo to the Deputy Director for Intelligence. It said:

> In the past several weeks a number of radar and visual sightings of unidentified aerial objects have been reported. Although this office has maintained a continuing review of such reputed sightings during the past three years, a special study group has been formed to review this subject to date.

O/CI [Office of Current Intelligence] will participate in this study with O/SI [Office of Scientific Intelligence] and a report should be ready about 15 August.[2]

On August 1, Edward Tauss, acting chief of the Weapons and Equipment Division, wrote to the Deputy Assistant Director for Scientific Intelligence. He said:

1. Pursuant to your request for overall evaluation of "flying saucers" and associated reports, the following is pertinent:

    a. Of 1000 to 2000 such reports received by ATIC, a large percentage are clearly "phoney". An equally large percentage can be satisfactorily explained as known flights of currently operational U.S. equipment (aircraft, weather balloons, etc.) and many others are undoubtedly of natural phenomena (meteorites, clouds, aberration of light caused by thermal inversion or reflections, etc.).

    b. Less than 100 reasonably credible reports remain "unexplainable" at this time; regarding these reports, there is no pattern of specific sizes, configurations, characteristics, performance, or location. The sources of these reports are generally no more or less credible than the sources of the other categories. It is probable that if complete information were available for presently "unexplainable" reports, they, too, could be evaluated into categories as indicated in "a" above.

2. Notwithstanding the foregoing tentative facts, so long as a series of reports remains "unexplainable" (interplanetary aspects and alien origin not being thoroughly excluded from consideration), caution requires that intelligence continue coverage of the subject.

3. It is recommended that CIA surveillance of subject matter, in coordination with proper authorities of primary operational concern at ATIC, be continued. It is strongly urged, however, that no indication of CIA interest or concern reach the press or public, in view of their probable alarmist tendencies to accept such interest as "confirmatory" of the soundness of "unpublished facts" in the hands of the U.S. Government.

4. The undersigned has arranged with the Commanding Officer of the Air Technical Intelligence Center at Wright-Patterson Air Force Base, Ohio, for a thorough and comprehensive briefing related to this subject on 8 August 1952. Subsequent to obtaining full details, a detailed analysis will be prepared and forwarded.[3]

Even at this early date, it was feared that the mere fact that the CIA was interested in flying saucers would be seen as "proof" they were real. Time would show this fear to be valid.[4]

After the August 8 meeting at ATIC, the CIA representatives wrote three summaries. The three briefing papers, dated August 14, 15, and 19, gave a summary of government knowledge of flying saucers in the wake of the 1952 flap. The August 14 paper went into the background of both the Air Force and CIA investigations:

> At this point, OSI felt that it would be timely to make an evaluation of the Air Force study, its methodology and coverage, the relation of its conclusions to various theories which have been propounded, and to try to reach some conclusions as to the intelligence implications of the problem—if any. In view of the wide interest within the Agency, this briefing has been arranged so we could report on the survey. It should be mentioned that outside knowledge of Agency interest in Flying Saucers carried the risk of making the problem even more serious in the public mind than it already is, which we and the Air Force agree must be avoided.
>
> In order to supply both breadth and depth to the survey we have reviewed our own intelligence, going back to the Swedish sightings of 1946; reviewed a large number of individual official reports, recent press and magazine coverage and the main popular books. Indexes of the Soviet press were scanned. We interviewed a representative of Air Force Special Study Group. Following this, we spent a day at Wright Field in a thorough discussion with the officers conducting the ATIC study and finally we took the problem to a selected group of our own consultants, all leaders in their scientific fields.

The briefing paper then dealt with "the four major theories."

> First, that it is a U.S. secret weapon development. This has been denied officially at the highest level of government and to make doubly certain we queried Dr. Whitman, Chairman of the Research and Development Board. On a Top Secret basis, he, too, denies it. However, in the light of the Manhattan District early super security, two factors might be mentioned which tend to confirm the denials—first, the official action of alerting all Air Force commands to intercept, and second, the unbelievable risk aspect of such flights in established airlanes.
>
> The second theory is that these are a Russian development. Though we know that the Russians have done work on elliptical and delta wing principles, we have absolutely no intelligence of such a technological advance as would be indicated here in either design or energy source. Further, there seems to be no logical reason for the security risk which would be involved and there has been no indication of a reconnaissance pattern. However, it should be mentioned that there is a totally unsupported thesis that this may be a Russian high altitude development of the World War II Jap balloon effort using preset flares and the resulting U.S. press reports to check flight tracks.
>
> The third theory is the man from Mars—spaceships—interplanetary travellers. Even though we might admit that intelligent life may exist elsewhere and that space travel is possible, there is no shred of evidence to support this theory at present. There have been no astronomical observations in confirmation—no slightest indications of the orbiting which would probably be necessary—and no tracking. However, it might be noted Comdr. McLaughlin (of the White Sands report), a number of General Mills balloon people and many others are reported to be convinced of this theory.

The fourth major theory is that now held by the Air Force, that the sightings, given adequate data, can be explained on the basis either of misinterpretation of known objects, or of as yet little understood natural phenomena.

The August 15 paper was an overview of the Air Force explanations of most sightings.

Before we elaborate upon the current explanations I would like you to keep in mind certain facts which are generally common to all reports.

First, is the earnestness of those making reports. These people are certain that they have seen *something.*

Secondly, objects sighted almost always are reported to be against the sky thereby providing no point of reference.

Thirdly, without a reference point, a valid estimation of size, speed, distance or relative motion is virtually impossible.

Finally, no debris or material evidence has ever been recovered following an unexplained sighting.

In each case of reported sightings exists the personal element. This is the combined effect of psychological and physiological factors which individually or together may have outstanding importance in the accuracy of a person's report. These factors generally cannot be determined adequately.

The psychological factors are:

Mental conditioning by newspaper stories of earlier reported sightings.

Individual emotional response with respect to the unknown.

Desire for publicity resulting in 'embroidering' of facts or complete fabrication.

Emotion of chase of interceptor pilots.

The major physiological factors are:

General physical condition of person at time of sighting: condition of fatigue, anoxia [lack of oxygen; a reference to the Mantell case].

Existence and extent of eye strain immediately preceding sighting.

Insufficient night adaptation.

The "psychological factors," were illustrated by a Skyhook sighting.

The time was near dusk. Captain Ruppelt was called out to witness a sighting of three red lights in the sky. Even through binoculars he could not determine their nature. An F-94 interceptor climbed to 43,000 feet. At this altitude the pilot could see clearly that the objects were a cluster of three Skyhook balloons still well above him, sailing an even course across the sky. By this time, telephone reports had started to come in. The objects were described as violently maneuvering "saucers" of various shapes and colors. Even "looping" maneuvers were reported. The medical staff at Wright Field, including the senior psychologist, witnessed the sighting. The next day the staff turned in a report stating that, despite the official statement that these objects were balloons, they felt that this was in error and that the sighting must have been of some other unknown origin.

It also went into the astronomical and other natural causes such as Venus and meteors, aircraft, the jet stream, and temperature inversions.

The paper suggested "little known natural phenomena" might be responsible for the remaining unknown sightings. These included atmospheric effects, ionization, radioactivity (from both cosmic rays and nuclear tests) and electromagnetic or electrostatic phenomena. It concluded, "Here we run out of even 'blue yonder' explanations that might be tenable, and, we are still left with numbers of incredible reports from credible observers."

The August 19 paper stressed what the CIA saw as the two dangers UFO reports posed.

> Earlier, we mentioned our search of Soviet press. ARTC made a similar search. With world-wide sightings reported, we have found not one report or comment, even satirical, in the Russian press. This could result only from an official policy decision and of course raises the question of *why* and whether or not these sightings could be used from a psychological warfare point of view either offensively or defensively. Air Force is aware of this and had investigated a number of the civilian groups that have sprung up to follow the subject. One—the Civilian Saucer Committee in California—has substantial funds, strongly influences the editorial policy of a number of newspapers and has leaders whose connections may be questionable. Air Force is watching this organization because of its power to touch off mass hysteria and panic. Perhaps we, from an intelligence point of view, should watch for any indication of Russian efforts to capitalize upon this present American credulity.
>
> Of even greater moment is the second danger, our air warning system will undoubtedly always depend upon a combination of radar scanning and visual observations. We give Russia the capability of delivering an air attack against us, yet at any given moment now, there may be a dozen *official* unidentified sightings plus many unofficial. At the moment of attack, how will we, on an instant basis, distinguish hardware from phantom? The answer, of course, is that until far greater knowledge is achieved of the causes back of the sightings . . . we will run the increasing risk of false alerts and the even greater danger of tabbing the real as false. This is primarily an operational research problem but as long as it exists it will have intelligence implications because of its bearing on air vulnerability.[5]

It is worth recalling that these briefing papers were classified "Secret." If the Air Force had "proof" and was covering it up, as Keyhoe claimed, it would have been included in the three briefing papers. Yet the Secret explanation was the same as the unclassified one—the vast majority of sightings were due to misinterpretation of conventional objects with a small percentage of unknowns. There was no proof, such as a crashed saucer.

After several months of study, the Assistant Director for Scientific Intelligence, H. Marshall Chadwell, wrote a memo on September 24, 1952, to CIA Director Walter Smith. The memo is worth quoting in full both because it gives a summary of the CIA's research and for the insight it gives to the reasons for the Agency's interest. It also puts into perspective later claims of CIA control of the "cover-up."

1. Recently an inquiry was conducted by the Office of Scientific Intelligence to determine whether there are national security implications in the problem of "unidentified flying objects," i.e. flying saucers; whether adequate study and research is currently being directed to this problem in its relation to such national security implications; and what further investigation and research should be instituted, by whom, and under what aegis.

2. It was found that the only unit of Government currently studying the problem is the Directorate of Intelligence, USAF, which has charged the Air Technical Intelligence Center (ATIC) with the responsibility for investigating the reports of sightings. At ATIC there is a group of three officers and two secretaries to which come, through official channels, all reports of sightings. This group conducts investigation of the reports, consulting as required with other Air Force and civilian technical personnel. A world-wide reporting system has been instituted and major Air Force bases have been ordered to make interceptions of unidentified flying objects. The research is being conducted on a case basis and is designed to provide a satisfactory explanation of each individual sighting. ATIC has concluded an arrangement with Battelle Memorial Institute for the latter to establish a machine indexing system for official reports of sightings.

3. Since 1947, ATIC has received approximately 1500 official reports of sightings plus an enormous volume of letters, phone calls, and press reports. During July 1952 alone, official reports totaled 250. Of the 1500 reports, Air Force carries 20 percent as unexplained and of those received from January through July 1952 it carries 28 percent unexplained.

4. In its inquiry into this problem, a team from CIA's Office of Scientific Intelligence consulted with a representative of Air Force Special Studies Group; discussed the problem with those in charge of the Air Force Project at Wright-Patterson Air Force Base; reviewed a considerable volume of intelligence reports; checked the Soviet press and broadcast indices; and conferred with three CIA consultants, who have broad knowledge of the technical areas concerned.

5. It was found that the ATIC study is probably valid if the purpose is limited to a case-by-case explanation. However, that study does not solve the more fundamental aspects of the problem. These aspects are to determine definitely the nature of the various phenomena which are causing these sightings, and to discover means by which these causes, and their visual or electronic effects, may be identified immediately. The CIA consultants stated that these solutions would probably be found on the margins or just beyond the frontiers of our present knowledge in the fields of atmospheric, ionospheric, and extraterrestrial phenomena, with the added possibility that the present dispersal of nuclear waste products might also be a factor. They recommended that a study group be formed to perform three functions:

    a. analyze and systematize the factors which constitute the fundamental problem.

b. determine the fields of fundamental science which must be investigated in order to reach an understanding of the phenomena involved; and

c. make recommendations for the initiation of appropriate research.

Dr. Julius A. Stratton, Vice President of the Massachusetts Institute of Technology, has indicated to CIA that such a group could be constituted at that Institute. Similarly, Project Lincon, the Air Force's air defense project at MIT, could be charged with some of the responsibilities.

6. The flying saucer situation contains two elements of danger which, in a situation of international tension, have national security implications. These are:

a. Psychological—With world-wide sightings reported, it was found that, up to the time of the investigation, there had been in the Soviet press no report or comment, even satirical, on flying saucers, though Gromyko had made one humorous mention of the subject. With a State-controlled press, this could result only from an official policy decision. The question, therefore, arises as to whether or not these sightings:

   (1) could be controlled,

   (2) could be predicted, and

   (3) could be used from a psychological warfare point of view, either offensively or defensively.

The public concern with the phenomena, which is reflected both in the United States press and in the pressure of inquiry upon the Air Force, indicates that a fair proportion of our population is mentally conditioned to the acceptance of the incredible. In this fact lies the potential for the touching-off of mass hysteria and panic.

b. Air Vulnerability—The United States Air Warning System will undoubtedly always depend upon a combination of radar screening and visual observation. The USSR is credited with the present capability of delivering an air attack against the United States, yet at any given moment now, there may be current a dozen official unidentified sightings plus many unofficial ones. At any moment of attack, we are now in a position where we cannot, on an instant basis distinguish hardware from phantom, and as tension mounts we will run the increasing risk of false alerts and the even greater danger of falsely identifying the real as phantom.

7. Both of these problems are primarily operational in nature but each contains readily apparent intelligence factors.

8. From an operational point of view, three actions are required:

a. Immediate steps should be taken to improve identification of both visual and electronic phantoms so that, in the event of an attack, instant and positive identification of enemy planes or missiles can be made.

b. A study should be instituted to determine what, if any, utilization can be made of these phenomena by United States psychological warfare planners and what, if any, defenses should be planned in anticipation of Soviet attempts to utilize them.

c. In order to minimize risk of panic, a national policy should be established as to what should be told the public regarding the phenomena.

9. Other intelligence problems which require determination are:
a. The present level of Soviet knowledge regarding these phenomena.
b. Possible Soviet intentions and capabilities to utilize these phenomena to the detriment of the United States security interests.
c. The reasons for silence in the Soviet press regarding flying saucers.

10. Additional research, differing in character and emphasis from that presently being performed by Air Force, will be required to meet the specific needs of both operations and intelligence. Intelligence responsibilities in this field as regards both collection and analysis can be discharged with maximum effectiveness only after much more is known regarding the exact nature of these phenomena.

11. I consider this problem to be of such importance that it should be brought to the attention of the National Security Council in order that a community-wide effort towards its solution may be initiated.[6]

Simply put, the CIA's concern was not with extraterrestrial spaceships, but rather with the possibility that the Soviets could exploit U.S. belief in flying saucers to create a flap to clog U.S. communications and intelligence channels to cover a surprise attack. The question became how to deal with it.

The Robertson Panel

On October 2, 1952, Chadwell wrote a memo to the CIA director. It summarized the September 24 memo and included several draft memorandums. A memorandum for the director of the Psychological Strategy Board suggested "that CIA, with the cooperation of PSB and other interested departments and agencies, develop and recommend for adoption by the NSC a policy of public information which will minimize concern and possible panic resulting from the numerous sightings of unidentified flying objects."

Not all accepted the need for a major CIA investigation of flying saucers. In an October 13, 1952, memo, James Q. Reber, Deputy Director for Intelligence Coordination, wrote:

Determination of the scientific capabilities of the USSR to create and control Flying Saucers as a weapon against the United States is a primary concern of CIA/OSI. Its review of existing information does not lead to the conclusion that the saucers are USSR created or controlled. . . .

The institution of fundamental scientific research is the primary responsibility of the Defense Department. . . .

It is far too early in view of the present state of our knowledge regarding Flying Saucers for psychological warfare planners to start planning how the United States might use U.S. Flying Saucers against the enemy.

When intelligence has submitted the National Estimate on Flying Saucers there will be time and basis for a public policy to reduce or restrain mass hysteria.[7]

On November 25, the Air Force gave the CIA another briefing. It was summed up in a December 2 memo by Chadwell:

At this time, the reports of incidents convinced us that there is something going on that must have immediate attention. The details of some of these incidents have been discussed by AD/SI [Assistant Director of Scientifc Intelligence] with DDCI [Deputy Director of Central Intelligence]. Sightings of unexplained objects at great altitude and travelling at high speeds in the vicinity of major U.S. defense installations are of such nature that they are not attributable to natural phenomena or known types of aerial vehicles. . . .

[OSI] is proceeding to the establishment of a consulting group of sufficient competence and stature to review this matter and convince the responsible authorities in the community that immediate research and development on this subject must be undertaken.

The tone of the memo implies that Chadwell, like some at Blue Book, believed the Extraterrestrial Hypothesis was a possibility.

The suggestion of a scientific panel to review the UFO situation was presented to the Intelligence Advisory Committee at its December 4 meeting. The IAC was made up of the directors of intelligence for the Air Force, Navy, Army, Atomic Energy Commission, State Department, Joint Chiefs of Staff, and an assistant to the FBI director. It concluded that the CIA should "enlist the services of selected scientists to review and appraise the available evidence in the light of pertinent scientific theories."

Chadwell contacted Dr. H. P. Robertson, a physicist with the California Institute of Technology, to set up the panel. In 1943, he had been appointed to decide if the V-1 flying bomb was a German hoax. He quickly determined it was real and posed a major threat to England.

Robertson gathered together a distinguished group of scientists. Dr. Samuel A. Goudsmit was a nuclear physicist with the Brookhaven National Laboratory. During World War II, he had been a member of the Alsos Mission, an intelligence unit that recovered documents, equipment and personnel involved with the German atomic bomb program. Dr. Lloyd V. Berkner was a geophysicist with Associated Universities. Dr. Luis Alvarez, from the University of California, was an expert in radar and electronics. The final member was Dr. Thornton L. Page, an astronomer at Johns Hopkins University.[8] Page was a long-time friend of Robertson's; Page said later, "He invited me because of our friendship and because I lived in D.C. requiring no travel expenses."[9] He was paid $50 for his work on the panel; this was the only time he worked for the CIA.

The two associate members were Frederick C. Durant III and Dr. J. Allen Hynek. Durant was president of the American Rocket Society and of the International Astronautical Federation. He was secretary of the "Robertson Panel" (as it became known) and wrote its report.[10]

The Robertson Panel opened at 9:30 A.M. on Wednesday, January 14, 1953, in Washington, D.C. Berkner was not present; he did not arrive until Friday afternoon. Robertson began by describing the evidence. ATIC had selected seventy-five cases from 1951 to 1952 as the best documented. There were also reports on sightings at Holloman AFB, the Green Fireballs, summaries of eighty-nine selected cases, and intelligence reports on Soviet interest in U.S. sightings. Robertson asked each member to look at cases within their specialty (Page looked at Green Fireballs, nocturnal lights and investigation programs). At first, Page took the subject lightly: "At the start I thought it was a lot of nonsense and said so. Robertson said 'Shut up Page' and proceeded to read the Terms of Reference for the panel—a serious report to the U.S. Government about the possible threats of UFOs. I shut up."[11]

After this, the panel watched two films. The first was taken at Tremonton, Utah, on July 2, 1952, by Navy Chief Warrant Officer Delbert C. Newhouse. It showed a group of twelve bright objects flying in pairs against a blue sky. The U.S. Navy Photograph Interpretation Center spent some 1,000 hours analyzing the film. It concluded the objects were light sources and not reflected light. From measurements of the objects' motion, it was concluded that the objects were moving at 653 mph if they were five miles away. Both conclusions would rule out seagulls or balloons. Page suggested that somebody visit the site with field glasses—believing the objects were, in fact, seagulls.

The second film was taken at Great Falls, Montana, on August 15, 1950. It showed two points of light flying on an even course above the skyline of Great Falls. They passed behind a water tower, indicating they were at a considerable distance. ATIC believed the two films were among the best evidence for UFOs being extraterrestrial spaceships. After seeing the films, the panel adjourned at noon.

When it reconvened at 2:00 P.M., the panel heard from Lt. R. S. Neasham and Harry Woo of the Navy Photo Interpretation Laboratory.

They described the analysis of the Tremonton film. Captain Ruppelt then described ATIC's investigation and efforts to improve the quality of reports. The first day's meeting ended at 5:15 P.M.

The Robertson Panel met again at 9:00 A.M. on January 15. Ruppelt concluded his briefing on Blue Book. Hynek described the Battelle Memorial Institute statistical study then underway. A number of case histories were discussed in detail. The morning's work was concluded with a film of seagulls in flight that tried to duplicate the Tremonton film.

When the panel returned at 2:00 P.M., they heard a briefing on Project Twinkle, the Air Force investigation of Green Fireballs. At 4:15 P.M., General Garland joined the meeting and made three suggestions: that greater use be made of Air Force intelligence officers, that efforts be made to declassify as many reports as possible, and that the ATIC analysis effort be increased. At 5:00 P.M., the meeting adjourned.

The morning session of January 16 opened at 9:00 A.M. and was spent in discussion of individual case histories. Dewey Fournet read a paper on UFO movements; he concluded the Extraterrestrial Hypothesis could be the answer. It was followed by considerable discussion of the cases he described. When the panel reconvened at 2:00 P.M., Lloyd Berkner was present for the first time. The afternoon session began with a review of the meeting's progress by Robertson and the tentative conclusions reached. A general discussion followed and tentative recommendations were considered. The members asked Robertson to write a draft report that evening for a review by the panel the next morning. The meeting then adjourned at 5:15 P.M.

The Robertson Panel's final day opened on Saturday, January 17. Robertson began the meeting at 9:45 A.M. by submitting the rough draft to the panel. The draft had been approved by Berkner earlier. The panel discussed and revised the draft. After the lunch break, the panel made some final changes. This completed, each member made specific comments that would be included in the minutes of the meeting. With this, the Robertson Panel completed its work and adjourned.[12,13]

The "Robertson Report" was as follows:

1. Pursuant to the request of the Assistant Director for Scientific Intelligence, the undersigned Panel of Scientific Consultants has met to evaluate any possible threat to national security posed by Unidentified Flying Objects ("Flying Saucers"), and to make recommendations thereon. The Panel has received the evidence as presented by cognizant intelligence agencies, primarily the Air Technical Intelligence Center, and has reviewed a selection of the best documented incidents.

2. As a result of its considerations, the Panel concludes:
   a. That the evidence presented on Unidentified Flying Objects shows no indication that these phenomena constitute a direct physical threat to national security.

We firmly believe that there is no residuum of cases which indicates phenomena which are attributable to foreign artifacts capable of hostile acts, and that there is no evidence that the phenomena indicate a need for the revision of current scientific concepts.

3. The Panel further concludes:
   a. That the continued emphasis on the reporting of these phenomena does, in these perilous times, result in a threat to the orderly functioning of the protective organs of the body politic.

We cite as examples the clogging of channels of communication by irrelevant reports, the danger of being led by continued false alarms to ignore real indications of hostile action, and the cultivation of a morbid national psychology in which skillful hostile propaganda could induce hysterical behavior and harmful distrust of duly constituted authority.

4. In order most effectively to strengthen the national facilities for the timely recognition and the appropriate handling of true indications of hostile action, and to minimize the concomitant dangers alluded to above, the Panel recommends:
   a. That the national security agencies take immediate steps to strip the Unidentified Flying Objects of the special status they have been given and the aura of mystery they have unfortunately acquired;
   b. That the national security agencies institute policies on intelligence, training, and public education designed to prepare the material defenses and the morale of the country to recognize most promptly and to react most effectively to true indications of hostile intent or action.

We suggest that these aims may be achieved by an integrated program designed to reassure the public of the total lack of evidence of inimical forces behind the phenomena, to train personnel to recognize and reject false indications quickly and effectively, and to strengthen regular channels for the evaluation of and prompt reaction to true indications of hostile measures.[14]

The minutes of the meeting (commonly called the "Durant Report") expanded on these comments:

> The Panel Members were impressed (as have been others (including O/SI personnel)) in the lack of sound data in the great majority of case histories; also, in the lack of speedy follow-up due primarily to the modest size and limited facilities of the ATIC section concerned.

The panel looked at eight cases in detail and about fifteen in less detail. The Navy Photo Interpretation Laboratory analysis of the Tremonton film was not accepted. Panel members had no less than eleven objections, which included the similarities between the motions, sizes, and brightnesses of the objects in the Tremonton film and that of the sea-gulls in bright sunlight. Other objections included the use of a copy rather than the original film, the intensity changes were too great for the Navy's analysis to be accepted, as well as use of incorrect equipment and questionable assumptions in making averages of the readings. The Great Falls movie was determined to be reflections from two F-94s known to have been in the area.

Fournet's presentation was also rejected, as it was based on "raw, un-evaluated reports." In several cases, terrestrial explanations had been suggested, and in the others, the sightings were so brief "as to cause sus-picion of visual impressions."

Among the more interesting cases the panel looked at were reports of excessive radiation detected at the same time UFOs were seen. The first occurred at Palomar Mountain in October 1949 when cosmic ray coun-ters went "off scale for a few seconds," apparently when a V-shaped for-mation of flying saucers was seen. The other was a series of observa-tions by the "Los Alamos Bird Watchers Association" between August 1950 and January 1951. In this case, cosmic ray coincidence counters reacted oddly. The circuit diagrams and records were available for these sightings and it was quickly pointed out "that the recorded data were undoubtedly due to instrumental effects that would have been recog-nized as such by more experienced observers." Based on the evidence presented:

> The Panel concluded that reasonable explanations could be suggested for most of the sightings and "by deduction and scientific method it could be in-duced (given additional data) that other cases might be explained in a similar manner." The Panel pointed out that because of the brevity of some sightings (e.g. 2–3 seconds) and the inability of the witnesses to express themselves clearly (semantics) that conclusive explanations could not be expected for every case reported. . . .
>
> . . . It was felt that there will always be sightings, for which complete data is lacking, that can only be explained with disproportionate effort and with a long time delay, if at all. The long delay in explaining a sighting tends to elim-inate any intelligence value. The educational or training program should have as a major purpose the elimination of popular feeling that every sighting, no matter how poor the data, must be explained in detail. Attention should be directed to the requirement among scientists that a new phenomena, to be accepted, must be completely and convincingly documented. In other words, the burden of proof is on the sighter, not the explainer.

The contrast between a normal intelligence problem and the investi-gation of UFOs was also noted:

It was the opinion of Dr. Robertson that the "saucer" problem had been found to be different in nature from the detection and investigation of German V-1 and V-2 guided missiles prior to their operational use in World War II. In this 1943–1944 intelligence operation (CROSSBOW), there was excellent intelligence and by June 1944 there was material evidence of the existence of "hardware" obtained from crashed vehicles in Sweden. This evidence gave the investigating team a basis upon which to operate. The absence of any "hardware" resulting from unexplained U.F.O. sightings lends a "will-of-the-wisp" nature to the ATIC problem. The results of their investigation, to date, strongly indicate that no evidence of hostile act or danger exists.

Although the Robertson Panel "concluded unanimously that there was no evidence of a direct threat to national security in the objects sighted," it did note some indirect ones:

Misidentification of actual enemy artifacts by defense personnel.
Overloading of emergency reporting channels with "false" information ("noise to signal ratio" analogy—Berkner).
Subjectivity of public to mass hysteria and greater vulnerability to possible enemy psychological warfare.[15]

Page later wrote that his "major contribution" was this warning about these indirect dangers.[16] The panel also seemed to feel the Air Force investigation was ill-suited to meet these indirect dangers:

. . . the Air Force has instituted a fine channel for receiving reports of nearly anything anyone sees in the sky and fails to understand. . . . The result is the mass receipt of low-grade reports which tend to overload channels of communication with material quite irrelevant to hostile object that might one day appear. The Panel agreed generally that this mass of poor-quality reports containing little, if any, scientific data was of no value. Quite the opposite, it was possibly dangerous in having a military service foster public concern in "nocturnal meandering lights". The implication being, since the interested agency was military, that these objects were or might be potential direct threats to national security. Accordingly, the need for deemphasization made itself apparent.

This "deemphasization" was to be accomplished through both "training" and "debunking":

The training aim would result in proper recognition of unusually illuminated objects (e.g., balloons, aircraft reflections) as well as natural phenomena (meteors, fireballs, mirages, noctilucent clouds). Both visual and radar recognition are concerned. . . . This training should result in a marked reduction in reports caused by misidentification and resulting confusion.
The "debunking" aim would result in reduction in public interest in "flying saucers" which today evokes a strong psychological reaction. This education could be accomplished by mass media such as television, motion pic-

tures, and popular articles. Basis of such education would be actual case histories which had been puzzling at first but later explained. . . . Such a program should tend to reduce the current gullibility of the public and consequently their susceptibility to clever hostile propaganda. The Panel noted that the general absence of Russian propaganda based on a subject with so many obvious possibilities for exploitation might indicate a possible Russian official policy.

Specific details of this debunking program included use of psychologists familiar with the mass mind, training films, and Walt Disney cartoons. The panel felt that this program of "training and debunking" would take one and a half to two years. "At the end of this time," it believed, "the dangers related to 'flying saucers' should have been greatly reduced if not eliminated."

The panel's comments ended with a reference to groups such as the "Civilian Flying Saucer Investigators" and the "Aerial Phenomena Research Organization":

> It was believed that such organizations should be watched because of their potentially great influence on mass thinking if widespread sightings should occur. The apparent irresponsibility and possible use of such groups for subversive purposes should be kept in mind.[17]

The Robertson and Durant reports were classified "Secret."

Aftermath

The Robertson Panel set the policy for Blue Book until the project ended sixteen years later. It committed the Air Force to a long-term public relations battle to convince the public that UFOs were not real. At the same time, its conclusions meant there was little money or priority for the struggle. The plans Ruppelt had been working on to take instrument measurements of UFOs were also unraveling. The Air Force had planned to set up several manned observation posts in northern New Mexico.[18] The Robertson Panel felt such posts were not useful. (Project Twinkle had produced only two useless frames after a year.) With a number of astronomical sky surveys underway, there seemed little point, and the plans were dropped.[19]

As a substitute, twin-lens Videon cameras were put in 100 air base towers. One lens was covered with a diffraction grid. Within weeks, however, the grids deteriorated and they were abandoned. A final plan was to have cameras photograph radarscopes at some thirty air bases.

This would provide a record of any unusual blips for later analysis. The results were disappointing.[20]

When Ruppelt organized Project Blue Book, he planned to make a study of the unknown reports to see if any common shapes, patterns or trends could be found. Out of 434 unknowns, only 12 cases had sufficient detail to be useful. Of the 12, not *one* had a shape identical to another. The report concluded:

> It is not possible, therefore, to derive a verified model of a "flying saucer" from the data that we have gathered to date. The point is important enough to emphasize. Out of about 4,000 people who said they saw a "flying saucer", sufficiently detailed descriptions were given in only 12 cases. Having culled the cream of the crop, it was still impossible to develop a picture of what a "flying saucer" is.
>
> In addition to this study of the good unknowns, an attempt was made to find groups of unknowns for which the observed characteristics were the same. No such groups were found.

Having failed to find any "marked patterns or trends," the study ended by saying:

> Therefore, on the basis of this evaluation of the information, it is considered to be highly improbable that any of the reports of unidentified aerial objects examined in this study represent observations of technological development outside the range of present-day scientific knowledge.[21]

The number of UFO sightings also declined during 1953. After a busy winter, reports fell off during the spring. Even the traditionally high month of July was quiet. The total for 1953 was 509 (42 unknowns).[22]

July also saw a change in Blue Book's organization. Ruppelt was given use of the 4602d Air Intelligence Service Squadron (AISS). This unit was trained to interrogate captured enemy aircrews; in peacetime they were limited to simulated exercises. Use of the 4602d AISS gave Blue Book the large number of field investigators it had lacked.[23]

In late summer the "Age of Ruppelt" ended at Blue Book. In August 1953, with the end of the Korean War, Ruppelt was released from active duty. Blue Book was turned over to Airman 1/C Max Futch. That an enlisted man was given command (even temporarily) showed how far Blue Book had fallen since the Great Flap.[24] (Dewey Fournet had left the Air Force before the Robertson Panel and Al Chop resigned in March 1953.)

The CIA's interest in flying saucers went into a similar decline. The CIA, the Office of Current Intelligence, the Weapons Division, and the Physics & Electronics Division all wanted to get rid of their UFO files.[25]

On May 27, Chadwell wrote Todos M. Odarenko, head of the Physics & Electronics Division, saying: "Responsibility for maintaining current knowledge of reports of sightings of unidentified flying objects is hereby assigned to your division."[26]

Odarenko was less than enthusiastic, noting in a July 3 memo:

> In view of the finding of the Board that a close inspection of the available material does not postulate a serious, direct threat to national security, and that no information has been obtained since the Board's conclusion to necessitate their modifications, it is concluded that:
> a. the project will be considered as inactive
> b. the incoming material will be reviewed periodically to segregate references to recognizable and explainable phenomena from those which come under the definition of "unidentified flying objects"
> c. all material on unidentified flying objects will be deposited in the files for future reference unless it raises an immediately recognizable problem of concern to national security.
>
> With the above premise it is planned to handle the project with a part-time use of an analyst and a file clerk. To provide filing facilities, one additional filing cabinet will be requested.[27]

A December 17, 1953, memo from Odarenko to the Assistant Director for Scientific Intelligence gave a summary of government interest in UFOs a year after the Robertson Panel. It was titled "Current Status of Unidentified Flying Objects (UFOB) Project" ("UFOB" was a term sometimes used in the early 1950s). The CIA's interest in flying saucers

> . . . has been confined to maintaining awareness of the activities of other agencies (notably the USAF) in the unidentified flying objects business and to maintenance of files. The Air Force continues to maintain, but with apparently decreasing emphasis, its interest in UFOBs. . . . The Navy, in spite of press reports to the contrary, is presently devoting only part of one ONI [Office of Naval Intelligence] analyst's time to maintaining cognizance of UFOB's. . . . The Army has evidenced little or no interest in UFOB's.[28]

The Robertson Panel was a reflection of the times. In January 1953, the Cold War was at its frozen depths—the Korean War continued in a bloody stalemate and Soviet nuclear development continued. Domestically, the fear of communism continued, Julius and Ethel Rosenberg had been sentenced to death for their roles as leaders of the atomic spy ring and McCarthy's witch hunt rolled on. The fears that civilian UFO groups could be used by the Soviets was an extension of the Age of Suspicion.

Looking at the larger picture, the Robertson Report was not really about flying saucers, it was about Pearl Harbor. Throughout the 1950s, the U.S. was haunted by the specter of a surprise Soviet nuclear attack. The Robertson Panel had not only warned that flying saucer reports could be used to hide a Soviet attack, but also called for improvements in intelligence gathering and analysis to detect signs that such an attack was imminent.

"Flying Saucers from Outer Space"

The years between 1951 and 1953 also saw publication of a second group of books on flying saucers. Gerald Heard's book *Is Another World Watching?* was published in 1951. He believed the saucers were from Mars. Because of the saucers' small size and ability to make right angle turns, he concluded they were flown by intelligent "super-bees" about two inches long. Only an insect could survive the G-forces.[29] Kenneth Arnold and Ray Palmer's *The Coming of the Saucers* was published in 1952. It was an embellished account of Arnold's original sighting, its aftermath, and the Maury Island Hoax.[30]

The second most influential of the 1951–1953 group of books was Donald Keyhoe's *Flying Saucers from Outer Space*. Published in October 1953, it would sell over 500,000 copies. Keyhoe asked Blue Book for classified sighting reports and Ruppelt arranged for their declassification.[31] All the information was filtered through Keyhoe's absolute belief that flying saucers were real and the Air Force knew it. One example of this is his description of the events leading up to the Samford press conference. Keyhoe "described" General Samford's inner turmoil as he agonized over what to tell the public. He could imply that the saucers were U.S. secret weapons, but the public might not believe it. "There was only one safe step, in the nation's present mood. The saucers would have to be debunked." The high speeds and maneuvers had to be explained away. "There was one loophole—the temperature-inversion theory publicized by Doctor Menzel. . . . Regardless of its merits, it offered the only out."[32] Ruppelt had a savage response to Keyhoe's description: "This bit of reporting makes Major Keyhoe the greatest journalist in history. This beats wire tapping. He reads minds."[33]

The Invasion of Washington was a major part of the book. Keyhoe rejected the idea that a temperature inversion could have caused the blips. To him, the one time all three radars picked up a blip at the same location was "proof" the objects were real. In fact, there should have been many multiple tracks if the objects had been solid targets. Repeatedly, National Airport showed targets over Andrews AFB that Andrews's own radar did not spot. Keyhoe's writing style was to make an assumption, then write as if it were a fact.

Keyhoe expanded his ideas on the Air Force cover-up. He thought there were three "groups." Group A represented the believers—"Most of the men in this group had seen all the evidence and were convinced the saucers were machines superior to any known aircraft." Group B was dubbed the "silence" group. They "also had seen the evidence, believed the saucers were real, but feared the effects of a public admission." Group C included the nonbelievers who had never looked at the evidence.[34]

The aftermath of the book's publication hardened Keyhoe's belief that "the lid" was coming down and that "Group B" had silenced those who wanted the public to be told the truth. Excerpts of the book appeared in the October 20 *Look*. The Air Force feared this would cause a new flap and pressured *Look* to include a disclaimer saying there was nothing unusual in the cases. Comments were inserted into the article that disputed Keyhoe's claims. The Air Force also accused Keyhoe of obtaining the Blue Book cases fraudulently. Keyhoe went to Al Chop who signed an affidavit that he had released the files. Eventually the Air Force backed down.

In the latter half of 1953, the Air Force changed its procedures to implement the Robertson Report. In August 1953, Air Force Regulation 200-2 was issued, replacing Air Force Letter 200-5 of April 1952. AFR 200-2 fed the suspicions of those who believed in an Air Force cover-up. It prohibited release of any information on a sighting until a solution was found. This was done to dampen public speculation and the risk of increased reports.

Far more sinister in the eyes of the believers was Joint-Army-Navy-Air Force Publication-146. JANAP-146 was issued in December 1953. Its title was "Canadian–United States Communications Instructions for Reporting Vital Intelligence Sightings." It established procedures for the relay of "information of vital importance . . . which in the opinion of the observer requires very urgent defensive and/or investigative action." The categories of such visual intelligence were hostile or unidentified aircraft, missiles, UFOs, submarines, ships, or ground parties which might indicate the beginning of an attack on the U.S. or Canada.[35,36]

The transmission of such reports was not only protected by the U.S. Communications Act of 1934 and a similar law in Canada, as are all government communications,[37] but because of their intelligence content, they were also protected by the U.S. Espionage Act and the Canadian Official Secrets Act. The penalties were one to ten years in prison or a $10,000 fine. These provisions were meant to "emphasize the necessity for the handling of such information within official channels only." There was, in fact, no requirement that the report be classified.[38]

Believers used these penalties to put a more sinister meaning on JANAP-146. The provisions for reports of airplanes, missiles, submarines, ships, and ground parties were ignored. UFOs were depicted as its only interest.[39] JANAP-146 became part of the flying saucer myth. Believers pointed to it and AFR 200-2 as the means by which the "silence group" enforced its "censorship" of flying saucer reports.

● ● ●

Flying Saucers from Outer Space and the other books filled out the basic flying saucer myth. They did not expand it by adding new features or "doctrines." That would be left to the most influential book of the 1951–1953 period—*Flying Saucers Have Landed* by Desmond Leslie and George Adamski. Adamski said the saucers were flown by the inhabitants of Venus. Adamski said he had talked to one of them.

The Contactee Era

> I was wondering, Watson, what on Earth could
> be the object of this man in telling us such a
> rigmarole of lies.
>
> —*The Adventure of the Three Garridebs*

George Adamski was born on April 17, 1891, in Poland. About a year later, the family emigrated to the U.S. Between 1913 and 1916, he was a member of the U.S. cavalry stationed on the Mexican border. Between 1916 and 1926, he worked as a maintenance man at Yellowstone National Park, a flour mill worker in Portland, and a concrete contractor in Los Angeles.

In 1926, he began teaching philosophy. During the 1930s, "Professor" Adamski founded a monastery in Laguna Beach, California, called "The Royal Order of Tibet." It had the special license needed during Prohibition to make wine for religious purposes. "I made enough wine for all of Southern California!" he later told two followers. "I was making a fortune." This ended with the repeal of Prohibition. If it had not been for that, Adamski explained, "I wouldn't had to get into this saucer crap."

During World War II, Adamski and his wife, Mary, helped run a four-seat hamburger stand owned by one of his students, Alice Wells. Called Palomar Gardens, it was several miles from the 200-inch Hale telescope. Adamski often gave lectures on Eastern philosophy, sometimes late into the night.[1]

According to Adamski's later account, he saw his first saucer on the night of October 9, 1946. He was watching a meteor shower when he saw "a large black object, similar in shape to a gigantic dirigible" hovering in the night sky. In August 1947, a procession of 184 saucers passed through the night sky above Mount Palomar.

Late in 1949, two men stopped at Palomar Gardens for lunch. They were Joseph P. Maxfield and Gene L. Bloom of the Naval Electronics Laboratory at Point Loma near San Diego. Adamski claimed they asked him to help photograph the saucers. Adamski rigged up a camera on his six-inch telescope and "succeeded in getting what I deemed at the time to be two good pictures of an object moving through space." He said he turned them over to Bloom.

In early 1950, Adamski became something of a local celebrity. On March 21, 1950, he gave a lecture on flying saucers to the Everyman's Club in La Mesa. He talked about the two photos he had given the Navy. A reporter with the *San Diego Journal* contacted the Naval Electronics Laboratory about the photos. They knew nothing about them.[2] Years later, Bloom said he and Maxfield had only stopped at the cafe for a brief lunch before going on to the Palomar Observatory. They were not there to ask for Adamski's help and, in fact, did not know of his interest in flying saucers before meeting him. They did not instruct Adamski on how to photograph the saucers nor did they accept any photos for analysis. Bloom flatly stated, "Everything Adamski wrote about us was fiction, pure fiction."[3]

The First Contactee . . .

Adamski continued to take saucer photos, with poor luck. He wrote later that, while taking his photos, he was "hoping without end that for some reason, some time, one of them would come in close, and even land. I have always felt that if the pilot within one of those ships would come out and we could meet, there would be a way for us to understand one another."

During 1951 and 1952, Adamski heard of flying saucers landing in the desert east of Mount Palomar. Adamski made a number of trips "hoping to make personal contact. . . . But without success." Then came Thursday, November 20, 1952. Traveling with Adamski were Dr. George H. Williamson and his wife, Betty, and Al and Betty Bailey. Driving their two cars were Alice Wells and Lucy McGinnis, his secretary. About noon, they stopped for lunch near Desert Center, California. Suddenly, they saw "a gigantic cigar-shaped silvery ship." Adamski said, "Someone take me down the road—quick! That ship has come looking for me and I don't want to keep them waiting!" Lucy McGinnis and Al Bailey drove Adamski about half a mile down the road. He told them not to come back for an hour unless he signaled. McGinnis and Bailey then rejoined the others to keep watch. The large craft left the area when several military planes appeared. Several minutes later, Adamski saw a small "scout ship" flying near the mountain, then hovering. Adamski took several pictures before it, too, was chased off by several planes.

Then Adamski saw a man standing in a ravine about a quarter of a mile away. The man had long, sandy hair that reached to his shoulders and was wearing what looked like a brown ski suit. Adamski suddenly realized he "was in the presence of a man from space—A HUMAN BEING FROM ANOTHER WORLD!" Using hand gestures, English, and telepathy, Adamski tried to communicate with the spaceman. He learned that the spaceman came from Venus. The alien's visit was friendly but he was concerned about radiation from nuclear testing that would both contaminate space and destroy all life on the Earth. The spaceman formed a mushroom shape with his hands and said "Boom! Boom!" Adamski also said that the spaceman's scout ship was brought to Earth by a big mother ship—much like "our own naval plane carriers." The aliens also believed in a "Creator of All." Adamski wrote: ". . . we on Earth really know very little about this Creator. . . . our understanding is shallow. Theirs is much broader, and they adhere to the Laws of the Creator instead of laws of materialism as Earth men do."

The alien also confirmed that saucers were coming from many planets, both inside the solar system and from other stars. Some of the landing attempts ended in crashes. Some of these had been caused by humans. Although some of the spacemen were walking the streets of Earth, there would be no public landings, the reason being that "there would be a tremendous amount of fear on the part of the people, and probably the visitors would be torn to pieces by the Earth people, if such landings were attempted."

On another subject, Adamski "ask[ed] him if any Earth people had been taken away in space craft. He smiled broadly, and in a half-way manner nodded his head in the affirmative."

Soon the hour was up and the "chat" drew to a close. The spaceman kept pointing to his feet. Adamski noted his shoes left strange marks in the ground and told him he would preserve them. The scout ship returned and hovered above the ground. The spaceman asked for one of the film holders, promising to return it. He boarded the scout ship and it took off.

The "contact" over, Adamski signaled the others to pick him up. Dr. Williamson made several plaster casts of the footprints. They also decided to drive to Phoenix to tell a newspaper of the contact. An account was published in the November 24 *Phoenix Gazette*. It was illustrated with sketches of the footprints and one very poor photo of the saucer.

But Adamski's supposed adventures had only begun. Remembering the spaceman's promise to return the film holder, Adamski kept watch with camera and telescope at the ready. At 9:10 A.M. on December 13, 1952, he saw the scout ship gliding noiselessly toward him. As it hovered, Adamski took two photos. One of the portholes opened and a hand extended out, dropped the film holder and waved good-by. As the saucer departed, it flew over one of the cabins on the Palomar Gardens property. There, one photo was taken of it by Sgt. Jerrold E. Baker with a Brownie Kodak camera. The three photos turned out well. When the film in the holder was developed, it was found to be covered with symbols like those on the footprint.[4]

Adamski wrote a sixty-page account of his contact and offered it to British writer Desmond Leslie. Leslie was impressed and tacked it onto the end of a book he had just completed. It was published as *Flying Saucers Have Landed* in September 1953. It sold quickly and a second and third printing followed in October. The book sold over 100,000 copies.[5]

If Donald Keyhoe defined the basic flying saucer myth, it was Adamski's tale that created the "Contactee Era" of the 1950s. It supplied "their" description (handsome), motivation (fear of nuclear tests), reason for not openly landing (fear of human fear), and, most importantly of all, their message of love to stave off the abyss of nuclear war.

. . . And His Skeptics

Not all were, shall we say, impressed by Adamski. Even before his contact, Adamski was known at Blue Book. After Adamski's "chat" with a man from Venus, Ruppelt paid a visit to Palomar Gardens as just another tourist. Ruppelt described Adamski's style:

> To look at the man and to listen to his story you had an immediate urge to believe him. Maybe it was his appearance. He was dressed in well worn, but

neat, overalls. He had slightly graying hair and the most honest pair of eyes I've ever seen.[6]

Adamski's other official recognition was more serious. On March 12, 1953, the Riverside *Enterprise* carried a story on Adamski's speech before the Corona, California, Lions Club. It said he began by saying his "material has all been cleared with the Federal Bureau of Investigation and Air Force Intelligence." Several days later, three FBI agents contacted him. Adamski denied making the statement and wrote a letter to the newspaper. He also wrote a statement saying he understood the implications of making false claims and that the FBI did not endorse individuals. It was countersigned by the three agents and a copy was left with Adamski.

Several months later, Adamski showed the document to an interviewer saying he had been "cleared" by the FBI. The Los Angeles Better Business Bureau complained and agents went to see him. They were to retrieve the document, "read the riot act to him in no uncertain terms," and warn him that legal action would be taken if he continued. Adamski later said he had been "warned to keep quiet."[7]

The most devastating exposé of Adamski was published by James W. Moseley in January 1955. Moseley found that several of those close to Adamski had information that cast doubt on his claims. He talked with Al Bailey, one of the witnesses to the November 20 contact. Bailey said he did *not* see the spaceman or the scout ship. He also said that a drawing of the spaceman in the book, supposedly made by Alice Wells as she watched through binoculars, could not, in his opinion, have been made at that distance. Nor was it made on that date. He did see the mother ship and some flashes of light in the direction Adamski was supposed to be during the contact. To the best of his knowledge, no one else saw more. He amplified this in a letter: "I am well aware of the placement and disposition of all members of the party that day. I also feel sure that no one saw any more than I did." Bailey's sworn statement was apparently based on Adamski's *original* manuscript. The version which appeared in the book had been edited, expanded, and "improved" by Clara L. John, a Washington, D.C., based friend of Adamski.

Moseley also received letters from Jerrold Baker. Baker had lived and worked at Palomar Gardens between November 12, 1952, and January 12, 1953, and was credited with taking the Brownie photo of the scout ship on December 13, 1952. Baker, in a sworn statement, denied he had taken the photo. In fact, it and three or four others had been taken by

Adamski on December 12 (not the 13th as claimed in the book). Baker also said the desert contact was preplanned. Baker explained, "I accidentally heard a tape-recorded account of what was to transpire on the desert, who was to go, etc., several days before the party left Palomar Gardens." In another letter, he gave more details:

> The tape recording I heard was a metaphysical discourse received through Professor Adamski approximately one week before the desert contact. I heard about ten minutes of the tape-recorded talk. . . . I was able to determine that the desert contact was not a mere stab in the dark or a picnic in the desert, but a planned operation.

Baker also told how Adamski had tried to talk him into keeping quiet about the photo. In a November 2, 1953, letter to Baker, Adamski wrote:

> Now you know that the picture connected with your name is in the book, too—the one taken by the well with the Brownie. And with people knowing that you are interested in flying saucers as you have been, and buying the book as they are . . . you could do yourself a lot of good. For you have plenty of knowledge about these things (i.e., saucers), whereby you could give lectures in the evenings. There is a demand for this! You could support yourself by the picture in the book with your name. Remember that you are as much publicized in the book as I am, as far as the picture is concerned. And having the knowledge you have of these things, you have your break right here.

Finally, Baker's wife, Irma, said that Adamski had changed his story from the first time she had heard it. She had taken notes, so was sure the changes had occurred. She also said Williamson had confirmed he did *not* see the spaceman during the November 20 contact. In a conversation with Adamski, he had said "that in order to get across to the public his teachings and philosophies, he couldn't be too 'mystical', as he put it, and that he must present all the happenings on a very material basis because that is how people want them." When she responded this "was as good as lying," he said, "Sometimes to gain admittance, one had to go around by the back door."

In addition to these accounts of Adamski's activies, Moseley also caught him in several misstatements about his relationship with Bloom, Al Chop and others. There were also "holes" in the story. The six people with Adamski were all close friends or "believers" which cast doubt on their independent confirmation. "Dr." Williamson's title was, like Adamski's "Professor," honorary. All this led Moseley to conclude:

> I do believe most definitely that Adamski's narrative contains enough flaws to place in very serious doubt both his veracity and his sincerity. Fur-

thermore . . . the reader will be moved to make for himself a careful re-evaluation of the worth of the Adamski book.[8]

Adamski's Imitators

By this time, more people had claimed to be "contactees." Two more books were published in 1954—Truman Bethurum's *Aboard a Flying Saucer* and Daniel Fry's *The White Sands Incident*. Bethurum was a maintenance mechanic whose education was limited to grammar school and several years of high school.[9] His contact occurred in July 1952 (before Adamski's contact), when he had been laying asphalt in the California desert. Bethurum claimed he was awakened one night as he slept near his rig by "about eight or ten small sized men . . . from four feet eight inches to about five feet tall." Unlike Adamski's spaceman, they spoke English. Nearby was a flying saucer and Bethurum was taken aboard to meet its female captain, Aura Rhanes. Bethurum said she was "tops in shapeliness and beauty" even though she was a grandmother. Aura explained she came from a planet called Clarion which was always behind the Sun and so could not be seen from Earth. The Clarionites had been coming to Earth for many years and were living among humans. The Clarionites feared nuclear war would cause "considerable confusion" in space. Aura spent much time, in Bethurum's account, describing the idyllic life on Clarion. The planet was untroubled by disease, politicians, taxes, and, of course, nuclear bombs. Humans could also enjoy such a society if they thought and behaved correctly. Unless they did, Aura said, "the water in your deserts will mostly be tears."[10,11]

The second contactee of 1954 was Daniel Fry. At the time of his contact, Fry was a technician working for Aerojet General at White Sands. Fry was self-educated in chemistry, physics, and electronics. On the night of July 4, 1950, Fry was walking on a remote part of the base. A flying saucer appeared in the sky and landed near him. He walked up to the saucer and touched it. In his account, the metal was slippery and a little warmer than the desert air. Suddenly, a voice said, "Better not touch the hull, pal, it's still hot!" Fry was frightened but the voice reassured him—"Take it easy, pal, you're among friends." The voice, which called itself "A-lan" invited him for a short ride aboard the saucer, to New York City and back. The saucer lifted off and headed east. All during the flight, Fry asked technical questions about the saucer. A-lan told him it was a "cargo carrier," magnetically powered with limited range.

It was remotely controlled from a mother ship some 900 miles above the Earth. Its purpose was to collect air and bring it back to the mother ship. The air would then be mixed with the visitor's own atmosphere to acclimate them to living on Earth. Over New York, it descended and circled the city. The saucer then headed west. The saucer landed back at White Sands after about thirty minutes.

Fry followed up *The White Sands Incident* in 1955 with *Alan's Message to Men of Earth*. Unlike the first one, this contact was mental, in the form of "a voice inside his head." Alan explained that physical science had developed much faster than social science or religion and mankind was no longer able to cope. Only by developing "understanding" between the nations of Earth could civilization survive. Alan also said that tens of thousands of years before, the lost continent of Lemuria had been destroyed in a war with Atlantis. The Earth was left devastated. A few survivors had fled to Mars. Fry said he had been picked as the messenger because a landing would upset the "ego balance" of Earth's civilization.[12,13]

1955 also saw the debut of the fourth of the major contactees—Orfeo Angelucci and his mystically oriented *The Secret of the Saucers*. Angelucci's adventures began on May 23, 1952, after he completed work on the night shift at Lockheed. A voice spoke to him from two fluorescent green balls of light. The "space brother" told Angelucci he was studying the "spiritual evolution of man" and expressed the fear that Earth's "material advancement" was endangering life's evolution.

His second contact came on July 23, 1952. He saw a flying saucer land in the dry Los Angeles River bed. It was igloo shaped and made of a translucent material. Angelucci boarded the saucer and was taken into space and saw the Earth through a transparent wall.

He did not meet a spaceman until August 2. Angelucci was out walking late at night when he heard footsteps and then the same voice from the earlier contacts. The space brother, named Neptune, told him Earth was called "the home of sorrows" and that a disaster called "The Great Accident" threatened to destroy the Earth in 1986. The space brothers were here to help the Earth. Scattered throughout the book were mystical descriptions of the situation on Earth and the space brothers' philosophy:

> For all its apparent beauty Earth is a purgatorial world. . . . Hate, selfishness, and cruelty rise from many parts of it like a dark mist. . . .
> Your teacher has told you, God is love, and in those simple words may be found the secrets of all the mysteries of Earth and the worlds beyond.

In January 1953, Angelucci said he had amnesia for a week and had been spiritually transported to another planet. There he met a beautiful spacewoman named Lyra and her friend Orion. Angelucci was told he had been a spaceman, also named Neptune, in his first life.[14]

1955 also saw the return of the original contactee with George Adamski's *Inside the Space Ships*. Adamski described how he met with Martians, Venusians, Jupiterians, and Saturnians in Los Angeles area bars and cafes. He would then be driven into the desert for rides aboard flying saucers. He claimed to have flown around the Moon and to the Venusian and Saturnian mother ships. There, he met with the 1,000-year-old elder philosopher of the space people. Adamski and "the Master" had long conversations about the Earth's place in the universe. The Master explained that the space people had come to Earth to save mankind from eventual atomic war and to stop the radiation from Earth's atomic testing from poisoning other planets. Adamski said he had been selected to carry this message to the Earth. Another such messenger was Jesus. Adamski also claimed that the Sun was not hot and that the far side of the Moon had an atmosphere, tree-covered hills, animals, and cities![15]

The fifth of the major contactees was a self-employed sign painter named Howard Menger. His book, *From Outer Space to You*, was published in 1959. Menger's first contact came in 1932 when he was walking in the woods. He met a beautiful, long-haired blonde girl sitting on a rock by a stream. She was dressed in a translucent ski suit. She told Menger she and her people had "come a long way" and "we are contacting our own." During World War II, he had several more contacts with the space people.

When the war ended, Menger went back to New Jersey to start his own sign painting company. On impulse, in June 1946, he returned to the site of the first meeting. Soon a huge, bell-shaped saucer landed and out stepped the woman he had met earlier along with two handsome spacemen in the by-now-standard metallic ski suits. The space people took Menger for several rides in their saucers. In August 1956, he landed on the Moon and was given a guided tour of the sights. Menger explained that the Moon had an atmosphere and he could breath with no problems. Menger was told he was a reincarnated Jupiterian put on Earth to do good deeds to benefit mankind.[16,17]

Among them, Adamski, Bethurum, Fry, Angelucci, and Menger defined the contactee myth: the claims, the features, and the message. They set the pattern for the other minor figures that followed their lead.

Outer Space Communications

Another branch of the contactee myth was based on "mental" contact with the space people. Such "Outer Space Communications" are part of a belief system that stretches back to before the Oracle of Delphi. At the time of Arnold's sighting, such groups as Meade Layne's Borderland Sciences Research Associates were continuing this tradition. It was a simple matter to incorporate flying saucers and space beings into their psychic messages from the great beyond. However, flying saucers were only a part of a much wider belief system, which included such things as religious mysticism, "Cosmic Consciousness," "Vibrations," "Re-embodiment," Eastern philosophy, end of the world prophecies, and a great "New Age"—a mystic golden time.[18]

A number of figures were involved with this aspect of the contactee era. "Dr." George H. Williamson (one of Adamski's witnesses) used a radio and a Ouija board to communicate with Martians. Mark Probert relayed messages from the "Inner Circle."[19,20] George King acted as "Primary Terrestrial Channel" for the "Interplanetary Parliament."[21]

The most influential of these figures was George Van Tassel. After graduation from high school, Van Tassel worked first as an airline mechanic, then for Douglas Aircraft, Hughes Aircraft, and Lockheed in flight testing. In 1947, Van Tassel leased an abandoned airport at Giant Rock, California.[22] Giant Rock was a sixty-foot-high boulder. Van Tassel built a small cafe beside it, and a runway was laid out on the wide valley floor. Planes could land, then taxi up to the cafe. Under Giant Rock, a room had been dug which was large enough to hold sofas, chairs, and a piano.[23,24]

It was in this room that Van Tassel, surrounded by his followers, the "Council of Twelve," made his mental contacts. He received his first such contact in 1951. It was from Ashtar, commandant of a space station controlled by the Council of Seven Lights of the planet Shanchea. Soon, he was "communicating" with not only Ashtar but also Zoltan, Desca, and others, linking them with an "Omnibeam." Many of the contacts were about biblical events such as the Star of Bethlehem. Van Tassel used the messages to build the "Integratron," a dome-shaped building that could prolong life, produce antigravity, and make time travel possible.[25]

In the early 1970s, "C" attended a "lecture" by Van Tassel at Giant Rock. "Dr." Van Tassel, as he was called, sat at a long table in the cafe. On his right was an "old guy" with a look in his eyes as if he was at a revival meeting. The students sat around the table. The walls of the cafe had photos of lenticular clouds. Van Tassel said that, long ago, Venusians came to Earth and mated with subhuman apes. The Venusians knew it was wrong but the fur-covered apes were so beautiful they could not help themselves. Humans are Venusian/ape hybrids. "C" called this "Van Tassel's version of original sin." Van Tassel also talked about himself: "I've been considered a crackpot for years. But now the scientific establishment is beginning to take me seriously." "C" said he spoke like a man who had gone through a long tunnel, and had now emerged to see the plains spread out before him.[26]

Flying Saucer Clubs and Saucerian Conventions

Van Tassel's impact on the flying saucer myth was due to his Giant Rock Convention. It was the largest and most widely publicized "Saucerian Convention."[27] The first Giant Rock Convention was held in March 1954 and attracted over 5,000 spectators. Giant Rock, and other conventions, gave the contactees a platform for lectures. Stalls were set up so spectators could buy books, tracts, photos, records, and souvenirs.

During 1952 the first flying saucer clubs had been organized. Among the early groups were the Civilian Saucer Investigators (CSI) and the International Flying Saucer Bureau. (IFSB). The CSI was technically oriented while the IFSB was a contactee group. Both groups folded within a few years. The longest lived of the early clubs was James and Coral Lorenzen's Aerial Phenomena Research Organization (APRO). It was also founded in 1952 and would continue until the end of the 1980s.[28,29] The new flying saucer clubs were soon caught up in the controversy spawned by the emergence of the contactees. Some groups accepted their claims, while others broke into factions. By the mid-1950s, there were over 150 contactee-type clubs.[30]

One such contactee-oriented group was studied by University of California, Berkeley sociologist H. Taylor Buckner. He followed the activities of a Bay Area flying saucer club for several years. It was founded by a late-middle-aged woman with a fourth grade education and the title "Reverend." The membership was elderly—the average age was 65 with very few under 50. Around ninety percent were women, either widows or single. The members' educational level was low. They did not learn in an orderly manner. Instead, they collected random knowledge and were unable even to put it into an orderly system of belief. Their physical and mental health was poor, even given the members' advanced age. Many were deaf, had poor vision, walked with sticks or had some other physical handicap. Hallucinations were quite common. The few men in the group were either young schizophrenics or were aged with advanced senility.

Buckner found all members had histories of involvement with several occult groups. A typical individual may have been a member of the Rosicrucian, Theosophistism, I AM, or other smaller cults. Buckner found a major difference between these occult groups and the flying saucer clubs. An occult group normally has a set body of knowledge and enforces conformity with these doctrines. But with flying saucers, "there are no externally verifiable facts . . . none of the many interpretations saucerians give can be refuted." Thus, the restrictions of most cults did not apply. Any idea, even one with no connection with UFOs, was embraced.[31]

The conventions and flying saucer clubs created a network. This network gave believers an opportunity to meet other believers and exchange ideas, rumors, and reports. It also provided another means, besides the occasional book, for the flying saucer myth to develop and spread. The clubs held meetings and conventions, published newsletters, and sought new members/converts. They also gave publicity to the contactees by sponsoring public appearances. Through this network, the scattered believers were linked, becoming more than the sum of their parts.

The contactees also used television and radio to spread their "message." This gave the contactees audiences of hundreds of thousands or even millions. For ratings-hungry networks or stations, the controversy the contactees sparked was an easy way to attract an audience. Steve Allen's *Tonight* show featured many contactees. The *Betty White Show* had Truman Bethurum as a guest several times. Long John Nebel's late-night radio show was the contactees' most regular platform. Menger's appearances on Nebel's show were the main reason he became a major figure.

For both the media and the contactees, this partnership was a Faustian one. The media got their ratings, but at the cost of sensationalism over substance. The attention the contactees gained also put pressure on their claims. Daniel Fry failed a lie detector test. A New York lawyer, Jules B. St. Germain, sent George Van Tassel several hoaxed flying saucer and occupant photos. After Van Tassel had insisted on their authenticity, St. Germain exposed them as his own hoax, putting Van Tassel into an indefensible position.

The Contactee Myth

It must be stressed that not all believers in UFOs also believed the contactees. Yet, they did gain a following. To understand why, one has to look at the hopes, fears, and mythology of the contactees' message—and at the world of 1950s America. The contactee myth offered an escape from what some saw as an "inevitable" nuclear war. The aliens came from utopian planets, untroubled by the problems of Earth. "They" did not live under the shadow of the bomb's mushroom cloud. The planets, as Angelucci put it, had "eternal youth, eternal spring, and eternal day."

These angel-like beings wanted to prevent war and stop nuclear testing, and to build the kind of utopian society "they" enjoyed. "They" also warned that radiation from nuclear tests threatened to contaminate other worlds and that nuclear war would upset the solar system's delicate balance.

It was this "message" (and the messenger) which held the central role in the contactee myth. "They" had selected the contactee to carry out this "Christ-like" mission to Earth. The contactees never said they were the son of God with God's word. They did claim to have been selected by angelic, superior beings from heavenlike planets. The contactee myth can be thought of as a messiah-based religion for an age when traditional religion had lost its meaning.

The contactee myth was a mixture of Christianity, mysticism, and the occult. The contactees said the space people worshiped an "Infinite Father" or "Infinite Creator." The space people had also sent Jesus to Earth.[32] In Van Tassel's book *Into This World and Out Again* he "verified" his mental communications by quoting extensively from the Bible.[33] Added to this was mysticism and occult beliefs—Atlantis, telepathy, reincarnation and the like. This mysticism was not an aberration but an integral part of the contactee belief system.

Despite the spectacular nature of their adventures, one is struck by how unimaginative and anthropomorphic the contactees were. All the space beings looked exactly like humans. The only thing "alien" about them was the men's long hair. The men were handsome, with fair, white skin and blonde hair. The women were all fantastically beautiful objects of male desire.[34]

Dr. David Jacobs, a pro-UFO historian, also noted a peculiarity in the development of the contactees' stories. First, Adamski said he talked to a space being. Bethurum entered a saucer and talked to its captain but did not lift off. Fry flew in a saucer but did not leave the atmosphere. Then

Angelucci went into space. This was followed by Adamski flying around the Moon. Finally, Menger landed on the Moon. This was a logical progression. However, each contactee claimed *his* adventures started *before* the earlier ones. Each contactee seemed to be trying to be the most important one.[35]

If the space brothers were "Technological Angels" there also had to be devils. Although their contacts with friendly aliens were more familiar, Adamski, Menger, and other contactees claimed there were also unfriendly aliens in league with evil humans, who were plotting against the human race. One version of this "Technological Devil" idea was the "Men In Black." They made their "debut" in Gray Barker's 1956 book *They Knew Too Much about Flying Saucers*. The book claimed that shortly before the International Flying Saucer Bureau closed,its founder, Albert K. Bender, told a friend that he had been "silenced" by three strange men in black suits. The book included other accounts of UFO investigators who had been forced into silence, going back to Harold Dahl's alleged run-in with a stranger in a black suit.[36]

Others chose more familiar bogeymen—"Dr." George H. Williamson claimed that "International Bankers" (a traditional anti-Semitic code word) were not only behind the "silence group," but were manipulating the world's economic, political, and social institutions. He wrote:

> Every king, president, or dictator on Earth is only a figure-head . . . a tool of the "Hidden Empire" . . . It matters not whether the "authority" is religious, political, or otherwise, for there is only one *hierarchy* . . . the International Bankers.[37,38]

The evil Men In Black were described as having dark skins and Oriental features.[39] Comparing this to the description of the tall, blond, Aryan space brothers, the racial stereotypes become obvious.

Two films also had an influence on the contactee myth. It is worth noting how similar Klaatu was to the space brothers "met" by the contactees. Klaatu was handsome, benign, wore a ski suit, warned that human wars posed a danger to both the Earth and the universe, and worshipped a "Creator of all Things." These were all themes Adamski would use a year later.[40] The other was the 1953 film *It Came from Outer Space*. The movie included a number of elements that appeared in later contactee stories—the desert, the misunderstood contactee, the hostile townspeople, and the fearful aliens. At the least, it gave a visual reality to meetings with aliens.[41,42]

The most important result of the contactees was to divide the believers. Keyhoe and others who wanted scientific respectability and acceptance for UFOs saw the contactees as a "lunatic fringe" who threatened to discredit them. There were now two enemies—the Air Force and the contactees. Keyhoe would wage this two-front war during the 1950s and throughout the 1960s.

The Flying Saucer Myth 1953–1956

Basic Beliefs

Disk-shaped alien spacecraft have been seen in the Earth's atmosphere for many hundreds of years.

These flying saucers are capable of maneuvers and speeds far beyond the capabilities of Earth aircraft and have been picked up on radar.

The aliens are here to observe human activities, such as nuclear testing, which concerns them and which may pose a threat.

The U.S. government has proof of the existence of UFOs and is covering it up.

The reason for this cover-up is to prevent panic.

The Contactee Myth

Certain humans have had contact, via personal meetings or mental telepathy, with "space brothers."

The "contactees" have also flown aboard flying saucers, traveling into space and to other planets.

The space brothers come from utopian societies which are free of war, death, disease or any other of the problems of mid-twentieth-century Earth.

The space brothers want to help mankind overcome its problems, to stop nuclear testing, and prevent the destruction of the human race.

This is accomplished by giving the contactee a message of peace and brotherhood, which he is to spread throughout the world.

Other sinister beings, the "Men in Black," are intent on covering up the existence of flying saucers. They will use any means, including threats and violence, to accomplish this goal.

The Rise of NICAP

> We must look for consistency. Where there is a
> want of it we must suspect deception.
>
> —*The Problem of Thor Bridge*

The years following the Great Flap of 1952 were a time of consolidation. For the Air Force this meant putting the Robertson Panel recommendations into effect. For the flying saucer clubs, it was both the beginning of a quest to make the Air Force "reveal" what it knew about UFOs and internal warfare over the contactee question. Keyhoe would play a central role in these events. In March 1954, the Air Force reorganized Blue Book. Capt. Charles Hardin was named head of the project. The 4602d Air Intelligence Service Squadron (AISS) also began training for its role as field investigators. The 4602d AISS was to do the preliminary screening of reports. Sightings they could not solve would be sent on to Blue Book for further analysis.[1]

Decreasing the number of unidentified sightings was an important part of Air Force policy. The Robertson Report stressed the need for public education to lessen interest in UFOs. The Air Force saw the problem as one of public relations. The sightings were blamed on the "Buck Rogers trauma"—technological advances in the postwar era, Cold War fears, and science fiction.[2] The goal of Blue Book was to lessen public hysteria in order to lower the number of reports and lessen the danger of missing signs of an impending Soviet attack. In the Air Force's public relations effort, stress was placed on the lower numbers of unknowns. An October 25, 1955, press release said that of the 131 sightings reported in the first four months of 1955, only three percent were listed as unknown. Air Force Secretary Donald A. Quarles said:

> . . . we believe that no objects such as those popularly described as flying saucers have overflown the United States. I feel certain that even the unknown three per cent could have been explained as conventional phenomena or illusions if more complete observational data had been available.

Also released were a summary of the Battelle Memorial Institute's statistical study which Ruppelt had started in 1952 and the Air Force study of the twelve best unknown sightings. Called "Special Report Number 14" it said:

> All available data were included in this study which was prepared by a panel of scientists both in and out of the Air Force. On the basis of this study it is believed that all the unidentified aerial objects could have been explained if more complete observational data had been available. Insofar as the reported aerial objects which still remain unexplained are concerned, there exists little information other than the impressions and interpretations of their observers. As these impressions and interpretations have been replaced by the use of improved methods of investigation and reporting, and by scientific analysis, the number of unexplained cases has decreased rapidly towards the vanishing point.
>
> Therefore, on the basis of this evaluation of the information, it is considered to be highly improbable that reports of unidentified aerial objects examined in this study represent observations of technological developments outside of the range of present-day scientific knowledge. It is emphasized that there has been a complete lack of any valid evidence of physical matter in any case of a reported unidentified aerial object.[3,4]

Yet, even as the number of unidentified sightings was going down, the number of reports was starting to go up again. There were 509 (42 unidentified) in 1953, 487 (46 unidentified) in 1954, 545 (24 unidentified) in 1955, and 670 (only 14 unidentified) in 1956. The monthly totals gave an unusual picture. In early 1954, there was a growth in reports.[5] This coincided with the end of the McCarthy Era. During the spring and early summer, the televised "Army-McCarthy hearings" had exposed to the public at large the emptiness of McCarthy's charges and his bullying tactics.[6]

For the next twenty-four months, June 1954 through June 1956, the number of sightings stabilized to around forty to fifty per month. On a more significant level, many of the fears of 1952 and early 1953 were gone. Stalin had died in March 1953 and the Korean War had ended four months later. The political environment was mixed; tensions remained high, but there seemed hope that a stable arrangment could be worked out.

The monthly totals did not show a significant upsurge until the summer and fall of 1956. This was the period of the 1956 presidential election. In addition, during October, England, France, and Israel attacked Egypt and the Soviets crushed the Hungarian revolt. Crises seemed to be coming on a daily basis and would do so for another eighteen years.

"The Flying Saucer Conspiracy"

Beginning with Keyhoe's assumption of an Air Force cover-up, the believers presumed anything the government said was part of this effort. Keyhoe's beliefs about the "conspiracy" were becoming more involved. In a March 1954 letter to Coral Lorenzen of APRO, Keyhoe wrote:

> Actually the Air Force is not the only agency involved; the CIA, National Security Council, FBI, Civil Defense, all are tied in at top levels. The White House, of course, will have the final word as to what people are to be told, and when.

As "proof" of this cover-up, believers pointed to the Air Force's refusal to allow access to the case files. The Air Force refusal was based on the Robertson Report and the fact the files contained information on intelligence procedures. The public relations effort was thus in conflict— the Air Force said UFO sightings were nothing more than misinterpretations, yet it refused to release the evidence. But there was also a problem in logic with the believers' position. The believers said the proof UFOs existed was in the Air Force files; yet they had never seen the files.

Keyhoe began, in 1954, to think of ways of forcing an end to the cover-up. Keyhoe believed that a "wide public demand" was needed. He wrote Lorenzen:

> If enough intelligent believers could get together and use all possible influence, through their congressmen, senators, and any other means at hand, it might force a quick policy change in Washington.[7]

Even at this early date, Keyhoe was thinking in terms of a mass organization. The alternative was to wait for "the big breakthrough"—a landing on the White House lawn or another big flap. For Keyhoe, use of a mass organization also meant *he* could control events.

Keyhoe's third book, *The Flying Saucer Conspiracy*, was a shrill attack on the Air Force. Keyhoe began by claiming "the censorship of flying saucer reports" had been "increasingly tightened." He said "this top-level blackout" was enforced by "two strict orders." JANAP 146 directed pilots to report UFOs "and keep these sightings secret." The other order, AFR 200-2, "carries court-martial penalties." AFR 200-2 "confines" UFO investigations to "three super-secret groups"—the Directorate of Air Force Intelligence, the 4602d AISS, and the Air Technical Intelligence Center (ATIC). Keyhoe flatly said, "Because of JANAP 146 and AFR 200-2, hundreds of new, dramatic encounters have been kept under cover."

Keyhoe believed the "cover-up" was directed by the "silence group." Having assumed the existence of this shadowy group, Keyhoe began "describing" their emotional responses and actions:

> I realized for the first time the silence group's cold determination. . . . a new crisis . . . forced the silence group into a desperate decision. . . . For three weeks the silence group stalled, nervously weighing the dangers.
> . . . a new series of events quickly jolted the silence group out of its complacency.
> . . . the silence group's wrath.
> . . . which shocked the silence group.[8]

These descriptions of the "silence group's" inner thoughts were a figment of Keyhoe's own imagination. As before, he took his beliefs about "their" reactions and stated it as a fact. *The Flying Saucer Conspiracy* marked a shift in Keyhoe's belief system. No longer were flying saucers the central theme; that now belonged to the silence group and its cover-up. For the next two decades Keyhoe's beliefs about this would dominate the flying saucer myth.

Keyhoe also added a new element; it was flying saucers that were causing planes and ships to vanish off the Florida coast. The "Bermuda Triangle" myth was still new in 1955. The first suggestion that something mysterious was occurring was in an Associated Press article on September 16, 1950. It claimed that six Avenger torpedo bombers and a search plane, three airliners and a freighter had been "swallowed up," "disappeared without a trace" or "vanished in the thin air." Two years later, the October 1952 *Fate* carried an article entitled "Sea Mystery at Our Back Door." Harold T. Wilkin mentioned the incident in his 1954 book *Flying Saucers on the Attack*. Keyhoe, and another writer, Morris K. Jessup, in his book *The Case for the UFO,* separately included the incidents the following year.[9,10] It would be another twenty years before the distortions would be exposed.[11,12]

The Flying Saucer Conspiracy was only one of a flood of flying saucer books in the middle years of the 1950s. Between 1950 and 1953, eight books were published (only one was a contactee book). From 1954 through 1956, a further eighteen were released. Contactee books made up a full fifty-five percent of the 1954–1956 books (ten out of eighteen).[13] These were the years Bethurum, Fry, Angelucci, Layne, Van Tassel, and "Dr." Williamson were following in Adamski's footsteps.

The only skeptical book in the group was Donald H. Menzel's *Flying Saucers*. His book looked at the various atmospheric phenomena (temperature inversions, mirages, etc.) he believed were responsible for most sightings. Menzel became the leading independent skeptic in the 1950s and 1960s. However, his frequent use of questionable mirage phenomena to explain some sightings lessened his effectiveness.

From a historical viewpoint, the most significant book was Capt. Edward J. Ruppelt's 1956 book *The Report on Unidentified Flying Objects*. As former director of Project Blue Book, Ruppelt was able to give an inside account of the Air Force's investigation. He revealed the existence of the Twining memo which established the Air Force investigation, the Estimate of the Situation, the splits in the Air Force during the 1952 flap, and the Robertson Panel. Ruppelt was not an apologist for the Air Force; he criticized its handling of the issue, particularly during the Project Grudge years. The overall tone has been called "semi-believer."[14] Despite this, *The Report on Unidentified Flying Objects* was the most authoritative of the early books. It should have ended the speculation about an Air Force cover-up. In fact, Ruppelt's statements were converted into support for the cover-up idea.

Flying Saucer Movies

The year 1956 was also both the peak and the end of the flying saucer cycle of movies.[15] The fading of the flying saucer cycle was best symbolized by *Earth vs. the Flying Saucers*. It was a satisfying thriller, but did not break any new ground. Rather than original concepts, it took plot elements from earlier, better films. The alien's threat, "Look to your Sun for a warning. Look to your Sun for a warning," for instance, was an obvious copy of the "Watch the skies" line from *The Thing*. The net result was a film that was no more than an imitation of the classics it drew on.[16]

Earth vs. the Flying Saucers clearly showed that the cycle had run out of steam. After coming in peace and trying (several times) to take over the world, there was nothing left for the UFOs to do. After 1956, flying saucer films went into decline. Subsequent films, such as the 1957 film *Invasion of the Saucer Men* were, at best, indifferent. The low point was the 1959 film *Plan 9 from Outer Space*—widely considered the worst movie ever made.[17]

The National Investigations Committee on Aerial Phenomena

Up to the end of 1956, the flying saucer clubs tended to be small, short-lived and local. A large percent had a contactee orientation which relegated them to the fringes. They had no role in the national scene. That was about to change. The most important flying saucer group of the 1950s and 1960s had modest roots. Originally called the Flying Saucer Discussion Group, it was organized in the spring of 1956 and met more or less monthly at the Washington, D.C., YWCA. The driving force behind it was Clara L. John, who had edited and "improved" Adamski's original contactee story. Another member of the group was T. Townsend Brown who had come to Washington looking for government funding for his "Winterhaven" project—an electric space propulsion system that worked on antigravity.

Like many other members of flying saucer clubs, John and Brown had thought about the need for an umbrella UFO group. The speaker for the July meeting, Morris K. Jessup, also thought this was a good idea so John put it on the agenda. The meeting was held at 8:00 P.M. on July 20, 1956. John's notes read:

> Today there are thousands of little research groups all over the world, as well as people working singly on this thing. The time has come to coordinate their activities into a pattern that will prepare humanity for this startling new event in human existence. . . . That is what these meetings are being called for. This, tonight, is our fourth meeting. We [have been] laying the ground work the last couple of weeks, and you here tonight are perhaps witnessing— and we hope will be participating in—a new step, an unprecedented history-making step.

The suggestion was accepted and Brown wrote a "Tentative Prospectus" for what he called the "National Committee for the Investigation of Aerial Phenomena." The purpose of the group was "to direct a united scientific investigation of aerial phenomena and to correlate the findings toward a broader understanding of the possibilities and technical problems of space flight."

On August 16, the Flying Saucer Discussion Group met and Brown presented his ideas. They were accepted and on August 29, Brown filed incorporation papers. The name of the new group was streamlined—it was now called the National Investigations Committee on Aerial Phenomena (NICAP).[18] With Keyhoe's help, Brown assembled a board of governors composed of a retired Army general, two physicists, two ministers, two businessmen, and retired Rear Adm. Delmer S. Fahrney.

NICAP was formally incorporated on October 24, 1956, and was immediately in financial difficulty. Brown estimated $85,000 a year was needed to cover costs. Memberships were set at $15.00. The membership did not develop and NICAP was on the brink of bankruptcy by the end of the year. Up to this point, Keyhoe had stayed in the background, but at a January 1957 meeting, Brown, already director, nominated himself for chairman of the Board of Governors. Keyhoe stood up and accused Brown of mismanagement and attacked his antigravity propulsion theories. Keyhoe issued an ultimatum—Brown would resign or Keyhoe would advise Admiral Fahrney and other board members to resign. The next day, the board forced Brown to resign and elected Keyhoe NICAP director with Admiral Fahrney as chairman.[19] Keyhoe now had the organization he had sought in order to wage war on the Air Force.

Keyhoe's first step was to gain publicity. The following morning, Admiral Fahrney issued a statement to the press which was carried in some 500 newspapers. This marked the start of Keyhoe's aggressive public relations campaign. To ease NICAP's financial problems, he cut the membership to $7.50, moved to a lower-rent office, and fired salaried employees.[20]

To give NICAP respectability, Keyhoe assembled a distinguished Board of Governors. In addition to Fahrney, there were Vice Adm. R. H. Hillenkoetter (CIA director from May 1947 to October 1950), Dewey Fournet (ex-Project Blue Book), J. B Hartranft (president of the Aircraft Owners and Pilots Association), retired Rear Adm. H. B. Knowles (a World War II submariner), Army Reserve Col. Robert B. Emerson, retired Marine Corps Lt. Gen. P. A. delValle (former 1st Marine Division commander), Dr. Marcus Bach (professor of religion at Iowa State University), Dr. Charles A. Maney (professor of physics at Deflance College), Rev. Leon LeVan, Rev. Albert Baller, columnist Earl Douglass, and syndicated radio commentator Frank Edwards (a frequent contributor to *Fate*). NICAP also had several "special advisers": Al Chop (ex-Project Blue Book), airline captain C. S. Chiles (of the 1948 classic Chiles/Witted sighting), Navy Capt. R. B. McLaughlin (author of the 1950 *True* article on the White Sands sightings), Warrant Officer Delbert C. Newhouse (who took the Tremonton, Utah, film), and Wilbert B. Smith (friend of Keyhoe and leader of an unofficial Canadian UFO study).

NICAP's membership grew and Keyhoe began putting together a nationwide network. Keyhoe's goals for NICAP were different from those Brown originally envisioned. The investigation of UFO sightings was now secondary. NICAP was to be a lobbying group for congressional hearings on UFOs and to pressure the Air Force to reveal that it had proof of their reality.[21]

In the first issue of *UFO Investigator* published in July 1957, NICAP made an extraordinary eight-point "offer" to the Air Force.

1. NICAP offered a regular department to the Air Force in the *UFO Investigator* to explain their official position.

2. NICAP agreed to urge witnesses who sent in confidential reports to also send them to the Air Force—if restrictions were lifted.

3. The NICAP board and panel of advisers would examine the UFO cases listed as solved by the Air Force. If they agreed with the solution, NICAP would publicly endorse them.

4. NICAP offered to set up a permanent Air Force liaison to clear up misunderstandings, establish the facts, and report the results to the public.

5. NICAP agreed to help expose hoaxes, as the Air Force had said it was not in a position to do this.

6. NICAP suggested that it help prepare the public for any conclusions which might be released later.

7. NICAP offered to make an evaluation of the Twining letter of September 23, 1947, which said UFOs were real, the 1948 Estimate of the Situation which said they were interplanetary spaceships, the "Fournet Report" on UFO maneuvers, and the 1953 report by a civilian panel (i.e., the Robertson Report).

8. NICAP agreed not to release any opinions on Air Force materials until they had been delivered to the Air Force.[22]

Taken together, the eight points implied NICAP wanted to "ride herd," as Ruppelt put it, on Blue Book. Points 3, 4, and 7 implied NICAP would have veto power over any Air Force solution to specific sightings. Point 6 reflected Keyhoe's belief that the Air Force was "preparing" the public for the unveiling of the "truth." This offer meant the Air Force would agree to become a junior partner to a small, private group which held beliefs the Air Force had rejected as both incorrect and dangerous. As Ruppelt put it, "This went over like a worm in the punch bowl."[23]

To understand the Air Force/NICAP wars, one must realize the conflicting assumptions of each. NICAP believed the Air Force had proof UFOs were real and all its efforts were aimed at forcing an admission. The Air Force took the narrow view that UFO publicity was the direct cause of sightings. Therefore, efforts were made to solve sightings and minimize publicity.

Capt. George T. Gregory, named Blue Book commander in April 1956, made a determined (and in the view of some, an excessive) effort to solve each case. The "probable" category was expanded to include reports where no information was provided that could eliminate an airplane, balloon or other causes, and upgrade reports from "possible" to "probable" and from "probable" to "identified." Most of the JANAP 146 reports were put into the insufficient data category without additional investigation.[24] The latter was ironic given Keyhoe's charge that this regulation was being used to "hide" sightings.

Given Air Force concerns over publicity, NICAP posed a special threat. With its distinguished board, it automatically gained a status the contactee groups lacked. Also, its quest for congressional hearings posed a threat of publicity beyond that of 1952. Televised hearings would have an audience of millions, front page coverage, and a circus atmosphere. They would also imply UFOs were a serious problem and the Air Force would be criticized for its handling of that problem.

At first, it seemed NICAP would quickly achieve its goal of congressional hearings. In July, Keyhoe received a call from NICAP's lawyer. He told Keyhoe that Sen. John McClellan's Senate Subcommittee on Investigations wanted to hold hearings on UFOs. Keyhoe met with the subcommittee's chief investigator, Jack S. Healey. The specific complaint Keyhoe and NICAP wanted Congress to investigate was that "by secrecy orders and pressure, Air Force Headquarters has muzzled hundreds of pilots and other UFO witnesses." Keyhoe attacked the Air Force's refusal to investigate sightings prior to 1947 (i.e., the Foo-Fighters and pre-Arnold cases). He complained about AFR 200-2 and JANAP 146. Keyhoe also charged that there was "an official Air Force policy to explain away sightings." Keyhoe finished by bringing up Ruppelt's discussion of the 1948 Estimate of the Situation and its conclusion that flying saucers were interplanetary spaceships.[25]

Fall 1957

The crisis atmosphere continued into the fall of 1957. The crisis was unfolding not in some far-off place like Egypt or Hungary but in the local
schoolyard. In 1954, the Supreme Court ruled "separate but equal"
schools were unconstitutional. The struggle over school integration
came to national attention in Little Rock, Arkansas, during September
1957. When a mob prevented nine black students from integrating Central High School, President Eisenhower ordered troops from the 101st
Airborne Division into Little Rock. The nine black students were escorted into the school by paratroopers.[26] The Battle of Little Rock marked
the start of an era of internal turmoil. The calm, complacent, and untroubled 1950s were over. The future would be far different.

In the early evening of Friday, October 4, 1957, the future arrived.

For America, the shock of the launch of Sputnik 1 ranked with that
of the Great Depression or the attack on Pearl Harbor. Sputnik carried a
great symbolic importance. Since Buck Rogers, space had been seen as
man's future, but a distant future—not just yet, not now. When that future did come, it was believed that America, with its frontier heritage
and technological achievements, would lead the way. Then came Sputnik. The future was here and it had not been made in America.[27] The
Sputnik crisis also brought an upsurge in UFO reports. The 1957 flap
was about to begin.

The 1957 Flap

> And then I gave a cry of exultation, for a tiny
> pin-point of yellow light had suddenly transfixed
> the dark veil . . .
>
> —*The Hound of the Baskervilles*

There was no hint of the storm that was about to break over Project Blue Book and the Air Force. For the first six months of 1957, UFO reports continued at the flat rate of 1954–1956. Summer brought the now-traditional upswing. With September and the Little Rock crisis, the number dropped. In October, and with the launch of Sputnik 1, there was a surge to 103. But this was only the prelude to the 1957 flap.[1]

Levelland

It began in earnest at 11:00 P.M. CST on Saturday, November 2. Pedro Saucedo, a farm hand and part-time barber, was driving his truck about four miles from Levelland, Texas. With him was a friend, Joe Salaz. The night was dark with a 400-foot ceiling, a complete overcast, and light drizzle. Heavy thunderstorms had just passed through the area. In his statement, he wrote:

> I saw a big flame, to my right, front, then I thought it was lightning. But when this object had reached to my position, it was different, because it put my truck motor out and lights. Then I stop, got out, and took a look, but, it was so rapid and quite some heat, that I had to hit the ground.

Saucedo later estimated the object was 200 feet long and 6 feet wide. He said it was torpedo-shaped, blue in color with yellow flames coming out the back. He estimated the object's speed at 600 to 800 mph as it passed 300 feet away. Saucedo said he watched it for two or three minutes before it burned out and disappeared. He got back in the truck and started it up. After the engine started, the headlights came back on.

Other witnesses were also seeing strange objects and having car problems. At about 11:50 P.M., a man, his wife, and two children were driving along State Farm Road 1073 (several miles from Saucedo's location). They had noticed occasional lightning and static on the radio. Then a bolt of lightning flashed to the southwest. At the same time, the car's radio and lights went out for one to three seconds. Both husband and wife remarked, "that was certainly a strong bolt of lightning to put out our lights and radio." They thought nothing more about it until the next evening.

The next sighting occurred about five minutes after midnight. A 19-year-old Texas Tech student was just outside Levelland when the car's engine, lights, and radio went out. He got out and checked, but could find no problem. He then saw the object and got back in the car. The Air Force summary said:

> SOURCE described the object as oval in shape and he thought that the size of the object was that of a baseball at arm's length. He estimated that the object was seventy-five to one hundred feet at its longest dimension. SOURCE stated that the object was white in color, with a greenish tint, possibly caused by the tinted windshield of SOURCE'S car.

He watched the object for four or five minutes until it rose straight up and out of sight. He could not estimate its speed or distance. He then restarted his car and drove slowly home. He did not report the sighting until the following afternoon. He recalled there were heavy clouds and light rain at the time.

In the meantime, Saucedo's sighting had been reported to the Levelland police and a Texas Highway Patrolman was out looking for the object. At 1:15 A.M., he was driving down Oklahoma Flats Road when "I saw a strange looking flash which looked to be down the roadway approximately a mile to a mile and one half, the flash went from east to west and appeared to be close to the ground. The flash lasted only a fraction of a second, and was red to orange red in color."

Fifteen minutes later, another police officer was driving farther down the same road, also looking for UFOs. He saw "just a streak of light one time." The light had a reddish glow and moved south to west in two seconds.[2]

The White Sands Sightings

The next event in the unfolding 1957 flap took place farther west at White Sands, New Mexico. At 2:30 A.M. MST on the morning of November 3 (two hours after the last of the Levelland sightings), an Army corporal and private first class were on patrol. The corporal wrote that he and the other MP

> noticed a very bright object high in the sky. We were proceeding north toward South Gate and the object kept coming down toward the ground. Object stopped approximately fifty (50) yards from the ground and went out and nothing could be seen. A few minutes later object became real bright (like the Sun) then fell in an angle to the ground and went out. Object was approximately seventy-five (75) to 100 yards in diameter and shaped like an egg. Object landed by the bunker area approximately three (3) miles from us. Object was not seen again.

The weather was cold, drizzling, and windy; no stars were visible. The two MPs continued on to the Stallion Site Camp where they reported the sighting to the Sergeant of the Guard. He went to the area but found nothing.

The second White Sands sighting took place that evening. At 8:00 P.M. on November 3, two other MPs were on patrol near the Trinity site (where the first A-bomb had been tested). The night was bright with some stars visible through scattered clouds. The Moon was also visible. Then

> we looked in the general area of the West Impact area, and seen a bright light leave the ground and proceeding slowly into the air. We watched it for a few minutes and then proceeded to Nip site, where we reached the Range Road. The object kept getting brighter, then dimmer, then out then proceed to get brighter again. On arriving at Nip site, we sat and watched it for a few minutes then it disappeared. We then proceeded to the PMO and notified the SGT of the Guard. On our way to the PMO we seen the object several times and then disappear again.

The other MP added that "it started blinking on and off" just before the light disappeared. He estimated the object "was two or three hundred feet long and just about as wide" and was four or five miles away.[3]

As these events unfolded, radio, television, and newspapers carried word of the November 2–3 Levelland sightings. The *El Paso Times* carried the story on November 4 and the story went nationwide the following day.[4] The headlines read EGG-SHAPED UFO STALLS CARS ON HIGHWAYS and FIERY FLYING OBJECT STOPS TEXAS TRUCKS. The articles claimed that fifteen to twenty people had called in the sightings. A patrolman was quoted as saying:

> They seemed to agree that this something was 200 feet long shaped like an egg and was lit up like it was on fire—but looked more like neon lights. They said it was about 200 feet in the air, and when it got close car motors and lights would go off. Everybody that called was very excited.[5]

There was no mention of the stormy weather in the area. Press accounts quoted a NICAP investigator as saying, "I think it's a space craft from some of the neighboring planets." He speculated that the machines inside the object "disturb the magnetic field of balance" which caused car engines to stall.[6]

The effect of the publicity was dramatic: during the six days following the Levelland sightings, the Air Force received some 300 reports. Most of the witnesses claimed to have seen "egg-shaped" objects similar to the press accounts of the Levelland sightings. The reports ranged from persons of some standing casually reporting a sighting to those who insisted that the "blue lights" had stopped their cars in heavy traffic in the middle of large cities in broad daylight.[7]

The Flap Spreads

The next major sighting was made near Orogrande, New Mexico, on November 4. At 1:00 P.M., James Stokes, an electronics technician from Holloman AFB, was driving along Highway 54. According to his later account, the car's radio began fading out. At the same time, the car began slowing down, as if it had battery problems. As the car stopped, he noticed several cars parked by the side of the road. Their occupants were standing beside them pointing to an "egg-shaped" object in the northeast sky. It was the color of mother-of-pearl, with a faint, purplish tinge. The object descended from 5,000 feet to between 1,500 and 2,500 feet. The object was three to five miles away and made two passes at a speed of 1,500 to 2,000 mph. Stokes noticed a distinct rise in body temperature—"kind of a heat wave"—as if it were a "giant sun lamp." He claimed to have been sunburned by the exposure. He discussed the sighting with two other motorists. Stokes took their names (but not license numbers). The two passes took three or four minutes.[8]

The following day, November 5, saw two widely publicized sightings—one significant, the other less so. The Coast Guard cutter *Sebago* was about 200 nautical miles south of New Orleans. At 5:10 A.M. CST, its radar picked up an unknown target at fourteen nautical miles range heading north to south. By 5:13 A.M., it had closed to two nautical miles. There was no visual contact with the target. It then reversed direction and headed back north. The target was lost at 5:14 A.M. At 5:16 A.M., a second target was picked up at a range of twenty-two nautical miles flying in a circular pattern. The target faded at 5:18 A.M. at a range of fifty-five nautical miles. The third target was picked up at 5:20 A.M., at a range of seven nautical miles and hovering. The contact lasted about one minute. The only visual contact was made at 5:21 A.M. The object looked like a "brilliant planet," with the now-standard egg-shape, and moved at a high rate of speed. The sighting lasted three seconds. In the press and TV coverage that followed, it was implied the radar tracks and the visual sightings were *all* caused by *one* unknown object.[9]

The same day the Air Force issued a press release. It did not deal with the flood of reports, but rather was a historical review of ten years of UFO studies. It was stressed that the number of unknowns was going down. The Air Force believed that "if more detailed objective observational data" was available on the unknowns, "these too would have been satisfactorily explained." The press release summed up the investigation by saying:

> Air Force conclusions for the ten years of UFO sightings involving approximately 5,700 reports were: first, there is no evidence that the "unknowns" were inimical or hostile; second, there is no evidence that these "unknowns" were interplanetary space ships; third, there is no evidence that these unknowns represented technological developments or principles outside the range of our present day scientific knowledge; fourth, there is no evidence that these "unknowns" were a threat to the security of the country; and finally there was no physical or material evidence; not even a minute fragment, of a so-called "flying saucer' was ever found.[10]

For the situation at hand it was irrelevant—there were no solutions or even mention of the Levelland, White Sands, or *Sebago* sightings.

Reinhold O. Schmidt

Late that same afternoon, a new contactee made his debut. Reinhold O. Schmidt, a 56-year-old grain buyer, drove into Kearney, Nebraska, "white-faced and asking to see a minister."[11] Schmidt told city officials that a little after 2:00 P.M., he saw a flash of light from the Platte River bed. He got within sixty feet of the river bank when his car died. He then noticed an object in the river bed, which looked like a Navy blimp. Then, Schmidt said, a flash of light came from the ship and paralyzed him. Two men came out, asked if he was armed, and made a fast search. Once the paralysis faded, Schmidt asked if he could see the ship. The two men said he could.

There were four men and two women aboard. They were dressed in normal clothing. The men wore brown or blue street suits, brown shoes, narrow-brim hats, and long ties. The women were dressed in white blouses and brown skirts, wore lipstick, had short brown hair, and silver chain necklaces with a pendant. All looked to be between 45 and 50 years old, were 5′ 4″ tall, and had dark complexions. They spoke English to him; among themselves, they used High German.[12] Unlike most aliens in contactee stories, the "crew members" did not have much to say. Schmidt quoted one as saying, "In time you will find out what we are doing" and "Tell the people we're doing no harm"—hardly an Adamski style peace and brotherhood message.[13]

After about twenty-five to thirty minutes, Schmidt said the aliens told him good-bye and wished him luck. After leaving the craft, Schmidt said it lifted off, propelled by two large fans at the ends. When it climbed above the trees, the object disappeared.[14]

Schmidt took the deputy sheriff, the Kearney police chief, and the Kearney city manager to the landing site. They found two sets of footprints approaching a single set. The three sets of footprints then advanced together and suddenly stopped. The police also found "a greenish-grease-like-fluid" at the spot where Schmidt said the object had landed.[15]

Schmidt's tale quickly attracted press attention; he spent the next sixteen hours talking with the press and being interviewed by the local radio and TV stations.[16] Late on the night of November 5–6, a taped interview of Schmidt was played on the Long John Nebel radio show.[17]

By the morning of November 6, the story had gone nationwide and the Air Force learned of the case. Two investigators arrived and Schmidt took them to the landing site. They noticed that, although Schmidt had said the object was only three feet off the ground, many dry weeds and scrub trees four to five feet high were unbroken where it had supposedly been. The oil spot was about twenty-four inches in diameter. The greenish oil covered dry leaves and a sample was taken from the pools made on the leaves. A quart motor oil can was found about thirty feet from the oil spot. It was identical to a can of motor oil in the trunk of Schmidt's car. A beer-type can opener found in his car made identical punctures to those in the can found near the oil spot.[18] A later analysis "proved that the oil residue in the cans and that in the field matched."[19]

The Air Force also found Schmidt had a lengthy criminal record—between 1932 and 1938 he had been arrested and fined several times for bad checks and crop thefts. He spent time in the Nebraska State Penitentiary for embezzlement in 1938–1939.

The Air Force concluded he had suffered a hallucination and had come to believe the incident had occurred. Newspapers and wire services carried news of Schmidt's background, exposure, and his refusal to take a lie detector test that same day.[20,21] Schmidt spent two weeks undergoing mental tests at the Hastings State Hospital before he was released.[22] The uninspired nature of Schmidt's story also indicated that the contactee myth was running out of steam. The originality was gone, leaving only pale imitations of Adamski.

The Air Force Investigates

On November 6, the Air Force was also investigating the other widely publicized cases. Each revealed omissions and flaws in the press accounts. At Levelland, the Air Force found only three persons (Saucedo, Salaz, and the Texas Tech student) who had witnessed the "blue light," not the nine Keyhoe had claimed. Also, there was no uniform description of the object.[23] Saucedo's account could not "be relied upon"—he had only a grade school education and "had no concept of direction and was conflicting in his answers." Only the student saw a hovering object while the others saw only streaks of light. In view of the stormy weather conditions (not mentioned in the press accounts) an electrical phenomenon such as Saint Elmo's fire or ball lightning seemed to be the most probable cause. The engine failures were blamed on "wet electrical circuits."[24]

In the White Sands case, the four witnesses were young (19 and 21) and were considered to be naive and impressionable. The investigation indicated the first sighting, in the early morning of November 3, was of the Moon. It set at 2:29 A.M. MST. The second, that evening, was Venus. At 8:00 P.M. it was 15° above the western horizon and was shining at first magnitude, brighter than most stars. In both cases, the broken clouds created the illusion that the objects were moving. The investigator concluded, "[The] account of the sighting has been magnified out of all proportion to its importance, and the attendant publicity has been more sensational than factual."[25]

The Orogrande, New Mexico, sighting (November 4) was deemed a hoax for several reasons. Stokes "made somewhat contradictory statements." Originally he said ten cars had been stopped; this later changed to eight. He also admitted experiencing radio fade-out in that area before. More importantly, Stokes had been examined at a hospital and no traces of a severe sunburn could be found. A search for the two witnesses "failed to disclose their whereabouts, nor could they be further identified, no other reports of such a sighting were made by anyone else." It was also "manifestly impossible" for him to have observed the object for as long as claimed if it was traveling at the estimated speed.[26] It was concluded the hoax had been inspired by the Levelland publicity.

The *Sebego* sighting was of four separate targets, not a single fantastically maneuverable one. Each time, the new target was in the opposite direction from the last one. The first target was traveling at only 250 mph while the second target's speed was 660 mph. This suggested they were caused by a prop and jet aircraft respectively. (The sudden appearance and disappearance of the targets also suggested false radar targets.) The area where the *Sebego* was sailing was the "scene of many flights and operations of Navy and Air Force" planes. It was not possible to "check the countless possible origins and their flight plans." The visual sighting was also thought to be an aircraft. (This was later changed to a meteor.)[27]

The Air Force solutions were made public on November 15 (thirteen days after the flap began). The summaries of the five widely publicized sightings were very brief. The Levelland account was only sixty words long. (The Air Intelligence Information Report was nineteen *pages* long.) There were none of the details in the original case files and none of the reasons behind the Air Force's conclusions—just a flat statement as to the cause. The two-page press release also contained a major error—the order of the White Sands sightings was reversed: it said Venus had been seen by the first patrol while the Moon was sighted by the second patrol.[28]

The dimensions of the 1957 flap can be seen in the monthly reports. Between January and September, 406 UFO sightings were reported. In October, 103 were submitted, while November saw 361 reports. This was greater than any month since July 1952 and almost equal to the previous nine months' total. In December, 136 were reported. The number remained high in January 1958 with 61. In February, it dropped to the "normal" level of 41. The total for 1957 was 1006 (14 unknowns).[29]

The context of the 1957 flap should also be considered. The upswing in reports followed the launch of Sputnik 1. A few hours after the Levelland and White Sands sightings, the Soviet Union launched Sputnik 2, which carried a dog named Laika. There could be no question about Soviet space leadership. The UFOs and Sputnik fought for headline space during the first two weeks of November. The final blow came on December 6, when the Navy's Vanguard satellite was lost in a launch-pad explosion. The U.S. was publicly humiliated. The first successful U.S. satellite, the Army's Explorer 1, was launched on January 31, 1958.[30] With this, the number of UFO sightings dropped.[31]

To the flying saucer myth, the 1957 flap added the idea that UFOs could "magnetically" stop cars.[32] Before a typical sighting would be a "light in the sky"—distant and aloof. The numerous "car stop" cases seemed to indicate that the UFOs were now "interacting" with humans.

The 1957 flap differed from the two earlier ones in an important way. The wave of sightings came on suddenly—only three days passed between the Levelland and White Sands sightings opening the flap, and Schmidt's contact, which effectively marked its end. Following this, the reports dropped off. There was not the slow buildup of sightings as there had been in 1947 or in the Great Flap of 1952.

NICAP's Battle for Congressional Hearings

> Never have I felt such a cold chill of
> disappointment, Watson.
>
> —*The Adventure of the Musgrave Ritual*

NICAP emerged from its first year under Keyhoe and the 1957 flap ready for the decade-long struggle to come. The January 1958 issue of *The UFO Investigator* carried "The True, Documented Story of the November UFO Crisis." The account of the 1957 flap included the Levelland, White Sands, Stokes, and *Sebego* cases. Interspersed with the sighting reports were charges that the Air Force had

> labeled a Coast Guard officer and Coast Guard radar experts as incompetent, . . . ridiculing hundreds of reputable and qualified observers, including even Air Force pilots, radarmen, guided missile trackers . . . CAA tower operators, airline pilots, and members of the armed forces whose duties require cool-headed thinking and an absolute lack of hysteria.[1]

NICAP at War

For NICAP to be successful in its goals, Keyhoe needed a wide audience. Television appearances could attract new members and spread his beliefs on UFOs and the Air Force cover-up. Keyhoe was invited to appear on an *Armstrong Circle Theater* program on UFOs. Keyhoe was not a happy guest, complaining that the Air Force spokesman and Dr. Menzel were getting twenty-five minutes while he had only seven minutes. The biggest problem was that he had to use a preapproved script. Keyhoe complained that the Air Force was pressuring the CBS producers over what he could say. He later wrote about the "censored script" and the "censored evidence." In reality, CBS did not want "any row on the program" or "an open battle with the Air Force" if the argumentative Keyhoe went beyond the script.

Keyhoe wanted to stress three "secret" documents on UFOs he said the Air Force was withholding. The section read:

> In 1948, in a "Top Secret" estimate, ATIC concluded the UFOs were interplanetary spaceships. In 1952, an Air Force Intelligence analysis of UFO maneuvers brought the same conclusion . . . interplanetary. In January, 1953, a report by a panel of top scientists at the Pentagon reached this conclusion: There is strong circumstantial evidence, but no concrete proof thet UFOs are spaceships. They recommended intensifying the investigation and telling the American people all the facts.

The first document was the rejected Estimate of the Situation, the second was Dewey Fournet's analysis which had been rejected by the Robertson Panel, while the third was the Robertson Report itself. The latter's conclusions were far different than those Keyhoe implied. When Keyhoe read this during rehearsals, the Air Force spokesman objected, saying that if Keyhoe said this on the air, he would stand up and deny it. The producers cut the lines and Keyhoe accused the Air Force of censoring the program.

The show, titled "UFOs: Enigma of the Skies," was telecast "live" on January 22, 1958. As Keyhoe began reading the script, his frustration boiled over and he began to ad-lib:

> And now I'm going to reveal something that has never been disclosed before. . . . For the last six months, we have been working with a Congressional committee investigating official secrecy about UFOs. If all the evidence we have given this committee is made public in open hearings it will absolutely prove that the UFOs are real machines under intelligent control.

Before Keyhoe finished the first sentence, his microphone was turned down so the home audience could not hear what he was saying. Millions of people thought the Air Force had (literally) "silenced" Keyhoe. He later claimed that "both CBS and the *Armstrong Theater* staff must have been warned by the Air Force: Don't permit any startling NICAP revelations, even if they have proof."[2] Keyhoe emerged as the winner of the *Armstrong Theater* battle. Believers would point to it as an example of "silencing." To the public at large, CBS's cutting off of the audio gave Keyhoe's appearance an impact much greater than anything he said.

Following the 1957 flap, Keyhoe had continued to work with the Mc-Clellan subcommittee. On February 14, 1958, the chief investigator told Keyhoe that the Robertson Panel had met under CIA sponsorship. It was the disclosure the CIA had feared. NICAP immediately wrote the CIA and requested a copy.[3] The "sanitized" text was released on April 9, 1958. It read:

> REPORT OF THE SCIENTIFIC PANEL ON
> UNIDENTIFIED FLYING OBJECTS
> 17 JANUARY 1953
>
> 1. The undersigned Panel of Scientific Consultants has met at the request of the Government to evaluate any possible threat to national security posed by Unidentified Flying Objects ("Flying Saucers") and to make recommendations. The Panel has received the evidence as presented by cognizant Government agencies, primarily the United States Air Force, and has reviewed a selection of the best documented incidents.
>
> 2. As a result of its considerations, the Panel concludes: That the evidence presented on Unidentified Flying Objects show no indication that these phenomena constitute a direct physical threat to national security. We firmly believe that there is no residuum of cases which indicates phenomena which are attributable to foreign artifacts capable of hostile acts and that there is no evidence that the phenomena indicate a need for the revision of current scientific concepts.
>
> 3. In the light of this conclusion, the Panel recommends: That the national security agencies take immediate steps to strip the Unidentified Flying Objects of the special status they have been given and the aura of mystery they have unfortunately acquired. We suggest that this aim may be achieved by an integrated program designed to reassure the public of the total lack of evidence of inimical forces behind the phenomena.4

Compared to the original text, certain changes are clear. There was no mention of CIA sponsorship or that the Soviets might use UFO reports as cover for an attack, which was the reason for both the panel's formation and its recommendations. This meant there seemed to be no reason for taking "immediate steps to strip" UFOs "of the special status . . . and mystery" they had gained over the years.

The Air Force sent NICAP a copy on April 10 and it was published in the June 1958 issue of *The UFO Investigator*. NICAP tried to put the best face on the document. They asked:

> Why did the CIA—and later the AF—evade any mention of the CIA link with UFO investigations? Was it because the CIA is the agency or part of a

high level group imposing UFO censorship? Is the Air Force investigation actually under CIA control?"

NICAP concluded:

Without the full report, no honest evaluation can be made of the brief Air Force summary.

It seems obvious from the CIA evasion that important facts about this long hidden study are being kept from the public.[5]

That NICAP should take such a position is understandable. The flying saucer myth's whole belief system was based on the idea that the government had some "secret knowledge" which "proved" the reality of UFOs. To accept the conclusion of the Robertson Panel that "there is no residuum of cases . . . which are attributable to foreign artifacts" and "that there is no evidence that . . . indicate a need for the revision of current scientific concepts" would be to reject the basis for everything NICAP and Keyhoe believed in. They simply *had* to question the conclusions of the Robertson Report.

Clearly, the CIA attempt to distance itself from UFOs had backfired. Instead, it did exactly what the CIA had feared—raise questions and suspicions that it had the "proof" Keyhoe sought.

Yet, the early months of 1958 also brought frustration in NICAP's quest for congressional hearings. In January 1958, representatives of the McClellan subcommittee discussed with the Air Force its UFO investigation effort. Chief counsel Donald O'Donnell was impressed and concluded the subcommittee should drop the issue.[6] Keyhoe got the bad news in mid-March via letter: "This committee has held several interviews on the subject of unidentified flying objects. . . . No public hearings are planned or contemplated. . . . The subcommittee does not intend to investigate the United States Air Force." Keyhoe concluded (not unexpectedly), "They've given in under pressure, obviously."[7]

Congressional interest remained, however. In June 1958, Ohio Representative John E. Henderson sent the Air Force a list of questions based on Ruppelt's *Report on Unidentified Flying Objects.* The Air Force decided to provide a special, comprehensive briefing for interested congressmen. At the briefing, the Air Force showed the congressmen the classified parts of the Robertson Report. The warning that the Soviets could exploit UFO reports seems to have impressed them. After the briefing, the congressmen said they would advise their constituents that publicity would be "unwise . . . particularly in an open or closed formal congressional hearing."

This did not completely end the matter, however, and in August the House Subcommittee on Atmospheric Phenomena requested a briefing on UFOs. The chairman, John McCormack, wanted a week-long closed and unrecorded hearing. When the hearings were completed, the sub-committee members complimented the Air Force witnesses and stated they were "definitely pleased" with their approach to the UFO problem and were "apparently satisfied."

To close off the possibility that NICAP and Keyhoe might try again, the Air Force established a new policy in 1959. The policy statement said that the Senate Permanent Subcommittee on Investigations had periodi-cally requested information and, after preliminary investigation, they indicated that it did not plan to hold hearings.[8] NICAP and Keyhoe had been frustrated in their attempts to gain congressional hearings. Howev-er, they would continue the quest with an obsessive determination.

NICAP vs. the Contactees

NICAP's war was also with other believers—the contactees. The first is-sue of *The UFO Investigator* carried an article entitled "Policy on Contact Claims Announced." It was a nine-point challenge to the contactees. The specific points were:

1. Would they submit their evidence to NICAP?

2. A request for any photographic negatives.

3. The names, addresses, and notarized statements of any witnesses.

4. Would the contactee sign a notarized statement that all his claims were true?

5. Would the contactee take a lie-detector test?

6. Would the contactee agree to appear publicly before a NICAP-sponsored panel?

7. If point 6 was not possible, would the contactee either appear be-fore a private NICAP meeting or answer on tape a list of NICAP ques-tions under oath?

8. If the contactee had been called a fraud or hoaxer, had the con-tactee filed a lawsuit for libel?

9. Any further comments and/or suggestions?[9]

As with the eight-point "offer" to the Air Force, NICAP seemed to want to be the final arbiter. On a basic level, NICAP's war with the con-tactees was a struggle for control of the flying saucer myth. If NICAP could establish hegemony over the believers, the "one, true doctrine" could be established and all "heretics" could be cast into the outer darkness.

NICAP sent letters to eight contactees—George Adamski, Orfeo Angelucci, Truman Bethurum, Daniel Fry, Mr. and Mrs. Howard Menger, George Van Tassel, and Buck Nelson (the latter claimed to have flown to the Moon, Mars, and Venus, had dinner with the planets' rulers, and sold packets of hair from a 385-pound Venusian St. Bernard dog). None of them accepted the "offer."[10]

Then, in August of 1958, the struggle took a different turn. Keyhoe received a late-night phone call. He was told that Adamski had flashed a NICAP membership card during a Los Angeles television appearance. When he checked the membership roll the next morning, he discovered not only Adamski, but Angelucci, Bethurum, Howard Menger, Nelson, Schmidt, and Van Tassel were all listed as honorary NICAP members.[11]

Keyhoe sent telegrams to the seven demanding they return the cards. They were told that the cards had not been authorized, were void, and any future claims of membership would be false pretenses. Keyhoe discovered that NICAP's administrator-treasurer, Rose H. Campbell, had sent the cards. (Campbell had long urged Keyhoe to accept contactee stories.)[12] She and another NICAP staff member resigned. They were replaced by Richard Hall, who acted as associate editor and de facto second-in-command at NICAP.[13,14]

The Contactees Fight Back

The contactees did not passively accept NICAP's try at doctrinal control of the flying saucer myth. One part of Adamski's efforts against NICAP was what became known as the "Straith Letter." In December 1957, Adamski received a letter written on official U.S. State Department stationery. It began, "My Dear Professor," and said that some people in the State Department felt Adamski's claims to have met a spaceman in the desert were true. It was signed "R. E. Straith" of the "Culture Exchange Committee." Adamski showed the "Straith Letter" around as official support for his claims. This, once more, attracted the attention of the FBI. He was told to stop and Adamski claimed he had been "silenced" (but apparently he kept showing the letter).

It was not until 1985 that the truth about the hoax came out. The hoax was not by Adamski but on him. It was the product of two writers, James W. Moseley and Gray Barker. They were close friends, and Moseley would go to Barker's home in Clarksburg, West Virginia, every few months to spend the weekend. On one such weekend, while very drunk, Barker and Moseley decided to have some fun. A young friend of Barker's had given him several sheets of State Department letterhead. The friend's father was a high State Department official. Barker typed up and signed a number of letters to believers in addition to Adamski. Neither "Straith" or the "Cultural Exchange Committee" existed. Moseley mailed the letters from Washington, D.C., on his way home. The FBI investigated the misuse of official letterhead. As Moseley later put it, had they been evil, they could have tried to start World War III with the stationery. Barker was questioned about the incident, but denied involvement. (Barker smashed up the typewriter and dumped the parts into several wells.) The father of the individual who gave Barker the letterhead later asked that the investigation be dropped.[15,16]

Unlike other contactees, Adamski also had a following overseas. Between January and June 1959, he lectured in New Zealand, Australia, England, the Netherlands (where Adamski had a two-hour audience with Queen Juliana), and Switzerland. In all, he had spent six months abroad and gained a worldwide audience, and, in the process, counteracted NICAP's efforts.

Adamski continued this with his third book, *Flying Saucers Farewell*. It followed the standard pattern of contactee books with chapters on "What I Have Learned from Interplanetarians" and "The Bible and the UFO." A major difference was the lack of any new tales of saucer rides. Adamski's focus was shifting. As he wrote:

> My preliminary studies, which began with the advent of flying saucers, have now been completed. Of course, this does not mean I intend to abandon the subject, but it does mean that a new program of greater intellectual expansion, along technical and philosophical lines, will be carried out by myself and my associates.
>
> The knowledge shared by our space brothers must now be put to work. I have been advised to proceed in two fields that are vital to our progress—space philosophy and technology—which, we will learn, are inseparable in establishing a peaceful, productive society.[17]

The contactee myth was clearly fading.

NICAP's Problems

NICAP's most difficult problem was not with the Air Force, Congress, or the contactees—it was staying alive. The 1957 flap and Keyhoe's radio and television appearances in early 1958 brought in new members.

Then things began to fall apart. The numbers of UFO reports dropped and membership sagged. Bills for printing, rent, office supplies and other expenses were overdue. To deal with the setback, the size of *The UFO Investigator* was cut from thirty-two to eight pages. The membership dues were cut again—from $7.50 to $5.00. (The few original $15.00 members had their membership extended to three years; the members who had paid $7.50 were extended to eighteen months.) Even so, the cash balance for 1957 was $1.40.[18]

NICAP's balance sheet reflects its major goal. The third largest expense ($2,275 for 1957) was rent. All other UFO groups, both before and after, operated out of founders' homes. Since the members' only real contact with the group was through the newsletter, rent was a nonproductive expense.

From Keyhoe's perspective, though, it was not. NICAP was a lobbying group. Its goal was congressional hearings which would make the Air Force reveal the "truth" of the UFO's reality. To lobby, NICAP needed an office in Washington, D.C. Lobbyists, however, were supported by business, labor, or some other special interest group. All NICAP had was its membership dues and contributions. It became clear early on that NICAP depended on the money and work of a small percentage of its members.

In 1959, the money problems continued—only 1,800 renewals and new memberships were received. Its income of $11,409.88 left a $485.12 deficit. This did not include printer's bills, deferred taxes, and office supplies.[19] NICAP was unable to keep up its publishing schedule. (Given the choice between lobbying and publishing, Keyhoe delayed the newsletter.) In 1958, four issues of *The UFO Investigator* were printed. In 1959, there were only two, and three each in 1960, 1961, and 1962. To make up for this, the length of membership was extended once more. This caused confusion to members. Because of the extended memberships, many did not know when to send their dues. By 1962, over 2,000 members out of 5,500 owed back dues totaling $12,000. (They were still receiving the newsletter, however.)[20]

Far more serious, from Keyhoe's viewpoint, was that NICAP's financial problems were interfering with its "Case for Congress" lobbying efforts. In 1960, Keyhoe planned to send every congressman a ten-page document titled "NICAP's Confidential Digest of Documented UFO Evidence." Five hundred copies were also to have been sent to leading newspapers, radio and television networks, commentators, columnists and influential citizens. In the end, only thirty-one copies were sent to Congress.[21]

In early 1960, Keyhoe's fourth book in a decade was published. *Flying Saucers Top Secret* covered the founding of NICAP, the 1957 flap, the quest for congressional hearings, the problems on the *Armstrong Circle* appearance, selected UFO sightings and speculation. There was a hint of failure in its tone; at every step, NICAP had been frustrated in its efforts. A large part of the royalties went to support NICAP.

Last Try for Hearings

Despite everything, in early July 1960, it seemed Keyhoe might yet get congressional hearings. Members of the Senate Committee on Prepared- ness, House Armed Forces Committee, House Science and Astronautics Committee, and the CIA all requested briefings on UFOs.[22] Keyhoe learned of the interest and considered it a major breakthrough. *The UFO Investigator* headlined it: SENATOR JOHNSON ORDERS UFO WATCH. The article quoted him as saying:

> "At my direction," Sen. Johnson told NICAP, "the staff of the Preparedness Investigations Subcommittee is keeping a close watch over new develop- ments in this field, with standing instructions to report to me any recent sig- nificant sightings of unidentified flying objects along with an analysis of the conduct and conclusions of the Air Force investigation of each such sighting."[23]

The briefings were held on July 13 and 15, 1960. Unlike past brief- ings, the congressmen were not fully satisfied. Congressman Richard Smart said he felt the Air Force was withholding information from both the public and Congress. He warned that his future responses to his con- stituents would be based on the Air Force meeting his demands.

Congressional interest remained high and, in the spring of 1961, House Majority Leader John W. McCormack said in an interview with a NICAP member:

> I feel that the AF has not been giving out all the information it has on Unidentified Flying Objects. These UFOs (the sightings that cannot be satis- factorily explained) much [sic] be in a very high state of development. Whether they come from some other planet we don't know. We can't say they come from another planet until we find life on another planet. On the evidence we have you can't pinpoint their source.
>
> So many expert witnesses have seen these objects that you can't disregard so many unimpeachable sources. Among the experts who insist that some of these objects constitute something real, something unknown, are pilots, other persons with special skills in this area, persons of great responsibility, ratio-

nal-minded witnesses. This is not all imagination. You can't rule out all these sightings as imagination producing a mistake in identity. You can't put it down to atmospheric phenomena. It might be well for the House Committee on Science and Astronautics to hold further hearings, either executive sessions or open hearings to bring the matter up to date.

All this led Keyhoe to conclude "that the UFO secrecy fight is nearing a climax," and that, as a headline put it, PROBE ASSURED.[24]

The reason for Keyhoe's optimism was a decision by McCormack. In 1961, he directed Congressman Overton Brooks, chairman of the House Science and Astronautics Committee, to investigate UFOs. Brooks selected Minnesota Congressman Joseph Karth as chairman of a three-man Subcommittee on Space Problems and Life Sciences. The hearings would be held in early 1962.[25]

Keyhoe learned of the "UFO Subcommittee," and quickly proposed that NICAP be allowed to present "proof that the Air Force has withheld, denied or untruthfully explained" sighting reports and "has given contradictory, misleading and untrue statements to Members of Congress, press media and the public." NICAP also wanted the right to question the Air Force. The Subcommittee would require the Air Force to answer all NICAP's questions.

Keyhoe also made recommendations on specific actions should the subcommittee decide the Air Force was covering up. This included "ending the censorship," and setting up, through "emergency legislation or . . . an Executive Order," a civilian "UFO Information Agency." This agency would release all evidence on UFOs from December 8, 1941, onward. The evidence would include intelligence reports and conclusions, visual radar, photographic astronomical information, opinions of witnesses, all UFO studies, all military, civil, private, and foreign UFO information, and all U.S. government documents and orders on UFOs. The UFO agency would have members of the press and media to speed the release of information. It would also have an Air Force consultant to delete "minor classified items" and "one NICAP representative to help expedite operations."[26] Like the earlier "offers" to the Air Force and the contactees, NICAP seemed as intent on securing its own power as it was on uncovering the "truth" about UFOs.

The Air Force, once more, sought to fend off the hearings. In August 1961, the Aerospace Technical Intelligence Center (ATIC) gave a briefing to House Science and Astronautics Committee staff member Richard P. Hines. The Blue Book procedures were explained and Hines was shown around the Aeronautics Systems Division. Hines explained that congres-

sional interest was due to pressure from "undisclosed sources" on Mc-
Cormack (this was presumed to be Keyhoe).

Hines was "favorably impressed" and a week later he told the Air
Force that Overton Brooks had decided not to hold hearings on UFOs.
Hines continued, "For this I am sure both you and I breathe a deep sigh of
relief." As a result the "'plantiffs' [i.e., Keyhoe] have begun their clamor
stimulated by notices in the press of our committee's interest in UFOs."

This was followed by a letter from Congressman Karth to Keyhoe
which blasted him for trying to "be-little," "defame," and "ridicule" the
Air Force. He further accused Keyhoe of "malicious intent." Karth said
he was no longer interested in holding hearings or "listening to head-
line-making accusations (prompted it seems by past gripes) in open debate between you and the Air Force." After saying that congressional
protocol required the Air Force and NICAP to testify separately, Karth
said he thought Keyhoe wanted the confrontation only to embarrass the
Air Force and to indulge in "grandstand acts of a rabble rousing nature
where accusations may be made THAT COULDN'T BE ANSWERED BY
ANYONE—the Air Force or NICAP."

Keyhoe backpedaled, offering to submit NICAP's "massive UFO evidence" and trying to soften Karth's harsh opinion, but the quest had
ended. At this same time, Overton Brooks died and the new chairman,
George P. Miller, had no interest in either UFOs or hearings.[27] Never
again would Keyhoe be this close to gaining his long-sought hearings.

NICAP's Critics

Among believers, there were many who were unwilling to give Keyhoe
and NICAP the dominating position they sought. One early critic was
Ray Palmer.[28] On the surface, Palmer's argument with NICAP was over
the contactee question. On a more basic level, it was personal rivalry.[29]
In May 1958, Palmer called NICAP a cover-up to hide the "real issue"
and implied that Keyhoe was a tool of the military.[30] Palmer's own credibility was damaged in December 1959 when he announced his own
"truth"—that flying saucers did not come from some other world, but
from secret bases inside the hollow Earth.[31] He won no converts; the
flying saucer myth was too well established for a revival of the Shaver
Mystery.

Another critic took the idea of a conspiracy to its farthest limit. Dr.
Leon Davidson, a chemical engineer who worked at Los Alamos, be-

came convinced everything about UFOs was a CIA plot. In Davidson's conspiracy theory, the early sightings were caused by secret test flights of the XF5U-1 "Flying Flapjack" over Air Force bases, V-2 launches, and Skyhook balloon flights.

During 1950, according to Davidson's theory, Allen Dulles and the CIA began using UFO reports as a psychological weapon to deceive both the American people and the Soviets. It was the CIA who set in motion the Great Flap of 1952; first by sponsoring the *Life* article "Have We Visitors from Space?," then by creating the Invasion of Washington by using electronic countermeasures to create the false radar images. The contactees were also a creation of the CIA. Adamski's 1952 "contact" was a CIA-arranged hoax, while his flight around the Moon was created by using movie special effects. The "saucer" remained on the ground; the views of Earth, space and the Moon were projections. At the same time, Keyhoe was being "fed" data from the government. The CIA was also setting up NICAP, the other flying saucer clubs, and the contactee groups.[32] It was a total, seamless conspiracy that covered everything, and was as insubstantial as a soap bubble. Dr. Davidson also gained no converts to his grand conspiracy theories.

Palmer and Davidson were critics NICAP could ignore. Another challenger posed a more significant threat. Both Keyhoe and NICAP had based a large part of their belief system on Capt. Edward Ruppelt's book *The Report on Unidentified Flying Objects*. At this same time, however, Ruppelt was becoming disillusioned with UFOs. In May 1958, he wrote a NICAP member: "I have visited Project Blue Book since 1953 and am now convinced that the reports of UFOs are nothing more than reports of balloons, aircraft, astronomical phenomena, etc. I don't believe they are anything from outer space."

Keyhoe wrote him and Ruppelt confirmed the statement, adding that he had always felt this way. Then in late May 1959, Ruppelt called Keyhoe and told him that he was updating the book and the Air Force was helping him. Keyhoe published an open letter in the June 1959 issue of *The UFO Investigator*. The introduction read: "In the past month, rumors that Capt. Edward J. Ruppelt has been pressured into debunking his own UFO book have been circulating in Washington." The letter seemed to be supportive of Ruppelt with such statements as:

> If you *are* under some terrific pressure, I want to help. NICAP will do all it can to expose the facts.
> They know you could prove your disclosures, so they've tried to discredit you. At times, it has amounted almost to a smear campaign.

Yet, at the same time, Keyhoe was putting his own pressure on Ruppelt:

> But perhaps you've been shown some way to "retreat gracefully." Don't let them trick you. If you try to retract, you will be bitterly attacked by many readers, including influential book reviewers, who hailed you for speaking the truth, for daring to put the record straight.
>
> If you insist you never believed in UFOs, you could even be accused—and I know it's not true—of writing your book solely for profit, without the slightest belief in the evidence you so carefully built up for your readers.

Keyhoe followed with a long list of statements selected to show Ruppelt as a believer and added that they "could come back to haunt you" and concluded: "Ruppelt must be under such severe pressure he feels he has no choice. He should be helped, if possible, not condemned."[33]

The "pressuring" of Ruppelt became part of the flying saucer myth. Reality was very different; years later his widow (Ruppelt died in late 1960) said his switch was caused by the continuing lack of any physical evidence, as well as by the contactees.[34]

Ruppelt could be explained away as having buckled under Air Force pressure. Not so another of NICAP's critics—the Aerial Phenomena Research Organization (APRO). Many NICAP members also had memberships in APRO. On the surface, both groups held similar beliefs, but there were deep doctrinal and personal splits between them. Coral Lorenzen (director of APRO) had worked at Holloman AFB in New Mexico for several years. While there, she found no evidence the Air Force was covering up UFOs. Between 1959 and 1961 she had begun to suspect that Blue Book was nothing more than a public relations "front" and "that if a cover-up was in effect, it was being accomplished at CIA level or higher."[35]

There was a more basic difference. APRO would accept "occupant cases," where a witness claimed to have seen a UFO pilot, when they felt the evidence warranted it. (The contactees were out of bounds.)[36] NICAP had much tighter limits on what kinds of sightings were acceptable. A UFO could be seen in flight or hovering, but NICAP was very reluctant to accept a landing. As for occupant cases, between 1957 and 1962, there was only one brief report. Even so, it said that the report of figures in the windows of a saucer "is still under evaluation"—far from an endorsement.[37]

The event which triggered the NICAP/APRO split was not a UFO sighting, but the 1962 recession. NICAP's monthly income fell to less than half its monthly expenses. Those people with dual memberships began dropping one or the other. In the July 1962 issue of *The APRO*

Bulletin, Coral Lorenzen wrote an editorial which called NICAP a lobbying group which was uselessly attacking the Air Force. The editorial caused a final split between APRO and NICAP. The two groups became bitter rivals. For NICAP, the split was a greater blow than the 1961 failure to gain congressional hearings. The split removed any chance NICAP could dominate the noncontactee flying saucer myth. The believers remained as before—small, fragmented groups mutually bickering among themselves as fiercely as they attacked the Air Force.

Air Force Activities 1957–1963

All this time, the Air Force and Project Blue Book were going through their own changes. In July 1957, the Air Defense Command disbanded the 4602nd Air Intelligence Service Squadron (AISS). Investigation activities were transferred to the 1006th AISS. Public relations activities were split between the Office of Legislative Liaison (for congressional inquiries) and the Office of Public Information (for the public). AFR 200-2 was also revised in February 1958; air base commanders would again handle the preliminary investigations. If ATIC requested a more extensive investigation, the 1006th AISS would conduct it. The revisions also tried to eliminate "any and all portions of" AFR 200-2, "which might provoke suspicion or misinterpretation by the public."[38]

Again, the changes amounted to little; Keyhoe still pointed to AFR 200-2 as "proof" of the cover-up.[39] Moreover, within a few months, funding for the 1006th AISS was cut, which limited its investigations. In July 1959, responsibility was then transferred (on paper) to the 1127th Field Activities Group. In reality, it made few investigations.

In October 1958, Maj. Robert J. Friend replaced Captain Gregory as head of Blue Book. This coincided with an internal debate over the future of the project. A study had recommended an increase of eighteen to twenty new staff members. The study noted that private UFO groups often reached witnesses and published sightings before the Air Force did. The Air Force investigators often lacked experience. These shortcomings all reduced the Air Force's credibility and caused embarrassment. The recommendations seemed to be aimed at actively combating NICAP and the other clubs. They were not carried out.

A year later, ATIC ordered another study of Blue Book's future. The study was completed in late September 1959. The first paragraph marked the eventual death of Blue Book:

Since the fall of 1947, the Air Force has conducted a project designed to determine if unidentified flying objects constitute a threat to national security, or if they offered any scientific and/or technical information which would be beneficial. The program, far from the original intent, has become an unproductive burden upon the Air Force, and specifically the Aerospace Technical Intelligence Center. The program requires financing and manning and has resulted in unfavorable publicity for the Air Force, and again more specifically the Aerospace Technical Intelligence Center. The Air Force needs to eliminate this costly, and to date unproductive, program. Complete elimination is desirable, but it should certainly be disassociated with the intelligence community where it is extremely dangerous to prestige.

The report noted that twelve years and 6,152 cases had failed to provide

the slightest evidence that these objects constitute a threat to national security, or are space vehicles controlled by men or alien beings from another world, nor has any real scientific and/or technical knowledge resulted.

Nor did the sighting reports provide early warning of an attack:

The methods by which UFO reports are forwarded is by TWX or telephone from military installations, and by letter or phone from civil organizations or private citizens. This, when compared with the reaction time necessary for survival in event of an attack using modern weapons, is ridiculous.

The study looked at two possible actions. The first was to immediately close down Blue Book. The other was to remove the UFO program from intelligence and transfer it to another Air Force agency. This would be coupled with a public education program (harking back to the Robertson Panel's recommendations). Removing Blue Book from intelligence had several advantages—Blue Book was "more or less open to public inspection," and it diminished the prestige of Air Force intelligence. This would also "strip this program of its aura of mystery" due to "the public's cloak and dagger attitude" about intelligence.

The question became where to place Blue Book. The two possibilities were within the Office of Public Information or the Air Research and Development Command (ARDC) which had responsibility for Air Force scientific activities. The study concluded that ARDC was preferred; if Blue Book was transferred to a public relations group, any intelligence or scientific value would be lost and "in time the UFO project would probably degenerate into a complete public relations program."[40]

ATIC acted on the recommendations; a letter was prepared and sent to ARDC on December 7, 1959. The letter noted the specific areas where the sightings could be of scientific interest—meteors and fireballs, space vehicles and missiles, radar, static electricity, meteorology, and upper air physics.[41]

ARDC's response was sent on February 5, 1960. It was to the point:

> We find that more than half of the program relates to phenomena of a non-scientific nature. The remaining portion, while possibly associated with scientific processes, does not include qualitative data and is therefore of limited scientific value. Considering the quality of data available from other sources, exploitation of the aerial phenomena observations would not significantly enhance our research programs.
>
> For the reason stated above, I do not believe that the transfer of the USAF Aerial Phenomena Program to ARDC is in the best interest of the Air Force.[42]

ATIC then tried to interest the Office of Public Information in taking over Blue Book. However, it too wanted nothing to do with UFOs, and the problems the believers caused.[43]

In 1962, there was a final attempt by the Air Force to rid itself of the UFO problem. It began when Edward R. Trapnell, the Assistant for Public Relations to the Secretary of the Air Force, attended a dinner with Dr. Robert Calkins, president of the Brookings Research Institute. The subject of UFOs came up; Dr. Calkins said he thought the Air Force should have somebody take an independent look at the subject.[44]

On April 6, 1962, Trapnell was briefed on Blue Book by Friend (now a Lt. Colonel), Dr. Hynek, and Major C. R. Hart of Air Force intelligence. Trapnell was told of the Robertson Panel. In the years since then, there had been no evidence found to change its conclusions. Trapnell was amazed to learn that the rate of UFO sightings was three times higher than it had been in the early days of the project. He observed "that this could grow into a life-time job unless headed off in some manner."

The means they discussed to avoid this broke little new ground— transferring Blue Book to NASA, the National Science Foundation, or the Smithsonian, under a new name like "Atmospheric Physics," or within the Air Force from intelligence to a scientific division. The third possibility was to contract it out to some private organization (such as Brookings).

Trapnell instructed the Foreign Technology Division (which had had overall control of Blue Book since 1961) to get the UFO files in order so a transfer could be made on short notice. Over the next several days, the options were analyzed. Friend believed a transfer to another government agency was not feasible. He noted:

It is my opinion that it will prove very difficult, if not impossible, to transfer this program to another agency because none of them want to inherit the public relations problem that goes with it. The final solution will probably be either to disband the project entirely and allow the Air Force to absorb it in the normal course of its overall mission or to contract it to some private organization, the contract being monitored by some agency within the Air Force's scientific structure.[45]

Another analysis, by Colonel Edward H. Wynn, found other difficulties. If another agency, such as NASA, could somehow be persuaded to accept the transfer, it "would only serve to convince a larger segment of the public" that UFOs were alien spaceships. An outside contractor would be much more expensive than Blue Book, would not relieve the Air Force of investigation duties, and would require the contractor be given information on "missile, satellite, and balloon data . . . special program and/or operations." The Air Force would also have to monitor the contract. Even after all of this, he noted, a contractor would not remove charges of an "Air Force cover up." "The public would still feel that an organization under contract to the Air Force was directed to make certain statements. We have experienced this on a smaller scale regarding statements made by Dr. J. Allen Hynek"[46]

Colonel Wynn concluded that the best approach would be to close down Blue Book as a special project. Any reports would be handled by the nearest Air Force base. The emphasis would be on "determining the threat potential," rather than solving each sighting. It was noted:

Discontinuation of the UFO project would not result in the loss of valuable information. For those incidents which may be significant other than as UFO sightings, reports are made to other Air Force elements through channels completely independent for those spelled out for UFO reports.

Based on experience gained from handling thousands of cases, it is believed that field organizations could determine the causes for approximately 75 percent of the cases and evaluate the threat potential of them all.[47]

Clearly, the Air Force wanted out of its involvement with UFOs. The rationale for the Robertson Panel's recommendations was fading. In the late 1940s and early 1950s, it was conceivable that the Soviets could have secretly built a disk-shaped aircraft that would be mistaken for a UFO. Now, with the U-2 and reconnaissance satellites, U.S. intelligence had a much better understanding of Soviet military power.

In the end, nothing really changed. In 1963, Colonel Friend was replaced by Maj. Hector Quintanilla as head of Blue Book. Whereas Friend had tried to close down the project, Quintanilla saw himself as a caretaker.

The failure to make any changes was understandable in bureaucratic terms. There had been no big event to spark a basic review, and both public and press interest was low. The number of sightings was also flat—627 reports in 1958 (10 unidentified), 390 in 1959 (12 unidentified), 557 in 1960 (14 unidentified), 591 in 1961 (13 unidentified), 474 in 1962 (15 unidentified), and only 399 in 1963 (14 unidentified).[48] Given these conditions, it was easier to leave Blue Book the way it was—to let it limp along with a staff of a single officer and an enlisted man, rather than take the unknown steps of either fighting NICAP in earnest, or closing the project down.

For the believers, it had been a difficult time. The flying saucer myth had been split into two competing versions—NICAP's and the contactee's. On a basic level, NICAP's myth was mechanistic. All it dealt with was the machines (i.e., UFOs). The contactees were not concerned with cold steel, but in spreading their "message" of peace and brotherhood.

In the end, neither myth would emerge triumphant. For the believers, and U.S. society as a whole, the next decade was to be a time of wonder and terror.

"The Sixties" were about to begin.

The Flying Saucer Myth(s) 1957–1963

Basic Beliefs

Disk-shaped alien spacecraft have been seen in Earth's atmosphere for hundreds if not thousands of years.

These flying saucers are capable of maneuvers and speeds far beyond those possible for earth aircraft and can be picked up on radar.

The aliens are here to observe human activities, such as nuclear testing.

Flying saucers have the ability to magnetically stop cars and cause sunburn on exposed skin.

The U.S. government has proof of the existence of UFOs and is covering it up.

The reason for this cover-up is to prevent panic.

The NICAP Myth

To enforce its cover-up, the Air Force has smeared reliable witnesses as liars and fools, pressured Edward Ruppelt to debunk his own book, and lied to both Congress and the public. The legal backing for the cover-up consists of AFR 200-2 and JANAP 146 regulations which carry harsh punishment for revealing a UFO sighting. The CIA, through the Robertson Panel, is also deeply involved with the cover-up.

The best way to end the cover-up is to hold congressional hearings at which the Air Force would have to reveal what it knows about flying saucers.

The sighting of UFOs by reliable witnesses such as airline pilots, radar operators and others is proof of their extraterrestrial nature.

There are no reliable reports of "contact" with aliens. All such claims are hoaxes or delusions.

The UFOs may be hostile, as they are thought to be possibly responsible for several aircraft crashes and disappearances.

The Contactee Myth

Certain humans have had personal and/or mental contact with space brothers.

These contactees have also flown aboard flying saucers, and traveled into space and to other planets.

The space brothers come from utopian societies which are free of war, death, disease or any other human problem.

The space brothers want to help mankind solve its problems, to stop nuclear testing and prevent the destruction of the human race.

This will be accomplished by the contactee spreading a message of love and brotherhood throughout the world.

Other sinister beings, the Men in Black, use threats and force to continue the cover-up of UFOs.

The Sixties

> Let us hear the suspicions. I will look after the
> proofs.
>
> —*The Adventure of the Three Students*

"The Sixties," the period between November 1963 and August 1974, both shaped and haunted the generation that came of age during that time. Before the Sixties had run their course, one president had been murdered, another had resigned in disgrace, men had walked on the Moon, and the U.S. had become involved and defeated in a war that destroyed the fabric of American society.

For the flying saucer myth, these years were also "eventful." Between mid-1965 and the end of 1967, there was a prolonged flap.[1] In the process, UFOs achieved a kind of respectability, then were cast into the outer darkness. The whole belief system, like American society itself, was shattered. The flying saucer myth reassembled from those fragments was very different from the NICAP and Contactee myths that had begun the decade.

Prologue to the Flap

The years before 1964 were grim ones for the UFO myth. NICAP had failed to gain the long-sought congressional hearings. In mid-1963, Congressman Carl Vinson of Georgia made the last inquiry to Blue Book until 1966. The pages of *The UFO Investigator* reflected Keyhoe's defeat in

Congress. In 1963, attacks on the Air Force were very limited and low-key. Keyhoe seemed to want to distance himself from his past flamboyant accusations.[2]

The contactees also faced difficulties in the early 1960s. Adamski's circle was torn by internal differences. In 1961, his long-time secretary, Lucy McGinnis, left because Adamski was practicing trance mediumship.[3] Adamski also damaged his own credibility, even with the "true believers." In March 1962, he claimed to have flown to Saturn. He also claimed to have met with President John F. Kennedy and Pope John XXIII.[4] By the spring of 1964, the situation at Mt. Palomar was an open palace revolt.

The Socorro Landing

April of 1964 saw a doubling in the number of sightings. One of these sightings would be prologue to the start of the Sixties flap. At about 5:45 P.M. MST on April 24, 1964, Socorro, New Mexico, police officer Lonnie Zamora saw a speeding car heading south out of town and he set off after it. According to Zamora's account, given soon after to FBI Special Agent J. Arthur Byrnes, Jr., he heard a roar and saw a flame in the sky about one-half to one mile away. He described the flame as being "bluish and sort of orange too . . . narrower at the top than at bottom . . . 3 degrees or so in width." The flame was slowly descending. He could not see the bottom of the flame as it was behind a hill. Zamora did not notice an object. The roar lasted about ten seconds.

His first thought was that a dynamite shack in the area had exploded. Zamora broke off the chase and turned west onto a rough dirt road. He had to make three tries to get over a steep hill. Once over the hill, he drove slowly down the gravel road, looking for the dynamite shack. After fifteen or twenty seconds, he saw "a shiny type object" sitting in a gully at a distance later found to be around 800 feet. Zamora stopped the police car for "only a couple seconds." He stated, "It looked, at first, like a car turned upside down. . . . Saw two people in white coveralls very close to the object. One of these persons seemed to turn and look straight at my car and seemed startled—seemed to quickly jump somewhat." Zamora first thought a white car had overturned. During the "possibly two seconds or so" he was looking at the two figures, he did not notice "any particular shape or possibly any hats or headgear." They looked normal in shape "but possibly they were small adults or large kids."

Zamora drove on and radioed the sheriff's office to report a possible auto accident. The dirt road went around a low hill and he lost sight of the object. The police car then came around the hill and stopped on a flat area that overlooked the gully, about 100 feet away. Zamora then said that as he hung up the radio mike and started to get out of the car, he heard "two or three loud thumps, like someone possibly opening or shutting a door hard."

Rather than an overturned car, Zamora said the "object" was egg-shaped, "alumimum-white in color," and twelve to fifteen feet long. It had no visible doors or windows and sat on short legs. Zamora did not see the two figures. He did notice a red "insignia" about 2.5 feet tall.

Zamora said he had only a brief time to see all this; as soon as he left the car, the object began to whine and emit blue and orange flames. The exhaust began kicking up dust. Zamora said he panicked and began running. He bumped into the left rear of the police car, knocking off his glasses (Zamora had relatively poor 20-200 vision). When he looked back at the object, he said it had lifted into the air and started flying to the southwest. It cleared the top of the dynamite shack by about three feet and continued at a low level until it disappeared over the distant mountains. Zamora called police headquarters and said, "Look out the window, to see if you could see an object." Zamora then asked if Sgt. Sam Chavez, head of the local office of the New Mexico State Police, could come alone to the site.

Once it was gone, Zamora said in his FBI statement, he "went down to where the object had been, and I noted the brush was burning in several places." Before Chavez arrived, Zamora made sketches of the object; the first drawing showed an egg-shaped object, with its long axis vertical, sitting on two legs. The second, closer drawing showed an elliptical object with the insignia and two legs.[5]

Sergeant Chavez arrived about three minutes after the object had disappeared. Chavez went into the gully with Zamora and found "four fresh indentations in the ground and several charred or burned bushes. Smoke appeared to come from the bush and [Chavez] assumed that it was burning, however no coals were visible and the charred portions of the bush were cold to the touch."[6] Chavez contacted the FBI, who notified the Army White Sands test site. They were soon joined by FBI agent Byrnes and Army Capt. Richard Holder who commanded a tracking station south of Socorro. Byrnes interviewed Zamora and Holder measured the "padprints" as they soon became known. Samples of the soil and charred bushes were also taken.

The indentations in the sand were arranged in a kite-shaped pattern.

Significantly, the distance between each was different—ranging from 115.5 inches to 177.5 inches. In the center of the "padprints" were several burned bushes. The burning seemed sporadic to Holder. Clumps of grass in close proximity to the burned area were untouched. By one of the padprints were several shallow, irregular impressions. These were labeled "foot prints," in the belief they were made by the two "occupants."[7,8]

This was not the first time a person had reported seeing UFO crewmen. Coral Lorenzen of APRO found twenty-nine U.S. cases (excluding contactees) prior to 1964. She noted, however, that in "some of these cases . . . the observers do not care to be identified, and others are cases which stretch the credibility of even the most seasoned UFO researcher."[9] In this case, however, the "occupants" were seen by a policeman and physical traces were found.

The Socorro Investigation

The Air Force learned of the sighting on April 26. Capt. Hector Quintanilla (Blue Book commander) called T/Sgt. David N. Moody (staff investigator) to request that it be investigated. Moody and the UFO Investigation Officer at Kirtland AFB, Maj. William Conner, headed to Socorro. Arriving at noon, they interviewed Chavez and Zamora and visited the landing site, reenacting the sighting and checking for radiation (none was found).

Moody described Zamora's account of the object as "vague," "the only specific detail being the red marking." The local radar stations showed no unidentified tracks. No helicopter flights took place in the area. They also learned that Coral Lorenzen and her husband had beaten the Air Force to town and had already interviewed Zamora, Chavez and Captain Holder. Neither Major Conner nor Moody could reach a conclusion as to the cause of the sighting. Moody called Captain Quintanilla that evening and told him of the situation.[10]

On April 28, Dr. Hynek went to Socorro. He interviewed both Zamora and Chavez for two hours. The next morning, the three of them went out to the landing site. They had not been there more than ten minutes when Ray Stanford of NICAP arrived and began taking photos and samples. Hynek also talked to other townspeople. The manager of the Whitting Brother's Service Station said that an unidentified tourist heading north on U.S. 85 had told him he had seen the UFO fly low over his car. He then saw a police car heading up the hill. Dr. Hynek concluded: "Zamora, although not overly bright or articulate, is basically sincere, honest, and reliable. He would not be capable of contriving a complex hoax, nor would his temperament indicate that he would have the slightest interest in such."

Given this, the question became what the object was. From the first, it was assumed to be a secret U.S. aircraft. Dr. Hynek wrote, "Both Zamora and Chavez appeared to me to be hoping that I could tell them that this had been a secret Air Force device, so that they could dismiss the whole thing from their minds." He warned that NICAP and other groups would try to use the sighting "as a lever for a congressional investigation." Hynek suggested:

> The object which produced this, if it was a new device under test or in maneuvers, be brought to same location and movies be taken of it departing in the manner described by Zamora, and under the same lighting conditions. This then could be played at any future hearings on flying saucers. This, it seems to me, could go a very long way towards exploding the myth of flying saucers, and might do more good than all the previous years of propaganda.[11]

He concluded that Chavez and FBI Agent Byrnes would have to be "in" on any hoax. All attempts to locate a secret aircraft which could explain the landing ended in failure. The unknown tourist was also never found. Chemical analysis of soil and brush samples showed no traces of propellent. With the character references for Zamora, Blue Book had no choice but to list the case as "unidentified."[12] This is the only landing/occupant case so listed in the Blue Book files.

Aftermath

As Hynek predicted, UFO groups were quick to endorse the Socorro landing. NICAP's account was published in the July-August 1964 issue of *The UFO Investigator*. It said, "Intensive on-the-spot investigations by NICAP and the Air Force have resulted in one basic agreement: That the object seen by a highly reliable witness cannot be explained as any known device or phenomenon." The article quoted Hynek as saying:

> . . . it is one of the soundest, best substantiated reports as far as it goes. Usually one finds many contradictions or omissions in these reports, but Mr. Zamora's story is simply told, certainly without any intent to perpetrate a hoax. The story, of course, was told by a man who obviously was frightened badly by what he did see. He certainly must have seen something.[13]

For NICAP to endorse a UFO landing/occupant case was a unique event—they had always avoided such reports as too similar to the contactees. NICAP Assistant Director Gordon Lore, Jr. said, "We still know of no other occupant case that we feel has been verified enough for us to call it 'authentic,' although a few look promising and could well be 'authentic.'"[14]

APRO's Coral Lorenzen wrote an article which detailed other landing and radar tracking reports from New Mexico that had been made in the wake of the Socorro sighting. She concluded:

> The spring 1964 flap impresses me as an intelligence operation carried out by the occupants of the UFOs either to show themselves preparatory to closer contact in the future or to find out the effect such contact would have on humans or how much we already suspect.[15]

As the Sixties flap grew, others would develop a similar belief.

The greatest impact of the Socorro sighting was on Dr. Hynek himself. He made two more trips to Socorro, in August 1964 and March 1965. The general opinion in town remained that the case was not a hoax, and that Zamora had seen a secret U.S. aircraft.[16,17] Unable to find a secret egg-shaped aircraft, and unwilling to believe Zamora had committed a hoax, Hynek slowly began to believe some UFO sightings were of extraterrestrial spaceships.[18]

There was one exception to the support for Zamora—Felix Phillips. He and his wife lived some 1,000 feet away from the landing site. They were at home at the time and heard no loud roar as Zamora reported. Phillips concluded the whole story was a hoax. Hynek rejected this, arguing that the Phillips house was downwind from the landing site and a strong southwest wind was allegedly blowing at the time. The hoax charge, Hynek wrote, "is not acceptable . . . because there are just too many bits of evidence that militate against [it]."[19]

Despite Hynek's endorsement, the case file and the subsequent investigation by Philip J. Klass cast doubt on Socorro. One was the lack of any radar tracking of the object—even though the local radar picked up cars on the road—and the lack of any traces in the soil samples. The sporadic burning and the intact twigs visible in photos were inconsistent with the intense flame and blast Zamora reported.

Phillips told Klass there were several windows open at the time of the alleged landing, yet he and his wife heard nothing. Zamora said he heard the roar from a distance of 4,000 feet over the sound of his own speeding police car. Yet, the Phillips house was only one-fourth that distance. The exact wind speed and direction is uncertain as Socorro did not have a weather station.

Zamora also changed his story in the years following the sighting. He later claimed to have heard only a roar but saw no flame when the object was landing and that the car radio was jammed until the UFO cleared the dynamite shack. Zamora also claimed to have seen a rock that had been melted by the intense heat.

The "padprints," which were the main evidence for Zamora's story, were also a problem. To fit the spacing of the marks, the object would have to have had four legs with unequal lengths and angles. This non-symmetrical landing gear would have been unstable. The padprints could have been made by lifting rocks from the sand and using a shovel. It would be a simple matter to make four marks at right angles to each other, quite another to make the distance between them equal.

The unknown tourist story was contradicted by the timing of the sighting—it would not have been possible to see the UFO flying over U.S. 85 and Zamora's car starting up the mesa at the same time—Zamora said he saw the flames from the top of the mesa, then headed for the area.

The final factor was where the "landing" took place. The site was between the two main roads into town—U.S. 60 and 85. The land itself was owned by Socorro's mayor. After the landing, the nearly impassable road was graded and plans were made to use the landing site as a tourist attraction. (The town lacked industry and was dependent on tourists.) The implication was the landing was a hoax, to bring in tourist dollars.[20]

The Sixties Flap Begins

In the wake of the Socorro "landing," the number of UFO reports shot up. With the fall, the number dropped. The final total for 1964 was 562 (19 unidentified). The long drought in interest in UFOs had ended. Keyhoe sensed the change and published an article in the January 1965 issue of *True* titled "U.S. Air Force Censorship of the UFO Sightings." He wrote:

> For the past three years, unknown to the general public, there had been a tremendous new wave of incidents in which [UFOs] have been sighted around the world. . . . The U.S. Government has been aware throughout that time that enigmatic alien craft of some kind are watching. . . . The new wave

of UFO appearances fully matches in magnitude the great "flying saucer" scare of the late 1940's and early 1950's, when it wasn't unusual for dozens of UFO sightings to be reported in a single week. UFO activity slowed down somewhat in the late 1950's. But now, suddenly, the UFOs are back—their numbers greater, their origin as obscure, their purpose as unfathomable as ever before.

The article was vintage Keyhoe. He went through all the old cases and made the same old charges about AFR 200-2 and the Air Force "tactic" of "total suppression." It concluded:

> Congressional hearings are almost bound to be held eventually—probably within the next year. The basic finding of those hearings—that we are indeed under surveillance of some kind by visitors from the universe—will undoubtedly startle and frighten many people throughout the world.[21]

With the article's publication, Keyhoe and NICAP embarked on an all-out publicity campaign.[22] Keyhoe and NICAP staff members appeared on the *Today* show, the *Tonight* show, *Open Mind,* and *The Mike Douglas Show* during late 1965 and early 1966.[23] Hand-in-hand with this effort were renewed attacks on the Air Force. *The UFO Investigator* carried articles with such titles as "AF Intimidates Witnesses," "New Sightings Put AF on Spot," and "If They Try to Silence You." It also spoke of "increased low-level approaches" of UFOs which indicated landings might "occur without warning," and "the increasingly ruthless treatment of capable, honest Americans" by the Air Force.[24]

Astronaut Sightings

The *True* article also introduced another element to the flying saucer myth. Keyhoe opened the article with "an eerie story." On April 8, 1964, the Gemini 1 spacecraft was launched on an unmanned test flight. Keyhoe claimed that during the first orbit "four spacecraft of unknown origin flew up to it." He continued that, while radar trackers watched, the four UFOs took up positions around Gemini 1 and paced it for an orbit, then flew off.[25] In reality, the radar tracks were of debris—pieces of the second-stage rocket engine nozzle lining. The formation flight occurred simply because they were in a similar orbit.[26]

The Gemini 1 story was reprinted in the May-June issue of the British magazine *Flying Saucer Review*. It was followed with a second article on astronaut sightings. It claimed that during the October 1964 Soviet Voskhod 1 flight, the three-man crew had seen UFOs while in orbit. It continued that "in Moscow there are, in fact, persistent rumours that [Voskhod 1] was repeatedly overtaken by extremely fast flying discs whick struck the craft violent shattering blows with their powerful magnetic fields." It added that during the Voskhod 2 flight in March 1965, the crew spotted an "unmanned mystery satellite" which passed within half a mile of their spacecraft. The article speculated that the UFO had caused Voskhod 2's off-course landing.

U.S. astronauts were also reported to have "spotted" UFOs in space. During an April 30, 1962, X-15 flight, NASA test pilot Joe Walker photographed "five or six cylindrical or discoidal objects." A second X-15 sighting occurred on July 17, 1962. Maj. Robert White reported seeing an object some thirty or forty feet away. During the Mercury 9 flight, the article claimed, astronaut Gordon Cooper had reported seeing "a green and red UFO streaking along in the opposite direction."[27]

At the same time the article was published, the most important astronaut sighting was made. The Gemini 4 flight was launched on June 3, 1965, with the crew of James McDivitt and Edward White.[28] About thirty hours after launch, McDivitt reported seeing an object about ten to twenty miles from the spacecraft (White was asleep). It seemed to be cylindrical with an arm sticking out. McDivitt tried to photograph the object, but it was lost in the Sun's glare after about thirty seconds. Twice, later in the flight, McDivitt saw distant point sources of light too far away to see any details.

At a press conference, McDivitt said, "I saw a white object and it looked like it was cylindrical and it looked to me like there was a white arm sticking out of it. It really could have been a reflection of another piece of it."[29] He also noted: "It looked a lot like an upper stage of a booster."

The North American Air Defense Command (NORAD) listed eleven objects near Gemini 4 at the time of the sighting, but the only large object was Pegasus 2. This was a Saturn I second stage fitted with two long meteorite detection "wings." Although it fit McDivitt's description, Pegasus 2 was 1,200 miles away, and thus would have been a point of light.[30] The photos did not clear up the question. NASA headquarters released several frames of film which showed an oval with a long tail. It was actully sunlight reflecting off a bolt on the smeared window.[31,32] The crews of Gemini 7, 10, 11, and 12 also saw small points of light from distant satellites or debris from their spacecraft or booster.

As the Sixties flap began, shadows were forming over American society. In the South, civil rights workers were attacked, several being killed. At the University of California, Berkeley, student protests had paralyzed the campus. In South Vietnam, the situation was deteriorating. Then, following an attack on the U.S.S. *Maddox,* Congress passed the Tonkin Gulf Resolution which authorized use of U.S. forces in Vietnam. In February 1965 the "Rolling Thunder" bombing campaign against North Vietnam began. This was a limited effort aimed at forcing the North Vietnamese to negotiate. By July 1965, 75,000 U.S. troops were in South Vietnam with another 50,000 on the way.[33]

UFO reports for January through June 1965 ran between 33 and 45 per month. With July, the number shot up to 135. There were 262 in August and 104 in September. These were the highest monthly numbers since the 1952 and 1957 flaps.[34] The most spectacular event took place on the night of August 1–2, 1965. The sightings began after sunset with reports of "multi-colored lights," "eggs," and "diamonds" being made throughout the Midwest. Many of the sightings were made by police officers. Deputy Sheriff Dan Carter of Canyon, Texas, thought "a plane had exploded. . . . The object appeared to go south, then disintegrated in all colors." At Wichita, Kansas, it was reported that the weather radar had tracked several "unidentified craft." The blips were described as "looking much the same as an airplane's might." They were "small and rather diffused"—brightening and dimming while they traveled at about forty-five miles per hour.

The August 1–2 sightings marked a shift in attitudes. The following morning, the Air Force issued a press release which stated the sightings were of Jupiter, or the stars Rigel, Capella, Betelgeuse, or Aldebaran. "The azimuth and elevations of the reported sightings support this conclusion." The Air Force statement was greeted with contempt; a UPI reporter in Wichita said, "Ordinary radar does not pick up planets or stars." The director of the Oklahoma Science and Art Foundation Planetarium said the Air Force statement "is as far from the truth as you can get. These stars and planets are on the opposite side of the Earth from Oklahoma City at this time of year."[35]

Some of the newspaper editorials following the August sightings seemed to endorse NICAP's conspiracy theories. The *Charleston Evening Post* said that "something is going on 'up there' and we rather suspect the Air Force knows it." The newspaper said the Air Force, when faced with a sighting, "immediately begins to crank out of the wild blue yonder the same prerecorded announcement it has been playing for 20 years: scratch, scratch, the Air Force has no evidence." The *Fort Worth*

Star Telegraph said the Air Force "can stop kidding us about there being no such thing as flying saucers." The *Orlando Sentinel* noted that writers had changed "from outright scepticism to at least tentative belief" in UFOs. It speculated that if the newspaper editorials combined with congressional interest, the Air Force would be forced to open its "classified" files.[36]

The editorial response to the August sightings was an early sign of an attitude that was to grow during the Sixties—a disbelief, even a contempt for any government or "official" statement. UFO believers had long embraced such an attitude. As this grew in mainstream publications and in the public at large, belief in UFOs flourished.

The number of sightings slowly trailed off after the summer. The total for 1965 was 887 (16 unidentified).[37]

The Wave of UFO Books

The upsurge in sightings and public interest resulted in a similar increase in UFO club membership, television programs with flying saucer themes, and UFO books. NICAP's membership doubled (on paper) to 11,000, while Van Tassel's Giant Rock Convention attracted some 2,000 people, more than twice previous years.[38]

Television was quick to use the flying saucer myth. In *Lost in Space*, the "Jupiter II" spacecraft was disk-shaped. *Voyage to the Bottom of the Sea* and *The Time Tunnel* featured alien invaders. The "Tomorrow is Yesterday" episode of *Star Trek* used a variation of the Mantell incident. The only UFO series was *The Invaders*. In it, David Vincent (Roy Thinnes), a young architect, discovered that aliens had infiltrated American society and government in order to make Earth "their world."[39,40]

The major impact of the August sightings was an upsurge of UFO books. Between 1965 and 1968, more than twenty-five books on UFOs were published. Jacques Vallee wrote *Anatomy of a Phenomenon* and *Challenge to Science*. Jim and Coral Lorenzen of APRO wrote four books—*Flying Saucers: The Startling Evidence of the Invasion from Space, UFOs over the Americas, Flying Saucer Occupants,* and *UFOs: The Whole Story*. Even reprinted contactee books and "potboilers" (such as the book that said Mantell was flying a "jet") sold well.[41] Of the wave of books, only four had a significant impact on the flying saucer myth.

The first of these was John G. Fuller's *Incident at Exeter*. Fuller, a columnist with *Saturday Review* magazine, described a series of local sightings in Exeter, New Hampshire. It began at 2:24 A.M. on September 3, 1965, when Norman Muscarello ran panic-striken into the local police station. He said he had been hitchhiking when he saw a UFO coming toward him across a field. Patrolman Eugene Bertrand took Muscarello back to the spot he had seen the UFO. As they walked into the field, horses in a corral began to whinny. They both saw "a brilliant, roundish object" that bathed the area in a red light. A second officer drove up and also saw the object.

Fuller talked with witnesses and soon noticed a particularity of the UFO sightings—many were seen near electrical power lines. One witness said, "We've often seen them come along these lines," while another said, "It went right down the power line. That's what it always seems to do—hover over the power lines."

On the evening of November 9, 1965, Fuller met with representatives of *Look*, which was to publish excerpts of his book on the sightings. At about 5:30 P.M. he noticed the lights flicker. Only later did he learn that most of the northeastern U.S. had been blacked out. Fuller immediately remembered all the references to "power lines" or "transmission lines" in his interviews. There were several reports of "objects" seen near power lines at the time of the blackout. Fuller declared the reason for the blackout was a complete mystery, and implied that UFOs were the real cause. This belief was soon incorporated into the flying saucer myth. The references to UFOs near power lines would also attract attention from another direction.[42]

Incident at Exeter had a cool, literate style which soon made Fuller a popular speaker on UFOs. In contrast, Frank Edwards's two books—*Flying Saucers—Serious Business* and *Flying Saucers—Here And Now!* were a mixture of wild UFO stories and fierce attacks on the Air Force and U.S. government for the "cover up." Even by the standards of UFO books, Edwards was not noted for scholarship—one believer called his research "shoddy at best."[43]

Edwards's style was a relentless dismissal of any prosaic explanations as silly lies put out by stupid government agencies. This was shown by his handling of the astronaut sightings in *Flying Saucers—Serious Business*. The Gemini 4 sighting was summed up in a single paragraph. The next four paragraphs were spent in attacks on what he called "The Department of Instant Explanations" and the Pegasus 2 explanation.

Edwards discussed another astronaut sighting that occurred aboard Gemini 7 in December 1965. The crew of Frank Borman and James Lovell reported seeing a "bogie." When Mission Control suggested to

Borman it was their Titan II second stage, he responded he could see it in another part of the sky. Other spaceflight-related UFO sightings involved the X-15. Edwards dismissed the explanation that they were "ice flakes" by saying, "If so, it is one of those extremely rare incidences where ice flakes flew in echelon formation and followed a plane at 2,000 miles per hour—which you may agree is pretty fast, even for an educated ice flake."[44]

In his second book, *Flying Saucers—Here And Now!*, Edwards expanded on the astronaut sightings. In his account of the Mercury 9 sighting, Edwards claimed the "greenish, glowing, disk-shaped thing" was also *seen* by *200* people at a tracking station. Edwards summarized the Gemini 4 sighting by saying, "If that incident did nothing else, it shows how excited the 'experts' were when McDivitt described that glowing egg-shaped thing that was being photographed as it circled the Gemini capsule, leaving a contrail behind it from its propulsion system." Edwards added details to the Gemini 7 sighting, saying the "bogie" was "unlike anything the men had ever seen before." He also said, "The men also reported that several miles ahead of their Gemini capsule, and across its line of flight, they could see hundreds of small glittering objects."

Edwards mentioned a sighting on the Gemini 10 flight. In his account, John Young and Michael Collins reported there were "two red glowing things" ahead of them. Young then radioed that the objects had disappeared and guessed they were satellites. Edwards's belief in an all-encompassing conspiracy entered his account of the incident:

> Friends of mine, who were present at the Space Center during this incident, tell me that the voice of Astronaut Young was cut off the intercom system for more than a minute as he began describing what he was watching. By the time he came back on the intercom he seemed to have been briefed, for that was when he "guessed" that he had only been seeing some satellites.

This led him to conclude:

> The reports from White and McDivitt had been embarrassing; the additional reports from Borman and Lovell added to the problem for the censors. By the time Young and Collins began reporting on the things they were watching, somebody's hand was on the switch, according to reports.[45]

Despite their differing styles, these three books were very much within the flying saucer myth, with their stories of UFO sightings and charges of a cover-up. It was the fourth book which brought about a fundamental shift in the belief system. It was John Fuller's *The Interrupted Journey*.

Interrupted Journey?

The contactees continued to be active in the 1960s, but the surge of reports seems to have overshadowed them. Adamski died of a heart attack on April 23, 1965, removing the major figure in the controversy.[46,47] New contactees kept appearing, however—on an October 1966 television appearance, "Reverend" Frank Stranges showed a "creature" about eight inches long that looked like "a wizened dehydrated little man with yellow glossy skin." Stranges claimed it had been dropped from a UFO. The "creature" was a devilfish—a kind of stingray. Another contactee was "Mel Noel" who claimed to be a former Air Force F-86 pilot with a secret unit which communicated with UFOs in 1952. "Noel" later admitted that was not his real name, and that he had never been a pilot, or in the Air Force.[48]

The basic split remained—for "mainstream" UFO believers the contactees were dismissed as hoaxes or delusions. Even an "occupant" case (like Socorro) was accepted only with reluctance. It was against this background, in October 1966, that Betty and Barney Hill's story of "two lost hours" aboard a UFO came to national attention.

The story began on the night of September 19–20, 1961. Betty and Barney Hill were driving home from a Canadian vacation, down U.S. 3 through the White Mountains to Portsmouth, New Hampshire. They expected to arrive home at about 2:30 or 3:00 A.M. Barney Hill, who was black, worked on the night shift at the Boston Post Office. He was intelligent, with an IQ of 140. He suffered from ulcers. Betty Hill, who was white, was a social worker with a case load as high as 120 assignments. Both were involved with civil rights activities.

As they drove through the White Mountains, sometime after midnight, there were no other cars on the road and all the hotels were closed. The night sky was described as clear with a nearly full Moon. To the left and below the Moon was a single bright star. As the car was just south of Lancaster, Betty noticed that another star, bigger than the first, had appeared between it and the Moon. The light seemed to be following the car, although they were not sure if this was only an illusion caused by the car's motion. Betty looked through binoculars and saw "a double row of windows." Excited, she told Barney repeatedly to stop the car. Barney seemed indifferent—dismissing the light as an airplane or a satellite.

Finally, he stopped the car and went out into a field with the binoculars. When he looked at the light he saw "at least a half a dozen living beings" looking back at him. All but one stepped back from the window. Barney focused on the one he dubbed "the leader" and saw eyes staring at him. Barney felt "certain he was about to be captured." Barney ran back to the car, shouting hysterically they were going to be captured, then drove off.

According to Betty's later account, a "beeping" sound started coming from the rear of the car and they felt "drowsiness" coming over them. Some time later, they heard the beeping sound again. Betty said to Barney, "*Now* do you believe in flying saucers?" He responded, "Don't be ridiculous. Of course not." They arrived home shortly after 5:00 A.M., but attached no importance to their late arrival.

Betty continued to think about the sighting and called her sister. The sister reinforced Betty's fears that the car or their clothing had been contaminated with radiation. She said a physicist had said an ordinary compass could show the presence of radiation. (This is untrue—a compass can only detect a magnetic field.) Betty quickly asked Barney where he had put the compass. He was not helpful, but finally, at Betty's insistence, he got it. When Betty went out to the car, she was surprised to find a dozen "shiny circles" on the paint of the car's trunk. She placed the compass on one of the spots and the needle went out of control.

Betty called Pease AFB to report the sighting. She also went to the library looking for UFO books. She checked out Keyhoe's *The Flying Saucer Conspiracy* and read it in one sitting.[49] Although the book was centered on the "Silence Group," Keyhoe also wrote about nearly a dozen occupant cases. Most were rejected outright. Keyhoe did give a limited acceptance to a series of UFO reports from Venezuela involving hairy dwarfs which tried to abduct several people.[50] On September 26, 1961, Betty wrote a letter to Keyhoe about the sighting. There was no mention in the letter of arriving home late. Starting ten days after the sighting, Betty began having a series of extremely vivid nightmares. These continued for five straight nights, then stopped. She wrote down a description of the dreams soon afterward, at the urging of her co-workers. The dreams were jumbled and events were not in "chronological order." In the dreams, the car came to a roadblock with eight to eleven men standing in the road. The car motor died, the men surrounded the car, and pulled Betty and Barney out. Betty recalled, "I am struggling to wake up; I am at the bottom of a deep well, and I must get out. Everything is black; I am fighting to become conscious, slowly and gradually, I start to become conscious. . . . Then I win the battle and my eyes are open."

Betty found herself in the woods. Barney seemed to be "sleep walking." They were surrounded by the aliens. She described them as being shorter than Barney (5' to 5' 4") with large chests and long noses "like Jimmy Durante." They had a gray complexion, blue lips, and black hair and eyes. All were dressed in blue uniforms. The "leader" reassured her several times that no harm would come to them.

Betty and Barney entered the saucer and were taken to different rooms. Here she met the "examiner," who asked her a number of questions. He did not seem to understand many of her answers, however. The examiner then said they were going to make some tests on Betty, reassuring her there would be no pain.

She was given a physical—her ears, throat, skin, and feet were examined. Hair samples were also taken. Next, she was asked to lie on a table. A machine was brought over which resembled an EEG. Attached to it were several wires; on the end of each was a needle. The needles were used to touch various parts of her body. During the examination, Betty's dress was removed "as it was hindering the testing."

In Betty's dreams, the aliens said the next examination was a "pregnancy test" and that it would not hurt. A very long needle was thrust into her navel and Betty felt intense pain. The two aliens were startled and the leader waved his hand across her eyes. The pain immediately vanished and Betty "became very grateful and appreciative to the leader; lost all fear of him; and felt as though he was a friend."

With this, the aliens decided to halt the testing and Betty began talking with the leader. Suddenly, the leader was called out of the room and Betty feared something had gone wrong with Barney's examination. The leader returned, opened Betty's mouth and touched her teeth. He expressed surprise that Barney's teeth could be removed while Betty's could not.

She laughed and explained that Barney had dentures. Betty said that as people got older, they lost their teeth. This astonished the aliens as they did not understand the term "old age." Betty then asked if she could have some proof of the experience. The leader agreed and Betty selected a large book. She opened it and "found symbols written in long, narrow columns."

She next asked where the aliens came from and the leader showed her a "sky map" with lines connecting the stars. Some of the lines were heavy, while others were broken. The leader refused to point out their home world when Betty was unable to point out the Earth's location on the map.

By this time in the dreams, Barney had been brought back, still in a daze. As they were about to leave, a disagreement started between the aliens. The leader took the book away from Betty. She protested, saying it was "my only proof." He said that was why he was taking it. He added that it had been decided they would not remember the experience. Betty "became very angry and said that somehow, somewhere, I would remember" and that there was nothing the leader could do to prevent her. The leader responded that might be possible but no one would believe her, and moreover, Barney would remember the experience differently. The aliens took them back to the car, and the UFO took off.

A month after the sighting, on October 21, the Hills met with Walter Webb of NICAP for a six-hour interview. Despite NICAP's reluctance to endorse even an occupant case, Webb was impressed with the story. A follow-up interview was held on November 25, 1961. On hand were C. D. Jackson and Robert E. Hohman of NICAP, and James McDonald, a retired Air Force major and friend of the Hills. The interview lasted a full twelve hours. At one point, Hohman asked, "What took you so long to get home?" It was a question that changed the whole flying saucer myth.

Both Betty and Barney responded strongly to the question: Betty said later, "I thought I was really going to crack up. I got terrified." Barney added, "I became suddenly flabbergasted, to think that I realized for the first time that at the rate of speed I always travel, we should have arrived home at least two hours earlier than we did. . . . Even if I allow more time than I know we took at those roadside stops, there still were at least two hours missing out of that night's trip." The Hills could not account for "the missing time period" and Betty began to wonder if her dreams were real experiences that had been so traumatic they had been blanked out.

At the same time, they began to tell their story to a UFO study group and their church discussion group.[51] Published accounts also began to appear—the January-February 1962 *UFO Investigator* had a brief account, while the March 1963 *APRO Bulletin* also had an article. Interestingly, Barney Hill told APRO that the "beeping" sound had continued for some thirty-five miles as they drove (rather than there being two sets of separate beeps).[52]

Barney's problems with ulcers and high blood pressure continued, and he was referred to Dr. Benjamin Simon, a noted Boston psychiatrist and neurologist who had extensive experience with the use of hypnosis. The first session was on December 14, 1963, and they continued for six months. Dr. Simon quickly decided that both Barney and Betty needed treatment.

At first, Dr. Simon thought Barney's illusions and fantasies were influencing Betty. After several sessions, however, it became clear that it was Betty who was influencing Barney, who, Dr. Simon felt, appeared to be more suggestible. Dr.Simon noted that while events Barney experienced were in Betty's story, very little of what happened to Betty was included in Barney's account. This was in contrast to their account of the drive—that was a joint experience, the "abduction" was not.

Interpretations and Meanings

Dr. Simon believed that Betty's dreams of being abducted were only that, dreams. They were not repressed memories of a real event. This was because the symbolism was standard for dreams. Dreams are not a replay of events. The "latent content" of dreams is disguised by symbols of unconscious conflicts, desires, wishes and problems. These, in turn are influenced by the patient's own history, conflicts, wishes, and problems.

One difficulty in interpreting Betty's dreams is the limited amount of patient history in the book—her relationship with her parents, for instance. What little is given makes it sound as if she had a rather lonely, unhappy childhood. When children frequently describe themselves as "bored," as Betty did, they often mean depressed. The union activities of her mother would be unsettling for a child. Her constant reading (her mother limited her to one book a day) is suggestive of a defense against conflict, depression, and looking for escape and gratification through fantasy. In contrast to Betty's mother, her father comes across as passive, much like Barney. Several times Betty forced Barney into taking actions he really did not want to do. This ultimately included accepting the "reality" of the "abduction."

As for the dream itself, the struggle to make this material conscious is suggestive of her trying to resolve conflict, and to escape depression. Many of the events in the abduction are symbolic of the affections of a parent—being escorted to the saucer, the benevolent nature of the leader, the examiner's questions about food in a room with a table. (Food = mother = nurturing = somebody taking an interest in her.) The leader and examiner are also taller than the other aliens which is symbolic of authority figures. Many of the symbols are obviously sexual in nature—the "Jimmy Durante" noses, the needles on wires, the removing of her dress because it "hindered the testing" (intercourse), the inserting of the needle into her navel, the pain and its sudden removal.

The final symbol is Betty being given a book, then it is taken away. This is as if her mother has come at the last minute, once again, to spoil her fun (i.e., escape) by taking away her book.[53]

Another reason Dr. Simon believed the abduction was not a real experience was the contradictions. The aliens did not understand the idea of "old age," "life span," or "year." Yet, when Betty was about to leave, the leader said "wait a minute." Such contradictions are common in dreams. Dr. Simon made no secret of his belief the event was not real. He wrote in the introduction to *The Interrupted Journey*: "Their existence (the UFO's) as concrete objects is of less concern to me than the experience of these two people showing the cumulative impact of past experiences and fantasies on their present experiences and responses."[54]

As with Fuller's earlier UFO book, *Look* magazine ran a two-part excerpt beginning in the October 4, 1966, issue. Although *Look* "hyped" the story as being true, Dr. Simon gave a far different behind-the-scenes view. In an interview with Philip J. Klass, Dr. Simon described a visit he had had with a *Look* editor before the articles were published. The editor asked him, "Do you believe the Hills were abducted by spacemen?" Dr. Simon responded "Absolutely NOT." Later the *Look* editor said, "If you had said you did believe it, I would have packed up immediately and gone home."[55]

Response

The response of UFO believers to the Hill's abduction story was mixed. For many, it was too similar to the contactee stories of the 1950s. NICAP and Keyhoe endorsed their UFO sighting, but not their abduction. Frank Edwards went farther—in *Flying Saucers—Here And Now!*, he included the Hill's story in a chapter on contactees such as George Adamski. Edwards wrote:

> The widely publicized story told by the Hills becomes another unsupported and unsupportable "contact" story to add to the long list of such tales. It has all the familiar elements of such stories—and all the familiar shortcomings. Lacking proof, it must be filed along with the other followers in the steps of George Adamski as "interesting if true."

He concluded by saying, "When the contactees are aboard, [the UFOs] travel at the speed of lie."[56]

On the other side was *Flying Saucer Review*, which had long published contactee stories. In the months before the *Look* articles, it had published a four-part series on the claims of a Brazilian farmer named Antonio Villas Boas. He claimed that on the night of October 15–16, 1957, a UFO landed near his tractor. Before he could escape, four small men captured him, dragged him into the saucer and stripped him naked. Soon after, a door opened and a naked female walked in. She then had sex with Villas Boas in what he claimed was a breeding experiment.[57] *Flying Saucer Review* tried to link the two cases.[58] Despite the attention it was given, the Villas Boas case drew more snickers than converts.

It is understandable why the Hill "abduction" would be lumped in with the contactees during the 1960s—Betty had "talked" with the spacemen. Yet there was a difference. Adamski and the other contactees were knowingly committing hoaxes. Although Dr. Simon did not believe Betty's story, he never felt the story was a hoax. Betty *believed* she had been taken aboard a flying saucer. The supposed event was only a dream.

There was another difference; the contactees were becoming a part of the past. The Hill abduction story would set the pattern for the future— a person sees a UFO, experiences "missing time," then tells stories of a medical exam under hypnosis. But not just yet.

The Sixties Roll On

In the nation at large, the events that shaped "The Sixties" rolled on. The Vietnam War continued to grow. By the summer of 1965, U.S. troops had begun "Search and Destroy" sweeps of the jungle. The air war over the North was subject to a long list of restrictions. As the war escalated, the antiwar movement grew on college campuses. The protests were not only against the war, but were becoming a rejection of the whole American way of life.

With the increasing domestic turmoil, the rejection and contempt for authority continued to grow. Just as 1966–1968 saw an increase of UFO books, those same years saw a flood of books which rejected the Warren Commission's conclusion that Lee Harvey Oswald acted alone when he killed Kennedy and Dallas Police Officer J. D. Tippit. The "conspirators" blamed in the books included such authority figures as a Texas oil man, the FBI, the CIA, the Secret Service, the Dallas Police, "right wingers," and "gangsters." These "conspiracy theories" soon gained wide acceptance.[59]

UFO reports continued to pour in. Past flaps had lasted one to three months followed by years of few reports. In contrast, the number of reports for 1966 was 1,112 (32 unidentified)—higher than 1965. This trend continued into 1967. That year's final total was 937 reports (19 unidentified). The Sixties flap had lasted from July of 1965 through November of 1967. In terms of numbers of reports, it surpassed the Great Flap of 1952.[60,61]

"The Big Breakthrough"

Starting with the Socorro "landing" of 1964, a conviction had begun to grow among believers that "The Big Breakthrough" was at hand. In the believers' view, low-level sightings (such as those at Exeter) and the upsurge in reports pointed to an impending "overt contact" by the aliens.[62] Frank Edwards believed the UFOs had a seven-step surveillance program:

Phase One—Brief, long-range observation over the past several thousand years.

Phase Two—Close-range observations starting with the Foo-Fighters during World War II, the ghost rockets, and the early UFO reports through 1953. Edwards believed these UFOs were "unmanned" and that they took photographs, gathered atmosphere samples, and located Earth's cities.

Phase Three—Starting in late 1953, Edwards thought, "manned" UFOs undertook more extensive studies. It was at this time the first "occupant" cases were reported. Other activities by the aliens included landings, buzzing cars, and interfering with electrical power systems.

Phase Four—Close approaches to determine if humans were hostile and to locate radar sites and military bases.

Phase Five—Brief landings in isolated areas to collect plants, animals, and, if possible, humans.

Phase Six—Landings and low-level approaches where the UFOs and occupants could be seen by the maximum number of people. This, in Edwards's view, would set the stage for the final step.

Phase Seven—Deliberate, carefully planned contact with humans.[63]

Edwards continued:

> . . . we are probably witnessing the sixth phase. . . . And if last summer's [1965] mass sightings were that sixth phase—or a major part of it—then the seventh phase . . . "Overt Landing" or deliberate contact, cannot be far away.

If we have, indeed, gone through six phases in nineteen years—then the final phase would seem to be due in the next two or three years.

Edwards concluded by saying, "It is my personal belief that the day is not far distant when these questions will be answered for us."[64]

In 1966, events seemed to be going the believers' way. The press and public had seemingly accepted the existence of both UFOs and the cover-up, the Air Force explanations had been discredited, and an independent scientific investigation was underway. The three years that followed Edwards's prediction saw not the big breakthrough, however, but the destruction of the flying saucer myth.

The Condon Report

> Holmes looked thoughtful. "I see, Watson. You
> are sketching out a theory by which everything
> they say from the beginning is false."
>
> —*The Valley of Fear*

The events which destroyed the flying saucer myth began at 8:30 P.M. on March 20, 1966. The sheriff's office at Dexter, Michigan, received a telephone call from Bob Wagner that a UFO was in a swamp. Wagner and two deputies went into the woods trying to locate the object. The police report said:

> While in the woods area, a brilliant light was observed from the far edge of the woods, and upon approaching, the light dimmed in brilliance. As the afore mentioned [sic] approached the upper ridge, and the edge of the woods, the brilliant light again appeared, and then disappeared. A continued search of the area was conducted, through swamp, and high grass, with negative results.

Before the deputies arrived, Frank Mannor (Wagner's father-in-law) and his son had also seen the lights and had headed into the swamp trying to find the UFO. They saw two small lights which went out, then reappeared 500 yards away. The police report said:

> Object was observed to be of a brown coloring, appearing to be quilted type outside surface. Object appeared to be flat upon the bottom, and cone shaped toward the top, however being low in height. Two small lights appeared to be at the outer edges of the object, glowing with a bluish-green light, and intensifying to a brilliant red in color. When the vehicle or object illuminated, the lighting was a yellow-white in color, and ran horizontal be-

tween the two outer lights, allowing some of the object to be viewed. Outer
body appeared to be rough in texture.

After watching for several minutes, the lights intensified, then went
out with a sound like a rifle ricochet. Mannor and his son said the object passed over them in an instant.[1]

The next night, March 21, 1966, a second sighting was made at Hillsdale, Michigan, by eighty-seven coeds at a Hillsdale College dorm, a civil
defense director, and an assistant dean. The incident began when a report was made from the women's dorm that blue, red, and white lights
were visible to the east near the ground. The State Police were called,
but found nothing. Reports of lights in a swampy area continued to
come from the dorm. The lights were later described as "a fairly bright
red light and two yellowish lights, resembling Christmas tree lights."
One witness reported seeing a convex-shaped object between the lights;
others saw only the lights.[2]

Swamp Gas

Word of the twin sightings spread nationwide within hours and Blue
Book was deluged with calls from newspapers, radio and television stations, and *Life* magazine.[3] Dr. Hynek was sent to investigate the sightings. The intense press interest made it almost impossible to interview
witnesses. None of the witnesses was able to adequately describe the
brightness or angular speed of the lights. Hynek later called the three
days "general bedlam."

Given the confusing accounts, Dr. Hynek had to look for common elements—both cases were associated with swamps, the lights were described as small, reddish yellow and green with a general yellow glow,
which moved slowly and smoothly, with a tendency to suddenly disappear in one place and reappear at another. The few accounts of the lights
having a shape were made from too great a distance to be reliable.

With press interest and excitement reaching a "fever pitch," Hynek
decided to hold a press conference on March 26, 1966. Several University of Michigan scientists suggested the sightings had been caused by
"swamp lights," also called will-o'-the-wisp or fox fire. These lights are
caused by decaying vegetation releasing methane, hydrogen sulfide and
phosphine. Impurities in the phosphine spontaneously ignite in contact
with air, creating a glowing light. The lights are dim, move erratically

and sometimes give off a "popping" sound (similar to the ricochet sound Mannor heard).[4]

Dr. Hynek's press conference was a critical event in the history of the flying saucer myth. He stated his conclusions and the reasons behind them. But all the press heard were the two words "marsh gas." Or, as the headlines later put it, "Swamp Gas."[5]

The result of the press conference was an immediate, almost universal, hostile reaction. The headline in a *South Bend Tribune* editorial read: AIR FORCE INSULTS PUBLIC WITH SWAMP-GAS THEORY. The *Richmond News Leader* said, "It is high time for the Air Force to cease suppressing any hard evidence relating to such phenomena" and called for it to halt the policy of attempting "to discredit the testimony of witnesses."[6] *The New Yorker* magazine was even more outspoken: "We read the official explanation with sheer delight, marveling at their stupendous inadequacy. Marsh gas, indeed! Marsh gas is more appropriate an image of that special tediousness one glimpses in even the best scientific minds."[7]

The incident struck a chord with both public and press. For one thing, the phrase "Swamp Gas" *sounds* funny, with its implication of a tenuous nature and a bad smell. A more important reason was the assumption that swamp gas was being given as the *only* explanation for *all* UFO sightings. But Hynek never said it was. In the introduction to his press conference, he clearly stated his solution was *only* for the Dexter-Hillsdale sightings. In the savage merriment that followed, that was ignored.

Because of the swamp gas controversy, UFOs again began to attract congressional interest. Michigan Congressmen Weston E. Vivian and Gerald R. Ford officially requested that the House Armed Services Committee hold hearings. Ford said, "The American public deserves a better explanation than that thus far given by the Air Force."[8]

The hearings were approved and held on April 5, 1966. Air Force Secretary Harold D. Brown, Dr. Hynek, and Major Quintanilla testified. Brown stated the official position—that there was no proof UFOs were extraterrestrial or were a threat. When Chairman L. Mendel Rivers asked if anyone in authority accepted the Extraterrestrial Hypothesis, Brown said no one in the Air Force or executive branch had expressed such a belief.

The most important part of Brown's testimony was that he was considering the recommendations of the Ad Hoc Committee to Review Project Blue Book.[9] Called the "O'Brien Committee" after its chairman, Dr. Brian O'Brien of the Air Force Scientific Advisory Board, the report was completed in March 1966. It recommended that rather than continue Blue Book's limited activities, the Air Force contract with a few universities to provide scientific teams to investigate selected UFO sightings. A university or nonprofit group would coordinate the teams. The O'Brien Committee concluded:

> It is thought that perhaps 100 sightings a year might be subjected to this close study, and that possibly an average of 10 man days might be required per sighting so studied. The information provided by such a program might bring to light new facts of scientific value, and would almost certainly provide a far better basis than we have today for decision on a long term UFO program.[10]

The members of the House Armed Services Committee repeatedly endorsed the idea of an outside UFO study. Secretary Brown took the "hint" and that same afternoon, as soon as the hearing was over, he ordered the Air Force Chief of Staff to carry out the O'Brien Committee recommendations. The next link in the chain of events had been forged.

The House Armed Services Committee hearing also marked the public break between the Air Force and Hynek. Deeply hurt by the swamp gas controversy and charges that he was the Air Force's puppet, he read a "daring" statement "which has certainly not been dictated by the Air Force." He said he felt there must be aspects of UFO reports worthy of scientific investigation. Dr. Hynek did not publicly support the idea of alien spaceships. In response to a question, he said, "Puzzling cases exist, but I know of no competent scientist today who would say that these objects come from outer space."[11,12] That was about to change.

Dr. James E. McDonald

In March 1966, as the swamp gas controversy grew, a new figure appeared. He would play a key role in the soon-to-begin university study. Dr. James E. McDonald was a senior physicist at the Institute of Atmospheric Physics at the University of Arizona in Tucson. He specialized in cloud physics and weather modification research.[13] McDonald was also an angry, aggressive, driven, manipulative and ambitious individual. He was a "believer" in UFOs, but had never made any public statements. With the swamp gas controversy, this changed. In late March and early April 1966, he tried to organize a small summer study (one to three people) of UFOs. This was superseded by the approval of the university study.

McDonald wanted very much to be a part of the study. In the words of a biographer, he "toots his own horn quite blatantly at this point by discussing his UFO work and academic areas of specialization which would make him an asset to a UFO study." McDonald wrote in one letter that he had heard that he was at the head of the list "to tilt with the little green men."

During the summer of 1966, McDonald made three trips to Wright-Patterson AFB to examine the Blue Book files. During his first trip, on June 6, 1966, he read a complete copy of the Robertson Report, which had been declassified in error. McDonald took notes. But when McDonald returned on June 30 and asked to photocopy the report, he was told authorization would be needed. On his third visit, he was told the CIA had decided to reclassify the document. He was shocked to learn the Robertson Panel had been sponsored by the CIA, and it only fueled McDonald's suspicions. He never made up his mind, however, whether there was a Keyhoe-style "cover-up," or it was a "foul-up" (i.e., the "evidence" had been overlooked rather than hidden).[14]

The first trip to Blue Book also marked the start of a feud with Dr. Hynek. After examining the Blue Book files, McDonald was convinced they contained "proof" UFOs were alien spaceships. He went directly from Wright-Patterson AFB to Northwestern University to confront Hynek. In a righteous rage, he pounded on Hynek's desk and said, "How could you sit on this information for so many years without alerting the scientific community?" McDonald considered Hynek to have been scientifically dishonest, calling him "the original Menzel."[15]

Most of McDonald's time was taken up by lectures on UFOs to campus groups, the Rand Corporation, and NASA. His goal was to quietly build interest and acceptance for UFOs within the academic and scientific communities. In this effort, he met with some success. McDonald also researched old cases, such as Kenneth Arnold's sighting, the Mantell incident, and the Invasion of Washington. As part of this, he received a $1,300 grant to make telephone calls to witnesses. It is important to note that none of these activities was publicized; McDonald had not yet made any public statement of his belief in UFOs. As the summer of 1966 continued, he slowly edged toward such a statement.[16]

That same summer, a new figure appeared on the UFO scene. He was Philip J. Klass, the senior avionics editor for *Aviation Week & Space Technology* magazine. In June of 1966, the Institute of Electrical and Electronics Engineers announced it would hold a public symposium on UFOs. Klass objected, and was invited to be a panelist. As research, he bought a copy of Fuller's *Incident at Exeter*. As he read it, Klass also noticed the large number of reports of UFOs seen near power lines. Klass had a degree in electrical engineering and had worked for ten years at General Electric before joining *Aviation Week*. He began thinking about coronas—clouds of glowing ionized air formed near power lines. Klass became convinced many UFO sightings were actually of ball lightning. Klass published two articles in *Aviation Week*.[17] As atmospheric electricity was part of his speciality, McDonald was quick to dismiss Klass's ideas, viewing him as an upstart journalist.[18] The two rivals were in place.

A Poor Choice of Words

During the summer of 1966, the Air Force was trying to find a university to undertake the UFO study. Harvard, MIT, the University of North Carolina, the University of California, and others all turned them down. McDonald offered to be a "traveling salesman" to find an interested university. This was his first attempt to involve himself in the study. It was clear most universities did not want the public relations problems, and felt the whole subject was "illegitimate."

The stalemate was broken when Dr. J. Thomas Ratchfort of the Air Force Office of Scientific Research asked the National Center for Atmospheric Research (NCAR) to conduct the study. He was turned down, but the center's director, Dr. Walter Orr Roberts, suggested the University of Colorado at Boulder. Ratchford then approached the university in August 1966. The study was worth $300,000 plus $13,000 to cover the school's overhead. (An extension raised the total to $525,905.) The university had suffered budget cuts and the money may have been a major factor in the school's interest.[19]

On August 9, 1966, Assistant Dean Robert Low wrote a memo to E. James Archer, dean of the graduate school, and Thurston E. Manning, vice president and dean of faculties, on the pros and cons of the UFO study. It would become one of the key documents in the flying saucer myth. It read:

> I have pondered the UFO project and talked to a number of persons about it. Here are a few thoughts on the subject.
> Branscomb is very much against it. Gordon Little thinks it would be a disaster. George Benton, likewise, is negative. Their arguments, combined, run

like this: In order to undertake such a project one has to approach it objectively. That is, one has to admit the possibility that such things as UFO's exist. It is not respectable to give serious consideration to such a possibility. Believers, in other words, remain outcasts. Branscomb suggested that one would have to go so far as to consider the possiblity that saucers, if some of the observations are verified, behave according to a set of physical laws unknown to us. The simple act of admitting these possibilities just as possibilities puts us beyond the pale, and we would lose more in prestige in the scientific community than we could possibly gain by undertaking the investigation. Little indicated you do these things sometimes if there is a real national need. You do them in spite of possible adverse consequences. But, in this case, there is no real national need. Branscomb compares the situation to Rhine and the ESP study at Duke.

Walter Roberts, on the other hand, very much favors our undertaking it. He tried to get Will Kellogg, who is associate director of NCAR for the Laboratory of Atmospheric Sciences, to undertake it. Kellogg is very interested and almost did. He felt, however, he was too committed to do it. Walt hopes very much that we will. He says that he has information that Colorado really is the first choice of the Air Force, that others have not been approached and turned it down. He thinks, contrary to Little, that there is a very urgent need to do it, and he feels that we will gain a great deal in favor among the right circles by performing a critically needed service. He said that we must do it right—objectively and critically—and avoid publicity and all that sort of thing. But having the project here would not put us in the category of scientific kooks.

Branscomb says it would be better if the National Academy takes a contract from the Air Force and then subcontracts the money to us to do the work. He feels it would look much better that way, and I agree. There are, however, measures short of this that would accomplish almost the same thing—i.e., having a very distinguished group of consultants and/or advisers, having a committee in the Academy to whom our final report could be submitted.

Comments:

The analogy with ESP, Rhine, and Duke is only partially valid. The Duke study was done by believers who, after they had finished, convinced almost no one. Our study would be conducted almost exclusively by nonbelievers who, although they couldn't possibly prove a negative result, could and probably would add an impressive body of evidence that there is no reality to the observations. The trick would be, I think, to describe the project so that, to the public, it would appear a totally objective study but, to the scientific community, would present the image of a group of nonbelievers trying their best to be objective but having an almost zero expectation of finding a saucer. One way to do this would be to stress investigation, not of the physical phenomena, rather of the people who do the observing—the psychology and sociology of persons and groups who report seeing UFO's. If the emphasis were put here, rather than on examination of the old question of the physical reality of the saucers, I think the scientific community would quickly get the message.

There is another reason, it seems to me, to do this. Except possibly in a field like optical meteorology, I can't imagine a paper coming out of the study that would be publishable in a prestigious physical science journal. I can quite easily imagine, however, that psychologists, sociologists, and psychiatrists might well generate scholarly publications as a result of their investigations of the saucer observers.

I have not, of course, heard the story presented by the Air Force people. That comes Wednesday morning, the 10th. Ed Condon and Will Kellogg *have* heard it, however, and they say the project is presented in a very reasonable light.

It is premature to have much of an opinion, but I'm inclined to feel at this early stage that, if we set up the thing right and take pains to get the proper people involved and have success in presenting the image we want to present to the scientific community, we could carry the job off to our benefit. At least, it ought not to be rejected out of hand.

Notes:

Walt Roberts pledged NCAR's cooperation and assistance, especially in optical meteorology, a very thinly populated field in the U.S. (in Boulder it is represented only at NCAR).

The University persons who have expressed an interest in the project so far are the chief types. We'll have to be sure, if we take on the work, that we can find properly qualified people who will actually do the work.[20]

The memo was filed away and forgotten—for a while.

At the same time, Dr. Edward U. Condon was being offered the job of project director. Condon was an internationally known physicist—he had written the first textbook on quantum mechanics in the U.S. and the standard text on atomic spectra. He also had the political credentials—during the Age of Suspicion he had been accused of being a communist. When it was over, Condon had emerged with both his scientific and personal integrity intact. In 1958 he had accused the U.S. government of downplaying the effects of nuclear fallout. Clearly, he was not a man who would submit to the demands of authority. Condon was reluctant, however, to do the study.[21]

As both the University of Colorado and Condon debated undertaking the UFO study, McDonald began to maneuver toward a public announcement. It was carefully planned with the help of NICAP. McDonald gave several local lectures at the University of Arizona in early October. These were in preparation for a speech before the American Meteorological Society on October 19, 1966, in Washington, D.C. In these lectures, McDonald stressed a number of points: Blue Book was completely inadequate, Congress and the public had been deceived—the percent of unknowns was actually thirty to forty percent, and that astronomical, geophysical, or psychological explanations failed to cover all sightings. McDonald concluded "the least unsatisfactory hypothesis" was that UFOs were extraterrestrial spaceships.

The results of the Tucson lectures were negative—Dr. Gerard Kuiper of the Lunar and Planetary Laboratory said he was unwilling to question scientific laws based only on a few reports of untrained observers. Worries were expressed about the lectures' effects on the University of Arizona's reputation. The press coverage was also disappointing, saying McDonald believed in "persons from outer space" and in current CIA involvement. He decided to adjust the Washington speech, highlighting Blue Book's scientific failures while downplaying the CIA angle. He also included an attack on both the Villas Boas and Hill abduction cases.[22,23]

Hynek was also "going public" with his increasingly pro-UFO views. Between June and December 1966, he wrote letters to Secretary of the Air Force Brown and *Science* magazine. He also wrote articles on UFOs for *Discovery* and *Saturday Evening Post* magazines and the introduction for Jacques Vallee's book *Challenge to Science*. He was much more cautious than McDonald, saying only that UFOs were worthy of scientific study and that the Blue Book investigation had not provided this. Hynek did not express a belief in alien spaceships; in the *Saturday Evening Post* article he wrote: "There is no incontrovertible evidence, as far as I can see, to say we have strange visitors. But it would be foolish to rule out the possibility absolutely."[24]

Despite Hynek's more "open-minded" stance, McDonald continued to express contempt for him. McDonald said of the letter to Brown, "I find the letter disappointingly full of equivocations." As for the introduction, he dismissed it as "a masterpiece in trying to cover his rear."[25] McDonald may have had several reasons for his feud with Hynek. Their personalities were incompatible—McDonald was a bull in a china shop, while Hynek worked quietly behind the scenes. By attacking Hynek, McDonald may have thought he could discredit Blue Book's scientific competence. By discrediting Hynek, he could also remove a potential rival. Hynek had worked on UFOs for eighteen years; if there was a big breakthrough, academics were more likely to turn to him, rather than McDonald, who had worked on the subject for less than a year. On a more basic level, the feud was a continuation of the past pattern of bitter rivalries between believers.

Both McDonald and Hynek were soon overshadowed. On October 7, 1966, the Air Force announced the University of Colorado had been selected to conduct the UFO study. Dr. Edward U. Condon would be program director while Robert Low was project coordinator. Dr. Franklin E. Roach, an astrophysicist with the Enviromental Sciences Services Administration, and Dr. Stuart W. Cook, chairman of the psychology department, were the principal investigators.[26] The battle was about to begin.

The Battle of Colorado

It quickly became clear what was at stake with the Condon Study. If the study reached a positive conclusion, then believers would have achieved the scientific acceptance they had long sought. If the conclusion was negative, they would lose what respectability they had gained during the mid-1960s. It was not clear, however, what the study's ultimate goal would be. Some felt it would be best to limit the project to a recommendation on follow-on studies. Others, including Dr. David R. Saunders, wanted to define the study as a test of the Extraterrestrial Hypothesis. There was a certain logic in this—since 1950, the question "Are flying saucers real?" meant "Are flying saucers alien spaceships?" It was this question that had given the flying saucer myth its impact. The problem, even Saunders admitted, was that the probability of finding proof was slim at best.

Another staff member, Michael Wertheimer, pointed out a problem—the specific qualities of an alien spaceship were unknown. Thus, even if any did exist, they could not be separated from the "miscellaneous" category. Saunders disagreed and Wertheimer called him a "quasi-believer" in front of the other staff members. In the end, Low agreed to a test of the Extraterrestrial Hypothesis in early March 1967.

The exchange highlighted yet another problem—many of the younger staff members *already* believed the Extraterrestrial Hypothesis. Saunders, for instance, fully accepted Keyhoe's cover-up ideas, writing later: "Almost from the first day of the Project, I had maintained that a 'government conspiracy' to conceal the 'truth about UFOs' from the public was an even *more* likely hypothesis than [the Extraterrestrial Hypothesis]."

This belief cast a shadow over the staff. Why, they asked themselves, if the CIA was covering up UFOs, were they allowing the Condon Study to go on. Rather than question their belief in a cover-up, they assumed someone on the study was "acting in a double role." Saunders added, "This created an inevitable undertone of mutual distrust and game playing, which did the Project no good at all."

From the start, Keyhoe was also suspicious—in October 1966 he had expressed doubts to Saunders that the Condon Study would be truly independent of Air Force control.[27] Publicly, NICAP expressed support for the study. The January-February 1967 issue of *The UFO Investigator* said:

> Having met most of the scientists involved, we are generally satisfied with their fair-mindedness and their thorough plans. . . . It is probably fair to say that the scientists on the project range from open-minded skeptics to moderately convinced "believers," which is as it should be.[28]

That there were "believers" and "skeptics" on the study was in direct violation of the provisions of the Air Force contract. It stated:

> The work will be conducted under conditions of strictest objectivity by investigators who, as carefully as can be determined, have no predilections or preconceived positions on the UFO question. This is essential if the public, the Congress, the Executive and the scientific community are to have confidence in the study.[29]

McDonald's First Moves

By late 1966, McDonald seems to have felt he was the most qualified scientist in the field of UFOs, and believed he was the logical person to head the massive follow-on study that was sure to result from a positive Condon Study. For now, he wanted to "guide" the Condon Study.[30,31] McDonald was kept informed about events within the study by a network of "moles."

McDonald also sought an invitation to brief the staff. He sent a copy of his October 19 speech to Condon but received no response. He continued his attempts, writing several times to Condon to offer his help with the study. Finally, on November 20, McDonald telephoned Condon and/or Low, then flew to Colorado for the briefing.

McDonald came away from the briefing feeling that the staff was poorly prepared and lacked physical science specialists. He also expressed amazement at the elementary topics in meteorological optics the staff found informative. In a November 29, 1966, letter to Hall at NICAP, he said, "Let's cross our fingers and watch carefully."[32] McDonald would do more than "watch carefully;" he would interfere with the Condon Study both directly and behind the scenes.

Mid-January to mid-March 1967 was an active period for UFO reports and the investigators were kept busy. At the end of April 1967, however, the number of new sightings ebbed. Although the Sixties flap continued to the end of the year, it was starting to fade. To cope with this, an "Early Warning Network" was established in May 1967. Local volunteers (mostly NICAP members) would notify the study when they heard of a UFO report. The goal was to have an investigation team at the scene within twenty-four hours.[33] Dr. Norman E. Levine, who joined the Condon Study in June 1967, was named head of the Early Warning Network. Levine had just received his Ph.D. in electrical engineering from the University of Arizona. Like Saunders, Levine was a believer and had close links with McDonald.[34]

Factions

As 1967 dragged on, the believers on the staff became increasingly upset about Dr. Condon's attitude. On January 25, 1967, Condon gave a speech at the Corning Glass Works. The Elmira, New York *Star Gazette* article read:

> "It is my inclination right now to recommend that the government get out of this business. My attitude right now is that there's nothing to it."
> With a smile he added, "but I'm not supposed to reach a conclusion for another year."

Several NICAP members were in the audience and sent Keyhoe accounts of the speech. To paper over the split between Condon and NICAP, Condon sent a letter to Keyhoe in which he said his comments had been taken out of context. Condon also limited any public statements.[35]

Internal problems also began to appear. The staff began to believe Condon was showing what they thought was a preoccupation with contactee cases. For believers who accepted the NICAP version of the flying saucer myth, even a mention of the contactees was offensive. To bring them into a discussion of flying saucers was seen as an attack on the "reality" of UFOs.[36] Nor was the staff only upset at Condon. In August 1967, Low went on a month-long trip to attend the International Astronomical Union meeting in Prague, Czechoslovakia. Saunders thought he should see Charles Bowen, editor of *Flying Saucer Review,* and French UFO writer Aime Michel. Instead, he went to Loch Ness. The staff was offended by Low's equating UFOs with the Loch Ness Monster.[37]

These incidents fed the suspicions of NICAP, McDonald, and the staff. McDonald wrote a letter to Philip Seitz, president of the National Academy of Science. McDonald complained the Condon Study staff was not aware of the dimension of the UFO problem and that it was too small an effort. McDonald was also starting to think about a public confrontation with Condon.[38]

The means by which the confrontation could be arranged was discovered in July 1967. A new staff member, Roy Craig, was preparing for two speaking appearances. Going through the files, Craig discovered Low's August 1966 memo. He showed it to Levine with the comment, "See if this doesn't give you a funny feeling in the stomach." It was passed around the office and then returned to the files.

At the same time, Saunders was thinking about the future of UFO studies. He was convinced there would be two or three strong cases by the end of the study. Saunders thought the Condon Study should prepare the public for such a "positive conclusion." To do this, he proposed ending the press blackout and releasing carefully selected material— both positive and negative. They would also initiate discussions, at first within professional groups such as the American Psychological Association, of the social problems the world would face if proof of aliens should be found. Both Condon and Low rejected the proposals. Condon said he did not understand what Saunders was talking about. Condon added that if proof was found, he would take it directly to the president. Saunders felt that Condon would issue a negative report even if positive evidence was found.[39]

In early August, McDonald again went to Boulder to brief the staff on the results of a trip he had made to Australia. He had interviewed some eighty UFO witnesses. During the presentation Condon fell asleep three times. McDonald wrote a letter to Mary Lou Armstrong, Condon's administrative secretary, to register his complaints. Armstrong wrote back saying that she expected a split would come in the spring of 1968. The exchange with Armstrong was not an isolated incident—McDonald could talk and write freely to certain staff members.[40] This was to be the key to McDonald's efforts.

On September 13, 1967, Condon made an after-dinner talk to former colleagues at the National Bureau of Standards. He regaled them with contactee stories. Several believers in the audience were, yet again, offended. One said that Condon, "made no attempt to stress the seriousness of the problem. . . . He made no sincere attempt to stimulate interest among the group." NICAP learned of Condon's remarks on September 20; Keyhoe called and withdrew support for the study.[41] On September 27, an interview with Condon was published. He said he was "disillusioned" with UFOs and almost wished he could drop the whole business.[42]

The staff was in open revolt; Saunders wrote later, "The battle lines were now clearly and openly drawn—Condon and Low against the rest of us." There was talk of a mass resignation of the staff. Saunders said the staff would "do whatever we could to preserve the scientific validity and respectability of the UFO question." The believers feared that the final report would be so negative "as to stifle" further UFO studies for "another 20 years" or more. The staff considered writing a positive minority report in hopes "that Condon would be forced to accept it on its merits."

The "Trick" Memo

It was at this point that Low's August 1966 "trick" memo entered the struggle between Condon and the staff. Saunders gave Keyhoe a copy the day before Thanksgiving. Saunders wanted Keyhoe and NICAP to understand he had "no illusions" about the "one-sided nature" of the study. He asked Keyhoe not to make it public "as long as there was any hope."[43] It was also at this time (if not earlier) that McDonald learned of the memo. He said later that several staff members had told him of its existence. Given his extensive covert links with the staff, he may have first heard of it soon after it was discovered.

On December 12, 1967, there was a secret meeting of McDonald, Hynek, Saunders, Levine, and Armstrong. Hynek had a cold so left early. At this point McDonald brought up the Low memo to Saunders and Levine. As he already knew about it, they decided to give him a copy. Once he had a copy, McDonald was quick to realize the weapon the Low memo could provide. On December 28, he wrote Aime Michel to say, "Some confrontation is going to have to be effected. This is difficult to engineer. A number of us are working on that problem and thinking about it as carefully as we can."[44] At this point, McDonald's goals seem to have changed. He became less interested in changing the direction of the Condon Study. Now, he wanted to discredit it.

On January 31, 1968, McDonald wrote a long letter to Low dealing with his many complaints about the study—Condon's negative attitude and statements, his not going on field investigations, his interest in contactees, his refusal to stress how serious the UFO problem was, the lack of communications between Condon, Low, and investigations staff, and finally, the failure to investigate "cover-up" cases. To illustrate these problems, McDonald quoted part of the memo, including the line, "The trick would be . . . ." He said, "I am rather puzzled by the viewpoints expressed there."

When Low read the portion quoting the memo he exploded in anger and made an appointment to see Condon. The next day, Saunders and Levine were called to Condon's office and fired for leaking the memo. Armstrong resigned on February 22, citing a lack of confidence in Low by the staff.[45]

The Condon Study's "near-mutiny" came to national attention with the May 14, 1968, issue of *Look*. The article, titled "Flying Saucer Fiasco," was written by John G. Fuller. It centered on the "trick" memo—a headline read, "A startling memo from Robert Low said 'the trick would be' to 'appear objective'." The subtitle read, "The extraordinary story of the half-million-dollar 'trick' to make Americans believe the Condon committee was conducting an objective investigation." The article depicted the Condon Study as being biased against UFOs from the start. It spoke of "the negative approach to the UFO problem," "Condon's and Low's prejudice," and said "the study was being gravely misdirected." The issue was made out to be one of scientific integrity, not a question of belief. Indeed, it was never made clear that Saunders and Levine were believers. The goal was to discredit the study's anticipated negative conclusions in advance.[46]

On April 30, Congressman J. Edward Roush (D-Ind) took to the House floor to attack the study. He said:

> The story in *Look* magazine raises grave doubts as to the scientific profundity and objectivity of the project conducted at the University of Colorado. The publication of this article will cast in doubt the results of that project in the minds of the American public; in the minds of the scientific community.
>
> We are poorer—$500,000 later—not richer in information about UFO's. Where do we go from here? I am not satisfied; the American public will not be satisfied.[47]

Roush was the tool McDonald would use for his next move to discredit the Condon Study.

The Roush Hearings

McDonald had first met Roush in February 1967 when they had a long talk on UFOs. McDonald followed up over the next several months with several letters to Roush, urging him to push for congressional hearings (Roush was a member of the House Committee on Science and Astronautics). In late April 1968, as the controversy over the "trick" memo began to build, McDonald again wrote to Roush, saying it was critical that Congress step into the UFO controversy. Roush responded by making two speeches attacking the Condon Study and wrote the Secretary of the Air Force and the Comptroller General.

Over the next several months, McDonald met with congressmen, staff members and aides. On June 3, he spoke to the Capitol Hill Burro Club, a group of Democratic staff members. The talk so impressed Morris Udall's staff that they convinced Udall to appear with McDonald on a local Tucson television program on UFOs. Then, on June 19, Udall arranged an appointment for McDonald with George P. Miller, chairman of the House Science and Astronautics Committee, who gave approval for the hearings. McDonald was surprised at how easy it had been.[48]

On June 28, Dr. Phyllis O'Callaghan, Roush's administrative assistant, called McDonald to ask for suggestions on a UFO seminar. This was seen as a precursor to the actual hearings. McDonald took the opportunity to stage-manage the whole seminar. He provided a list of participants—Dr. J. Allen Hynek, Dr. Robert Hall, Dr. R. M. L. Baker, Jr., Dr. Carl Sagan, Dr. Robert M. Wood, and himself. All but Sagan were pro-UFO. McDonald and O'Callaghan discussed the pros and cons of each person. Several weeks later, Wood cancelled out. McDonald told O'Callaghan that Dr. Jim Harder of University of California, Berkeley's Engineering Department would make an effective witness. McDonald then wrote Harder about the seminar, and prepared the wording of the invitation he wanted O'Callaghan to send. McDonald was also given use of Roush's phone credit card to arrange the appearances.

The UFO Symposium was held on July 29, 1968. Speaking were Hynek, McDonald, Sagan, Hall, Harder, and Baker. Written statements were submitted by Menzel, Stanton Friedman, Frank Salisbury, and Roger Shepard. Hynek's statement was low-key while Sagan limited his remarks to the possibilities of extraterrestrial life. The others were strongly pro-UFO. McDonald said that the subject of UFOs "now needs to be very rapidly brought out into the open as a problem demanding very serious and very high-caliber scientific attention." Harder said "the physical reality of UFOs has been proven beyond a reasonable doubt." He added that they were "interplanetary" and used propulsion systems based on "an application of gravitational fields that we do not understand."

The token skeptic was Dr. Menzel. Originally, he had not been scheduled to appear. When he learned of the seminar, he protested he was "amazed . . . that [Roush] could plan so unbalanced a symposium,

weighted by persons known to favor Government support of a continuing expensive and pointless investigation of UFOs without inviting me."
In his statement he called UFOs "a modern myth" and reiterated the
large number of conventional objects that could be mistaken for a flying
saucer.[49,50]

The Roush hearings were the high point of the effort to gain respectability for flying saucers. Never again would UFOs command so august a body. It was also the high point of McDonald's efforts; he had
arranged the congressional hearings the believers had long sought. He
had succeeded where Keyhoe had failed. The U.S. Congress had become
a tool of his effort against the Condon Study. But in six months it would
all be gone.

Even as the Roush hearings were unfolding, McDonald was running
into trouble. McDonald's 1967 trip to Australia was paid for by the U.S.
Navy's Office of Naval Research. McDonald defended this by saying UFO
sightings could provide information on ball lightning and other atmospheric effects. However, Klass found numerous comments by McDonald
that atmospheric phenomena accounted for only a tiny percent of UFO
reports. This was a clear contradiction, and Klass accused McDonald of
using Navy funding to "bootleg" his UFO research.

In retrospect, it is clear McDonald did use ONR funds to support his
UFO studies, albeit with the knowledge of his contract supervisor. This is
supported by a letter he wrote regarding his 1968 ONR contract:

> On that point, let me ask you if it isn't possible now for ONR to "make me
> an honest man" with respect to my UFO research. In view of the somewhat
> altered climate of opinion about UFOs, can't we bring my work out in the
> open and make it an explicit part of my next year's work?

Later in the letter, he added:

> I have run out of my $1,300 of local money many weeks ago, and am now
> operating (primarily on telephone tolls and travel) on my ONR funds. It looks
> like the contract funds will go to a flat zero by the end of the contract period,
> incidentally.[51]

Despite the "trick" memo, the Roush hearings, and the ONR controversy, interest in UFOs was fading. It was 1968, and the world was going
mad.

1968: Year of Madness

By January 1968, U.S. forces in Vietnam were approaching 500,000. On
January 30 the Viet Cong launched the "Tet Offensive" in every major

city in South Vietnam. It was a failure, and by the end of February 1968, the Viet Cong had been destroyed as a military force.[52] This did not matter—at home, Tet was depicted as an American defeat. The battle had broken whatever will remained inside the Johnson administration to continue the war. On March 31, President Johnson announced a partial bombing halt over North Vietnam and his own withdrawal from the presidential campaign. In July, negotiations began in Paris with the North Vietnamese. Most of the early discussions were on the shape of the table.

At home it was a bloody spring. On April 4, 1968, Martin Luther King was shot and killed by James Earl Ray. King's death set off the worst rioting in U.S. history—168 cities suffered arson, looting, and killings. Then, on June 4, Robert Kennedy, having just won the California and South Dakota primary elections, was shot and killed by Sirhan Sirhan. The spring semester of 1968 saw major demonstrations at 101 colleges.[53] Political dialogue was replaced by obscenities, terrorism, and violence.

Secretary of State Dean Rusk asked "whose side are you on?" Protesters marched under Viet Cong flags. Across the land, a chasm of hate and bitterness yawned. It was a chasm which could never be bridged. American society had been splintered.

The UFO reports for 1968 reflected this turning inward. Only 375 sightings were sent to Blue Book. This was the lowest number since 1951. Only three were listed as unidentified. This was the first presidential election year since 1952 that did not see a large upsurge in monthly UFO reports in the late summer.[54,55]

The Condon Report and After

The final report of the Condon Study was completed in the fall of 1968. Before it was publicly released, a panel of the National Academy of Science would review the study. McDonald had continued his attempts to discredit it. During the spring, he wrote several letters to academy president Seitz saying, "I think it will be scientifically undesirable to let the Condon Study run its course." McDonald also had Roush write the NAS asking it to investigate.

This effort resumed in October 1968 when McDonald wrote O'Callaghan asking that she use Roush's office to learn more about the NAS review panel. McDonald wanted to contact them to provide his views on both the Condon Study and the UFO phenomenon. In this effort he was frustrated—the names of the panel members were kept secret.[56]

The Condon Report was released on January 9, 1969. It was a massive document—963 pages in the paperback edition. Condon was to the point:

> Our general conclusion is that nothing has come from the study of UFOs in the past 21 years that has added to scientific knowledge. Careful consideration of the record as it is available to us leads us to conclude that further extensive study of UFOs probably cannot be justified in the expectation that science will be advanced thereby.

The controversy surrounding the Condon Report has continued among both skeptics and believers, overshadowing its accomplishments. One of the more significant cases looked at was the reentry of the Zond 4 booster on March 3, 1968. At about 9:45 P.M. EST, hundreds of witnesses from Kentucky to Pennsylvania saw two, three, or more flaming objects with golden-orange tails. Two of the reports described it as a cigar-shaped spaceship with a row of lighted windows. One witness said, "It was shaped like a fat cigar. . . . It appeared to have rather square shaped windows. . . . It appeared to me that the fuselage was constructed of many pieced or flat sheets . . . with a 'riveted together look'. . . . The many 'windows' seemed to be lit up from the inside."

The "windows" were, in fact, the burning booster fragments. This was called the "airship effect": the tendency of a witness to a bright fireball to "see" a cigar-shaped object outlining several brightly lit "windows" which were actually glowing meteor fragments. The similarity between the Zond 4 and Chiles-Whitted sightings was obvious. The report noted:

> The present discussion provides definitive evidence that fireballs can be described in *just* the way reported by Chiles and Whitted. The investigator is faced with the perfectly conceivable possibility that Chiles and Whitted, suffering from the "airship effect", became excited and reported a misconception—a cigar-shaped object with windows and flames—just as a fraction of witnesses to spectacular fireballs are now known to do.[57]

One investigation that was to have great future impact on the flying saucer myth was the death of Snippy the horse. It had been found on September 9, 1967, with all skin and flesh on the head and neck gone. The cut at the base of the neck "couldn't have been the work of a sharp hunting knife" as it was too smooth. No blood was found in the carcass or on the ground. Word soon spread. There were reports of crushed brush, more dead horses in the area, landing pad marks, radioactivity, and exhaust burns. There was speculation that Snippy had been "zapped" by a flying saucer's death ray. The stories soon attracted the attention of the Condon Study, NICAP, and APRO.

The Condon Study investigator found the horse had a severe infection in its rear leg and flank. A cut was found in the neck—apparently from someone who had tried to put the suffering horse to sleep. Birds used the cut to get at the flesh and stripped the neck and head. There were no exhaust burns or radiation. NICAP endorsed the finding, saying it "has been determined to be neither a UFO case nor especially mysterious." APRO, on the other hand, clung to the idea that a UFO had been responsible, even denying the horse had an infection.[58] The death of Snippy introduced the idea that UFOs were killing and mutilating animals for their own ends.

Despite such positive points, there were also problems. A major one was that several of the sections were background, historical, or had limited connection with UFOs. One example of this was the chapter on astronaut sightings, "Visual Observations Made by Astronauts." It was little more than a text on manned astronomical observation in space. Of the thirty-three pages, only a little more than three were on the UFO sightings. Solutions were given for only three sightings. The Mercury 9 sighting was caused by the night airglow: the light given off by the gasses in the upper atmosphere. The Gemini 11 crew had seen the Soviet scientific satellite Proton 3, while the Gemini 12 astronauts saw four pieces of equipment they had jettisoned several orbits earlier. It concluded there were only three astronaut sightings that could be considered unidentified. They were:

Gemini 4—The cylindrical object.

Gemini 4—Observation of a bright moving object, fifty hours into the flight, that was above the spacecraft and appeared to be in a polar orbit.

Gemini 7—Sighting of a "bogie" and many illuminated particles in a polar orbit.

This opinion was based on the belief Pegasus 2 was too far away for the first sighting and that no satellite had been identified as being the cause of the second sighting. (There was also mention, in passing, of a "light" seen off the China coast at another point in the flight.) As for the Gemini 7 sighting, it was noted that although the objects might be fragments from the Titan II second stage, this would be impossible if they were truly in a polar orbit.[59]

Although all the astronaut sightings, except the three listed above, were dismissed, there were no details. In effect, the claims went unchallenged. Moreover, since the Gemini 4 sighting, the most famous and significant of the reports, was listed as unidentified, their status continued to grow.

Another problem was the sighting cases that were investigated. They were a mixture of trivial sightings, hoaxes, and good reports. As such, they were representative of what the Air Force had been dealing with for twenty-two years. Of the ninety-one cases looked at, however, thirty were listed as unidentified. This was thirty-three percent, far higher than the Air Force rate. The believers, operating under the assumption that unidentified = alien spaceships, thought this negated the study's negative conclusion. McDonald, Hynek, Fuller, and Keyhoe all made this point.[60,61]

A member of the Condon staff, Michael Wertheimer, pointed out the flaw in this reasoning. He said, "There is a logically indefensible jump between the assertion that people are seeing things they don't understand and the assertion that these reports constitute proof of or evidence for an extraterrestrial intelligence origin of the objects reported."[62]

In the end, what was actually *in* the Condon Report was overshadowed by the controversy that surrounded it. There was blame on all sides. McDonald never liked anything the study did. He sought to manipulate the study, undermine it, and finally provoked the controversy over the "trick" memo. Although academia is noted for fierce internal warfare, McDonald's conduct went beyond the acceptable.

At the same time, Condon and Low cannot escape blame. Condon should have realized how provocative his comments were to believers. Condon subsequently acknowledged he had underestimated what he was getting into:

> I had some awareness of the passionate controversy that swirled around the subject, contributing added difficulty to the task of making a dispassionate study. The hazard proved to be much greater than was appreciated at the outset. Had I known of the extent of the emotional commitment of the UFO believers and the extremes of conduct to which their faith can lead them, I certainly would never have undertaken the study.[63]

Low lacked the experience to manage so complex a study. Moreover, the plan to conduct a complete reinvestigation of UFOs was too ambitious. It might have been better to ask NICAP, APRO, and other groups to recommend five or ten cases each. This would have eliminated the charge they had not looked at the "good" sightings. Low was also naive about the believers. He admitted to one person that he knew Saunders and Levine were believers when they joined the study. He thought the evidence that UFOs were not real would be so compelling that they would come around.[64]

At the same time, Saunders, Levine, and the other believers showed their own brand of naiveté. Having given McDonald the memo and been found out, Saunders still thought he and Condon could come to an agreement over the handling of the study.

There is a final note—the public controversy over the Condon Study always centered on the use of the word "trick" in Low's memo. Scientists often use the word "trick" in the sense of "problem," "difficulty" or "task." It was later confirmed Low used the word in this sense.[65] But there was a far more important misunderstanding. Saunders acted under the assumption that Condon had seen the memo and that it had established policy for the study. In fact, both Condon and Archer denied ever seeing the memo. After learning this, Saunders wrote later, "I understood why Condon had been so upset with our action. . . . it never crossed my mind that he didn't know of it." He added that had he known Condon was unaware of the memo, he would have acted differently.[66]

The final assessment of the Condon Study is this: it was impossible for the different factions to come together in a common effort. Their views were so divergent they could not understand each other. The Condon Study was a microcosm of the Sixties.

The End of Blue Book

With the Condon Report's finding that the study of UFOs had no scientific justification, the end of Blue Book was assured. This was formally decided at a meeting in March 1969.[67] The announcement was made by Air Force Secretary Robert C. Seamans, Jr. on December 17, 1969. He stated, "The continuation of Project Blue Book cannot be justified either on the ground of national security or in the interest of science." Based on the Condon Report, the NAS review, past UFO studies, and twenty-two years of investigation, the Air Force concluded:

No UFO had given any indication of a threat to national security.

There was no evidence any unidentified sightings represent technological developments or principles beyond the range of present-day knowledge.

There was no evidence UFOs were extraterrestrial vehicles.[68]

Even before the end of Blue Book, the number of sightings had dwindled to the lowest point since 1947. Only 146 reports were submitted to the Air Force during 1969 (one was unidentified). In all, the Air Force had received 12,618 reports with 701 unidentified (5.56%). Of the unidentified cases, 43.2% (303 out of 701) were from the Great Flap of 1952.

So ended the Air Force's twenty-two-year struggle with the flying saucer myth. In retrospect, Air Force involvement had kept the subject alive. By dismissing UFOs, yet maintaining an investigation unit, it fed suspicions. Ultimately, it is clear the Air Force was fighting an unwinnable battle. It was going against the popular belief and desire to believe in UFOs. "Saucer activists," as the *New York Times* called them, welcomed the end of Blue Book. NICAP said, "The Air Force decision opens the way for a fresh look at the UFO problem." NICAP felt a high-level federal/private agency with "the right people" should take over UFO investigations. NICAP added, "UFO's can now be given the serious scientific attention they require, free from military considerations."[69] Soon, though, NICAP too, would be gone.

The Fall of NICAP

The Sixties flap had caused NICAP's membership to peak at 12,000. Keyhoe felt the rising membership meant that the constant threat of bankruptcy was past. Starting in early 1967, however, public interest in UFOs started to fade. With this came a sudden drop-off of new members and renewals. NICAP's income lagged behind costs. On August 14, 1967, Keyhoe sent out an emergency fund-raising letter, warning that NICAP would have to suspend operations unless help was received immediately. Ironically, one of the "very bad effects" of this would be "crippling of the influential Colorado University UFO Project, which depends on NICAP for most of its factual evidence." (The break was still a month off.)[70]

Despite the return of NICAP's money problems, Keyhoe still had ambitious plans. In the fall of 1968, Keyhoe began discussions with several congressmen about "Operation Lure." Keyhoe had been thinking about it since the spring of 1958.[71] A UFO landing field would be built in an isolated site in the southwest. There would be buildings with educational displays and several dummy UFOs. These would be used to attract the flying saucers' attention. Keyhoe believed that within "a few days" a UFO would "undoubtedly" land. This would lead to the first face-to-face contact with the aliens.[72]

Events in early 1969 brought an end to Keyhoe's plans. NICAP membership continued to drop, down to 7,800 members, and bankruptcy again loomed. In April, Keyhoe sent out another letter requesting money. A survey of the ex-members found that they had grown tired of articles on the Condon Report and "our fight against secrecy." The ex-members said they had joined NICAP to learn more about UFOs, but soon got bored with all the Condon Report articles. Keyhoe's obsession with the "UFO cover-up" had, in the end, alienated NICAP's own membership.[73]

The April appeal failed to pay off the bills. On July 28, five of the nine NICAP staff members were laid off, office space was cut, files stored, and pay was delayed. Yet back bills still totaled $10,374 while total income through September amounted to under $23,000, not enough to cover operating expenses, let alone salaries.[74,75]

With NICAP on the brink of disaster, the Board of Governors stepped in. Although Keyhoe had made much of their rank and status, they had been only ornamentation for NICAP. The group, in fact, had not held a formal meeting since 1960. They found NICAP had been withholding Social Security taxes, but had not been sending them to the government. Moreover, only a fraction of the membership was currently paying dues. Yet, they continued to be sent *The UFO Investigator*, sometimes for years.

In early December 1969, a few days before the Air Force closed down Blue Book, Keyhoe was forced out as NICAP director by the board. The meeting was stormy and Keyhoe was furious about the "coup." He remained on the board but never attended a meeting. Col. Joseph Bryan III was named acting president. He and two other board members, J. B. Hartranft, Jr., and Maj. Dewey Fournet, Jr., took over as caretakers.[76]

Although NICAP lingered on into the early 1980s, the departure of Keyhoe marked its end as a force in the flying saucer myth. Despite the board's efforts, NICAP membership continued to drop, going from 12,000 (on paper) in 1967 to only 4,000 in 1971. APRO also underwent a similar drop in membership. It went from 4,000 in 1967 to 2,000 in 1971. The only group which showed any growth was the Midwest UFO Network. MUFON had split off APRO in 1969 (earning it Coral Lorenzen's unending hate). Most of the new members were ex-NICAP. In 1970, MUFON had several hundred members. As the group went nationwide in the 1970s, the name was changed to the Mutual UFO Network.[77]

The Death of McDonald

The evaporation of interest in UFOs took its greatest toll on McDonald. Throughout 1969 and 1970, he continued to speak out on UFOs, but his efforts fell on deaf ears. McDonald's own scientific career was at a halt. Between 1951 and 1966 he published sixty-four scientific papers. After 1966, when he was working full time on UFOs, there were none.[78] The strain was beginning to show. In the fall of 1970, McDonald gave a lecture to a NICAP audience at which he seemed more intense and tense than at earlier lectures, even to the point of being on the verge of a nervous breakdown.[79]

One of McDonald's fields of research was weather modification. He was asked by the NAS to study the effects of a planned fleet of 500 supersonic transports (SSTs) on the Earth's atmosphere. In November 1970, he concluded that the water vapor in the SSTs' exhaust would deplete the ozone layer and cause some 10,000 additional cases of skin cancer. McDonald testified before the House SST hearings in March 1971. His statement was terribly tedious and dull, a lecture on complex chemical reactions. As a result, most of the congressmen were dozing off or bored.[80]

Suddenly, Congressman Silvio Conte (R-Massachusetts) pointed out McDonald was an expert on UFOs and believed the Northeast Blackout of 1965 had been "caused by those flying saucers." McDonald responded that he thought there was a correlation between UFOs and blackouts that was worth study. During the exchange, several congressmen and spectators openly laughed at McDonald. Conte kept after McDonald, trying to equate his belief in UFOs to his SST theories. McDonald protested that there was no link between the two.

The next day Conte quoted a portion of McDonald's 1968 testimony in which he said some occupant cases might be valid. Conte then said, "A man who comes here and tells me that the SST flying in the stratosphere is going to cause thousands of skin cancers has to back up his theory that there are little men flying around the sky. I think this is very important."[81] McDonald was deeply hurt by the comments.

The final straw for McDonald was a personal crisis unrelated to his belief in UFOs. In May 1971, he attempted suicide. He shot himself in the head, but survived. He was placed in a Veteran's Administration hospital, blind and unable to remember why he had tried to kill himself. Several weeks later, the final act took place. McDonald's eyesight and memory had partially returned. On Sunday June 13, 1971, he got dressed, left the hospital and then hailed a taxi. He asked the driver to take him home. When they arrived, McDonald went inside and got the .38 caliber revolver he had used in his first suicide attempt. He then had the taxi drive him to the outskirts of Tucson. There he shot himself—a note was found by the body. He was 51.[82,83]

The Condon Report, the end of both Blue Book and NICAP, and the tragic death of McDonald left the flying saucer myth shattered. It would take a full decade before the flying saucer myth reassembled itself from the separate, contradictory fragments.

The Flying Saucer Myth 1964–1972

Disk-shaped alien spacecraft have been seen in the Earth's atmosphere for thousands of years.

These flying saucers are capable of speeds and maneuvers far beyond those of Earth aircraft.

These UFOs have been seen by such reliable witnesses as airline pilots and astronauts and have been tracked on radar, which proves their extraterrestrial nature.

UFOs have left traces at their landing sites. These include padprints, radiation, and metal samples.

Flying saucers have the ability to cause blackouts, magnetically stop cars, and cause sunburn.

UFOs may be hostile, and may be responsible for several aircraft crashes and disappearances.

There have been cases where dead animals have been found with cuts too smooth to have been caused by a knife and all their blood gone. This is believed to have been caused by UFOs.

The Air Force is covering up proof of the UFOs' existence.

The CIA is deeply involved with this cover-up.

The Air Force has fouled up its investigation of UFOs.

The aliens are here to observe human activity.

The aliens are here to save humanity from nuclear destruction.

There have been no reliable reports of "contact" with aliens.

Some people have had personal and/or mental contact with space brothers, flown aboard flying saucers, and traveled to other planets.

Some people have been taken aboard UFOs and been subjected to a medical examination. This may be part of a breeding experiment.

Sinister beings, the Men in Black, use threats and force to continue the cover-up of UFOs.

The Flying Saucer Myth in the 1970s

Snap goes our third thread, and we end where we began.

—*The Hound of the Baskervilles*

With the signing of the Paris Peace Agreement on January 15, 1973, ending the decade-long Vietnam War, it seemed the pain might finally end. These hopes were in vain; the Sixties still had a year and a half to run. On June 17, 1972, several men had been arrested trying to bug the Democratic National Headquarters in the Watergate building. By the spring of 1973, the "Watergate Scandal" had begun to break, and congressional hearings were underway. It was at this same time that a story began to circulate that would mark the resurgence of the flying saucer myth from the years of darkness.

The Aurora, Texas, Crash

One of the most remarkable stories to come out of the 1896–1897 "Mysterious Airships" reports was published in the April 19, 1897, *Dallas Morning News*. It read:

> Aurora, Wise County, April 17—About 6 o'clock this morning the early risers of Aurora were astonished at the sudden appearance of the airship which has been sailing throughout the country. It was travelling due north, and much nearer the earth than before. Evidently some of the machinery was out of order, for it was making a speed of only ten or twelve miles an

hour, and gradually settling towards the earth. It sailed over the public square and when it reached the north part of town collided with the tower of Judge Proctor's windmill and went to pieces with a terrific explosion, scattering debris over several acres of ground, wrecking the windmill and water tank and destroying the judge's flower garden. The pilot of the ship is supposed to have been the only one aboard, and while his remains are badly disfigured, enough of the original has been picked up to show that he was not an inhabitant of this world.

Mr. T. J. Weems, the U.S. Signal Service officer at this place and an authority on astronomy, gives it as his opinion that he was a native of the planet Mars. Papers found on his person—evidently the records of his travels—are written in some unknown hieroglyphics, and cannot be deciphered. This ship was too badly wrecked to form any conclusions as to its construction or motive power. It was built of an unknown metal, resembling somewhat a mixture of aluminum and silver, and it must have weighed several tons. The town today is full of people who are viewing the wreckage and gathering specimens of strange metal from the debris. The pilot's funeral will take place at noon tomorrow. Signed F. E. Hayden.[1]

As with the other "airship" reports, the Aurora, Texas, crash was forgotten until the 1960s. The January/February 1967 issue of *Flying Saucer Review* carried an article titled "Airships Over Texas" by Donald B. Hanlon and Jacques Vallee which included the crash story. As a postscript, the magazine published a letter from the two authors. The letter stated they had brought the story to the attention of Dr. Hynek due to its unusual nature. He sent a friend to Aurora where he located Oscar Lowry who had been eleven when the crash supposedly occurred. Lowry pointed out several major flaws in the newspaper story. T. J. Weems was not a U.S. Army Signal Service officer, but the town blacksmith. Also, Judge Proctor's farm never had a windmill. Additionally, a chart of the Masonic Cemetery showed no unidentified graves. Lowry said that F. E. Hayden was a local cotton buyer and writer who was concerned over the decline of Aurora. It had been by-passed by the railroad, suffered an epidemic, a fire had destroyed the west half of town, and boll weevils had wiped out the cotton crop. Lowry speculated that Hayden read the other airship stories and wrote the account to make Aurora a tourist attraction.[2]

This was not the only investigation in the late 1960s of the Aurora crash. Wise County historian Etta Pegues interviewed several old-timers. Mrs. Robbie Hanson flatly said, "It was a hoax. I was in school that day and nothing happened." Pegues added that if the story had been true, "Cliff D. Cates would have included it in his *Pioneer History of Wise County* which he published in 1907. It would have sold him a billion copies. Also, if it had been true, Harold R. Bost would have included it in his *Saga of Aurora*. It would have been the highlight of his theme. But neither men [*sic*] mentioned it because it had been forgotten as any other piece of fiction would have been forgotten."[3] So the matter rested— the Aurora crash was deemed a hoax. Throughout the 1960s, crashed UFO stories were still dismissed by believers.

This began to change in the spring of 1973. Haydon Hewes of the International UFO Bureau brought the story to the attention of Bill Case, aviation writer for the *Dallas Times Herald*. Starting in March of 1973, Case wrote a series of articles on the "crash." Case talked with Brawley Oates, who had lived on the former Proctor farm since 1945. He was quoted as saying, "I've heard this story all my life." Oates said that when he and a nephew had sealed the well under the windmill, they found a large amount of metal.[4] C. C. "Charlie" Stephens, who was 86, said his father had seen the "airship" as it flew low over the area before the crash. G. C. Curley, 98, said "two friends" had gone to the crash site and later told him about the wreckage and "torn up body." Mrs. Mary Evans, 96, was quoted as saying her mother and father would not let her see the crash site, but told her about it later.[5]

The "evidence" was not limited to the second-hand recollections of old-timers. By mid-May 1973, Fred N. Kelly, "a scientific treasure hunter," had found several pieces of metal. He said, "I've never seen any metal like that in 25 years of experience." Case headlined it as "'UFO' alloy unknown back in '97" and "UFO site metal described as 'puzzling,' 'unusual'." The "UFOlogists" as they called themselves, sought a court order to exhume the UFO pilot's "grave." It had been located through use of a metal detector. It was speculated the "spaceman" had been wearing a metallic suit. A "unique handmade headstone" was found at the spot.[6,7]

The publicity surrounding the Aurora crash story saw UFO groups taking sides. Dr. Hynek said the hoax conclusion was "highly improbable."[8] MUFON and NICAP both supported the crash story, while APRO deemed it a hoax. This was an unusual role-reversal. APRO had long been willing to accept more exotic UFO reports, while NICAP had not.[9]

The end came on July 4, 1973. The *Dallas Times Herald* carried the headline, "Grave believed UFO pilot's at Aurora, entered, robbed." The "grave robbery" occurred before dawn on June 14, 1973. MUFON investigator Earl F. Watts said the headstone was removed, then "The grave robbers probed down into the grave through the hole left by the stolen tombstone." The bone fragments and metallic clothing were removed.[10]

With this, the Aurora crash case began to fall apart. A photo cast doubt on the "spaceman's tombstone." It showed only a crude triangular area with several circles in the center. Rather than a cigar-shaped UFO, it appeared to be a crack caused by a plow blade. Hewes was also becoming disillusioned, saying that, "It appears now that the incident was exploited for publicity." Kelly had dropped out of sight. The International UFO Bureau had also tracked down the "eyewitnesses" Case had quoted. Evans complained, "They wrote that up to suit themselves. I didn't say it this way." Stephens insisted he had never said his father had seen the airship. "G. C. Curley" was actually named A. J. McCurley and was teaching school in Oklahoma at the time.[11]

In retrospect, it is clear there is nothing to back up the story of the Aurora "crash" except the single newspaper article. There were no follow-up articles, no photos, no police reports, no letters or diaries mentioning the crash, no samples of the wreckage, nor were the spaceman's papers ever published. The other airship stories in the *Dallas Morning News* were all "tall tales." There is no evidence the newspaper or its readers ever believed it was more than that.[12]

Through the spring and summer of 1973, word of the Aurora crash stories spread far and wide. Frank X. Tolbert, a Dallas columnist, wrote in June, "When I was in Colorado and New Mexico recently I heard more talk about the Aurora [crash] than I did about Watergate, and I understand the yarn of the 1897 visitor from another planet rivals Watergate for space in European publications."[13]

The Aurora UFO crash story set the stage for the 1973 flap.

1973—The Last Flap

It had been an eventful summer—the nation had been glued to the televised Watergate hearings. The sordid disclosures, the cover-up, and the lies crowded out everything else. By late August, the hearings had adjourned. At this time, there was an upsurge in UFO reports from Georgia. By early September, the Georgia flap had spread to surrounding states, and it seemed the whole South was in the grip of a flap. By the end of September, UFO reports were coming from all over the country.[14,15]

By early October, events had started to overshadow the Southern flap. A bribery scandal engulfed Vice President Spiro Agnew which forced him to resign. On October 6, the Egyptian and Syrian armies attacked Israel, starting the Yom Kippur War.[16]

Then, on the evening of October 11, two shipyard workers, Charles Hickson, 42, and Calvin Parker, 19, from Pascagoula, Mississippi, said they had been abducted. They said they were fishing on the Pascagoula River when they heard a "zipping" sound. When they turned around, they saw a blue-gray glowing object hovering a few feet above the ground. The two men said they were paralyzed with fear as they watched a door appear in the side of the UFO and three occupants come out.

They were unlike any reported before. They were about five feet tall, with gray, wrinkled skin. Their heads came directly out of their shoulders, with no neck. Their "ears" and "noses" were sharp points, while their "eyes" and "mouths" were like "slits." Their arms ended in crablike claws. The creatures did not walk, but according to Hickson, "They came at us in a gliding motion."

The creatures floated across to Hickson and Parker. Parker said, "They were upon us before I knew it. . . . I fainted as soon as they touched me." Hickson said, "The two things took me by the arms. I seemed to become weightless." Parker was carried by the third "occupant." In his account, Parker remained unconscious throughout the whole abduction and had only a vague memory of what allegedly happened.

Hickson remained conscious and said later that he and Parker were separated once inside the UFO. Hickson said he was laid out in midair; there was nothing to support him as he floated. The creatures began a medical examination. According to Hickson, "There was a large, optical-like device that came out of the wall." The object, "like a big eye," floated in midair without any support or wires.

After twenty to forty minutes, the examination was complete and Hickson and Parker were returned to the pier where they had been fishing. The three creatures floated back to the UFO and it took off. Hickson went to his car and had a stiff drink of whiskey. He and Parker decided they had to tell somebody, so they went to the *Mississippi Daily Press*. The paper's offices were closed, so they called the sheriff's office. After they came in, sheriff's officers spent several hours questioning them.[17]

APRO learned of the "abduction" the following morning. One of their consultants, Dr. James Harder, went to Mississippi to interview the two men. There he was joined by Dr. Hynek. They talked to Hickson and Parker on October 12 and 14.[18] Harder later gave their story a ringing endorsement: "There is no reasonable doubt that the craft came from outer space. . . . The experience of Hickson and Parker was a real one. It was not a hallucination."

Harder speculated the creatures were "cosmic anthropologists": "My theory is that the Earth is a cosmic zoo. We are cut off from the rest of the universe. Every so often the keepers come in to make a random check of the inhabitants of that zoo. . . . There is nothing to suggest that the UFO occupants have harmful designs on humanity."[19] Hynek was more restrained, saying only, "There is no question in my mind that these two men have had a very terrifying experience."[20]

The Air Force took a hands-off attitude toward the "abduction." On October 12, Hickson and Parker underwent a physical at Kessler AFB to check for any radiation contamination. None was found. When the Pascagoula sheriff sought further Air Force help, he was refused. An Air Force public information officer at Elgin AFB explained the post–Blue Book policy—"If anyone feels threatened, we send them to the local police. If they want a scientific investigation then we refer them to the nearest university." When the sheriff called the Pentagon, he was told, "The Air Force will investigate only if there has been a direct threat to our national security. Nothing has taken place to jeopardize national security."[21]

The Pascagoula abduction received national network exposure when Hickson appeared on the *Dick Cavett Show* on November 2. Cavett introduced Hickson by saying he had just passed a lie detector test. Several weeks later, both Hickson and Parker appeared on the *Mike Douglas Show*. During mid-October 1973, the NBC and CBS evening news, the *Tomorrow* show, the *Today Show*, the *CBS Morning News*, the *New York Times*, the *Los Angeles Times*, and the *Washington Post* all carried stories on the flap.[22,23]

The Pascagoula Investigation

With the end of Blue Book, investigation of the Pascagoula abduction was left to private individuals. Two very different investigators looked at the case—Philip J. Klass, an editor with the very establishment *Aviation Week & Space Technology* and Joe Eszterhas, a writer with the counter-culture magazine *Rolling Stone*. Eszterhas noted the UFO "landing site" was in the direct view of two twenty-four-hour toll booths. Both operators said they had not seen anything on the night of the "abduction." The site was also a mile from the Ingalls West Bank Facility shipyard. Its security cameras also observed nothing.

Eszterhas also learned Hickson had been fired from the Ingalls shipyards for "conduct unbecoming a supervisor" on November 20, 1972. According to Eszterhas, he "was borrowing money from the boys working under him, then paying them back by trying to finagle them promotions."

Soon after Hickson and Parker's story was publicized, local attorney Joe Colingo signed a contract with them to handle appearances and the selling of their personal story. Money seemed to be a central concern; Colingo told Hickson and Parker, "You ain't gonna talk" to any reporters "because none of them wants to pay." Colingo asked Eszterhas, "how much you think we can make on their Exclusive Story?" He responded that this would depend on how well it could be verified. Colingo replied, "A million, you think? I figure if we sell magazine and book and movie rights to one of the big studios, that can be a lot of money. I wish to hell *Life* magazine was still in business."[24]

Klass's investigation cast doubt on the lie-detector test Hickson "passed." The polygraph operator had been in practice only a year. He had not been certified by his training school and would not be, owing to his failure to complete his intern training. A licensed operator told Klass he felt the polygraph operator was "inexperienced" and added, "Judging from what he told you, I doubt whether he can tell whether the subject is telling a lie or telling the truth." The test itself was superficial—in a case of this type, the test should last a full day. The operator who tested Hickson told Klass he had run a series of four tests, each lasting only three to five minutes. After the first test, the operator announced, "Hell, they're telling the truth!" Colingo had exaggerated the operator's experience—saying he had given "thousands" of tests over "several years" and claimed the test of Hickson had taken "about three hours."

Klass noted several inconsistencies in Hickson's account. He first described the creature's mouth as a "hole." Later, he called it a "slit." On the *Mike Douglas Show,* he said his eyes had been hurt by the bright lights inside the UFO, comparing it to "a welding flash." He claimed it persisted "for about three days." Yet, he did not mention any such eye injury when examined at Keesler AFB the day after the alleged incident.[25]

As Eszterhas put it, Colingo "waited for the million dollar book and movie offers for their Exclusive Story. He waited and waited and waited and waited and waited and he's still waiting. 'I don't understand it,' Joe

Colingo said, 'their Exclusive Story is bigger than Watergate and nobody wants to buy it'."[26] The Pascagoula abduction became the next step in the growing acceptance of abduction reports.

The 1973 flap peaked in mid-October. Reports continued at a high level in November, then dropped off in December. Events had intervened; angered by U.S. support of Israel, Arab countries cut off oil sales. Gas prices doubled, unemployment rose, the economy stagnated, and inflation reached double-digit rates. Many suspected it was all a plot by the "oil companies." With the new year, UFO reports again increased between January and April 1974.[27]

Looking back, it is clear that the 1973 flap marked a basic shift in the flying saucer myth. Most of the reported sightings were of "lights in the sky." But the two cases which attracted the most attention were the Aurora "crash" and the Pascagoula abduction. The 1973 flap marked the start of a shift away from (mere) UFO sightings. By June 1974, the flap was over. Impeachment Summer had begun.

"Before the Year Is Out . . ."

During the Watergate hearings, it was learned that a recording system had been installed in the Oval Office. On July 24, 1974, the Supreme Court ruled that Nixon had to turn over the tapes to Congress. The same day, the House Judiciary Committee opened impeachment hearings. Then, on August 5, the White House released transcripts of three subpoenaed conversations, which clearly implicated Nixon in the cover-up. On August 8, 1974, Nixon announced he would resign. The following day, Vice-President Gerald R. Ford was sworn in as president. The Sixties were over.

For the believers, the years 1974 through 1977 were an optimistic time. There was a feeling that the government would soon reveal "proof" UFOs were "real." The predictions began in April 1974 with the book *Beyond Earth: Man's Contact With UFOs*. The authors, Ralph and Judy Blum, said flatly, "We predict that by 1975 the government will release definite proof that extraterrestrials are watching us."[28]

On August 25, 1974, the *National Tattler* carried an interview with James Lorenzen of APRO. He said, "A program has been undertaken that will over the next few months make it obvious that the government has reversed its position." He said the "government will release all its information within the next three years." Lorenzen implied that

Watergate was behind this. It would be done "so it won't be left with a red face, again lessening government credibility." It would be done "little by little" to avoid panic.[29]

On October 15, 1974, Robert S. Carr, a retired mass communications instructor, held a press conference. He said, "Five weeks ago I heard from the highest authority in Washington that before Christmas the whole UFO cover-up will be ended. There will be public admission that UFO's always have been real, and that for the past 25 years the United States government and the Air Force have known they were piloted by human-like beings."

A year later, the October 27, 1975, issue of *Midnight* quoted Robert Berry of the 20th Century UFO Bureau as saying, "The government will tell us what's been going on, in a series of television documentaries over a period of months. . . . The entire story is slated to be disclosed by the 200th anniversary of independence on July 4, 1976.[30]

Despite the failure of all these predictions, the belief in an imminent disclosure continued. During the 1976 presidential campaign, the Democratic candidate, Jimmy Carter, said he had seen a UFO in 1969. Believers concluded that with one of their own in the White House, proof was at hand.

This seemed to be confirmed on April 18, 1977, following Carter's election, when the magazine *U.S. News & World Report* carried the following item in their "Washington Whispers" column:

> OFFICIAL WORD COMING ON UFO'S: Before the year is out, the Government—perhaps the President—is expected to make what are described as "unsettling disclosures" about UFO's—unidentified flying objects. Such revelations, based on information from the CIA, would be a reversal of official policy that in the past has downgraded UFO incidents.[31]

Word of the report spread and the White House was deluged with letters from UFO believers. In July 1977, the White House press office asked presidential science adviser Frank Press for help with the UFO mail. Press wrote NASA Administrator Robert A. Frosch asking if the agency could answer the mail. Press also suggested it might be time for a new UFO study.[32]

NASA was agreeable about answering UFO mail, but was very reluctant to undertake any kind of UFO study. Frosch had firsthand experience with the bitter nature of the UFO debate. He had been head of Navy research and development during the controversy over McDonald's use of ONR funding for his UFO research. As a compromise, Frosch suggested a review of UFO literature for the previous ten years to determine if any further investigation was worthwhile.[33,34]

NASA made its formal response on December 21, 1977. In a letter to Press, Frosch said NASA was willing to analyze any "unexplained organic or inorganic sample." It continued, however:

> There is an absence of tangible or physical evidence available for thorough laboratory analysis. And because of the absence of such evidence, we have not been able to devise a sound scientific procedure for investigating these phenomena. To proceed on a research task without a disciplinary framework and an exploratory technique in mind would be wasteful and probably unproductive. I do not feel that we could mount a research effort without a better starting point than we have been able to identify thus far. I would therefore propose that NASA take no steps to establish a research activity in this area or to convene a symposium on this subject.[35]

Years of Drift

NASA's refusal to become involved with UFOs marked the end of the expectations of government disclosures. Carter's UFO sighting evaporated at this same time. It was identified as Venus by Robert Sheaffer in May 1977. American society was drifting in the 1970s. After the pain of Vietnam and Watergate, people turned inward. These were the years of the "Me Generation" and the "Age of Narcissism." People no longer believed in anything: in government, in society, in the future, or in themselves.

One reflection of these years of drift was the various "New Wave" UFO theories. These held that flying saucers were not "nuts and bolts" alien spaceships, but rather "psychic projections" that were "willed" into existence. The mind projects an image of a UFO into the sky, which becomes solid and "real." Some took this to an extreme—that "our entire reality" was only a "projection from the collective unconscious." Moreover, the whole structure of reality could be changed simply by people "wishing" it. The idea that there was no such thing as objective reality, that it was solely a product of one's own mind, is, to say the least, egocentric.

The New Wave gained a degree of acceptance for a time, but remained a fringe element of the flying saucer myth. For nearly three decades, flying saucers had been alien spaceships; it was too late to make so basic a change in the myth. By the end of the 1970s, the New Wave had crested.[36]

The Bermuda Triangle

During the 1950s and 1960s, both Keyhoe and NICAP held that some aircraft crashes and disappearances had been caused by UFOs. With the 1970s, the "Bermuda Triangle" myth took on a life, and identity, of its own. Between 1970 and 1974, there were no less than nine books on the subject. These included John Wallace Spencer's *Limbo of the Lost* and *No Earthly Explanation,* Richard Winer's *The Devil's Triangle,* and Charles Berlitz's *The Bermuda Triangle.* Articles appeared in not only such sensationalistic magazines as *SAGA,* but also such mainstream publications as the *Miami Herald Sunday Magazine, Catholic Digest,* and *Cosmopolitan.*

The Bermuda Triangle myth was never fully defined as to the cause of the disappearances. Although many writers blamed UFOs, others suggested "space warps," "atmospheric aberrations," "parallel universes," or "magnetic anomalies." Others blamed more supernatural causes such as a "jinx."

And then in 1975, it all came to a screeching halt. Lawrence David Kusche was a librarian at Arizona State University. He examined newspaper accounts, Lloyd's of London records, and Coast Guard, Navy and Air Force investigations. The results, published in his book *The Bermuda Triangle Mystery—Solved,* were devastating. In several cases, the incident had never actually occurred. In others, the ships and aircraft had been lost during bad weather. In one case, the ship was seen to sink; in others, distress signals were sent. In still others, wreckage was found which indicated the loss was due to the normal hazards of sea and sky. Several occurred in the Gulf of Mexico or the Pacific—far from the Bermuda Triangle.

Kusche also found that writers on the Bermuda Triangle had simply copied from earlier books and articles, rather than doing original research. In the process, the incidents were embellished, the names of ships were misspelled, and the dates of incidents were in error, sometimes by as much as a year. He stated flatly, "The Legend of the Bermuda Triangle is a manufactured mystery."[37] Kusche's book discredited the Bermuda Triangle; by the end of the decade, it too had faded from the flying saucer myth.

UFOs in Space

Still another element of the flying saucer myth which originated in the 1960s, but which grew in the 1970s, was the astronaut-sighting stories.

Within weeks of the Apollo 11 crew's return to Earth, a bootlegged tape and transcript began circulating. In it, the crew described "installations" on the Moon and UFOs "lined up in ranks on the far side of the crater edge." It was published in the *National Bulletin* magazine for September 29, 1969. The headline read "Phony Transmission Failure Hides Apollo 11 Discovery . . . Moon is a UFO Base!"[38]

As the transcript spread through the UFO network, more Apollo/UFO stories appeared. *The APRO Bulletin* for March/April 1970 included an account of astronaut sightings. The most influential report in the early 1970s appeared in the May 1970 issue of *SAGA*. It claimed that on November 15th, the day after Apollo 12 was launched, the crew of Charles Conrad, Richard Gordon, and Alan Bean saw two flashing lights as they were 150,000 miles from the Earth heading for the Moon. At first they and the ground thought the objects might be the S-IVB third stage or the SLA (Spacecraft Lunar Adapter) panels. Conrad then, according to the *SAGA* account, remarked he saw one of the objects speed off—something that space debris could not do. UFOs were also seen after the Apollo 12 Lunar Module *Intrepid* returned from the Moon. On the way home, the article said ". . . 11:47 A.M. on November 24th, the spokesman for Apollo 12 reported, in a startled voice, that they were all watching a bright red object flashing brilliant against the Earth."[39]

In 1974, a New Zealand UFO newsletter claimed that, from the launch on July 16, 1969, until Apollo 11 passed the midway point to the Moon, it was followed by a single UFO. The second sighting occurred on July 19 (the day before the landing) while Apollo 11 was orbiting the Moon. The UFO was described as "two objects in close formation." The third was made by Michael Collins when he spotted several objects on the Moon's surface from orbit. The fourth sighting occurred after the Lunar Module *Eagle* lifted off the Moon when a UFO passed under it.

The same year, a Japanese UFO group, called the Cosmic Brotherhood Association, published a series of photos taken during the second alleged sighting. They showed the lunar horizon and above it, two glowing balls of light. Because one was larger than the other, they looked like a "snowman." The snowman photo reached the U.S. in the weekly tabloid *Modern People*. The article was reprinted the next year in *UFO Report* magazine.[40] Also in 1974 was the release of a documentary and book entitled *UFO's Past, Present and Future*. The book featured a short chapter on astronaut sightings and had color photos taken during Gemini and Apollo missions of small blobs of light against the blackness of space.[41]

One of those keeping the astronaut sighting stories in the public eye was Dr. James Harder. At a 1975 UFO symposium at the University of

Santa Cruz, he said a UFO "followed Apollo 12 on three orbits around the Moon" and that "NASA suppressed the UFO incident for fear of panic." Harder said he learned of the sighting from "a member of the space team" who he refused to identify. Harder also rejected the Proton 3 solution to the Gemini 11 sighting, saying that Proton 3 would have been in another direction.[42]

UFO researcher George Fawcett compiled a listing of sixteen astronaut sightings which was published in the March 17, 1974, issue of the weekly tabloid *National Tattler*. In 1975, the list was also published in Dr. J. Allen Hynek and Jacques Vallee's book *The Edge of Reality*.[43]

This was the high point in acceptance of the astronaut sightings. There was now a challenge to the whole genre. It came from James E. Oberg, an ex–Air Force Captain, computer expert, flight controller at the Johnson Space Center, and a prolific writer on space. In 1976, he turned his attention to the astronaut sightings. The results were eye-opening—the names of crewmen, and the dates of missions were grossly in error. As with the Bermuda Triangle stories, each writer had only copied the earlier tales.

The two X-15 sightings, despite what Frank Edwards had said, were ice breaking off the X-15's skin. Major White described it as "about the size of a piece of paper." Both sightings took place near the high points of the flights when the X-15 was in space. The ice flakes had the same ballistic trajectory as the X-15 and would seem to follow it, thus explaining the "formation" flight.

Turning to the two Soviet reports, Oberg found the Voskhod 1 sighting was a hoax by some "highly questionable" Italian tabloids. The story was then picked up by *Die Andere Welt* and then *Flying Saucer Review*.[44] A NORAD investigation identified the satellite which caused the Voskhod 2 sighting. The cosmonauts said it passed within 200 meters of their spacecraft at 1412 Greenwich Mean Time (also called Zulu or Z). NORAD conducted a "correlation exercise" to identify the second satellite. It found only one object passed within 124 miles of Voskhod 2. This was object #1286, a six- by three-foot fragment from their booster which was tumbling at a rate of once every 112 seconds. The report concluded:

> At 1412 Z it passed within 4.5 kilometers of Voskhod II. Assuming the Soviet reporting of the sighting to have been made in good faith, it would appear that the lack of reference for measurement of size and distance contributed to the Cosmonauts reporting this sighting as another satellite rather than a fragment from their own operation.[45]

Next was the Gemini 4 report—Oberg found there were several facts unknown to the Condon Report. First, McDivitt's eyes were red and teary due to a reaction with the cabin atmosphere and a massive accidental urine spill. Another was that, a few hours before the sighting, McDivitt had seen the Titan II second stage but was, at first, unable to recognize it owing to the Sun's glare. The booster was only ten miles away. Moreover, the point in the orbit where the UFO was sighted was the same at which the booster was repeatedly seen earlier in the flight.

Oberg concluded that McDivitt, teary-eyed and dazzled by the Sun's glare, had seen the Titan II second stage but had not recognized it. This error was compounded when the NORAD list did not include the Titan II. Oberg believes this was because the computer was asked to compare Gemini 4's orbit to *previously* launched satellites, *not* its own debris. The other Gemini 4 sightings mentioned in the Condon Report were satellites.[46] The Gemini 7 sighting, also endorsed by the Condon Report, was caused by debris from the stage separation—pieces of metal, explosive bolt fragments, frozen fuel droplets and paint chips. The crew's belief they were in a polar orbit was in error.[47] The Gemini 10 sighting, despite Edward's cover-up charges, was also of debris.

The Gemini 11 report proved to be the most controversial. At the time, NORAD identified the satellite as Proton 3 and the Condon Report accepted this. Dr. Harder then reopened the issue in the mid-1970s. When Oberg reexamined the tracking data, he found that Proton 3 was in an unstable, decaying orbit. Gemini 11 had also made an orbital maneuver. When these two factors were combined, Oberg believed the Proton 3 was close enough to explain the sighting.[48]

This was challenged by UFOlogists Bruce Maccabee and Brad Sparks, who made a complex calculation of the two orbits, which indicated Proton 3 was too far away at the time of the sighting for it to have been seen. Oberg accepted this.[49,50] Since then, no one has reexamined the tracking data or compared Gemini 11's orbit to those of any other satellite or debris.

The multiple reports of sightings on the Apollo 11 and 12 missions were due to booster debris, misunderstood transcripts, and hoaxes by UFO groups. Oberg easily showed the *National Bulletin* transcript was a "crude hoax" from internal evidence alone. It was filled with what Oberg called "technical sounding gibberish"—"field distortion," "625 to the fifth," "auto-relays," etc. The object seen by the crew on the way to the Moon was right on the edge of visibility. It was tumbling and was indistinguishable from debris. The mention in the New Zealand account of

Collins's sighting of "weird white objects" was based on a loose rewording of his actual comments. He was looking for the Lunar Module on the Moon's surface. He doubted the object (possibly a boulder) was the LM because it would be tilted and Armstrong and Aldrin had not reported any such tilt. There is no mention of fleets of UFOs.

These two reports could be simple misinterpretations of the astronauts' comments. Not so the "snowman" report. The Japanese photos came from 16mm color film magazine F. Viewing the original film shows numerous glares and reflections in the LM's window—there is no possibility of their being solid objects in space. The Japanese UFO group took stills from the film, then cropped and airbrushed out the other reflections leaving only the "snowman." The supposed astronaut comments, speculations, and actions concerning the snowman UFO were embellishments added later based on the forged photos.[51]

The story of the Apollo 12 sightings is more complex. The sighting on the way to the Moon, in which a UFO follows the spacecraft, then suddenly speeds off, was based on an honest misunderstanding of the transcript by the two *SAGA* writers. Conrad was discussing the location of the SLA panels based on their separation velocity. He doubted Houston's estimate that they were only 300 nautical miles away because he saw one of the SLA panels "leaving the area at a high rate of speed . . . like it got a lot more than a foot per second or so" *33 hours earlier* when he performed the turnaround maneuver to pull the LM free of the S-IVB third stage. The flashing object did not suddenly accelerate as Conrad talked with the ground.

There were only two alleged UFO sightings on Apollo 12 with any validity. The first occurred as the LM *Intrepid* was jettisoned in lunar orbit after Conrad and Bean had returned to the CSM *Yankee Clipper*. Three objects were seen by millions of television viewers and filmed by a movie camera. Dubbed A, B and C, they were: A—a small segment of the docking channel, B—part of the docking ring, and C—part of the electrical harness. The other Apollo 12 sighting was of "a light of indistinct shape" seen as the crew headed back to Earth: it was the reflection of the full Moon off the Earth's ocean.[52]

Thus, only one astronaut sighting, Gemini 11, can be considered unidentified. In this case there is the complicating factors of the Proton 3's decaying orbit and the possibility that the sighting was of some other satellite or debris from Gemini 11 itself, such as the Extravehicular Life Support System used on a space walk during the first day in orbit.[53] As the ELSS had been jettisoned from Gemini 11, it would be in a parallel orbit. Of the other reports, most were distortions or outright hoaxes.

Aftermath

The astronaut sightings received another burst of publicity in 1979, during the tenth anniversary of the Apollo 11 flight. This allowed Oberg to trace the process by which the astronaut sightings became part of the flying saucer myth. It began in 1976 with publication in France of UFOlogist Maurice Chatelain's book *Our Ancestors Came from Outer Space*. Writing about the Apollo 11 sighting, Chatelain claimed that "only moments before Armstrong stepped down the ladder to set foot on the Moon, two UFOs hovered overhead." He also claimed that the Apollo 13 mission had carried a nuclear weapon to make seismic measurements of the Moon. The explosion in an oxygen tank was, according to rumors, due to an attack by UFOs.

The story then traveled from France to the Soviet Union, when on November 24, 1977, Vladimir G. Azhazha gave a lecture to NOVOSTI news service employees. Azhazha, using Chatelain's book as his source, said that "the American astronauts who visited the Moon saw a gigantic cylinder 1500 meters long there" and that, after the landing, the Apollo 11 crew reported, "Directly across from us, on the other side of the crater, there are other spacecraft observing us." Azhazha continued: "The Moon is evidently a transhipment [*sic*] base for UFOs and every Apollo which has flown to the Moon has been under the 'observation' canopy of the UFOs. It was not by accident that the American astronauts were not successful in their attempt to explode a nuclear device for scientific purposes on the Moon. Instead the oxygen cylinder on Apollo exploded."

The September 9, 1979 *Sunday Mirror* and the September 11 *National Enquirer* then picked up the story, headlining it "Aliens On Moon When We Landed." The authors, Eric Faucher, Ellen Goodstein, and Henry Gris, wrote, "The astronauts saw UFOs and even photographed them, but the stupifying close encounter has been kept completely under wraps by NASA until now . . . NASA's coverup was so massive that the news has taken ten years to reach the American public—and had to be first disclosed by Soviet scientists, who found out about it two years ago."

The source of the report was Vladimir Azhazha. He was quoted as saying, "I am absolutely certain this episode took place." The article said Azhazha "refused to identify the source of his information—but he and other Soviet space experts say the encounter has been common knowledge among Russian scientific circles." "Independent corroboration" of the Soviet account came from *Maurice Chatelain*! The circle was now complete—the story had been passed from Chatelain to Azhazha and back to Chatelain.[54] Following the 1979 publicity, the astronaut sightings virtually disappeared from the flying saucer myth.

One irony about the astronaut sightings is that despite the claims and wild charges of a "NASA cover-up," *all* the sightings were based on publicly released transcripts, films and still photos, rather than secret inside sources. It was the UFO believers who put their own interpretations on them, or at worst, distorted and fictionalized the events.[55]

Redefining the Myth

Despite the 1973 flap and the expectations of imminent disclosures, it was clear that, a decade after the Condon Report, the flying saucer myth was still in disarray. The old order was shattered, the old patterns lost, and many believers were drifting into other areas. The old UFO groups were also in decline. NICAP was a pale shadow of its former power and none of the other groups, such as APRO and MUFON could fill the vacuum it left. Keyhoe's final book, *Aliens From Space,* published in 1973, was a plea for recognition from a world that no longer cared. It contained all the old suspicions and accusations, but the fire seemed gone.

The power to shape the myth had now shifted to the individual UFOlogists. Accordingly, there was no central focus as each followed his own interests and they fought among themselves. Dr. Hynek, with his academic credentials, Blue Book experience, and public appearances, was the most familiar figure. Yet neither he, nor the group he founded in 1974, the Center for UFO Studies (CUFOS), was comparable to Keyhoe or NICAP.

Another growing influence was tabloids such as the *National Enquirer* and newsstand UFO magazines. They had had a major role in publicizing the astronaut sightings. These stories also underlined how widespread the flying saucer myth now was. They had gone from the U.S. to New Zealand and Japan, back to the U.S., then to France, the USSR, and again back to the U.S.

The destruction of both the Bermuda Triangle and the astronaut sightings only underlined the momentum now on the side of the skeptics. In 1976, the Committee for the Scientific Investigation of Claims of the Paranormal (CSICOP) was organized. CSICOP soon took a major and controversial role in attacking belief in UFOs.

So, as the 1970s neared a close, the flying saucer myth was still struggling to redefine itself after nearly a decade of disappointments. The process was already underway; three major themes were emerging—cattle mutilations, abductions, and crashed saucers. By the early 1990s, they would combine into something dark and sinister—the alien myth.

The Flying Saucer Myth 1973–1979

Basic Beliefs

Disk-shaped alien spacecraft have been seen by millions of people around the world for hundreds or thousands of years.

These UFOs have fantastic maneuverability, including the ability to make 90° turns, and speeds beyond those of Earth aircraft.

The UFOs are undertaking reconnaissance of military bases including nuclear facilities. They have been known to hover over electrical lines, apparently drawing power from them. They may also have caused the New York blackout of 1965. The UFOs also have the power to stop car engines.

The aliens are interested in human activities and may fear the threat humans pose to their safety.

The UFOs are known to land, leaving padprints, burn marks, high levels of radioactivity and similar physical traces.

UFOs are also suspected of causing the mutilation of animals.

On some occasions, the crewmen have been seen in or near the flying saucers.

The U.S. government knows the flying saucers are real, has proof and is covering it up in an effort directed by the CIA.

The reason for the cover-up is to prevent panic.

Beliefs Gaining Acceptance

Some people are forcibly taken aboard UFOs and subjected to medical examinations.

Beliefs Declining in Acceptance

UFOs are not "nuts and bolts" spacecraft but rather are psychic projections from the human mind that become real objects.

U.S. and Soviet spacecrews have seen and had contact with UFOs in Earth orbit and on the Moon.

Ships and aircraft are mysteriously disappearing off the coast of Florida, due to UFOs, or some type of geophysical anomaly.

Dead Cows

"I suppose, Watson, we must look upon you as a
man of letters," said he. "How do you define the
word 'grotesque'?"

—*The Adventure of Wisteria Lodge*

The first of the elements that would shape the future of the flying
saucer myth was "cattle mutilations." In the spring of 1973, there were
sporadic reports of mysterious deaths of cattle in Minnesota, South
Dakota, and other midwestern states. Certain parts of the cows' bodies
were removed: the tongue, sex organs, udder, anus, rectum, and sometimes the eyes and ears. The cuts looked "too smooth" to have been
made by predators. Rather, they seemed to have what became known as
"surgical precision." The cows seemed to have fallen over dead, with no
struggle. It was also said there were no tracks around the dead cows.

Then, in the spring and summer of 1974, there was an upsurge in reports of such "classic mutilations" or "mutes" from ranchers in Kansas,
Nebraska, Oklahoma, and Iowa. The county sheriffs were confused and
unable to catch the perpetrators. Fear and anger quickly spread among
the ranchers. Two new elements were added—the dead cows reportedly
had been drained of blood, and there had been sightings of black, unmarked helicopters in the areas of the mutes. Rumors began to spread
that the mutes were being done as part of secret government or military
testing of chemical and biological weapons.

Even as the tales of government conspiracies spread, doubts were being cast on the mutes. Necropsies (animal autopsies) showed the cows
had died of natural causes and then been chewed on by scavengers. The

sheriffs and ranchers did not accept this conclusion—they knew what they had seen.

During May and June of 1975, mutes began to be reported in eastern Colorado. The *Bush Banner* newspaper pushed the idea of secret government activities. The editor, Dane Edwards, sometimes devoted the whole issue to the subject. The *Gazette-Telegraph* claimed the mutes were done by a huge, nationwide, fantastically rich Satanic cult bent on a "1,000 year reign of terror and darkness." The organs and blood were used in their rituals. In mid-August 1975, another article quoted a local UFO group as claiming flying saucers were responsible.[1] When the Colorado Bureau of Investigation found that the mutes were the result of scavenger damage, the local sheriffs and press began to charge the CBI was part of the cover-up.[2]

By the end of October 1975, UFOs began to be reported from northeast Colorado. With the approach of winter, the number of mute reports fell off. When they returned the following spring, the number of mute reports was far lower. UFO sightings, in contrast, were coming in regularly and they had become one of the possible "causes" for the mutes.

In the late fall of 1975, the mute wave spread to northern New Mexico. The *Albuquerque Journal* noted reports of "ghost copters" buzzing ranches. They could not be traced by the FAA or military. Some believed the cows were being lifted into the air by the helicopters/UFOs, mutilated, then dropped.

One of those caught up in the mute wave was Gabe Valdez, a New Mexico State Policeman in Dulce, New Mexico. He received his first mute report on June 13, 1976. According to his subsequent police report, there were two sets of three pad prints near where the dead cow was found. Smaller tripod prints followed the cow to where it fell. Radiation was found at the site. The year 1977 was relatively quiet, but there was an upsurge in mute reports the following year. One aspect of the New Mexico wave would have a profound impact on the development of the flying saucer myth. A New Jersey psychic talked about a secret government conspiracy involving military teams carrying out the mutilations using manned helium balloons. There were also references to secret underground bases. When Valdez heard the tapes, he suggested that several of her vague comments referred to places near Dulce.[3]

Valdez's investigation was attracting interest. On December 30, 1978, Senator Harrison Schmitt (R-New Mexico) said he would try to get the FBI involved. On April 20, 1979, a conference on mutes, sponsored by Senator Schmitt, was held in Albuquerque, New Mexico. Four days later, in a separate move, the Law Enforcement Assistance Administration provided a $50,000 grant to the First District Attorney's Office for an investigation of the mutes. Ken Rommel, a twenty-eight-year veteran of the FBI, was named investigator.[4,5]

The Network

As these events unfolded, a loose network of private individuals interested in the mutes had formed.[6] By the late 1970s, these "mutologists" had two major theories (the Satanic cult having fallen out of favor). The first was a government conspiracy to test biological weapons. The stories centered on the "VX toxin," an organism designed to kill Orientals only. The supposed program had begun in 1961, when the U.S. involvement in Vietnam was growing. In 1970, when biological weapons were banned, the program went underground. Open air testing on private land was conducted by "rogue researchers." The mutologists said the lymph glands, blood, eyes, ears, and tail were taken to monitor the spread of the organism through the cow's body. It was claimed that the eyes and mucous membranes of the cows were chemically similar to those of Orientals.

The story was first told by Dale Edwards, editor of the *Bush Banner* newspaper. In the fall of 1975, he had disappeared, claiming to have been threatened. He was hidden for a time by George Erianne, a Colorado Springs private eye. Edwards tape recorded parts of a book manuscript on the mutes and left it with Erianne. In 1976, Erianne was the source for a number of newspaper and magazine articles on "Project Jerome," as he said it was called.[7] It was claimed the helicopters were fitted with lights and a "feathered blade" to make them appear to be UFOs, in order to divert attention.[8]

A variation of the government conspiracy theory was that the cows were mutilated to monitor a secret spill of biological weapons, chemical waste, or radiation, such as from the Gasbuggy underground nuclear test, near Dulce, New Mexico. Another version was that corporate conspirators were conducting "geobotanical" prospecting. The cattle, so the theory went, picked up trace elements from the plants they ate. By "sampling" their tissues, the locations of mineral deposits could be located.

The other major theory was UFOs. This went back to Snippy's death in 1967. The speculation was that the UFO occupants were mutilating the cattle as a "teaching exercise," sending some sort of divine message.[9]

Most of the mutologists came from UFO backgrounds. Tom Adams was one example. In 1970 he was a student at East Texas University and a member of a UFO group at the school.[10] He had also done a class project on Snippy in a social psychology course. In November 1974, he heard about a mute in Texas and thought it might be related to Snippy. He later explained how the mute network formed: "The network already existed, I didn't have to create it. It was in operation through people we were already connected with UFOlogically. When the mutes came along they just naturally fell into that network."

In 1978, Adams began publication of *Stigmata*, a quarterly mute newsletter. It did not "push" any particular theory.[11] This reflected the undecided position of many mutologists. It was clear the mute myth was not yet fully defined. One aspect that had been defined was the scale of the mute wave. Between 1973 and 1978, it was estimated some 10,000 cattle had been mutilated.[12] It was this frequently quoted "body count" which gave the mute myth its importance.

"A Strange Harvest"—The Myth Defined

As befit an age when perceptions were shaped by what was seen on television, it was a documentary which defined the mute myth. Called "A Strange Harvest," it was first telecast on May 25, 1980, by KMGH-TV in Denver. It was produced, written, narrated, and directed by Linda Moulton Howe.[13] "A Strange Harvest" was heavily weighted toward the UFO theory. One rancher said, "We didn't know what could have happened unless it was a flying saucer or something." An investigator with the Trinidad, Colorado, District Attorneys Office said, "I'm inclined to agree . . . that who is doing this now is very possibly creatures not of this planet." The show ended with Howe quoting a psychic that the mutes were part of "the formulation of a serum-like concoction which will be returned to mankind during a time of need."[14] "A Strange Harvest" defined the mute myth as part of the larger flying saucer myth. It was shown at a MUFON conference in Houston and was well received. *Stigmata* also reflected this shift; issue number 10, mailed in May 1980, carried an article titled "Mute Site Indentations" which compared marks in the ground reported near mutes to "recognized UFO landing traces." This was the high point of the acceptance of the mute myth.

Two Investigations

In the spring of 1980, two investigations of the mutes were underway. The first was Ken Rommel's official study, the other was a private one by two writers, Daniel Kagan and Ian Summers. The Rommel Report was published in May 1980, while Kagan and Summers's book, *Mute Evidence,* followed in 1984. Rommel stated that "all of the mutilations investigated by me were caused by and totally consistent with what one would expect to find from normal predation, scavenger activity, and decomposition of a dead animal." He noted that the areas removed in a "classic mutilation" were exactly the same as those first consumed by birds and scavengers. Despite claims the "surgery" was too precise to have been done by animals, many scavengers can leave cuts as smooth as a knife. It required a microscopic examination to tell the difference. In one case, dog tracks were found leading from a dead cow, yet it was declared a "classic mutilation." The "bloodless" bodies were caused by the blood draining into the lower half of the cows' bodies. It then congealed and dried out.

Reports that several mutes had broken legs from being dropped were not supported by an examination. Rommel also noted that if a cow had been dropped, it should have landed with the removed eye against the ground half the time. He found it was always the eye facing upward that was removed, the side accessible to scavengers. A report of radiation at a mute site was useless without measurements of the normal background reading. Natural radiation can vary considerably. Yet it was just such unsupported assumptions, inconsistencies, lapses of judgment, and errors upon which the mute myth rested.

Rommel also looked at the various theories. "Flakes" from a UFO were found to be acrylic/latex house paint. The government conspiracy idea rested on the belief that something that large had to be done by the government. It was never explained why the government did not simply buy the cows or why they were left to be found. Prospecting via sampling animal tissues was not practical, as oil and gas deposits in New Mexico were 3,000 to 5,000 feet underground. No trace could enter the food chain. Another argument of the mutologists was that ranchers could tell the difference between a mute and normal scavenger damage. Rommel found otherwise—several times he pointed out to ranchers that the cuts were quite jagged and they agreed. When they were then asked why they had reported it, they responded "they had read about livestock mutilations . . . and wanted to make sure that this wasn't one of them."

Rommel concluded: "There is simply no concrete evidence to support the theory that mutilations are being conducted as experiments by highly skilled individuals using precision instruments. The facts cited to support this belief are at best questionable, and in many cases involve incredible flights of fantasy."

While Rommel's investigation was to determine if a crime had occurred, Kagan and Summers's was more wide-ranging. They had first heard of the mutes during a book tour. They thought it was an interesting mystery and made contact with the network. Initially impressed, they were soon disillusioned. They found the mutologists had no experience or knowledge in veterinary medicine, cattle biology, causes of death, and research or police procedures. None was a rancher or had been raised on a ranch. "Not one of their testimonies," they noted, "would be acceptable as expert or even informed in a court of law." Yet, their speculations had influence over sheriffs, ranchers, newspapers, and the public at large.

Also illuminating was the mutologists' response to the Rommel Report. He was accused of being "mentally ill," having lied, having been paid off to cover up the truth, and having committed fraud as part of an official investigation. No evidence was offered to back up these charges, only "enraged but weak and pointless insults."

Kagan and Summers discovered that "Dale Edwards" was an alias, one of many, of a petty criminal who conned his way on to the newspaper. His story was a clumsy lie—"VX" was a nerve gas, not a bacteriological agent. The claims of similarities between cattle and Orientals was absurd. There were no biochemical differences or any genetic traits that were race specific. The scientific "facts" were so absurd that it was clear neither "Edwards" nor Erianne had any "inside information."

One of the most devastating discoveries they made was the source of the estimate of 10,000 mutes. Two mutologists had gotten together in 1978. They added up the number of mutes in one Colorado county in 1976 along with the numbers of reports from other areas. Then one of them remembered hearing that the Colorado Cattlemen's Association had said something to the effect that their group would only let one in four mutes be publicized, so they multiplied the number by four. They then took the numbers from New Mexico and other states to arrive at 10,000 since 1973. Kagan and Summers found the procedure so inaccurate as to be completely useless. *None* of these reports had been confirmed by laboratory tests, yet the estimate had been published over and over again until it had become a "fact." It was based only on guesswork and rumor. Moreover, with the 10,000 estimate discredited, the whole justification for the mute myth was gone. Without those thousands of dead cows, there was nothing to stand on.

Of primary importance were the social aspects Kagan and Summers discovered. A map of the 1975 Colorado mute wave showed it started in the western part of the state, around Colorado Springs, and moved east and north, ending around Sterling, Colorado, in 1976. This was exactly the pattern mass psychology would predict. Fads start in cities, then spread outward to more rural areas.

From meetings with ranchers, Kagan and Summers concluded they had been "programmed" to "see" mutes. They found a dead animal and, with one look, *knew* it was a mute, without even having to examine it. They *already* believed that sinister forces were cutting up cattle. And because they believed, the ranchers denied, distorted, and ignored any indications it was not mysterious. Northern New Mexico (which included Dulce) was also a very superstitious area. Rommel observed, "You've got surviving Indian religions and all the old Spanish folklore, and the people are susceptible to strange stories." The situation was similar in Arkansas, which underwent a mute wave in 1978 and 1979. This was an area with both fundamentalist attitudes and a long folk tradition of witchcraft. It was easy for people to believe in devil-worshiping cattle mutilators.

Clearly, the mutes touched a deep emotional chord. Kagan and Summers noted, "The whole point was that the believers . . . *needed* the cattle mutilations to be bizarre, they needed them to remain a mystery, they *needed* a Rommel to hate." Kagan and Summers noted that the ebb and flow of the mute myth exactly matched the self-doubts of American society. It first came to public attention in the spring of 1973, as the Watergate scandal broke, and reached its peak in the late summer 1974, nearly at the same time as Nixon's resignation. The 1975 Colorado mute wave began in June, two months after the final U.S. withdrawal from Vietnam. It was also during the 1975 wave that reports of mysterious helicopters began. The helicopter was the most familiar image of the Vietnam war. "The last helicopter out of Saigon" was the final image of America's defeat. The symbolism fit with the ideas of military conspiracies. The year also saw the start of congressional investigations into past CIA activities. This included secret drug tests, assassination attempts against foreign leaders, and domestic intelligence. At one point, the CIA

was called a "rogue elephant." All this could only fuel belief in both secret biological weapons and an evil government.

Relatively few mute reports were made during the Bicentennial year
of 1976. The resurgence of mute reports came in 1978 and continued
into the spring of 1979. The economy worsened during 1978 with unemployment reaching a record level. Dissatisfaction with an inept Carter
administration was also growing. The end of the year brought the mass
suicide at Jonestown.[15] The years 1975 through 1978 also saw a resurgence of books claiming a conspiracy was behind the Kennedy assassination. It was both a reflection of and fed the atmosphere of suspicion
and conspiracy.[16]

Kagan and Summers also found a deeper correlation than a simple
chronology. In reality, the cattle mutilation phenomenon had nothing to
do with dead cows. What was actually being done (or not done) to the
cows was irrelevant. Instead, the dead cows were only the means for
uncontrolled speculation as to the mythic agents responsible.

The "suspects" in the mutes were a list of the popular "demons" of
the 1970s. The government, military, and CIA were subjects of contempt and hatred for their actions in the Vietnam war. Energy companies were resented for their wealth and power. Suspicions lingered over
their role in the 1973 oil crisis. Rumors that it had all been a fake were
popular. They were also seen as destroyers of the land, strip mining and
spilling oil—why should they not be responsible for the mutes? Cults
also had a role in the demonology of American society in the 1970s. Indian "holy men" with vast followings and the "Moonies" soliciting money at airports were familiar and sinister figures. Less visible were a large
number of small groups of "Satanists." Stories of strange rituals and
even human sacrifice spread. Jonestown showed the terrible reality of
messiah cults, totalitarian leaders, and brainwashed followers.

The stories of UFOs were the flip side to this list of popular villains.
As with the contactee myth, the UFO occupants were "the good, all-
knowing, all-saving, all-delivering superior consciousness." The mutes
were done to save mankind. The mute myth was so flexible the believers could pick and choose freely between the different ideas.

The Fading of the Mutes

Even as the myth was being defined, the mutes were fading. The pattern had been a surge in mute reports with the spring thaw. This failed

to happen in 1979 or 1980. The mutologists began to shift their emphasis, talking about a "silent siege." There were still thousands of mutes, but ranchers were reluctant to report them. No evidence was offered, and it seemed as if the mutologists were trying to take the drop in reports and turn it into a bigger mystery. This decline continued during the winter of 1981. *Stigmata* pushed the silent siege idea, Howe emerged as the mute myth's leading personality, and the UFO version became dominant.[17,18]

Although it was now a part of the flying saucer myth, the mute myth differed in several ways. First, it never developed the kind of national following UFOs had from the start. In part, this may be because it had only regional appeal limited to cattle-raising areas. Additionally, there had not been a big case, such as the Arnold sighting had been, to suddenly bring the mutes to national attention. Rather, the mute myth had developed slowly among the ranchers, sheriffs, and the network. A more practical difference was that a dead cow could be taken to a laboratory and analyzed. This was not possible for a conventional UFO sighting.

Although the mutologists were of the UFO subculture, they were not, by and large, major figures. Rather, they seemed to be a group of people interested in UFOs and other fringe beliefs who used the mutes to carve out a niche for themselves. The mainstream UFO groups took little interest—APRO was ambivalent and Hynek said nothing substantial on the subject.[19]

The image one gets in retrospect was of the development of a parallel myth—connected to the flying saucer myth, but still apart, existing outside it. This parallel myth was a mixture of the old and new. This can be seen in an article Howe wrote shortly before "A Strange Harvest" was rebroadcast in September 1980. She suggested "the poisons in our water, vegetation, and animal life" were affecting the UFO aliens too. This was very much in the contactee tradition, simply replacing "fallout" with "pollution." On the other hand, Howe wondered: "Is there a war going on out there with real Chewbakas and Leias and Darth Vaders who want this planet for different reasons but don't want us to know what's going on until there's a victor?"[20]

The mute myth introduced the idea of a systematic, ongoing genetic sampling program. According to the mutologists, it was only the "best" cattle which were being mutilated.[21] The extreme rhetoric, the attacks on the U.S. government and the belief in its inherently evil nature, turned the myth in a sinister, political direction. The result was an immense conspiracy theory, one that would include not only UFOs and mutes, but the Kennedy assassination, exotic test aircraft, secret treaties, underground cities, international bankers, shadowy "whistle blowers," and "the Jews." It would come to supersede the classic flying saucer myth.

Abductions and
Abductionists

These strange details, far from making the case
more difficult, have really had the effect of
making it less so.

—A Study in Scarlet

Between publication of John Fuller's *The Interrupted Journey* in 1966 and
the 1973 flap, UFO believers had an ambivalent attitude toward the Hill
abduction.[1] With the Pascagoula abduction in October 1973, this attitude began to change. The first step in this change came with the December 1974 issue of *Astronomy* magazine. It carried an article titled
"The Zeta Reticula Incident." Ohio schoolteacher Marjorie Fish believed
she had identified fifteen of the stars on the "star map" Betty Hill had
described. The aliens' home world was a planet of Zeta 2 Reticuli—a
double star system.[2]

This was challenged in the August 1976 issue of *Official UFO* by an article by Robert Sheaffer. He examined the planetary positions for the
night of September 19, 1961. Sheaffer found the Moon was two days
past full. Below it, just as Betty had described, was Saturn. Above Saturn, only 4 1/2 degrees away, was Jupiter. It was exactly where Betty
said the bright "UFO" was located. Sheaffer noted, "If an unknown craft
had actually been present, the Hills would have seen three objects near
the Moon—Jupiter, Saturn, and the UFO. Since they saw only two, this
proves that no unusual objects were present at the time."

Sheaffer also looked into the Fish "star map." He noted Fish matched
only fifteen out of twenty-six stars on the Hill map. Another eleven
stars (40%) were left out. Charles W. Atterburg, an amateur as-

tronomer, had produced a map which matched twenty-five of the twenty-six stars. The stars on his map were, however, different from those on the Fish map. (Epsilon Indi was the "home star.")[3] There is a basic flaw in any attempt to use the Hill abduction to prove the existence of UFOs. If, as Sheaffer concluded, Betty and Barney Hill became frightened because they mistook Jupiter for a UFO, then everything else—the dreams, the star map, and the whole abduction story—was only a psychological reaction to a frightening experience, not the key to understanding the aliens' "relationship" with humans. All this did not matter; a year before the Sheaffer article was published, a film version of the Hill abduction had been shown. It would have a major impact on the growth of abduction reports.

"The UFO Incident"

Soon after *The Interrupted Journey* was published, seven offers for movie rights to the book were submitted.[4] In the early 1970s, the actor James Earl Jones became interested, and wanted to take an option. Dr. Benjamin Simon, whose approval was needed, met with Jones for a day to hear his views on the project, and gave the go-ahead.[5]

"The UFO Incident" was shown on NBC-TV on October 20, 1975. Jones played Barney while Estelle Parsons had the role of Betty. Unlike the book, the film went into much greater depth with their psychological problems and the stresses of their interracial marriage. Barney came across as overwhelmed and uncertain, with a fear of not being in control and a deep need for approval. It was clear that Barney's fearful reaction when he "saw" the "aliens" through the UFO's "windows" was a reflection of his own personal problems. The film was an examination of two people trying to cope with a difficult situation—very little of which had to do with the UFO sighting.[6]

Certain liberties were taken in telling the Hills' story. The Dr. Simon in the film was depicted as uncertain about the reality of the abduction story. The real Dr. Simon had no such doubts—in an interview on *The Today Show* he said, "It was a dream. . . . The abduction did not happen."[7] In a letter to Klass, he stated flatly: "The abduction did not take place but was a reproduction of Betty's dream which occurred right after the sighting. This was her expression of anxiety as contrasted to Barney's more psychosomatic one."[8]

One aspect of the film would influence popular images of UFO occupants. The aliens were depicted as short, with smooth gray skins, bald, with slightly pointed heads, and having large, slanted eyes.[9]

The Travis Walton Abduction

Two weeks after *The UFO Incident* was telecast, the next major abduction case began. On November 5, 1975, Michael H. Rogers, a Forest Service contractor, reported that one of his brush clearing crew, Travis Walton, age 22, had been abducted. The crew had been thinning timber in the Sitgreaves National Forest. They had finished work at 6:00 P.M. (about dusk) and begun the drive back to Snowflake, Arizona, via the village of Heber. As the truck headed down a rough logging road, Allen Dalis, age 21, who was sitting in the rear of the truck, reportedly saw a yellow glow in the heavy timber. When the truck reached a clearing, both Dalis and Travis Walton said they saw a UFO hovering about 100 feet from the road. Walton, who was sitting by the door on the passenger side, yelled for Rogers to stop the truck. Walton jumped out of the still-moving truck and ran toward the UFO. As he neared it, Rogers said, there was a blue-green flash, like a bolt of lightning which "blew him back ten feet." Rogers said later that he panicked and drove off, leaving Walton behind. After driving about a quarter of a mile down the road, Rogers stopped and the crew began debating going back to rescue Walton. After seeing a streak of light which suggested the UFO had left, they agreed to go back. When they returned to the site, however, there was no trace of Walton.

Finally, they abandoned the search and drove back to Heber. One of the crew called Undersheriff L. C. Ellison around 7:45 P.M. After hearing the story, Ellison called Navajo County Sheriff Marlin Gillespie. He and his deputy, Kenneth Coplan, drove to Heber. The three policemen, Rogers, and two crew members returned to search for Walton. (Three crewmembers refused.)

The search was abandoned soon after midnight. Rogers and Coplan went to notify Mary Kellett, Walton's mother. She was living in a ranch house about fifteen miles from the UFO site. Her reaction seemed strange to Coplan. He told Klass, "When Rogers told the mother what had happened, she did not act very surprised. She said, 'Well, that's the way these things happen'." Kellett notified her daughter, Mrs. Grant Neff, who also took the news calmly.

Starting on the morning of November 6 and continuing through November 9, several searches were conducted of the Turkey Springs area. No trace of Travis Walton was found—there was no blood, no ripped clothing, nor any trace of burning on the dry wood pile or pine needles.

While the search for Travis Walton was underway, Rogers and Duane Walton (Travis's older brother who acted as a surrogate father, owing to Mrs. Kellett's two failed marriages) were interviewed by Phoenix UFOlogist Fred Sylvanus. Throughout the sixty-five-minute interview, neither expressed any concern about Travis's fate. Duane said he was "having the experience of a lifetime!" Travis had not acted impulsively, Duane said, but as part of a long-standing plan between the two brothers:

> Travis and I discussed this many, many times at great length and we both said that [if either ever saw a UFO up close] we would immediately get as directly under the object as physically possible.
>
> We discussed this time and time again! The opportunity would be too great to pass up . . . and whoever happened to be left on the ground—if one of us didn't make the grade—to try to convince whoever was in the craft to come back and get the other one. But he [Travis] performed just as we said he would, and he got directly under the object. And he's received the benefits for it.

For the police, this was a missing persons report. In any such case, the possibility of foul play must be considered. Accordingly, on November 10, Rogers and the five other members of the crew took a lie detector test. The test was conducted by C. E. Gilson of the Arizona Department of Public Safety. Because this was a possible criminal investigation, three of the four questions were whether Travis was killed or injured by one or more of the crew. The fourth question, added at the last minute, was "Did you tell the truth about actually seeing a UFO last Wednesday when Travis Walton disappeared." All six answered "no" to the first three questions and "yes" to the UFO question. Gilson concluded five were truthful. The result for the sixth, Allen Dalis, who was the first to see the UFO, was judged "inconclusive." Gilson concluded: "These polygraph examinations proved that these five men did see some object that they believe to be a UFO and that Travis Walton was not injured or murdered by any of these men, on that Wednesday (5 November 1975). If an actual UFO did not exist and the UFO is a manmade hoax, five of these men had no prior knowledge of a hoax. No such determination can be made of the sixth man whose test results were inconclusive."

A few hours later, just after midnight on November 11, Travis returned.

"Gross Deception"

Travis called his sister's house from a gas station in Heber, Arizona. Duane Walton and Grant Neff drove to pick him up. They found him collapsed in the phone booth. As word spread of Travis's return, Duane began to get phone calls. Among them was one from Coral Lorenzen who offered APRO's assistance. Soon after, she was called by the *National Enquirer* and asked for an appraisal. Lorenzen suggested that Travis and Duane be "sequestered" in the Scottsdale Sheraton Inn. The *National Enquirer* agreed to underwrite the cost in exchange for the exclusive story.[10]

On November 12, Duane and Travis were in a suite at the Scottsdale Sheraton Inn. The following day APRO's James Lorenzen and Dr. James Harder met with the Waltons. They were joined by several *National Enquirer* reporters. One of the reporters, Jeff Wells, later described the "four days of chaos" he experienced. Duane was described as "one of the meanest and toughest-looking men I've ever seen." He warned them, "Nobody is going to laugh at my brother." The *National Enquirer* reporters reassured him and offered a $1,000 initial payment. If the story was good and Travis passed a lie-detector test, the amount could reach the five-figure range. Travis was a very different picture. Wells wrote, "Our first sight of the kid was at dinner in the motel dining room that night. It was a shock. He sat there mute, pale, twitching like a cornered animal."[11]

On November 15, Travis underwent a lie-detector examination. It was administered by John J. McCarthy, who had twenty years of experience and was the senior examiner in Arizona. McCarthy's examination lasted some four hours. He first listened to tapes of Travis describing his abduction. Then he conducted a lengthy preliminary interview with Travis. He learned Travis had experimented with marijuana, speed, and LSD, and had been convicted of stealing and forging payroll checks in 1971. McCarthy also went through the questions to make sure Travis could answer them with a simple "yes" or "no."

With Travis wired up to the lie detector, McCarthy began by asking Travis "baseline" questions (where he was born, etc.) to establish that he would respond in a significant manner when he told a lie.

With this completed, McCarthy asked nine questions on the UFO story. He found Travis was lying. Moreover, Travis was holding his breath before the questions, trying to fool McCarthy. The test was completed shortly after 4:00 P.M. McCarthy called Travis's responses "gross deception" and said it was the plainest case of lying he had seen in twenty years. Wells heard Duane yell, "I'll kill the sonofabitch!" Wells later recalled "the office was yelling for another expert and a different result."

The following day, McCarthy completed his formal report, stating, "Based on his [Travis's] reactions on all charts, it is the opinion of this examiner that Walton, in concert with others, is attempting to perpetrate a UFO hoax, and that he has not been on any spacecraft."

Walton's abduction story suffered another blow a few hours after he failed the McCarthy lie-detector test. APRO had invited Dr. Jean Rosenbaum, a psychiatrist, and his wife Beryl, a psychoanalyst, to examine Travis. They arrived on the evening of November 15 and spent several days with Travis. Dr. Rosenbaum, his wife, and another psychiatrist all concluded the "abduction" was a psychological aberration. Dr. Rosenbaum said that the story "was all in his own mind. I feel that he suffered from a combination of imagination and amnesia, a transitory psychosis—that he did *not* go on a UFO, but simply was wandering around during the period of his disappearance." This should have been the end of the case. It was not.

On November 22, Travis Walton and James Lorenzen appeared on Phoenix television station KOOL. In this and subsequent appearances, Travis described two different kinds of aliens. The first looked like "well-developed fetuses." They were about five feet tall and wore tan-brown robes. Their skins were described as "white like a mushroom." Their heads were domed and lacked hair. Their eyes, Travis said, were large and they had long fingers with no fingernails. The others looked like a normal human (hair, facial features, etc.) and were dressed in blue. Lorenzen said Travis had been examined by doctors and psychiatrists who had rejected the idea of a hoax. What he did not say was that the psychiatrists were convinced Travis was simply fantasizing. Lorenzen also did not say a word about the failed lie-detector test.[12]

The December 16, 1975, *National Enquirer* carried an article titled "5 Witnesses Pass Lie Test While Claiming . . . Arizona Man Captured by UFO." Dr. Harder said "after considering all the known facts" he was convinced Travis Walton had been taken aboard a UFO.[13] Again, there was no mention of the failed lie-detector test.

On February 7, 1976, APRO announced that Travis and Duane Walton had passed a lie-detector test administered by George J. Pfeifer. (Mrs. Kellett also later passed another test given by Pfeifer.) These tests, along with those given earlier to the six crewmen, became the centerpiece for the July 6, 1976, *National Enquirer*. The Walton case was selected by the tabloid's "Blue Ribbon Panel" as "1975's Most Extraordinary Encounter With a UFO." The $5,000 prize was split between Travis and the six crew members. The case received ringing endorsements from Dr. Harder, Dr. Frank Salisbury, Dr. R. Leo Sprinkle, and Dr. Hynek.[14]

As with past cases, different UFO groups had divergent opinions on the Walton abduction. William Spaulding of Ground Saucer Watch (GSW) labeled the case a hoax as early as November 15, 1975. NICAP expressed doubts, while MUFON noted, "Because of inconsistent factors, it is impossible to determine whether the case is authentic or a hoax." APRO, not surprisingly, said, "The Travis Walton case is one of the most important and intriguing in the history of the UFO phenomena."[15,16]

The Walton Investigation

Philip J. Klass became suspicious about the Pfeifer test when he read the account in the December 1975 issue of *The APRO Bulletin*. The first question was "Before November 5, 1975, were you a UFO buff?" Travis answered "No" and Pfeifer concluded he was telling the truth. This contradicted extensive evidence; Dr. Rosenbaum told Klass, "Everybody in the family had seen some [UFOs] and he's [Travis] been preoccupied with this almost all of his life. . . . Then he made the comment to his mother just prior to this incident that if he was ever abducted by a UFO she was not to worry because he'd be alright."

Klass called Pfeifer's former employer, Tom Ezell & Associates (Pfeifer had left shortly after the Walton test to set up his own practice). Ezell examined Travis's charts and told Klass that APRO and the Waltons had told Pfeifer the specific questions they wanted asked. This was counter to standard practice; the examiner frames the specific questions. Ezell stated, "Because of the dictation of the questions to be asked, this test should be invalidated." After looking at Travis's chart, Ezell added, "The reactions on the chart, to my way of interpretation, would not be readable. You would not be able to say if he [Travis] is telling the truth or if he's lying."

The lie-detector test of Rogers and the other crewmen had similar flaws. The single UFO question was an afterthought. Gilson told Klass, "That one question does not make it a valid test as far as verifying the UFO incident." Gilson also had second thoughts about his "inconclusive" verdict on Allen Dalis. During press interviews, Dalis had described the

UFO in great detail. Yet, Dalis told Gilson he had become so frightened he "ducked down in the seat and didn't see any blue-green flash. So he wasn't even being truthful to start with; what he originally claimed he saw he [later] admitted to me he didn't see any of it."

Klass found Duane Walton evasive about their past interest in UFOs, Travis's criminal record, the secret McCarthy lie-detector test, and who framed the questions for the Pfeifer test. Klass also talked with Lorenzen and found similar evasions and falsehoods. Klass asked, "Do you know if Travis has taken any other polygraph tests?" Lorenzen replied, "No, never." (Klass learned of the secret test from Ezell and had already talked with McCarthy when he made the calls.)

The question now became why Travis should undertake so elaborate a UFO hoax. Klass found a possible reason. In the spring of 1974, Rogers had won a Forest Service contract to clear 1,277 acres in the Turkey Springs area. His bid was less than half the high bid. The crew got a late start and, despite an extension, it was clear that Rogers could not meet the November 10 deadline. The reason for the failure was that Rogers's crew was secretly "moonlighting" on two other better paying subcontracts. This was done without the knowledge of his Forest Service contract officer.

Under standard practice, the Forest Service withheld ten percent of the contract fee pending completion. The first extension resulted in a $1.00 per acre penalty; if he asked for another extension, there would be additional penalties. If he defaulted on the contract, most of the money would be lost. Rogers had already defaulted on one contract—a second could endanger future business. Either way, the financial picture looked bleak.

On October 20, NBC telecast *The UFO Incident*. Both Rogers and Travis Walton admitted watching the show. Klass believed this planted the idea. If the contract could not be completed owing to external causes, the withheld money could be returned without a default going on the contractor's record.

On November 18, 1975, Rogers wrote the Forest Service to tell them he could not complete the work because of the UFO abduction "which caused me to lose my crew and will make it difficult to get any of them back on the job site." The Forest Service put the remainder up for bids and later released the withheld money.[17,18]

After five months of investigation, Klass made public his conclusions. Copies of his June 20, 1976, White Paper were mailed to the *Arizona Republic*, a Phoenix newspaper; *The Star*, a tabloid rival of the *Enquirer*; and

NICAP, GSW, MUFON, and APRO. The July 12 *Arizona Republic* was the first to publish Klass's investigation. *The Star* carried a two-page article in its August 10 issue. NICAP published excerpts of the White Paper and stated, "The indications are that a hoax has been perpetrated." GSW, and later MUFON, also published all of the White Paper. The *National Enquirer* ignored the new information.

APRO responded by slandering McCarthy, calling him "unbelievably incompetent" and accusing him of breaking "some of the most elementary rules of the polygraphic profession." APRO concluded by saying, "Describing this test as meaningless . . . is really being too kind. It was badly botched by the tester. Sometimes long years of experience can serve to crystallize bad habits."[19]

APRO's "stonewalling" was, in the end, successful. Many UFOlogists came to accept the Travis Walton abduction as valid. Dr. Hynek said, "Walton's story seems more consistent than that of his detractors." APRO prospered while NICAP continued to decline.[20]

The Walton case marked the final step in the acceptance of abductions. They were no longer viewed as akin to contactees, but as a "mainstream" belief. No longer were abductions "one-time" events. In fact, the Walton case was only one of a number of abduction claims made in the wake of *The UFO Incident*. In these cases, a person had seen a UFO, but it was not until *after* seeing the film, several months later, that they "realized" they had had a period of "missing time." Under hypnosis, they would "remember" having been taken aboard a UFO and being subjected to a physical examination. As these "abductions" were only recognized after seeing the movie, skeptics argued that the claims were inspired (consciously or unconsciously) by the film itself, not by a real event.

Although the pattern of the abduction myth was set, there remained one aspect not yet defined. In each abduction, the description of the aliens was different. In one case, they were described as having fingers covered with feathers. Another had three webbed fingers and a thumb.[21] Size varied from several inches to ten feet tall. One researcher noted that out of fifty-one abduction cases, eight "UFOnauts" had slanted or wrap-around eyes. Yet, the eight alleged beings differed in every other physical characteristic. The only common feature was a roughly human shape—head, two arms, and two legs. Even here there were exceptions. A truck driver reported being abducted by large "boxes" with mechanical arms which hurt when they touched him.[22] This remaining aspect, the lack of a common description for the aliens, would be defined by the best flying saucer movie ever made.

Close Encounters of the Third Kind

Although many films had used flying saucer themes, *Close Encounters of the Third Kind* was the only one to fully understand the flying saucer myth. The story is one of ordinary people trying to cope with mythic experiences. Roy Neary (Richard Dreyfuss) is a power company lineman who sees a UFO. He finds himself the victim of subliminal messages which cause him to undertake obsessive, bizarre actions which cause his family to leave. Neary finally realizes he is to go to Devil's Tower, Wyoming. He embarks on an arduous cross-country journey. Overcoming obstacles, he is rewarded with a meeting with the aliens. As the multicolored mothership lifts off with Neary aboard, he rises above his own mundane, earthly existence.[23]

In earlier films, the flying saucers were sources of danger. In *Close Encounters of the Third Kind*, the meeting with the aliens was not to be feared, but to be anticipated. It was this "sense of wonder" that was so lacking in such films as *The Thing* or *Earth vs. the Flying Saucer*.[24]

Close Encounters of the Third Kind defined the shape of the aliens. In the film, "they" were short, with large heads, slanted dark eyes, and light gray skins. Their noses were small and their ears were only small holes. The aliens' bodies were elongated and very thin. The fingers were also long. Their overall appearance was that of a fetus. By the early 1980s, this "shape" would come to dominate abduction descriptions.

The Growth of Abduction Reports

Certain UFOlogists began to specialize in abduction cases. The first such "abductionist" was Dr. R. Leo Sprinkle, a psychologist at the University of Wyoming. Sprinkle was frequently quoted by the tabloids and was on the *National Enquirer*'s Blue Ribbon Panel. Sprinkle's role was critical in shaping both the development of the abduction myth and its acceptance. His "hypnotic sessions with UFO abductees" began in 1967 and 1968 with three cases. It was not until 1974 that Sprinkle had another abduction case (reflecting the post-Condon Report decline in interest). In 1975 there were two cases. There were three cases each in 1976 and 1977 (after *The UFO Incident*). In 1978 (after *Close Encounters of the Third Kind*), Sprinkle worked with ten subjects, while in 1979 there were eighteen abductees. In 1980 he held the first of his annual conferences for UFO abductees and investigators.

This increase in abduction reports was not limited to Sprinkle. UFOlogist David Webb noted that a 1976 search of UFO literature (covering nearly thirty years) showed only 50 abduction-type cases. Yet, over the next two years, about 100 *more* cases were reported, bringing the total to some 150.[25] By the end of the 1970s, the total number of cases exceeded 200.[26]

While attention was centered on the growth of abduction reports, a more subtle trend went unnoticed. Starting in the 1970s, people simply stopped *seeing* UFOs. No more daylight disks, no "trace cases," and even non-abduction "occupant" reports had practically disappeared.[27] The flying saucer myth had become separated from the flying saucer itself.

This upsurge in abduction reports was a worldwide phenomenon. Jose Inacio Alvaro was an 18-year-old Brazilian UFO buff. Early on the evening of March 2, 1978, the power failed in his neighborhood. When he went outside to check, Alvaro was amazed to see "an ashen colored, smokey sort of ball." He said, "It was huge and bright like the Sun; I couldn't focus my eyes." Soon after it disappeared, the power came back on. Alvaro was so excited he decided to take a bus to his father's house. Once there, he said later, he saw the UFO again and walked out into a nearby field. The next morning he awoke in the field. Alvaro knew about abduction stories, and he wondered if this had happened to him. Under hypnosis, Alvaro recalled having sex with a female UFO pilot. She was naked, tall and plump with light almond-shaped eyes and long, silvery hair. Alvaro said, "Her breasts were fuller than the breasts of a female from Earth." Alvaro quivered with pleasure as he told the story. The story was repeated in a second session soon after.

The UFO sighting was actually caused by fuel vented from the Soviet Molniya 1-39 booster. As the fuel cloud expanded, it was illuminated by the Sun which was below the horizon. And, as Oberg so dryly put it, "On the ground thousands of observers began freaking out, one worse than most."[28]

Budd Hopkins

With the 1980s, a new abductionist appeared—an artist named Budd Hopkins. Long interested in UFOs, the rise in abduction reports attracted Hopkins's attention in 1976. He met "Steven Kilburn." Kilburn had a vague memory of being afraid of a stretch of road, but no UFO sighting. To this point, people claiming to have been abducted said they had seen a UFO and/or occupant. This was followed by a period of "missing time." The "abduction" itself was "remembered" under hypnosis. Kilburn had no such memory. When he was hypnotized, however, Kilburn said he was grabbed by a "big wrench" and was taken aboard a UFO.

To Hopkins, this implied a person could be an "abductee" *without* any overt memory. Hopkins began asking people if thay had "uneasiness," recurring dreams, or "any event" which might indicate an abduction. It was no longer necessary for a person to have "missing time." *Anyone* could now be an abductee and not realize it. Hopkins believed there might be tens of thousands of abductees—what he called "an invisible multitude."

Hopkins published his conclusions in his 1981 book *Missing Time*. He believed "a very long-term, in-depth study is being made of a relatively large sample of humans." The "human specimens" were first abducted as young children. "Monitoring devices" would be implanted in the abductee's nose. This was described as a tiny ball on a long rod. The ball was left in the nasal cavity. The young abductees were then released with no memories of the (alleged) events. Years later, Hopkins believed, once the abductees reached puberty, they would be abducted a second time.

The aliens in Hopkins's abduction cases all followed the shape of those in *The UFO Incident* and *Close Encounters of the Third Kind*—large heads, thin bodies, slanted eyes, and gray skin. The book had several drawings of what became known as "the Grays." *Missing Time* completed the process of defining the shape of the aliens.

Hopkins also speculated on the alien's motivation. He noted several abductees had scars from childhood. He believed tissue samples were being taken. Hopkins suggested the aliens needed a specific genetic structure. Hopkins also suggested the aliens were taking sperm and ova samples. These, he continued, might be for experiments in producing human/alien hybrids.[29]

This expanded the abduction myth; it was now much more "intrusive." In the Pascagoula case, Hickson claimed he was passively "scanned." Now, tissue samples were being taken which left scars. The alleged abductees also showed emotional scars from their supposed experiences—long-lasting anxiety and fear. The "monitoring devices" were a further intrusion. The taking of sperm and ova was, symbolically, the most intrusive of all. Humans were depicted as helpless before the aliens' overwhelming power, reduced to a lab rat.

Hopkins further developed these themes in his 1987 book *Intruders*.

In September 1983, he received a letter from "Kathie Davis." She had read *Missing Time* and wrote him to describe a dream she had had in early 1978 of two small beings in her bedroom. From Davis's accounts and twelve other abductees, Hopkins came to believe the aliens had an unmistakable interest "in the process of human reproduction" going back to the Villas-Boas case.

Hopkins described the process as follows—female abductees were identified as donors during their childhood abductions. The implants allowed the aliens to "track" them. When they reached puberty, they would be reabducted. Ova would be removed, its genetic structure altered with alien characteristics, then replanted back in the human. The female abductees would carry the "baby" several months, then again be abducted. The human/alien child would be removed and brought to term.

Males were not immune to such breeding abductions, according to Hopkins. "Ed Duvall" recalled under hypnosis a sexual encounter with a hybrid alien. In this and other cases, a "suction device" was placed over the penis to remove the sperm. None of these breeding abductions could, according to Hopkins, be described as an erotic experience. "It was very perfunctory," Duvall said, "a detached, clinical procedure."

Once the hybrid children were born, the humans who had "donated" sperm or ova were (yet again) abducted and "shown" their "offspring." The aliens even encouraged the humans to hold the "babies" in a kind of bonding exercise, according to Hopkins. Four women either dreamed or remembered under hypnosis being shown a tiny baby—gray in color and oddly shaped. Kathie Davis claimed to have seen two of her *nine* hybrid children and been allowed to name them. Nor did this cycle of abductions end here. Hopkins claimed the children of abductees were themselves targets for abductions.

Some of Hopkins's abductees gave their impressions of why the aliens were doing these things. "Lucille Forman" had the impression of an alien society "millions of years old, of outstanding technology and intellect but not much individuality or warmth . . . the society was dying . . . children were being born and living to a certain age, perhaps preadolescence, and then dying." The aliens were desperately trying to survive, through both taking new genetic material and exploiting human emotions.

Hopkins painted a progressively darker picture of the "relationship" between humans and aliens. "The UFO phenomenon," Hopkins wrote, "seems able to exert nearly complete control over the behavior of the abductees." He continued that the "implants" had "a controlling function as receivers" and that the abductees can "be made to act as surrogates for their abductors." It is a basic tenet of the abduction myth that these alleged events were truly *alien* experiences—that they are not based on science fiction nor psychological aberrations. Hopkins said, "None of these recollections in any way suggests traditional sci-fi gods and devils . . . the aliens are described neither as all-powerful, lordly presences, nor as satanic monsters, but instead as complex, controlling, physically frail beings."[30]

Dr. David Jacobs (a pro-UFO historian) said in a 1986 MUFON paper, "Contactee stories were deeply rooted in a science fiction model of alien behavior [while] abductee stories have a profoundly alien quality to them that are strikingly devoid of cultural programmatic content."[31]

Thomas E. Bullard said that Betty and Barney Hill had no cultural sources from which they could have derived their story, that they were "entirely unpredisposed."[32]

Entirely Unpredisposed?

Consider the following story—a group of men are in a rural area, at night, when they are abducted. They are rendered unconscious, loaded aboard strange flying machines, and taken to a distant place. They are then programmed with false memories to hide the time they were missing. One of them is converted into a puppet of his abductors. They are then released with no overt memories of what happened. But, years later, two of the group begin having strange, surreal dreams about what was done to them.[33]

This story has many elements of abduction stories—loss of control, loss of memory (i.e., one's soul), and loss of humanity. It is not an abduction story. It has nothing to do with UFOs. It is the plot of the 1962 film *The Manchurian Candidate*.

Despite Hopkins's and Jacobs's claims, the abductee myth has numerous similarities with science fiction. Martin Kottmeyer has noted a number of these. In the film *Killers from Space* an abductee has a strange scar and missing memory. In *Invaders from Mars*, the Martians use implants to control humans. This includes not only adults, but their children as well. In the "Cold Hands, Warm Heart" episode of *The Outer Limits*, an astronaut (William Shatner) orbiting Venus loses contact with Earth for eight minutes. After returning to Earth, he has dreams that he landed on Venus and saw a Venusian approaching the ship. His body also starts changing into a Venusian.

"Dying planets" such as "Lucille Forman" described are a standard feature of science fiction—in H. G. Wells's masterpiece *War of the Worlds,* the Martians attacked because Mars was dying and Earth seemed their only hope for survival. Similar "dying planet" themes appeared in the films *This Island Earth, The 27th Day, Killers from Space,* and *Earth vs. the Flying Saucers. The Invaders* were "alien beings from a dying planet."[34,35]

Crossbreeding between humans and aliens was a common science fiction film plot. They include *Devil Girl from Mars, I Married a Monster from Outer Space, The Mysterians, Village of the Damned, Mars Needs Women,* and the *Alien* film series.[36,37]

The shape of aliens in abduction stories is well within the traditions of science fiction. The "bug-eyed monsters" of 1930s and 1940s pulp magazines often had large, bald heads. This was the shape of the projected image of the Wizard in the *Wizard of Oz.* The aliens in the film *Invasion of the Saucer Men* were "bald, bulgy-brained, googly-eyed, no-nosed," fitting the sterotyped image of UFO aliens. Kottmeyer noted that this "prompts worries that abductees are not only plagiarists, but have bad taste as well." In the 1960s, television series such as *The Twilight Zone* and *The Outer Limits* often featured dome-headed aliens.[38] The original pilot for *Star Trek,* "The Cage" (telecast as the two-part episode "The Menagerie"), had short, large-headed, gray-skinned, bald, physically weak aliens with the power to control human minds.

The reasoning behind this particular shape was best expressed by an *Outer Limits* episode called "The Sixth Finger." The story involves the forced forward evolution of a human (David McCallum). As he evolves, his brain grows, his hair recedes, he becomes telepathic, and can control humans. The idea is that apes have small brains, are hairy, and strong. Modern man, in contrast, has a larger brain, has limited body hair, and is weaker. It therefore seems "right" that a future man would have a huge brain, no hair, and be physically frail.

All these similarities between science fiction concepts and the abduction myth caused Kottmeyer to write, "It seems more sensible to flip Hopkins' allegation around. He says nothing about the aliens of UFO abductions resembling 'sci-fi'. I ask, is there anything about UFO aliens that does not resemble science fiction?"[39]

A final note—Hopkins describes a half human/half alien being lacking the ability to feel emotions. It is just such a being which is the most famous character in all of science fiction—Mr. Spock of *Star Trek*. How "logical."

Questions about Hypnosis

Hopkins's abductees had no overt memories until they were hypnotized. The question becomes whether the abduction story is only a product of being hypnotized. A controlled test of hypnotic abduction accounts was conducted in 1977 by Dr. Alvin H. Lawson, a UFOlogist and English professor at California State University, Long Beach. He and others were dissatisfied with the hypnotic regression of abductees. They decided to ask a group of people with no significant UFO knowledge to imagine an abduction under hypnosis. The hypnotic sessions were conducted by Dr. William C. McCall, an MD with decades of clinical hypnosis experience. Lawson and the others had expected the imaginary abductees would need prompting. The result was quite different—Lawson wrote later:

> What startled us at first was the [subject's] ease and eagerness of narrative invention. Quite often, after introducing the situation—such as, "describe the interior"—Dr. McCall would sit back and the [subject] would talk freely with no more prompting than an occasional, "what's happening, now?"

Lawson compared four imaginary abduction accounts with features of four "real" abduction stories. The chart was an exact match. He concluded:

> It is clear from the imaginary narratives that a great many apparent patterns may originate in the mind and so be available to a witness—whether imaginary or "real". If a person who is totally uninformed about UFO's suddenly finds himself in the abduction sequence, it seems safe to assume that the individual's own sensibility will be able to provide under hypnotic regression, pattern details of his encounter which he may or may not have actually experienced in a "real" sense.[40]

The implication of the Lawson study was not that there was a massive number of covert abductions. Rather, it shows that nearly anyone can, under hypnosis, provide an abduction story. Not surprisingly, abductionists and UFO groups have criticized and ignored the Lawson test.

The typical questioning during an abduction hypnotic session goes far beyond "what happening, now." While researching the book *Mute Evidence*, Daniel Kagan was hypnotized by Dr. Sprinkle. During the session, Dr. Sprinkle said, "Imagine yourself in a spacecraft." There were no UFO images in the recurring dream Kagan was describing. Kagan was so shocked by the attempt to insert a UFO that he came out of the trance. Kagan concluded:

> Sprinkle had just demonstrated how much he had probably been responsible for the UFO imagery reported by so many of his hypnotic subjects. It meant that none of Sprinkle's case histories could be taken seriously, because his role as hypnotist could have been the single most powerful factor in introducing UFO images into the subjects' memories.[41]

Another factor is that many of the stories originate with dreams. The dreams are real, but are they dreams of real events? One indication that they are, in fact, only dreams is the wildly irrational and contradictory nature of the stories. This includes one case in which an "abductee" reported hearing a voice from inside a UFO cry out, "I am Jimmy Hoffa!" Other psychological factors include the abductee's own mental state (even "normal" people can have hallucinations) and such organic brain disorders as temporal lobe epilepsy. Finally, there are the effects of personal experiences: under hypnosis, one abductee gave an extremely outlandish description of the aliens; when the hypnotist asked, "Are you sure?" the abductee responded, "No . . . that was something I saw in the Sunday comic section." Clearly, hypnosis is not the foolproof truth-finding technique the abductionists make it out to be.[42]

In retrospect, it seems clear that the flying saucer myth was always an attempt to find a relationship with the aliens. Earlier myths were about contacts/interactions/struggles between humans and humanlike supernatural beings. Even the conservative Keyhoe had "Operation Lure." The contactees had their own "relationship," rooted in the world view of the 1950s. When this faded, it was replaced, in the 1960s and 1970s, by the abduction myth, yet another attempt to find a relationship with mythological beings.

This human/alien relationship exactly mirrors society's changing attitudes toward authority, science, and sex. During the contactee era of the 1950s, the grandfatherly "Ike" was president. By the mid 1980s, authority was seen as absolutely evil. Science in the 1950s was seen as utopian. By the 1980s, this had changed into the belief science was anti-human. In 1978, Jose Inacio Alvaro described his alien sexual encounter as being pleasurable. By the 1980s, with the specter of AIDS haunting the bedroom, Hopkins was depicting it as a joyless, technological rape.

The function of mythology is to allow a society to relate to the larger world. This has not changed.

Cosmic Debris

I think we have now fairly gone over the old
ground, have we not? But you spoke of some
fresh developments.

—*The Adventure of the Creeping Man*

By the mid-1970s, it had been two decades since Scully's book *Behind the
Flying Saucers* had been exposed as a hoax. Therefore, when the Aurora
UFO crash story began to circulate in the spring of 1973, it seemed fresh
and new. In October 1974, Robert S. Carr, a retired teacher of mass
communications at the University of South Florida and southern director of NICAP, held a press conference. He claimed that for the past twenty-five years, the Air Force had had twelve alien bodies in deep freeze at
Wright-Patterson AFB. Two UFOs, both captured in 1948, were hidden
at the base, according to Carr.[1]

It was simply an embellished version of the Aztec, New Mexico, crash
story Scully had told. Carr claimed there were twelve aliens aboard the
Aztec saucer (Scully said sixteen). The saucer had a small hole in the
transparent plastic dome which had allowed the air to escape. The aliens
were described as being three to four feet tall, having perfect teeth, and
eating a "white square biscuit wafer" which was "fed to guinea pigs who
thrived on them." Manuals, written in an alphabet the Air Force could
not decipher, were also found aboard the UFO. All these story elements
were taken directly from Scully's long discredited tale. "A second disk
was found near Farmington, New Mexico," Carr said. "It was half-
burned with decayed bodies . . . it had little scientific value," he continued.[2]

Crashed Saucer Stories Grow

Between the Aurora crash and Carr's resurrecting of the Scully story, the dam had been broken—after a quarter century, crashed saucer stories were "respectable" again. A major figure in this acceptance was Leonard H. Stringfield. In 1977, his book *Situation Red, The UFO Siege* was published. It included ten pages on crashed saucer stories. One such story was that of "Fritz Werner," who claimed to be a former engineer at Wright-Patterson AFB. He swore that "during a special assignment with the U.S. Air Force on May 21, 1953, I assisted in the investigation of a crashed unknown object in the vicinity of Kingman [Arizona]. . . . A tent pitched near the object sheltered the dead remains of the only occupant of the craft. It was about four feet tall, dark brown complexion, and had two eyes, two nostrils, two ears, and a small round mouth."

Subsequent investigation showed some major holes—"Werner" had earlier told his story to a group of schoolchildren. Of more importance, several of the story elements were drawn directly from Scully—the proving ground landing site, the researchers coming from Phoenix, the aluminumlike material of the saucer, its interior arrangement, and the "dark brown" skin of the alien "caused by exposure to our atmosphere" when air "rushed through that broken porthole window."[3]

Stringfield presented his stories at a MUFON convention at Dayton, Ohio, in July 1978. He described nineteen "retrievals of the third kind." His sources were twenty-two privates, majors, colonels, and civilian professionals who (allegedly) had seen or had taken part in the UFO recoveries. He said that "Blue Berets"—a special Air Force UFO retrieval unit—rushed to recover the debris and bodies. The bodies were described as beige or gray humanlike beings, about four feet tall, who were hairless, sexless, and did not eat. The local *Dayton Journal Herald* was critical, noting "no starship wreckage was displayed, no preserved bodies were shown and no sources were named." It called the stories "anonymous second and third-hand accounts."[4]

The following year, *Flying Saucer Review* endorsed the crashed saucer stories. This even extended to Scully's story. The magazine's editor, Gordon Creighton, wrote, "The Scully book was dynamite, and it naturally created a sensation. It was therefore imperative that Scully be stopped in his tracks, and a feverish and powerful campaign was at once launched to damn and discredit him utterly. That campaign was 100% successful."[5]

The same issue of *Flying Saucer Review* carried the first of three installments of Stringfield's 1978 MUFON paper. Several of the stories were "friend of a friend" type accounts—they had happened to a neighbor of the person telling the story to the UFOlogists. In several of the cases, the original witness was dead.

The credibility of Stringfield's research was called into question by his handling of the Scully crash story. In his opening remarks he said, "So completely was Scully's retrieval story put down that some researchers today wonder, in retrospect, if the book and/or its exposure were contrived."[6] Later Stringfield described the evidence Carr had collected on the Aztec "crash." Carr said he had found five eyewitnesses to the recovery. One (now dead) was a surgical nurse at the alien's autopsy. Another was a high-ranking Air Force officer. Two others were aeronautical engineers who described the UFO's structure and systems. The final witness was an Air Force enlisted man who had been a guard.[7]

None of Stringfield's other crashed saucer stories were so well documented. Yet, no other retrieval story was so thoroughly discredited as Scully's Aztec crash. Rather than deal with the documented facts about the hoax, some believers descended to innuendoes that the exposure was part of the evil Air Force/CIA cover-up. The reality, that *True*, the magazine which had defined the flying saucer myth, had published the story, went down a UFOlogical "memory hole."

"Tomato Man"

During the late 1970s and early 1980s, crashed saucer stories continued to circulate. One centered on a 1948 UFO crash in Mexico. The crash was described by Stringfield as having occurred about thirty miles inside Mexico, across from Laredo, Texas. U.S. troops recovered a ninety-foot diameter UFO and the single crewman. The alien was described as being 4.5 feet tall, hairless, and lacking thumbs. The story was told by a man who said his uncle had taken part in the recovery, and by the uncle himself, who was described as a retired colonel. A third witness, described as an F-94 pilot flying out of "Dias AFB" in Texas, said the UFO was detected over Washington State traveling 2,000 mph. It made a 90° turn and headed over Texas. The F-94 pilot said he saw it pass over his fighter. The UFO then disappeared from radar. The "Dias AFB" radar operators had tracked the UFO and determined it had come down some thirty miles south of the border. The F-94 pilot landed and, with another pilot, took a light plane to the crash site. By the time they arrived,

U.S. troops had secured the area and had covered the saucer with a canopy. The two pilots were called to Washington, D.C., and were sworn to secrecy.[8]

The 1948 crash story was further embellished with more details over the next two years. Two photos of the burned body of the alien pilot (dubbed "Tomato Man") were published in the *Cleveland Plain Dealer* newspaper and *The Globe* tabloid in the summer of 1980. The photos were described as part of a series of thirty-nine photos taken by a Navy photographer flown in from White Sands. The crash was said to have occurred on July 7, 1948. The U.S. military unit was invited to the crash site by the Mexican government.[9,10]

The "Tomato Man" crash story was an obvious hoax—even with three "independent" witnesses. There was no "Dias AFB." The runway at *Dyess* AFB was not built until 1953. The prototype F-94 did not fly until July 1949 (a full year after the "crash"), and did not enter service until late 1950.

As for the photos, Oberg identified the "alien" as being the burned body of an Air Force pilot killed in a plane crash.[11] The photos were also examined by the Air Force Museum. They stated, "Using tubular construction, [the debris] could well be of 1930s or 1940s vintage and might be a trainer, but there is no way to be sure." Both Oberg and the Air Force Museum noted an odd "artifact." The Air Force Museum wrote, "Presumably you noticed the pair of eye glasses near the center of one of the prints." Lying under the "alien" body were the frames of a pair of aviator-style sunglasses.[12]

The acceptance of the crashed saucer stories was a reflection of the changes in UFOlogy in the 1970s. One UFOlogist noted that the "psychic and [New Wave] theories . . . so popular in 1970, have by 1979, almost been supplanted by a return to extraterrestrialism, crash-disc theories, and government conspiracy paranoia."[13]

"The Roswell Incident"

The next step in the development of the crashed saucer stories was a book—*The Roswell Incident*—written by Charles Berlitz and William L. Moore. It was centered on the July 1947 report that the Army Air Force at Roswell, New Mexico, had recovered debris from a crashed "flying disk." The next day, it was identified as coming from a weather balloon.

Berlitz and Moore rejected the balloon explanation. Instead, they claimed that at about 9:50 P.M. on the evening of July 2, 1947, a flying saucer was seen over Roswell by Dan Wilmot and his wife. Wilmot said, "All of a sudden a big glowing object zoomed out of the sky. . . . It was going northwest [toward Corona, New Mexico] at a high rate of speed." It was described as oval-shaped, "like two inverted saucers faced mouth to mouth," and glowing as if internally lit.

Berlitz and Moore then claimed that, north of Roswell, the saucer ran into a severe thunderstorm over the ranch of William W. "Mac" Brazel. It changed course to the south-southwest, but was hit by a lightning bolt. The bolt damaged the saucer, causing a large amount of debris, which then fell to the Brazel ranch, to be blown off the saucer. Brazel himself heard an odd explosion. The severely damaged saucer cleared the mountains, but crashed on the Plains of San Agustin, west of Socorro, New Mexico, killing the crew.

The next morning, July 3, 1947, the saucer was discovered by Barney Barnett, a civil engineer, and a group of archaeological students from the University of Pennsylvania. While they were looking at the damaged saucer and its dead crewmen, an Army officer drove up and ordered them out of the area. He also told them not to talk about what they had seen.

That same morning, about 150 miles away, Brazel discovered the fragments scattered over a field. According to an account by his son (Mac Brazel having died in 1963) the debris field was a quarter of a mile long and several hundred feet wide. Mac Brazel did not think much of it at first, but the next day, he decided to have a closer look. He picked up some of the debris and took it back to the ranch house. That evening, July 4, 1947, Brazel went to his nearest neighbor's house, but he was not interested in seeing it.

The evening of July 5, 1947, Brazel went to Corona, New Mexico, and, for the first time, learned from his uncle, Hollis Wilson, about the flying saucer flap that was sweeping the country. Both Wilson and a friend thought the debris might be from a "flying disk." Brazel was not convinced, but felt the debris was unlike anything he had seen before. The next day, July 6, Brazel drove into Roswell. While there, he told Sheriff George Wilcox about the debris. Sheriff Wilcox, in turn, called Roswell AAF.

Maj. Jesse A. Marcel, the base intelligence officer, took the call. Marcel met with Brazel and decided it should be reported to Col. William H. Blanchard, the base commander. They decided, according to Marcel's 1979 account, that some unusual type of aircraft might be involved.

Marcel should go out and see about it. Marcel and an Army Counter Intelligence Corps agent followed Brazel out to his remote ranch, arriving very late that afternoon.

The next morning, July 7, they went to the debris field. Marcel said he did not see a "complete machine," but rather "a lot of wreckage." They loaded it in the Jeep carry-all the CIC agent was driving and Marcel's 1942 Buick staff car. They were finished by that afternoon.

Marcel later described the debris as unusual. There were small beams, three-eighths to one-half inches square, which looked like balsa wood but were not. He said there was also a great deal of "parchment-like" material that was brown in color and extremely strong. There was also a large number of pieces of "a metal like tinfoil." This metal, according to Marcel, could not be dented, even when hit with a sixteen-pound sledgehammer. When the pieces were reassembled, they covered an area of about ten square feet. They did not have any idea of the object's shape. Marcel also said he could not find anything "that resembled instruments or electronic equipment." The debris was covered "with symbols that we had to call hieroglyphics." They were pink and purple and looked as if they had been painted on the debris. Marcel's son, then 11, also recalled the markings. He said his father arrived home on the evening of July 7. Major Marcel brought some of the debris into their house and tried to fit some of the pieces together.

On the morning of July 8, 1947, Colonel Blanchard ordered the base public information officer, Lt. Walter Haut, to issue a press release that the AAF had recovered a crashed flying disk. The text read:

> The many rumors regarding the flying disc became a reality yesterday when the intelligence officer of the 509th Bomb Group of the Eighth Air Force, Roswell Army Air Field, was fortunate enough to gain possession of a disc through the cooperation of one of the local ranchers and the sheriff's office of Chaves County.
>
> The flying object landed on a ranch near Roswell sometime last week. Not having phone facilities, the rancher stored the disc until such time as he was able to contact the sheriff's office, who in turn notified Major Jesse A. Marcel of the 509th Bomb Group Intelligence Office.
>
> Action was immediately taken and the disc was picked up at the rancher's home. It was inspected at the Roswell Army Air Field and subsequently loaned by Major Marcel to higher headquarters.

That afternoon, the debris was loaded on a B-29 for the flight to Wright-Patterson via Carswell AAF at Fort Worth, Texas. According to Marcel's account, Brig. Gen. Roger Ramey, commander of the 8th Air Force, "took control" when the plane landed at Carswell. Ramey told

Marcel to bring the debris up to his office. It was spread out on brown paper and *one* photo was taken of Marcel with the real saucer debris. After the press left, according to Marcel, the real debris was replaced with parts from a balloon. The press was then allowed to photograph the balloon debris while General Ramey and his aid Col. Thomas DuBose examined it. Ramey announced the debris was from a Rawin Target weather balloon. This was a set of foil and balsa wood radar reflectors carried aloft by several helium-filled balloons. Brazel was forced into silence. Marcel claimed the real debris was already on its way to Wright-Patterson when Ramey made his statement.[14] Berlitz and Moore claimed this was the start of a cover-up which has continued to this day.

Roswell Analyzed

Unlike other crashed saucer stories, the "Roswell Incident" does not rely on "friend of a friend" or anonymous third-hand sources. There are contemporary newspaper accounts, documents, and the AAF press release. There is no doubt something was found. The question becomes *what.*

The story has two elements—one documented, the other not. Barney Barnett's story of finding a crashed saucer and its dead crew is unsupported by any documentation or additional witnesses. Barnett's wife's diary indicates he was far from the Socorro area during July 1947. None of the University of Pennsylvania archaeologists ever came forward. Barnett told the story to two close friends in February 1950. It was from them Berlitz and Moore learned of his crash story.

In contrast, Mac Brazel's discovery of the odd debris in a field, and the events that set in motion, are documented. However, some of the evidence contradicts the story told in *The Roswell Incident.* During the late afternoon of July 8, 1947, Brazel was interviewed by the *Roswell Daily Record* newspaper. In the account published the next day, Brazel said he had found the debris on June 14, not July 3. More important, his description of the debris was very different from that of Marcel thirty-two years later. Brazel was quoted as saying it "consisted of large numbers of pieces of paper covered with a foil-like substance and pieced together with small sticks much like a kite. Scattered with the materials over an area of about 200 yards were pieces of gray rubber. All the pieces were small."[15] The article continued:

When the debris was gathered up the tinfoil, paper, tape, and sticks made a bundle about three feet long and 7 or 8 inches thick, while the rubber made a bundle about 18 or 20 inches long and about 8 in thick. In all, he estimated, the entire lot would have weighed maybe five pounds . . . . considerable Scotch tape and some tape with flowers had been used in the construction. No strings or wire were to be found but there were some eyelets in the paper to indicate that some sort of attachment may have been used.[16]

Further evidence that the debris was, in fact, from a balloon and not a saucer is found in the photos taken in Ramey's office. Marcel claimed that one photo was taken of him with the real "saucer" wreckage. The others were of the substituted balloon debris. In fact, seven photos were taken—*two* with Marcel. A careful examination shows the same debris in all the photos. This casts doubt on the claim of a switch.

The photos also refute claims the foil material was rigid. In one photo a triangular piece is propped against a chair. One edge has an S-shaped curve. In the next photo it is being held by Colonel DuBose; the same edge is now shaped like a parabola. Obviously, it is bending under its own weight. In the two photos of Marcel, he is holding a piece of debris. According to his own account, this was the "real" debris. Yet, he has folded over one section to show the white backing. The debris also shows numerous dents. It is actully paper-backed foil. In several places the foil is peeling off from the paper backing. On the spars, regularly spaced tufts of the foil paper are visible, indicating it was stapled to the spar. Foil paper and wooden spars were used in the radar reflector of the Rawin Target.[17]

The debris was also identified as a Rawin Target by Warrant Officer Irving Newton, who was in charge of the base weather office and the flight center at Carswell. He told Moore, "It was cut and dried. I had sent up thousands of them." Newton also explained how General Ramey had become involved: "I was later told that the major from Roswell had identified the stuff as a flying saucer but that the general had been suspicious of this identification from the beginning and that's why I was called."[18]

Several formerly classified documents also confirm that the debris was from a balloon. One was from the "Combined History, 509th Bomb Group and Roswell Army Air Field, July 1–July 31, 1947." It read: "*The Office of Public Information* was kept quite busy during the month answering inquiries on the 'flying disc', which was reported to be in possession of the 509th Bomb Group. The object turned out to be a radar tracking balloon."[19]

The second document was a teletype message from the Dallas FBI office on July 8, 1947. The text read:

Flying disc, information concerning. _____, Headquarters Eight Air Force, telephonically advised this office that an object purporting to be a flying disc was recovered near Roswell, New Mexico, this date. The disc is hexagonal in shape and was suspended from a balloon by a cable, which balloon was approximately twenty feet in diameter. _____ further advised that the object found resembles a high altitude weather balloon with a radar reflector, but that telephonic conversation between their office and Wright Field had not borne out this belief. Disc and balloon being transported to Wright Field by special plane for examination.[20]

Another document made a much more serious challenge to the validity of the whole Roswell incident. Ironically, it had been made public at least a decade before *The Roswell Incident* was published. It was the memo from Gen. Nathan Twining to the Air Force chief of staff of September 23, 1947 (almost three months after Roswell). A part of the Twining memo was quoted in *The Roswell Incident,* including the statement that "the phenomenon reported is something real and not visionary or fictitious." Berlitz and Moore added, "It is understandable that the Twining memo makes no reference to the Roswell disc."[21]

Despite what Berlitz and Moore imply, the Twining memo *does* deal with the Roswell incident—but in a negative way. What they left out was the statement that there was a "lack of physical evidence in the shape of crash-recovered exhibits which would undeniably prove the existence of these objects."[22] Not only the Twining memo, but the Estimate of the Situation, the 1952 CIA documents, the Robertson Report, and the whole history of Sign, Grudge, and Blue Book are inconsistent with the secret recovery of a crashed saucer.

The Historical Context

An aspect of the Roswell incident which seems to have been overlooked is its historical context. The events took place only two weeks after Arnold saw the nine disks. In early July 1947, no one—not the Army Air Force, not the FBI, not the public, not the believers—had any idea what the "flying disks" were. The two leading theories were U.S. or Soviet secret weapons. The Extraterrestrial Hypothesis did not become popular until the following year, thanks to Ray Palmer and *Fate*. When

Roswell AAF issued the press release, there was no reason to connect the debris with alien spaceships.

Decades later, when Roswell was rediscovered, it had to conform to all the elements of the flying saucer myth—disk-shaped alien spaceships, little aliens, and, of course, the government cover-up—all of which sprang up *after* 1947. One can see this in the way extraneous stories were brought in to convert Brazel's discovery into an acceptable crashed saucer story.

If the debris had been found on June 14, rather than July 3, for instance, it would not be possible to use the Wilmots' sighting the previous night as "confirmation." Barney Barnett's story was needed to provide the crashed saucer itself. Recall that Marcel said he did not find any electronic components. Neither he nor Brazel found any control panels, computers, seats, dead aliens, or atomic engines. The debris was only tinfoil, paper and sticks—not the sort of things interstellar spacecraft would be made of. One UFOlogist pointedly asked how Brazel could have decided it was from a "flying disk."[23] The answer is that when Mac Brazel looked at the debris, he did not have any preconceptions. Thus, any odd-looking debris would be seen as possibly coming from a crashed disk. It did not have to look like it came from an alien spaceship, it just had to look strange.

The Barnett story also provided the cover-up. One implication, were the story true, is that nine days after the Arnold sighting, the government *knew* they were alien spaceships and had *already* decided to cover this up. Recall that Barnett did not say he reported the saucer—the military arrived soon after he "found" it.

Similarly, *The Roswell Incident* included various stories about the saucer being stored at Edwards AFB. The sources were Meade Layne and Gerald Light of the Borderland Sciences Research Association (an occult/contactee group), Mrs. Frank Scully, and Desmond Leslie and George Williamson (both associated with George Adamski).[24]

If all these extraneous stories are removed, one is left only with a few fragments in a field.

Redlight, Stealth, and Crashed UFOs

Many of the crashed saucers were described as being intact. It was only a matter of time before it was claimed that the U.S. was both flying captured UFOs and using their technology. On April 5, 1980, "Mike" contacted a MUFON member. Mike claimed to have worked between 1961 and 1963 as a radio maintenance man at the nuclear test site and "Area 51"—the secret flight test center at Groom Lake, Nevada. He further claimed that a UFO was test flown at Area 51 under the code name "Project Redlight." Mike saw the UFO only once. It was on the ground and partially hidden behind a building about one-half mile or more away. He said it was twenty or thirty feet in diameter and a dull silver color. Several times, when "IT," as Mike called the saucer, was about to take off or land, he was taken into a building, out of sight of the runway. Each time, Mike said, he heard no noise. He also said a friend at a radar site at Tonopah, Nevada, told him he was always picking up UFOs, but was told to ignore them. The radar targets went from one edge of the screen to the other in three sweeps of the antenna. The project ended abruptly in 1962, when, he believed, the UFO crashed.

Mike's story was very vague—he never saw the "UFO" in flight and his one "sighting" on the ground was at a considerable distance. It might have been a radar test target or components for the A-12 mach 3 reconnaissance aircraft, then being assembled and test flown at the Groom Lake site. The high speed radar tracks may have been from A-12 test flights.

Mike's story generated considerable interest among UFOlogists. They filed Freedom of Information Act requests seeking declassification of Project Redlight documents. No such project could be found.[25] Indeed, the Air Force *denied the existence* of any documents related to crashed saucers. When the UFOlogists appealed, they were told that the Air Force was not denying access to the documents (which was legal if the government could show their release would endanger national security) but rather, it specifically denied the *existence* of any such records.[26]

One argument against the crashed saucer stories was that, despite having them for thirty years, the U.S. still used conventional jets and rockets.[27] Then, several months after "Mike" appeared, believers thought they had such an example of a UFO-based aircraft. In August 1980, Defense Secretary Harold Brown announced that the U.S. had developed "stealth" aircraft which could not be detected by radar. This was due to the aircraft's shape and use of radar-absorbing materials.[28] This announcement of an "invisible" aircraft also attracted the interest of UFOlogists. Press accounts described the stealth aircraft (erroneously) as possibly looking like "a manta ray."[29] A letter to *Flying Saucer Review* wondered if stealth technology had been developed from a crashed UFO.[30]

On July 11, 1986, an F-117 stealth fighter crashed near Bakersfield, California, killing its pilot, Maj. Ross E. Mulhare.[31] The crash site and the airspace above it were placed off-limits. Air Force spokesmen would not say what kind of aircraft had crashed. A newsletter of the Citizens Against UFO Secrecy (CAUS) drew a "parallel here to the handling of UFO incidents." People in the crash area said the Air Force guards wore "blue berets" which CAUS found "very reminiscent of Len Stringfield's quick deployment group used in crash retrieval UFO cases."[32] CAUS further noted that a disk shape had been found to have good stealth properties in the 1950s. Several cases were described where UFOs had been reported flying off the wingtips of aircraft, yet were not picked up on radar. CAUS supposed the Air Force had noted this ability of UFOs and decided to develop a similar aircraft. Thus, stealth aircraft were developed from studies of UFO capabilities, not necessarily from crashed saucer debris.[33]

Another version of the stealth/UFO link was the direct opposite of that envisioned by CAUS. Ground Saucer Watch (GSW) advocated what it called the "Federal Hypothesis." GSW argued that the few valid UFO reports were caused by secret testing of advanced aerospace technology. It was the stealth aircraft that were the basis of UFO reports. GSW further claimed that some in the government and CIA "deliberately mislead" the public about UFOs. This group "wanted everyone to believe in 'flying saucers' to create a ruse to cover the testing."[34] GSW's "Federal Hypothesis" was similar to Dr. Leon Davidson's idea that UFOs were a psychological warfare program directed against the American people by the CIA—that the government was not merely covering up the truth, but was actively manipulating the flying saucer myth, for its own evil ends.

Long and Sinister Shadows

By the mid-1980s, crashed saucers, abductions, and cattle mutilations had achieved a wide level of acceptance among believers. That acceptance would cast long and sinister shadows across the flying saucer myth. Believers were quick to see the dark implications of the crashed saucer stories. In 1980, a letter writer to *Flying Saucer Review* noted that *if* these stories of crashed saucers and captured aliens—both dead and alive—*were* true,

> it means that for about 30 years the U.S. and probably other governments have been in full possession of all the facts and concrete evidence necessary to identify UFOs. . . . It also means scientists have had three decades to study the design and mechanics of the retrieved UFOs, and so the government agencies concerned must have developed a UFO-type propulsion system of their own years ago.
>
> This would mean the whole NASA and Soviet space programmes must be seen as a complete fraud—a joint Soviet-American charade to hoodwink the public. . . . government agencies must have been secretly in contact with and visiting civilisations on other planets for about 20-odd years. This would mean many of the UFOs seen in recent years would be of Earth-origin, and there must be some hideous secret conspiracy too terrible to reveal to the world at large.[35]

The letter writer said, "I find this extremely hard to believe," and noted the impossiblity of keeping all this secret unless "those in charge of the conspiracy of silence are so completely powerful and so utterly ruthless that no-one can defy them and survive." Others, however, were more than willing to become ensnared in this "vision of dark and furtive power."[36]

The Flying Saucer Myth 1980–1986

Disk-shaped alien spacecraft have been seen around the world for thousands of years. These UFOs have fantastic maneuverability and speeds far beyond that of earthly aircraft. They are conducting reconnaissance of the Earth. They have landed, leaving pad prints and other traces. They have also drawn power from electrical lines, resulting in blackouts, and have caused cars to stop.

The aliens are described as having gray skin, and are short, with large, bald heads, and thin, elongated arms, legs, and bodies.

Despite their great mental and technological abilities, the aliens are physically weak and sickly. Both the aliens' society and their planet are dying.

To save themselves, the aliens are abducting humans, removing sperm and ova, then combining them with their own genetic material in order to produce alien/human hybrids.

The memories of the abductees are erased so they have no knowledge of what was done to them. The abductee is left with "Missing Time." In some cases, the hidden memories reemerge in dreams. These "dreams" can be probed through hypnotism to learn what occurred. This indicates many thousands of people have been abducted.

The aliens use implants in the noses of the abductees to track and possibly control them.

The aliens are also mutilating cattle in a systematic genetic sampling effort.

Flying saucers have crashed and the debris and dead crewmen have been recovered by the U.S. government.

These UFOs have been test flown and the technology derived from them used to develop the stealth fighter and other advanced weapons.

The U.S. government has been covering up these facts for forty years, ruthlessly slandering witnesses, coercing them into changing their stories and giving up evidence, and otherwise forcing them into silence.

This effort is controlled by the CIA.

Aliens among Us

> Its invisibility, and the mystery which was
> attached to it, made this organization doubly
> terrible. It appeared to be omniscient and
> omnipotent, and yet it was neither seen nor
> heard.
>
> —*A Study in Scarlet*

In the early 1980s, the flying saucer myth had three separate, distinct threads—abductions, crashed saucers, and the mutes. Yet, in the dark depths of the flying saucer myth, these diverse threads were being interwoven to make a whole new mythology. This "alien myth" would both encompass and overshadow the old flying saucer myth. In the end, the alien myth would, itself, become submerged in a witch's brew of fascist conspiracy theories, hate, and paranoia.

Beginnings

It was from the mute myth, with its images of death, dismemberment, and conspiracies, that the alien myth would first emerge. It began with a man named Dr. Paul Bennewitz, a physicist and president of a small electronics company in Albuquerque, New Mexico.[1] Bennewitz was also a UFO investigator with APRO. Jim and Coral Lorenzen believed he was "prone to make great leaps of logic on the basis of incomplete data." They felt Bennewitz had already decided what he was going to find before he investigated.[2]

In August of 1979, Bennewitz and Dr. Leo Sprinkle began investigating an abduction case. A mother and her young son were driving along a rural highway near Cimarron, New Mexico. During three hypnosis sessions, the woman said they observed two or more UFOs and a calf being abducted. Both the woman and her son were also abducted and taken to an underground base. The woman, under hypnosis, said she saw the calf being mutilated. The woman also said she had seen a vat containing body parts floating in a liquid. In another vat was the body of a human male. The woman said she was examined and small metallic objects implanted in the bodies of both her and her son.[3]

Bennewitz was convinced by August 1979 that the implants were used to control the abductees' actions. He also believed it might be possible to detect the electromagnetic signals he thought the aliens were using to control the alleged abductees. He called the effort "Project Beta" and reported to APRO in late 1979 that he had picked up low-frequency electromagnetic signals from UFOs. Bennewitz wrote a program for his personal computer to "translate" the signals. (He later claimed he had been helped by the aliens.)[4]

By mid-1982, Bennewitz had woven the basic threads of the alien myth. There were, according to Bennewitz, two types of aliens—the malevolent "Grays" and the more friendly "Highs" ("Nordic-type" aliens also called "Talls" or "Blonds"). Bennewitz also used the term "Extraterrestrial Biological Entities" (EBE) for the Grays.[5,6] Bennewitz claimed that the Grays were responsible for the cattle mutilations. The Grays needed the blood and organs for the building of humanoids by gene-splicing. The material was taken from live cattle to maintain their supply of DNA.[7] They had also abducted and implanted hundreds of thousands, even millions, of people.

The Grays had, according to Bennewitz, entered into a secret treaty with the U.S. government. The Grays were allowed to conduct mutes and abductions without interference. They were also allowed to build a secret underground base near Archuteta Peak outside Dulce, New Mexico (the site of a mute wave in the late-1970s) and three other areas. In exchange, the government was provided alien space technology and weapons. The Grays violated the treaty, Bennewitz continued. The weapons were defective or made to fail. The Grays' double cross left the Earth helpless against their invasion. Already, there had been battles between the Grays and the U.S. military. The Grays' intent was to reduce the human race to slaves or cattle.[8,9]

Bennewitz saw himself on a one-man crusade to warn the world of this alien plot to take over the Earth. He wrote letters and made phone calls by the hundreds. With his degree, along with a convincing and compelling style, Bennewitz began influencing other UFOlogists. He met with Linda Moulton Howe and John Lear (son of Learjet inventor Bill Lear) who would have key roles in the spread and embellishment of Bennewitz's ideas.[10]

Other UFOlogists were less impressed—Bennewitz had photos which he claimed showed a crashed UFO, burned wreckage, and the entrance to the alien base. All that others could see were rocks, trees, and shadows. His computer program assigned words, sentence fragments, and even whole sentences to the various individual pulses in the signals. When the text elements were broken up, reshuffled, and reassembled, the "new" message was the same. Dr. Hynek and the Lorenzens expressed doubts about Bennewitz's claims. The split between the old flying saucer myth and the new, darker alien myth had begun.

Bennewitz himself was becoming increasingly erratic—he claimed the aliens were coming through the walls at night and injecting him with chemicals. Finally, he suffered a mental breakdown and was hospitalized.[11]

In retrospect, it is clear the alien myth was a product of the troubled mind of Dr. Paul Bennewitz. Beyond this point, one enters a swamp of suspicions, hoaxes, claims of disinformation, deception, and lies—a place where every source is tainted, "official documents" are not what they are claimed, and nothing is as it seems.

William Moore, Richard Doty, and the Birth of MJ-12

The next major figure in the development of the alien myth was Sgt. Richard C. Doty, a special agent with the Air Force Office of Special Investigations at Kirtland AFB. In September 1980, Doty wrote a report on a series of unidentified lights seen over the Kirtland test range.[12]

By February 1981, Doty had a working relationship with William Moore, then a member of APRO's board of directors. At that time, Doty gave Moore what became known as the "Project Aquarius Document." This *seemed* to be a November 7, 1980, teletype message from AFOSI headquarters in Washington, D.C., to the Kirtland AFB OSI office. The message, classified Secret, dealt with the analysis of several UFO photos taken by Bennewitz. According to the text, analysis of one photo "revealed object to be saucer shaped, approximate diameter 37 feet. Object contained a trilateral insignia on the lower portion of object." The document also *seemed* to reveal the nature of the U.S. government's UFO activities. It stated:

> Ref your request for further information regarding HQ CR 44. The following is provided: Capt Grace 7602 AINTELG/INS contacted and related following: (S/WINTEL) USAF no longer publicly active in UFO research, however USAF still has interest in all UFO sightings over USAF installation/test ranges. Several other government agencies, lead by NASA, actively investigates [*sic*] legitimate sightings through covert cover. (S/WINTEL/FSA) One such cover is UFO Reporting Center, U.S. Coast and Geodetic Survey, Rockville MD 20853. NASA filters results of sightings to appropriate military departments with interest in that particular sighting. The official U.S. government policy and results of Project Aquarius is still classified Top Secret with no dissemination outside official intelligence channels and with restricted access to "MJ TWELVE." Case on Bennewitz is being monitored by NASA/INS, who request all future evidence be forwarded to them thru AFOSI/IVOE.[13]

This was the first time the terms "Project Aquarius" and "MJ-12" were mentioned. In time, they would dominate and shape the flying saucer myth.

This process began within a year. In January 1982, Moore met with Robert Pratt, a former *National Enquirer* reporter, and told him about Project Aquarius and MJ-12. Moore said the information had come from a "Deep Throat" source. Despite the supposedly reliable source, Pratt felt it would be impossible to prove Moore's claim. They decided to write a novel, called *The Aquarius Project,* to pass the story off as fiction. Moore would supply the information, Pratt would do the writing, while Doty was understood to be a silent third-party with the right to review the manuscript. The central figure was an AFOSI agent.[14] It was finished in late 1983, but was never published.

In the late spring of 1982, Moore was hired by KPIX-TV, in San Francisco, as a consultant for a UFO special. In June, Moore brought Jaime Shandera (a television producer) and Stanton Friedman (nuclear physicist and UFO lecturer) into his research efforts.[15] Moore supplied KPIX-TV with a copy of the Project Aquarius Document. On August 6, 1982, Bob Peters of KPIX-TV called the Air Force to ask about it. An AFOSI investigation indicated it was a forgery, with numerous flaws in style and format. Moore subsequently admitted the Project Aquarius Document was not authentic, in that he had retyped it and added an official-looking date stamp.[16]

In January 1983, Doty met with Ron Lakis, a KPIX-TV producer; Peter Gersten, a lawyer involved with FOIA requests for UFO documents;

and Moore. Doty told them that the OSI was deeply involved with UFOs, and that he had been assigned to investigate UFOs for the past five or six years. He also claimed to have access to presidential UFO briefing papers.

Doty's claims were similar to those of Bennewitz. He talked about the secret treaty allowing mutes and abductions in exchange for alien technology. Project Aquarius dealt with the government/alien contacts. The National Security Agency (NSA) was trying to communicate with the aliens. Unlike Bennewitz, Doty said the aliens were benevolent. Doty said he knew of three UFO crashes—Roswell, and one each in the 1950s and 1960s; bodies had been recovered. Doty also said the government had infiltrated UFO groups and was feeding them "disinformation." This claim, like the alien myth, grew over the coming years. He also said the government was "programming" the public, using movies and television, to accept the alien's presence on Earth.[17]

Linda Howe and the Presidential Briefing Paper

The next major development in the evolution of the alien myth occurred in April 1983. Linda Moulton Howe proposed a documentary titled *UFOS: The E.T. Factor* to Home Box Office. Howe went to Albuquerque to meet Doty on April 9, 1983, at the Kirtland AFB AFOSI office. Doty gave her several sheets of paper titled "Briefing Paper for the President of the United States of America." Doty said his superiors wanted her to see the document; she could read it and ask questions, but not take notes.

The briefing paper described several UFO crashes—in 1946, 1947, 1949, and several in the early 1950s. Some of the sites were Aztec, New Mexico; Kingman, Arizona; and in northern Mexico. Two different crashes occurred at Roswell. The briefing paper said radar had disabled the UFOs' guidance systems. The UFOs and alien bodies were taken to Los Alamos and Wright-Patterson AFB. The "EBEs" had gray skin, long arms, and clawlike nails with webbing between their four fingers. Their noses and ears were small holes.

In 1949, a UFO crashed near Roswell. Six aliens were found, one still alive. An Air Force officer took the survivor to Los Alamos. Over the next three years, until he died on June 18, 1952, "Ebe" told the officer about his civilization and the aliens' role in human evolution. This was done both via telepathy and verbally. Ebe came from a planet in a binary star system about fifty-five light years away from Earth.

The EBEs have been coming to Earth for at least 25,000 years in order to manipulate the DNA of existing terrestrial primates and other life forms. The specific intervals Howe remembered were 25,000, 15,000, 5,000, and 2,500 years ago. The briefing also stated, "Two thousand years ago extraterrestrials created a being" that was to teach humans about love and nonviolence.

The briefing paper concluded with a list of projects related to government UFO research. First was "Project Garnet." It stated that all questions and mysteries about the evolution of *Homo sapiens* had been answered and the project had been closed. "Project Sigma" was described as an effort to communicate with the aliens. "Project Snowbird" dealt with research and development of alien technology. This included test flights of a recovered UFO. The final entry was for the now-familiar Project Aquarius. It was described as an overall effort to accumulate all the available information on the aliens. The paragraph stated that some data collected in Project Aquarius had been used in the U.S. space program.

The paper also talked about another group of aliens—the "Talls." When asked, Doty said, "They tolerate each other," and said there was some kind of friction between them.

Doty explained to Howe that she was being shown the briefing paper because she would soon be given several thousand feet of film of crashed saucers, alien bodies, the live "Ebe," and a meeting between aliens and humans at Holloman AFB. This meeting occurred at 6:00 A.M. on April 25, 1964. One UFO landed while two others hovered overhead. The Air Force officer who befriended "Ebe" and two scientists greeted them. Several alien bodies were returned. Doty implied humans were returned and others went aboard in an "exchange program." The Socorro "landing" had been an error; a mistake had been made in the time and location of the meeting and the aliens landed outside Socorro. The second try, Doty claimed, came off without a hitch.

Howe met with Doty that evening at a Mexican restaurant. Doty expanded on what the "briefing paper" had said. Doty said the "Ebans" lived like Pueblo Indians in houses carved out of soil and rock. Their planet was a hot desert world. Howe asked if the binary stars were Zeta Reticula (as in the Fish map) but he refused to say. Howe asked, "How do you know how they live? Has someone from here been to their planet?" Doty responded, "Something like that. You might say we have research scientists studying their planets like they study ours."

Doty said no one knew why Ebe died. They had tried to save him, sending signals to the Ebans. When he died, the Air Force officer cried—Doty compared it to the film *E.T.* Howe asked if Ebe had said anything about God. Doty responded, "He said our souls recycle, that reincarnation is real. It's the machinery of the universe." In the end, no film was released, due to "political reasons," Doty claimed.[18] The so-called presidential briefing paper introduced additional terms and ideas into the growing alien myth.

Paranoia Strikes Deep

Unseen by the larger society, the flying saucer myth was becoming possessed by an increasingly paranoid vision. It had its roots in the political turmoil of the 1960s. On the Left, it was popular to talk about the "Military Industrial Complex." This was seen as a small group of the rich and powerful who "really ran things." The Vietnam War, the Cold War, and the arms race were the result of their "virtual conspiracy" to enrich themselves and keep their power. By the late 1970s, this attitude of trendy nihilism had become academic orthodoxy. It also found a receptive audience among some UFO believers.

The link between political nihilism and UFOs was first forged in the May 1979 issue of *Second Look* magazine. It carried an inteview with Victor Marchetti, an ex-CIA official and co-author of the anti-CIA book *The CIA and the Cult of Intelligence*. Part of the interview dealt with UFOs. Marchetti noted that the released CIA documents indicated only a routine interest in UFO reports. "However," he noted, "few such reports were released—and that implies a cover-up!" His theory was that

> we have, indeed, been contacted—perhaps even visited—by extraterrestrial beings, and the U.S. government, in collusion with the other national powers of the Earth, is determined to keep this information from the general public. The purpose of the international conspiracy is to maintain a workable stability among the nations of the world and for them, in turn, to retain institutional control over their respective populations. Thus, for these governments to admit that there were beings from outer space . . . [could] erode the foundations of the Earth's traditional power structure. Political and legal systems, religions, economic and social institutions could all soon become meaningless in the mind of the public. The national oligarchical establishments, even civilization as we know it, could collapse into anarchy. Such extreme conclusions are not necessarily valid, but they probably accurately reflect the fears of the "ruling classes" of the major nations.[19]

Not surprisingly, the mutologists were quick to embrace this political interpretation. Some began talking about "connections" between mutes, mass murderers, and "unanswered questions in both Kennedy and the King assassinations."[20,21] In 1986, *Stigmata* published "The Occult, MIB's, UFOs and Assassinations." It asked:

> . . . is the ever continuing search for clues and hints to the "truth" leading as-sasso-buffs into an area populated by umbrella men, mystery tramps, and the elusive men-in-black (MIBs), those strangely dark-clothed characters who have terrorized UFO investigators since 1947?

The whole UFO/conspiracy "link" was "established" through Fred Lee Crisman. He and Harold Dahl were involved in the Maury Island Hoax. The article claimed Dahl "vanished" after talking with Kenneth Arnold. Crisman was suddenly recalled to duty in the Air Force and sent to Alaska and then Greenland. The two Air Force officers, Davidson and Brown, "were killed" after finishing their investigation. The article con-tinued that slag samples collected by Crisman and Dahl were switched and others were stolen from Ray Palmer's office. Paul Lance, a Tacoma newspaper reporter who helped Arnold, died soon afterward. Arnold was nearly killed when his plane's engine failed. All this, the article im-plied, was part of some vast conspiracy. Nor did it end there. On Novem-ber 22, 1963, three "mystery tramps" were arrested by the Dallas Police soon after President Kennedy's assassination. The article claimed one of them had been "identified" as Fred Lee Crisman. He was also called be-fore the New Orleans Grand Jury during D.A. Jim Garrison's "investiga-tion."[22]

The effect of this was to "link" the flying saucer/alien myth with the conspiracy subculture—a loose network of conspiracy theorists "for whom every death is suspicious, and every little incident has a labyrinthine political, social, and historical context." A common theme was the "Nazification of America"; comparisons were drawn between the rise of fascism in 1920s Germany and postwar American society. Their tortuously reasoned theories depicted a world where evil forces controlled every event.[23]

"Executive Briefing/Subject: Project Aquarius"

Also in 1986, what *seemed* to be several pages from a Top Secret briefing on Project Aquarius began to circulate. The cover was labeled "EXECU-TIVE CORRESPONDENCE," while another page was a list of code names for UFO-related projects. The text read:

> 2. (TS/ORCON) PROJECT SIGMA: PROWORD: (_____). Originally es-tablished as part of Project _____ in 1954. Became a separate project in 1976.

Its mission was to establish communication with Aliens. This Project met with positive success when in 1959, the United States established primitive communications with the Aliens. On April 25, 1964, a USAF intelligence Officer, met with two Aliens at a prearranged location in the desert of New Mexico. The contact lasted for approximately three hours. _____, the Air Force officer managed to exchange basic information with the two Aliens (Atch 7). This project is continuing at an Air Force base in New Mexico. (OPR: _____).

    3.(TS/ORCON) PROJECT SNOWBIRD: PROWORD: (_____). Originally established in 1972. Its mission was to test fly a recovered Alien aircraft. This project is continuing in Nevada. (_____).

    4. (TS/ORCON) PROJECT _____: _____. Originally established in 1968. Its mission was to evaluate all UFO ____ information pertaining to space technology. PROJECT POUNCE continues. (_____).[24]

The pages were part of a ten-page document. Moore claimed he had been shown the document and allowed to photograph it. The document is similar, but not identical, to the so-called presidential briefing paper shown to Howe. The "Executive Briefing" refers to the April 25, 1964, "contact," the capture of "EBE" and his death on June 18, 1952. It also said:

> EBE reported that 2,000 years ago his ancestors planted a human creature on earth to assist the inhabitants of earth in developing a civilization. This information was only vague and the exact identity or background information on this homo-sapien was not obtained. Doubtless, if this information was released to the public, it would cause a world-wide panic.

However, there are differences—only three UFO crashes were listed: in 1947 (four bodies), 1949 (when EBE was captured), and another in 1958 (the saucer was found abandoned in the Utah desert). EBE's home world was identified as Zeta Reticula; Howe said Doty would not say if this was true. The study of human evolution was called "Bando;" Howe said it was called "Garnet."[25] During the mid-1980s, "MJ-12" and "Aquarius" appeared with increasing frequency in UFO newsletters. In May 1987, they came to public attention.

The MJ-12 Forgeries

On May 29, 1987, Moore, Jaime H. Shandera, and Stanton T. Friedman released copies of "Briefing Document: Operation Majestic 12" which purported to be a preliminary briefing for President-elect Eisenhower. The document was dated "18 November, 1952" and the briefing officer was Adm. Roscoe H. Hillenkoetter (MJ-1). The "Majesty 12" group had been set up by President Truman following the crash at Roswell. The original twelve members (all dead by 1987) were Admiral Hillenkoetter, Dr. Vannevar Bush, Defense Secretary James V. Forrestal, Gen. Nathan F. Twining, Gen. Hoyt S. Vandenberg, Dr. Detlev Bronk, Dr. Jerome Hunsaker, Sidney W. Souers, Gordon Gray, Dr. Donald Menzel, Gen. Robert M. Montague, and Dr. Lloyd V. Berkner. Following Forrestal's death, he was replaced by CIA director Gen. Walter B. Smith on "01 August, 1950."

Following the report that a rancher had found a crashed saucer,

on 07 July, 1947, a secret operation was begun to assure recovery of the wreckage of this object for scientific study. During the course of this operation, aerial reconnaissance discovered that four small human-like beings had apparently ejected from the craft at some point before it exploded. These had fallen to earth about two miles east of the wreckage site. All four were dead and badly decomposed due to the action by predators and exposure to the elements during the approximately one week time period which had elapsed before their discovery.

. . . the disc was most likely a short range reconnaissance craft. This conclusion was based for the most part on the craft's size and the apparent lack of any identifiable provisioning. . . . A similar analysis of the four dead occupants was arranged by Dr. Bronk. It was the tentative conclusion of this group (30 November, 1947) that although these creatures are human-like in appearance, the biological and evolutionary processes responsible for their development has apparently been quite different from those observed or postulated in homo-sapiens. Dr. Bronk's team has suggested the term "Extra-terrestrial Biological Entities", [sic] or "EBEs", [sic] be adopted as the standard term of reference for these creatures until such time as a more definitive designation can be agreed upon.

No "wings, propellers, jets . . . wiring, vacuum tubes or similar recognizable electronic components" were found in the wreckage. Writing found aboard could not be deciphered. The "document" continued:

On 06 December, 1950, a second object, probably of similar origin, impacted the earth at high speed in the El Indio—Guerrero area of the Texas—Mexico boder [sic] after following a long trajectory through the atmosphere. By the time a search team arrived, what remained of the object had been almost totally incinerated. Such material as could be recovered was transported to the A.E.C. facility at Sandia, New Mexico, for study.[26]

Although eight attachments were listed, only one was included—a memo for Defense Secretary Forrestal from President Truman. Dated September 24, 1947, it established the MJ-12 group. Moore said the document was sent to Shandera on a roll of undeveloped 35 mm film in

December 1984. They spent the next two years trying to authenticate the document.

In 1985, they discovered, at the National Archives, an unsigned carbon copy of a memo for General Twining from Robert Cutler, special assistant to the president, dated July 14, 1954. It dealt with "NSC/MJ-12 Special Studies Project." The text read: "The President has decided that the MJ-12 SSP briefing should take place *during* the already scheduled White House meeting of July 16, rather than following it as previously intended."[27]

Moore said it "unquestionably verifies the existence of an 'MJ-12' group in 1954."[28] To some it was the long-sought "smoking gun." But to others, it was "too good to be true."

The National Archives noted numerous problems with the "Cutler Memo." The "document" was classified Top Secret, yet it lacked a Top Secret register number. It was labeled "Top Secret Restricted Information," yet this classification was not used at the National Security Council until the Nixon administration, nearly two decades later. The memo did not have a government watermark—documents created by Cutler while at the NSC had an eagle watermark on onionskin paper used for carbon copies. There was no NSC meeting on July 16, 1954, and there were no NSC records dealing with MJ-12, Majestic, UFOs, flying saucers, or flying disks. There was no listing in President Eisenhower's Appointment Books for a special meeting on July 16, 1954. Even when he had off-the-record meetings, the Appointment Books listed the time of the meeting and the participants. Finally, Robert Cutler was not even in Washington, D.C., or the U.S. on July 14, 1954. He was visiting military bases in Europe and North Africa between July 3 and 15. A genuine memo, also dated July 14, 1954, was signed by James S. Lay.[29]

The so-called MJ-12 briefing paper shows numerous errors of style, facts, and content. The most glaring error was the "01 August," "07 August," and "06 December." The author has never seen an "0" prefix before a single digit date in the text of a government document. The backers of the MJ-12 documents have offered no examples, either. The use of a comma after the month is also in error—it should be "6 December 1950." Both Klass and CAUS noted, however, that Moore had used the same particular date format since the fall of 1983. This includes not only personal letters and papers, but also retyped official documents.[30,31,32]

There are also errors in the classification markings. CAUS discovered that the lettering of the "TOP SECRET/MAJIC EYES ONLY" marking on the briefing document was identical in style to that used by Moore on his return address stamp. This rubber stamp, unlike real classification stamps, used removable lettering. One obvious indication of this is the letter "I." In both the "MAJIC" and the "WILLIAM" and "OLIVE" of Moore's return address, the "I" is raised slightly.[33] The warning against copying the document does not match the wording on real documents from 1952. Additionally, Top Secret documents have page count statements—"This document has ___ pages," and each page is numbered "Page ___ of ___ Pages." This is because Top Secret documents must be checked periodically to ensure no pages are missing. There are no such page counts on the MJ-12 briefing.

Factual errors include a reference to "Roswell Army Air Base (now Walker Field)." This should be Roswell Army Air *Field* and Walker *AFB*. Army Air Base was a term not used after 1943. "Field" was not used after 1947 when the Air Force became an independent service.[34]

The document also has particularities of style; use of the words "media" (rather than "press"), "impacted" (as a verb), and "Extra-terrestrial" rather than "alien." These terms were not popular until the 1960s. Others include misspelled words such as "boder," non-American punctuations (", and ". rather than ," and ."), hyphenating "homo-sapiens" (also in the Aquarius briefing paper), and the lack of commas.[35]

The membership of Hillenkoetter and Menzel also raises questions. Hillenkoetter was CIA director from May 1, 1947 until October 7, 1950.[36] Yet, in November 1952—over two years later, he was still chairman of MJ-12. Interestingly, one newspaper account calls him "then CIA Director"; the hoaxer may have made the same mistake.[37] After retiring from the Navy in May of 1957, he joined the board of NICAP!

Menzel, another supposed MJ-12 member, wrote three anti-UFO books. James Moseley, who knew him personally, said that "he made Phil Klass look like a hard-core believer!"[38] Moseley also found evidence that Menzel and Hillenkoetter did not know each other—something that would be impossible if they had worked together in the MJ-12 group.[39] Clearly, Menzel had been included as an act of revenge for his past activities.

The final blow came in early 1990, when Klass showed that the Truman memo of September 24, 1947, was a forgery. The "Harry Truman" signature was *identical* to that on an October 1, 1947, letter to Vannevar Bush. The "H" showed a distinctive skid mark. It is impossible for two signatures to be identical. A document examiner also told Klass the memo was typed on a Smith-Corona typewriter first sold in 1963—a full fifteen years after the memo was supposedly typed.[40,41] By the early

1990s, most believers had come to the conclusion the documents were forgeries. Yet, MJ-12 had taken on a life of its own.

The MJ-12 forgeries were simply the latest example in a continuing theme—the distrust of "secret societies" as "elitist cabals," a privileged brotherhood counter to American principles. As in Masonic orders or occult "hierarchal magic" groups, the "Majic Twelve" are high priests or enlightened masters of a mystery religion in which levels of security clearances replace levels of initiation. Only the President and his 12 Disciples know the final answers to these mysteries. This sinister, secret group also controls knowledge that might enable them to control the world.

That, in turn, leads to parallels with other historical conspiracy "documents," including The Protocols of the Elders of Zion. This long-discredited anti-Semitic forgery described twelve Jewish elders meeting in a cemetery to discuss plans to secretly conquer the world. Five of the original MJ-12 "members" had Jewish-sounding names (with Donald Menzel as Judas).

Strawberry Ice Cream

The year 1987 saw not only the MJ-12 documents, but publication of Budd Hopkins's *Intruders*, Whitley Strieber's *Communion*, which described his torment at the hands of alien "visitors," and *Light Years*, on the contactee Eduard Meier, who claimed to have gone back in time and met with Jesus Christ. *Communion* reached number 1 on the *New York Times* best seller list by May 1987. It was a degree of interest in UFOs not seen since the 1973 flap aftermath. (All that was missing were UFO sightings.)

On October 14, 1988, *UFO Cover-Up? Live!* was telecast. The program featured "Falcon" and "Condor." It was claimed they were two of Moore's "Deep Throat" sources. Their faces were hidden and their voices were electronically disguised. Far from giving authority to the program, they brought ridicule from skeptics and believers alike. Falcon claimed, "Presently, as of the year 1988 there is one extraterrestrial being. He's a guest of the United States government." Condor claimed an agreement had been signed between the U.S. and the aliens. Part of this was a base in Nevada at "an area called Area 51 or Dreamland." He said, "The extraterrestrials have complete control of this base." Condor added, "The aliens enjoy music, all types of music, especially ancient Tibetan style music. . . . their favorite dish or snack is ice cream—especially strawber-ry."[42] CAUS called it, "an amazingly inept move." Several people, in-cluding Gersten, Howe, and ex-AFOSI agents, identified "Falcon" as Doty.[43]

The credibility of both Doty and Moore suffered. In early 1985, a few weeks after the documents were mailed, Doty was tranferred from Kirt-land AFB to West Germany and assigned to counterintelligence duties. Doty's superiors became suspicious that some of his reports of contacts with communist agents were faked. Doty flunked a lie-detector test, was removed from the AFOSI, and transferred back to Kirtland AFB in late 1986. He spent his final year in the Air Force as a "food services special-ist," managing the mess hall. In a March 3, 1988, letter to CAUS, Doty denied showing Howe the presidential briefing paper. He further stated that, "I know of no secret Government investigation of UFOs. I have never heard of MJ-12 or any secret Government agency that investi-gates UFOs." Howe responded by signing a sworn statement that what she had said about Doty was true.[44]

Moore also damaged his reputation. In October 1987, Moore claimed his high-level intelligence contacts told him and Shandera to fly to Washington, D.C. They would be met by someone who would take them to a wooded area. They would then be allowed to interview and film "EBE-3." They went to Washington, but no one met them.[45]

Moore's speech before the 1989 MUFON convention inflicted further damage.[46] In a long, rambling statement, Moore claimed that since Sep-tember 1980, he had acted as an unpaid double agent for the govern-ment. Moore said he had been approached by a "well-placed" individual who claimed to be connected with a government UFO project. "The Fal-con," Moore claimed, represented a group of people who opposed the UFO cover-up. The Falcon offered to provide Moore with information meant to end the cover-up. Doty would act as liaison between the Fal-con and Moore. As part of this "exchange," Moore said he provided the government information on APRO and Bennewitz.

Moore further claimed that Bennewitz had been the victim of a gov-ernment "disinformation" effort. The stories of secret treaties, malevo-lent aliens, underground bases, technology exchanges, and battles with the aliens were intended to discredit Bennewitz. This disinformation, Moore claimed, resulted in Bennewitz's breakdown. Moore also claimed that "at least *some*, quite possibly a substantial portion" of the informa-tion given by Falcon and Condor in *UFO Cover-Up? Live!* was also disin-formation. Moore added, "I am equally convinced that some of it is true." Moore justified his involvement with this disinformation effort as an attempt to learn about the cover-up.[47]

Moseley observed that the speech "sunk [Moore's] credibility to a new low."[48] Some believers, however, accepted the idea that the government was feeding "disinformation" to UFOlogists. Whenever a document or UFO sighting proved false, the situation could still be salvaged by saying it was a carefully conceived government disinformation effort.[49] CAUS noted, however, "Given the current sad state of affairs with the credibility of UFOlogy, one wonders whether the government considers UFOlogists important at all!"[50]

There was another effect, not realized in 1989. With the belief in disinformation came a growing interest by some UFOlogists in intelligence activities, particularly those that could be connected with conspiracy theories. It was now time for the dark visions to flower.

Cosmic Debris—Continued

As the alien myth emerged in the late 1980s, the crashed saucer stories continued to expand and be embellished. In 1987, William S. Steinmen and Wendelle C. Stevens published *UFO Crash at Aztec*. It was an expanded version of Scully's tale. One anonymous "witness" described seeing the saucer hitting a cliff. Another person said, "If news of this vehicle's water driven engine got out to the whole scientific community, that would be the end of the oil industry."

One of the book's sources was Dr. Robert Sarbacher, a one-time consultant to the Research and Development Board. In September 1950, he had talked with Wilber Smith, a Canadian scientist and UFO researcher. Sarbacher told him that a small group under Vannever Bush was then investigating UFOs. He also told Smith that Scully's book was "substantially correct." Sarbacher added that UFOs were "classified two points higher than the H-bomb. In fact it is the most highly classified subject in the U.S. government at the present time."

In a 1983 letter to William Steinman, Sarbacher added, "Certain materials reported to have come from flying saucer crashes were extremely light and very tough." The aliens, Sarbacher understood, were of "very light weight. . . . I got the impression these 'aliens' were constructed like certain insects." He noted, however, "I had no association with any of the people involved in the recovery and have no knowledge regarding the dates of the recoveries."[51]

Despite such authoritative-sounding statements, the Aztec "crash" remains a hoax by two con men. Additional research was done, ironically by Moore, in the early 1980s. He discovered Silas M. Newton had been in trouble with the law as early as 1928. Leo GeBauer had been investigated for violation of the White Slave Traffic Act, was a Nazi sympathizer, and operated under at least eleven aliases.[52] Newton's later activities were equally dubious. Newton was charged (but later acquitted) in 1959 with selling $125,000 in worthless securities in a uranium mine.[53] As late as 1970, he was under indictment on two counts of grand theft. At the time of his death, in Los Angeles at age 83, in December 1972, there were some 140 civil suits pending against him. These totaled $1,350,000 and charged him with salting mines and pumping oil into wells to deceive investors. Newton's estate totaled $16,000. GeBauer died, also in poverty, in Colorado in late 1982.[54]

The Roswell Incident also grew during the 1980s. Some 300 witnesses came forward to claim they had seen or heard something about the recovery. Yet, despite all the added "information," what really happened at Roswell became less clear. Berlitz and Moore's original 1980 version said the UFO was struck by lightning over Mac Brazel's ranch, creating the debris field, then crashed some 150 miles away. In their 1991 book, *UFO Crash at Roswell*, Kevin D. Randle and Donald R. Schmitt claimed the UFO came down only a few miles from the debris Brazel found. The saucer was discovered by aerial reconnaissance and, on July 8, 1947, the Army sealed off the whole area. The saucer and the bodies of four dead aliens were recovered.[55] This was very much like the events described in the MJ-12 document.

In contrast, Stanton Friedman and Don Berliner's 1992 book, *Crash at Corona: The U.S. Military Retrieval and Cover-Up of a UFO*, claims that *two* saucers crashed due to a midair collision. One of the UFOs disintegrated over the Brazel's ranch, leaving four dead aliens. The second UFO flew on to the Plains of San Augustin where it crashed. Three of the aliens were killed while one survived. This was directly counter to the MJ-12 documents which said nothing about a second saucer or a surviving alien. Ironically, Friedman was the most outspoken defender of the MJ-12 documents.[56] The differing versions of the Roswell Incident pitted Moore vs. Randle/Schmitt vs. Friedman/Berliner, and CUFOS vs. MU-FON.[57]

In a normal historical problem, the more information one has, the clearer the chain of events becomes. Not so with Roswell; there the picture becomes ever more clouded and confused. One writer noted, "Like all good stories, Roswell expands to accommodate whatever you bring to it. That's the nature of myths and legends—they're detailed enough to seem real, yet fuzzy enough to stay always just beyond the reach of objective proof. . . . Roswell grows a little with each retelling.[58]

Aurora

In the late 1980s, reports began to circulate of an aircraft flying at high altitude and high speeds above the Mojave Desert in the early morning hours. The aircraft produced a "pulsing" sound and a "linked-sausage-shaped smoke trail" in flight. On takeoff, it was said to make "a sound like the sky ripping." It was speculated this was the "Aurora" aircraft—capable of mach 5–8 and 250,000 feet.[59]

A series of articles on the Aurora began to appear in the technical press starting in December 1989. It was described as an unmanned, elongated, diamond-shaped vehicle about 110 feet long and 60 feet wide. Its surface was covered with black ceramic tiles. The tiles were described as having a "scorched, heat-streaked appearance," and coated with "a crystalline patina" due to prolonged exposure to high temperatures. It was claimed, "A burnt-carbon odor emanates from the surface." The tiles on the rear section were pockmarked from the external-burning engine. Fuel was sprayed across the rear fuselage and ignited. The shape of the rear fuselage acted like a rocket nozzle to produce thrust. One source called this an "impulse motor." The Aurora carried 121 nuclear warheads in individual ports on the vehicle's underside.[60,61] Later articles claimed that Aurora looked like the XB-70 bomber. Still later, its shape changed to a large delta.

The nontechnical press began to pay attention to Aurora in 1992. The *Los Angeles Times* noted that on five occasions between June 1991 and April 1992, Los Angeles residents reported brief rumbles. They were not from an earthquake, but rather from sonic booms. All five rumbles occurred at 7:00 A.M. on Thursdays.[62] *Time* magazine's "Grapevine" reported Aurora was being flown out of a Royal Air Force base at Machrihanish, Scotland. It claimed the plane was code-named "Senior Citizen."[63]

Despite such authoritative-sounding claims, most of the "details" about Aurora—what it looked like and even what it smelled like—had their origins with people who believed in the secret bases and that black aircraft like Aurora were actually "reverse engineered" from crashed saucers. As for Aurora itself—a senior government official told the author that when the articles started to appear, they caused a major uproar within the government. An investigation was made at a high level, and despite diligent checking, no evidence of its existence was found. He officially stated that no such aircraft (as described in the articles) had been developed or flown.[64]

Aliens among Us

The final step in the development of the alien myth was the emergence of "The Whistleblowers." This was a group of people who claimed to have secret knowledge of the aliens. The first of these "whistleblowers" was John Lear. On December 29, 1987, he issued a statement claiming the "horrible truth" was that the U.S. government had sold out the human race to the evil EBEs. During 1969–1971, he said, MJ-12 and the aliens agreed that abductions and mutes would be covered up in exchange for alien technology. MJ-12 would be given a list of abductees. The secret base was set up at Groom Lake in 1972–1974.

But, Lear claimed, the aliens suffered from a genetic disorder which caused their digestive systems to fail. To survive, they used "an enzyme or hormonal secretion" obtained from both human and animal mutes. This was mixed with hydrogen peroxide and spread on the aliens' skin. Lear further claimed that "it became obvious that some, not all, but some of the nation's missing children had been used for secretions and other parts required by the aliens." Lear also claimed that "cows and humans are genetically similar. In the event of a national disaster, cow's blood can be used by humans."

Lear said that between 1979 and 1983, MJ-12 began to realize they had made a terrible error in dealing with the aliens. The first indication was "the Dulce massacre" in 1979, when sixty-six Special Forces soldiers were killed in a failed attempt to rescue humans held in the Dulce base. This "Grand Deception" by the aliens sent MJ-12 "into utter confusion and panic." It was decided, Lear claimed, that development of a weapon to destroy the aliens would be continued under the guise of the Strategic Defense Initiative, "which had nothing whatsoever to do with a defense for inbound Russian nuclear missiles." Lear concluded, "Is the more sinister and most probable situation that the invasion is essentially complete and it is all over but the screaming?"[65]

Lear's claims were a mixture of the tales told by Bennewitz and Doty, combined with an overwhelming sense of hopelessness and helplessness. There was no hope of survival; in an interview, Lear said, "They're going to march us just exactly like the Holocaust."[66]

It was Lear who introduced the next of the whistleblowers. In July 1988, Robert Lazar, who said he was a scientist working in New Mexico, contacted Lear, who gave him a "five-hour lecture." Over the next several months, they corresponded. In late September, Lazar called Lear and said he had independently verified Lear's information, using a classified library.[67]

Lear then introduced Lazar to George Knapp, a reporter with Las Vegas station KLAS-TV. On November 10, 1989, the station began a series of reports on Area 51, based on Lazar's stories. Lazar said he had been shown classified reports on UFOs, photographs and autopsy reports on the aliens, and photos of saucers. He was told the project was called "Majestic" and was run by the Navy. Lazar said there were nine saucers at "S-4." He said one had a large hole in the top and bottom, as if it had been hit by a four- or five-inch shell. Lazar said he realized they were from outer space when he looked inside and saw small chairs. Lazar saw them being test flown on several occasions. The UFO's underside glowed with a blue light and hissed. After lift-off, it became silent. The saucers were powered by an antimatter reactor which created an antigravity field. The reactor was powered by "Element 115."[68] Security at S-4 was described as oppressive—Lazar said he was hit in the chest, screamed at, and had M-16s pointed at him.[69]

Lazar's story had some holes—he underwent lie detector tests, but the results were inconclusive. He claimed to have vivid recollections about the alien technology, but had forgotten large blocks of time. Lazar's educational background could not be confirmed, and he was not a member of the American Physical Society or the American Nuclear Society. More serious, in August 1990, Lazar pleaded guilty to one count of pandering (a felony) and was placed on three years' probation.[70]

Milton William Cooper

The alien myth reached its final form through another of Lear's proteges—Milton William Cooper. In early 1989, Cooper and Lear issued an "Indictment" of the U.S. government, charging it "with murder and treason against the people and Constitution of these United States," due to the secret alien treaty. They accused the president, vice president, CIA director, NSA director, certain cabinet members, MJ-12 members, the

Jason Society, the directors of the Senior Interagency Group, the president's national security adviser, and others, going back to 1953, with being part of this "joint government and alien conspiracy." They demanded the government

> cease aiding and abetting and concealing this Alien Nation which exists within our borders. We charge the government to cease all operations, projects, treaties, and any other involvement with this Alien Nation. We charge the government to order this Alien Nation and all of its members to leave the United States and this Earth immediately, now and for all time, by June 1, 1989, and we charge the government to enforce this order. We further charge the government to make a complete disclosure of its alien involvement to the American people prior to April 30, 1989 and to make a full accounting for its actions. We charge the Congress to order this to be done and we charge the Congress to enforce this order.

If the U.S. government ignored their charges, Lear and Cooper said,

> we hereby swear upon the Constitution that we will not rest until these crimes are exposed to the American people. We swear on the Constitution that all guilty parties shall be brought to justice. We swear that we will persist until our death to accomplish these ends in the name of humanity, the Constitution of these United States of America, and in the name of all true patriots who have gone before us, we do so swear.[71]

Cooper defined the alien myth in his "The Secret Government: The Origin, Identity, and Purpose of MJ-12," dated May 23, 1989. Cooper claimed that some twenty-seven UFO crashes occurred between 1947 and 1953. A total of ninety-one alien bodies and five live aliens were recovered. Two UFOs were recovered near Aztec, New Mexico, in 1948. Aboard the saucers was a large number of human body parts. A classification above Top Secret was placed on flying saucer information. When Secretary of Defense James Forrestal began to talk about "the alien problem," he was forced to resign, was admitted to Bethesda Naval Hospital under the pretext of a mental breakdown, and was then murdered by CIA agents.

President Truman kept all U.S. allies, including the Soviet Union, informed, and plans were made to defend the Earth against alien attack. Because of the extreme difficulty of keeping these efforts secret, Cooper claimed a "secret society" called the "Bilderburgers" was set up in Geneva, Switzerland. The Bilderburgers, Cooper claimed, eventually became a secret world government, "that now controls everything."

In 1953, Eisenhower became president. To cope with the alien problem, Eisenhower asked Nelson Rockefeller to plan a secret organization.

According to Cooper, asking for Rockefeller's help was "the biggest mistake Eisenhower ever made for the future of the United States and most probably all of humanity." Within a year the MJ-12 group was set up. (Cooper said "MJ" stood for "Majority.") The membership was split between the government and the Council on Foreign Relations. MJ-12 was staffed with people having backgrounds not only in the Council on Foreign Relations, but also the Jason Society (a group of elite scientists), members of the secret "Skull and Bones" and "Scroll and Key" societies of Yale and Harvard, and the Trilateral Commission (Cooper claimed the name of the latter came from the alien's "Trilateral" flag).

In 1953, Cooper claimed that astronomers detected large objects heading toward the Earth. They subsequently went into a very high orbit above the Earth. At the same time, a race of blond humanlike aliens, the Nordics, contacted the government to warn against the aliens in the huge orbiting spaceships. The Nordics also warned that mankind was on the road to self-destruction. Humans must learn to live in harmony and stop polluting the Earth. They offered to help with mankind's spiritual development, but at the price of destroying all nuclear weapons. The offer was rejected.

Later, in 1954, Cooper claimed that a race known as the "Large-nosed Grays" landed at Holloman AFB. They stated they had come from a planet of the red giant star Betelgeuse. Their world was dying and they needed a new home. A second landing was made at Edwards AFB, with Eisenhower in attendance. He and the Large-nosed Grays signed a treaty for bases and technology exchanges. (Cooper also talked about two other kinds of aliens—the Grays, who work for the Large-nosed Grays, and a red-haired humanlike type called the "Orange.")

By 1955, Cooper said it was clear the aliens were cheating on the treaty—human and animal mutilations were being done to provide the aliens with the glandular secretions, enzymes, blood, and genetic experiments they needed to survive. MJ-12 also discovered that not all abductions/contacts were being reported, and not all abductees were returned. It was also learned that the Large-nosed Grays had created the human race and had long manipulated it through religion, secret societies, witchcraft, satanism, magic, and the occult. MJ-12 decided to continue diplomatic relations with the aliens until the Earth was able to develop weapons able to destroy them. Overtures were made to the Soviet Union to join forces to save humanity.

Two weapons were developed. The first was Project Joshua—a low-frequency sonic cannon meant to destroy the saucers. The other was

Project Excalibur—a missile carrying a 1-megaton nuclear warhead which could penetrate 1,000 meters of hard-packed soil to destroy the alien bases.

By 1957, a new problem appeared, according to Cooper. A study indicated that by the year 2000, the Earth would no longer be able to support human life owing to overpopulation and pollution. The Jason Society developed three plans. "Alternative 1" envisioned use of nuclear explosions to blow holes in the stratosphere to allow the heat and pollution to escape into space. This was rejected as not being likely to work. "Alternative 2" proposed the building of vast underground cities to house selected survivors. The rest of humanity would be left to fend for itself. "Alternative 3" was to use the alien technology to establish colonies on the Moon and Mars. All three alternatives envisioned using birth control, sterilization, and deadly microbes to slow the growth of the Earth's population. Cooper claimed that AIDS was one part of this effort. The joint U.S./Soviet leadership decided to begin work on Alternatives 2 and 3.

Cooper said there were areas on the Moon in which plants grow and change with the seasons. The Moon also has an atmosphere dense enough for humans to survive with only an oxygen tank. Clouds also form in the Moon's atmosphere. By the time President Kennedy announced the goal of landing a man on the Moon, a joint alien/U.S./Soviet Moon base already existed. On May 22, 1962, Cooper claimed, a space probe landed on Mars and confirmed the planet could support life. Work on the Mars base began soon after. By the late 1980s, whole cities existed on Mars. The "official" space program was nothing more than a cover story. The Aurora was used to go into orbit, while alien-supplied UFOs carried humans to the Moon, Mars, Venus, and other planets.

All this cost money, and MJ-12 used several sources. One was to corner the illegal drug market. "The ruling powers," Cooper claimed, approached an oil company president named George Bush to help with this effort. Cooper claimed that "the CIA now controls all the worlds [sic] illegal drug markets." Another source was "a public charade of antagonism" between the U.S. and the USSR, "when in fact we are the closest allies." The money appropriated for national defense was secretly diverted to MJ-12.

To keep all these secrets, MJ-12 ordered the murder of President Kennedy when he threatened to reveal the selling of drugs and the alien presence on Earth. Cooper claimed that Kennedy's Secret Service driver turned around and shot him. All witnesses near enough to see the killing were themselves murdered within two years. MJ-12 also ordered President Nixon to resign over the Watergate scandal. When he refused, a military coup was launched to force him out. The Warren Commission, Rockefeller Commission and the Church hearings into CIA misconduct, as well as the Iran-Contra hearings, were nothing more than efforts to cover up the MJ-12 power structure.[72]

"Wild Ravings"

Cooper claimed he learned all this while in the Navy during 1970–1973. In fact, one can trace the various elements back to Bennewitz and Doty. Examples of this include the alien treaty, the secret base(s), the firefight at Dulce (which Cooper said took place in 1969, but still with sixty-six casualties), and the landing at Holloman AFB. Many UFOlogists flatly rejected the Lear/Lazar/Cooper stories. Moseley called them "wild ravings," while CUFOS suggested they represented another kind of contactee story. Rather than meeting aliens, they claimed to have seen secret documents describing the aliens.[73] Cooper's claim that the Moon has an atmosphere and plant life is straight out of Adamski. The "Alternative 3" story that was the cornerstone of Cooper's conspiracy theories was a BBC "April Fools" documentary. Some UFOlogists, however, took it seriously.

Jacques Vallee found it absurd that a civilization billions of years ahead of ours was unable to synthesize an enzyme. Moreover, Chicago slaughterhouses would be more than pleased to sell cattle organs. Lear's claim that cattle blood could be used in human transfusions was also ridiculous—a person would die within minutes from immunological shock. When he was told the alien base at Dulce was "the size of Manhattan," Vallee asked, "Who takes out the garbage?" (A better question would be "Where's the Dirt?") Even underground, a base that big could not be hidden—it would produce waste, require water, and have a massive heat output.

Yet, despite such absurdities, Cooper and the others developed a devoted following. Vallee noted they were "some of the best horror stories I had heard since my childhood days when my mother read me *Grimm's Fairy-Tales*."[74] But it was more than that. The alien myth is intensely political, with something for every extremist—Ultra-Right, Ultra-Left, and Nihilist.

On the Ultra-Right, there are the references to the "Constitution" and "true patriots." Cooper claimed MJ-12 was secretly undermining American society with drugs and gun control laws. MJ-12 was also planning to impose martial law and suspend the Constitution. The "secret alien army of implanted humans" (one in forty of the population) and "all dissidents" would be rounded up and sent off to concentration camps. These one-mile-square camps had already been built and the operation had already been rehearsed in 1984 under the code name "REX-84." Just substitute "Communist Conspiracy" for "MJ-12" and one has the standard Ultra-Right claims of the 1950s.

There are other, more obvious signs; Cooper said the Council on Foreign Relations and the Trilateral Commission "not only control but own this country." This includes "major foundations," "all of the major media and publishing interests," "all the major corporations," "the upper echelons of the government," and of course, "the largest banks." The Council on Foreign Relations, and its offshoots in each country, Cooper claimed, are controlled through the Bilderburgers. It, in turn, controls a vast network of banks and holding companies with Jewish-sounding names. His drawings of the "Large-nosed Grays" were compared to racist stereotypes of Jews in Nazi posters. In his book *Behold a Pale Horse,* Cooper includes the text of the Protocols of the Elders of Zion, a long-exposed anti-Semitic forgery.[75,76]

In 1991–1992, Cooper's claims began to shift. The UFO material was dropped; he now claimed it was a hoax in order to create an "external threat." This would be used to set up a World Dictatorship under the U.N. (another long-time Ultra-Right bogeyman). Within two years, a "New World Order" would be set up and U.S. sovereignty would be lost. The "saucer technology" was actually based on captured Nazi saucers.[77]

There were also religious aspects—Cooper compared the Nordic aliens to angels and the Grays to demons. About the alien treaty, he said, "After all, the Bible talks about a pact with the Devil in the last days, after Israel is reinstated. Leading to Armageddon."[78]

At the same time, there are elements of the alien myth to appeal to the extremist Ultra-Left. The idea the CIA is involved with drug sales is a popular one on the Ultra-Left. The belief that the world is really run by a small group of the rich and powerful is central to Ultra-Leftist ideology. Cooper's claim that the government is planning to round up "Dissidents" and ship them off to concentration camps is enough to send a thrill of pleasure through the heart of any Ultra-Leftist. If one believes that the U.S. government is evil, it is not that great a leap to believe it is allied with the aliens to enslave the world. The idea that modern weapons technology is "alien" or "nonhuman," that it came from outside, would have appeal to those who came of age during the sixties. Indeed, several UFOlogists who expressed support for the alien myth had backgrounds as "Peace Activists."

It is also a central idea of the Ultra-Left that a right-wing conspiracy was behind the assassination of President Kennedy. Cooper's list of MJ-12 members—Nelson Rockefeller, the Council on Foreign Relations, and the "Eastern Establishment"—are also bogeymen of the Ultra-Left. (Extremes do tend to meet.) The effect is to create a link between UFOs and conspiracy theories. *UFO* magazine carried an article which suggested possible "links" between the "October Surprise," the Iran-Contra arms deal, the BCCI bank scandal, the Lockerbie airliner bombing, Area 51, and the antigravity theories of T. Townsend Brown, NICAP's original founder. It was claimed there is a "war" between two elements of the intelligence community—a CIA group called "Aquarius" (around a "power center" called MJ-12) and a Naval group called "COM-12," which was trying to preserve constitutional government. The source was in jail awaiting trial on drug charges.[79]

Finally, the idea that EVERYTHING—the origins of the human race, the structure of the U.S. government, the Cold War, the arms race, and conditions on other planets—was a lie would appeal to an increasingly nihilistic mood.

Closing the Circle

One common thread running through each telling of the alien myth is the underground bases. The number and size of these bases have grown over time. Besides Dulce and Groom Lake, other sites include Albuquerque, Santa Fe, Taos, Sunspot, and Roswell, New Mexico; Colorado Springs, Colorado; Catalina Island, Mount Shasta, the Nevada nuclear test site, and the Tejon Ranch area near Edwards AFB.[80,81] These bases are described as underground cities, with millions of aliens. It has been implied that their population is a significant percentage of the official population of the U.S.

These secret bases give the alien myth its sense of helplessness and terror. "They" are here, millions of "them," waiting in the bases. It is akin to an all-powerful occupying army, yet one that cannot be seen or heard.

The underground bases relate to many classic myths, such as the

Labyrinth—the prison for a monstrous human/"alien" hybrid. Another is Hell—a subterranean place where strange, misshapen beings (aliens) plot the downfall of mankind. These beings have both supernatural powers (superior technology) and willing human assistance (the government). These beings offer great power (the technological exchange) but the reward for helping them is eternal damnation (the "Grand Deception"). These beings also perform cruel acts against their helpless victims (mutes, abductions, and the genetic experiments). Because this is a technological mystery religion, the "sacred places" are known by code names—words of power—MJ-12, Area 51, and S-4.

Real examples of underground bases, such as NORAD headquarters inside Cheyenne Mountain, presidential nuclear bunkers, and underground nuclear testing in Nevada (near Area 51) create a link between secret power and nuclear weapons. Add that the alien base is located at a place called "Dreamland," and it all creates powerful images that speak to the fears of many people.

There are also the images of the underground bases of Science Fiction—*Fantastic Voyage, Forbidden Planet, Wargames, The Andromeda Strain*, and *Fail Safe*. In *The Time Tunnel*, there was the stunning image of a car driving toward the viewer, then suddenly diving into the ground, where the "billion dollar time machine" is hidden.

●　　●　　●

It is also the underground bases that bring the circle to a close. After five decades, after a long, strange journey through this modern mythology, we find ourselves where we began—with the Deros in their underground world of madness, pain and fear.

The Alien Myth 1987–1993

Disk-shaped alien spaceships have been seen for thousands of years. These UFOs have fantastic maneuverability and speed beyond those of earthly aircraft. They have landed, leaving pad prints, causing blackouts, and stopping cars. They have crashed, leaving debris and both live and dead aliens.

The aliens, called the "Grays," are described as short, with gray skin, large bald heads, and thin, elongated arms, legs and bodies. They are physically weak and sickly, and are suffering from genetic disorders.

To survive, the Grays abduct humans, remove sperm and ova, and combine them with their own genetic material in order to produce alien/human hybrids. The abducted humans have implants placed in their noses to allow the aliens to control them. There are millions of such abductees. They have no knowledge of what was done to them as their memories have been erased. The Grays have also mutilated cattle and humans as a source of the enzyme they need for food.

MJ-12 has made a pact with the Grays. The Grays agree to provide technology, which has been used to build such advanced weapons as the B-2, F-117, and Aurora. In exchange MJ-12 agreed to build huge underground bases. The Grays were also allowed to conduct mutes and abductions. The money needed for the alien projects is provided through the sale of drugs by the CIA and George Bush.

Through MJ-12, the Council on Foreign Relations, the Trilateral Commission, the Bilderburgers, and international bankers have become a "Secret Government" controlling every aspect of society, policy, and economics.

To maintain this, the Ruling Powers have used murder to remove anyone who stood in their way. This includes President Kennedy and assassination witnesses.

The Ruling Powers, in league with the Grays, are planning to set up a one-world dictatorship, under the guise of a "New World Order." Abductees and others will be rounded up and forced into concentration camps.

The Real Aliens

> "What is the meaning of it, Watson?" said Holmes solemnly as he laid down the paper. "What object is served by this circle of misery and violence and fear?"
>
> —*The Adventure of the Cardboard Box*

To understand both the flying saucer and alien myths, one must consider the times in which they originated. Both the years 1947–1952 and 1987–1992 were marked by what has been called a "paranoid style" in politics, in which debate is replaced by "suspiciousness and heated exaggeration." Such times are marked by feelings of a society under seige by outside forces ("alien" forces). Events seem to be spinning out of control, and there is a deep suspicion as to who is to blame. It has been said that paranoia is the last refuge of hope. One is not the helpless victim of titanic, impersonal events—there is a reason, someone is to blame. More importantly, because someone is manipulating events, it is possible to change them.

One result is "savior politics" where people turn to an "outsider," transforming an excess of disgust with the system into an emotional binge of enthusiasm for a "man on horseback" who will set everything right. The years 1947–1952 was such a time. Senator Joe McCarthy, General Douglas MacArthur, and even Eisenhower were such outsiders. Forty years later, it was again a time of paranoid politics. This time the political saviors were outsiders like Oliver North and Ross Perot.[1,2]

Both Keyhoe and Adamski could also be seen as such "outsiders," intent on setting things right. Keyhoe said the Air Force was lying about flying saucers. What Keyhoe was also saying was that if believers followed him, he would compel the Air Force to admit the cover-up. Keyhoe would justify their faith in the flying saucer myth. Adamski said he had talked with alien beings from utopian planets. They had none of the problems that beset America in the early 1950s. Adamski said he had been given the knowledge to make Earth just such a utopian planet, if they followed him.

Like Keyhoe and Adamski, the "prophets" of the alien myth were outsiders. Lazar claimed to have "escaped" from the evil place called Dreamland with the secret of the saucers. Cooper said he had seen the truth in classified documents, and was telling the world, even at the risk of his life.

Old Secrets

Because the flying saucer myth was defined at a time of suspicion and paranoia, it is frozen in the attitudes of that era. For the flying saucer myth, it will always be January 1950. One example of this is the key idea of a cover-up. Keyhoe said in 1950 that the Air Force knew flying saucers were alien spaceships. Ever since then, this has been an article of faith, learned by rote.

As support for this idea of a complete, seamless cover-up, believers sometimes point to a quote by Ruppelt. He noted that in July 1947 the "security lid was down tight." Any inquiries "got the same treatment that you would get today [1956] if you inquired about the number of thermonuclear weapons stock-piled in the U.S.'s atomic arsenal."[3] Believers have argued that this level of security has been maintained all these decades.

The first H-bombs in the U.S. stockpile were five EC-14 weapons in February 1954. Between April and September 1954, five EC-17 and ten EC-24 H-bombs were added. These weapons were preproduction prototypes, lacking drogue parachutes and having arming and fusing systems that were simplified to the point of being dangerous to the bomber crews. All twenty EC (for "Emergency Capability") weapons were removed from the stockpile in October and November 1954. Deliveries of the 200 MK-17s and 105 MK-24s began in October 1954. In April 1955, the first of some 1,200 MK-15 H-bombs was delivered. This was followed in December 1955 by the first of 275 MK-21 bombs.[4,5]

In 1956, what you have just read was Top Secret. Had it been published in 1956, it would have represented a major security breach. But that was then, and this is now. The passage of time means this information is no longer worth keeping classified. Secrets, like everything else, get "old." Documents and information related to such (once) Top Secret projects as the Verona decoding of KGB cables, reconnaissance balloons, the U-2 overflights, the SR-71, and reconnaissance satellites have long been declassified.[6–10] Some specific details are still classified, yet there can be no doubt of the existence of these projects. Were a UFO cover-up real, not merely specific details but even its existence have been kept secret for nearly five decades.

In the late 1970s, UFOlogists filed Freedom of Information Act requests against the CIA, DIA, FBI, and NSA for classified UFO documents. Most of the documents were declassified, yet some documents were withheld on national security grounds. The NSA, for instance, withheld 156 documents. The UFOlogists filed an appeal, which went to the U.S. Supreme Court. The NSA gave its reasons in a Top Secret (Codeword) court petition. The Supreme Court agreed and the documents were withheld. When the NSA petition was declassified, most of the text was blacked out. UFOlogists have pointed to this as "evidence" the NSA is covering-up "proof" of UFOs. Yet, like the Blue Book files in the 1950s, they have not seen the documents.

One UFOlogist who had seen the documents was Tom Deuley. At the time of the FOIA request, he was an NSA employee. Because of his interest in UFOs, he was one of those selected to review the NSA's UFO documents. He later stated:

> I believe I saw or held copies of the large majority of the documents [that were] withheld in the FOIA suit. Though there may have been exceptions among the documents I did not see, none of the documents I was aware of had any information of scientific value. . . . I did not see any indication of official NSA interest in [UFOs]. . . . I did not see any exchange of material indicating any form of follow-up activities. . . . I did not see any indication of real involvement other than the existence of the documents themselves.[11]

There is a more subtle aspect—the NSA withheld 156 documents. Yet, in 1992, the U.S. government released 1.3 *million* documents on allegations that U.S. POWs are still being held in Vietnam. Moore claimed that the U.S. recovered a crashed UFO and several alien bodies in July 1947. Friedman claimed that two UFOs, seven bodies, and one live alien were recovered. The effort to analyze such a find would involve tens of thousands of people and billions of dollars. And all this produced was 156 documents?

UFO Flaps and Social Factors

One element in the development of the flying saucer myth was the UFO flaps. These occurred in 1947, 1952, 1957, 1965–1967, and 1973. Believers have always argued that such flaps are independent of social factors, the implication being they were outside the Earth.

A study by Otto Billig indicated that there was, in fact, a specific relationship. It was vague, poorly defined crises which caused the flaps. When the crisis was clearly defined, such as during the 1962 Cuban Missile Crisis, the number of sightings went down. The year 1947 saw the developing Cold War and fears of communist subversion. The Great Flap of 1952 marked the Cold War's frozen depths, the stalemated Korean War, development of the H-bomb, and the McCarthy era. The 1957 flap followed Little Rock and the launch of Sputnik. The Sixties flap was a time of civil disorder on college campuses and the inner city, and the internal conflicts caused by the Vietnam War. Finally, the 1973 flap saw the Watergate scandal and the resulting breakdown of faith in government. In each case, the threat was what might happen, not what was happening. Another example of this was presidential election years. Between 1952 and 1964, each election year saw an upsurge of UFO reports during the summer and early fall. This upsurge was much greater than the usual summer upturn. Presidential campaigns create just such ill-defined fears.

This pattern also extended to the pre-Arnold flaps. The 1890s were a turbulent period in U.S. history. An economic depression began in 1893 and continued for the next four years. Working men felt threatened both by foreign immigrants and the "Plutocrats." The Populist Party wanted to ban industrial development and return to a lost, mythical agrarian Eden. The Populists also warned of foreign Anarchists and a tyranny of the rich few. It was in 1896–1897, with the depression at its height, that the "Mysterious Airships" flap occurred. In popular novels, such as Populist Ignatius Donnelly's *Caesar's Column,* the airship was a technological engine of destruction, raining poison gas bombs on a terrorized population.

This pattern extends back through the Middle Ages and back to Biblical times. Ezekiel's Wheel is often described by believers as a UFO. What is left out is the social situation of 592 B.C.—the people of Israel had been defeated, the Babylonians had taken Jerusalem and the Israelites had been reduced to slavery. Their society was spiritually and politically bankrupt. Then, as now, people looked to the skies, seeking salvation and escape from dark and threatening forces.[12]

Another question then comes to mind—why have there been no more UFO flaps since 1973? Certainly there have been ill-defined crises since then—the drift of the Carter administration, fears of an imminent nuclear war in the early and mid-1980s, the Iran-Contra scandal, the events leading up to the Gulf War, and five presidential elections.

One possibility is that the flying saucer myth itself has changed. In the 1970s and 1980s, the emphasis shifted to abductions, crashed saucers, and mutes. "Lights in the sky" sightings, which made up the bulk of UFO reports, were no longer seen as important. Popular culture also reflected this change—flying saucer movies, like *Close Encounters of the Third Kind,* were replaced, in the 1980s, by films with "alien among us" themes. These included *Strange Invaders, The Hidden, They Live,* and *Alien Nation.*

Alien Nation

At first glance, one would have to be truly "alienated" to believe in secret bases and a treaty between the U.S. government and the Grays. In reality, there are segments of American society in which such beliefs are middle-of-the-road. The late 1980s and early 1990s saw an increasingly brittle, angry, and conspiratorial world view. One book described how "movies and television have propagated images and themes that support militarism, imperialism, racism, sexism, authoritarianism, and other undemocratic values."[13] A historian claimed that cartographers had intentionally used the Mercator map to foster an imperialistic attitude toward the third world.[14] Several academics wrote books and articles supporting the idea that Korean Airlines flight 007 was on a spy mission when it was shot down by the Soviets in September 1983.[15] "Afrocentrism" claims that Africa was the actual source of Western mathematics, biology, architecture, astronomy, and medicine. These achievements were stolen by Ancient Greece and covered up by a conspiracy that has continued ever since. Western culture, freedom, and individual liberty is nothing more than a conspiracy by dead white males to maintain their power and privileges.[16,17]

Part of this attitude is a widespread rejection of science, technology, and even the process of analytical thinking. Radical feminists refer to scientific inquiry as "the rape of nature." They declare, "Mind was male. Nature was female, and knowledge was created as an act of aggression—a passive nature had to be interrogated, unclothed, penetrated, and compelled by man to reveal her secrets." Leonard Jeffries, one of the Afrocentrists, praised the destruction of Space Shuttle *Challenger* because it would deter whites from "spreading their filth throughout the universe."[18] Such attitudes are found off campus as well. An aide to a San Diego city councilman said the 200-inch telescope on Mount Palomar "would make a good restaurant. . . . I would say, 'Nice restaurant, Palomar under the stars'."[19]

The alien myth both reflects and is intertwined with this atmosphere. It is based on a belief that government and society are manipulated by evil forces—in this case, the Grays rather than a fascist military-industrial complex. Both UFO skeptics and believers are seen as tools of this conspiracy. The alien myth is nihilistic, and rests not on independent inquiry, but on the revealed truth of the whistleblower. It is not considered polite to point out the contradictions in the stories. One does not ask who takes out the garbage at Dulce.

One example of the interweaving of the alien myth and extremist political beliefs is the idea that AIDS is a man-made "genocide weapon" against blacks. The original appearance of a race-specific biological weapon was a part of the mute myth and the Project Jerome story. This was in the mid 1970s, before the discovery of AIDS. Around 1980, the Soviets began to claim the U.S. had developed some kind of "ethnic weapon" that killed only nonwhites.[20] In 1983, the Soviets began spreading the story that AIDS was developed in a Pentagon lab.[21] Between 1985 and 1987, the Nation of Islam began to claim that Jewish doctors were infecting black infants with AIDS and were plotting to "rule the world."[22]

In 1989, with the emergence of the alien myth, there was a flurry of articles on AIDS in UFO publications. Cooper claimed the joint U.S.-Soviet leadership created AIDS to eliminate undesirable elements. *Stigmata* published an article saying AIDS was "man-made."[23] *Flying Saucer Review* carried an article suggesting AIDS was an "Alien Induced Disease Syndrome," created by the Grays, through the blood and tissue taken during cattle mutilations and the sperm and ova taken during the abductions. The intent was to kill off the human race. The magazine's editor added that AIDS might be an effort by "our owners" to cull the "herds" of "any undesirable taints."[24] In 1992, a black activist, who believed the stories of AIDS as a genocide weapon, made an unintentionally ironic comment, "this is not outer-space thinking."[25]

The Future

What then is the future of the flying saucer and alien myths? In early 1992, several UFOlogists gave their differing views. Tal LeVesque said, "a high-tech Fascist takeover of the planet is underway." He predicted more "disinformation" and that death threats would force some UFOlogists out of the field. Gary Schultz, director of the Secret Saucer Base Expeditions, which makes trips to a site near Area 51 said, "1992 is apparently going to be a pivotal year for UFOlogy, and perhaps for other areas of interest and study. For example, it will be the year that the elitists intend to pull off the grand unification of Europe."

A number of UFOlogists talked "in hushed tones" about a plan by a "super oligarchy" to stage a landing as a precursor to an official announcement of the alien presences.

At the other end of the spectrum, Richard Hall, an ex-NICAP official, said, "My immediate reaction is 'how many times have we heard this before?' I can remember at least three and perhaps four times where somebody predicted that something was coming down in the next year or two or three, and that the government would open up, or something else definitive would happen, and of course it never did."

Barry Greenwood added, "I think the subject is in big trouble." Greenwood pointed out there was a general disinterest in the subject. Public belief in UFOs dropped below fifty percent—apparently the lowest point since the 1940s. Greenwood and others blamed the fixed, absolutist viewpoints that had come to dominate the field.[26] The wide range of views indicate how splintered the subject of UFOs has become.

Because the alien myth *is* so political, it is not surprising that it was incorporated into the belief system of extremist groups. On the Ultra-Right, *The Phoenix Liberator* carries "channeled" messages from "Commander Hatonn," supposedly an alien in orbit around the Earth. His communications are diatribes about Reaganomics, medieval history, and Jews. Hatonn claims America is controlled by a "secret government" run by "The Committee of 300" and "international bankers." The Holocaust never happened, according to Hatonn—the photos of mountains of bodies were actually of Germans interned after the war by Eisenhower and allowed to starve. The tattooed numbers were a fabrication, Hatonn says. Other "information" ranges from the Protocols of the Elders of Zion to the claim that the June 1908 Tunguski explosion in Siberia was actually a 30-megaton bomb built by a secret society of British and German scientists. Some of Hatonn's messages were taken directly from the writings of Cooper.[27]

Obviously, "Hatonn" is simply a device to give an alien authority to standard Ultra-Right claims. Parallels can be drawn with the contactees. Then the brotherhood platitudes came from the "space brothers," giving them an authority that Adamski, hamburger cook and handyman, lacked.

The Ultra-Left also makes use of UFOs. Louis Farrakhan, leader of the Nation of Islam, said in 1990 that he had been taken aboard a wheel-shaped UFO in 1985 which carried him up to the "Mother-Wheel." There he had advanced warning of the U.S. attack on Libya. He claimed, "During the confrontation in the Gulf of Sidra . . . a bright orange object was seen over the Mediterranean. The Wheel was, in fact, present and interfered with the highly sensitive equipment of the aircraft carrier, forcing it to return to Florida for repairs."[28]

The overriding factor in the future development of the flying saucer and alien myths is the impending turn of the century. Traditionally, these are times when there are popular expectations of great changes in society. As this is also the turn of the millennium, there are sure to be predictions of the end of the world and the Second Coming. Given the current attitudes, such thinking is sure to move the mythology in a darker direction.

One can project that the conspiracy theories will grow ever more grandiose, the aliens ever more demonic, and humans ever more powerless. One could also expect to see people claiming to be on a mission from God to save the world from the alien menace. Finally, as the belief system becomes more akin to outright paranoia, one might expect talk about a cosmic unity between humans, God, and the aliens, if only as an escape from the ever darker alien myth.[29]

The Mythological Experience

Each person goes through life attempting to make order of the events and phenomena around him. Humans need order, which comes both from knowledge and myth. The flying saucer and alien myths are really about how one makes order out of his world. The *idea* of disk-shaped alien spaceships becomes the symbol for hopes and fears about the world.

We watch the skies seeking meaning. In the end, what we find is ourselves.

Glossary

AAF	Army Air Force; Army Air Field
AFOSI	Air Force Office of Special Investigations
AISS	Air Intelligence Service Squadron
ANG	Air National Guard
ARDC	Air Research and Development Command
ATIC	Air Technical Intelligence Center, changed to Aerospace Technical Intelligence Center
APRO	Aerial Phenomena Research Organization
CAA	Civil Aeronautics Administration
CAUS	Citizens Against UFO Secrecy
CBI	Colorado Bureau of Investigation
CSI	Civilian Saucer Investigators
CSICOP	Committee for the Scientific Investigation of Claims of the Paranormal
CSM	Command and Service Module
CUFOS	Center for UFO Studies
DIA	Defense Intelligence Agency
EBE	Extraterrestrial Biological Entities
ELSS	Extravehicular Life Support System
FOIA	Freedom of Information Act
GSW	Ground Saucer Watch
IFSB	International Flying Saucer Bureau
LM	Lunar Module

MIB	Men in Black
MUFON	Midwest UFO Network; Mutual UFO Network
NAS	National Academy of Science
NASA	National Aeronautics and Space Administration
NCAR	National Center for Atmospheric Research
NICAP	National Investigations Committee on Aerial Phenomena
NORAD	North American Air Defense Command
NSA	National Security Agency
NSC	National Security Council
OCI	Office of Current Intelligence
ONR	Office of Naval Research
OSI	Office of Special Investigations
TID	Technical Intelligence Division
UFO	Unidentified Flying Object
UFOB	Unidentified Flying Object

Source Notes

In order to reduce the amount of note numbers in the text, paginations for consecutive citations from the same source are often ganged together and listed in the source note for the last citation in the series.

Chapter 1

1. Daniel Cohen, *The Great Airship Mystery* (New York: Dodd, Mead & Co., 1981).
2. Martin Gardner, *Fads and Fallacies in the Name of Science* (New York: Dover Publications, 1957), chaps. 4, 5.
3. Donald H. Menzel and Lyle G. Boyd, *The World of the Flying Saucers* (Garden City, N.Y.: Doubleday & Co., 1963), 1, 2.
4. Anders Liljegren, "Project 1946: The 'ghost rocket' documents released by the Swedish Defence Staff," *Flying Saucer Review* 32, no. 1 (1986): 23.
5. David Michael Jacobs, *The UFO Controversy in America* (New York: Signet Books, 1975), 30, 31.
6. Cohen, *Great Airship Mystery*, 178, 179. The term "Foo-Fighter" came from the comic strip "Smoky Stover." A running gag was the saying, "Where there's foo there's fire."
7. Philip J. Klass, *UFOs Explained* (New York: Random House, 1974), 90, 91. Among the B-29 crewmen who thought Venus was a Japanese night fighter was Edward J. Ruppelt—later head of Project Blue Book.
8. Liljegren, "Project 1946," 19–23.
9. Jacques Vallee, *Anatomy of a Phenomenon: UFOs in Space* (New York: Ballantine Books, 1974), 47–52.
10. Cohen, *Great Airship Mystery*, 181.
11. Liljegren, "Project 1946," 19–23.
12. Jacobs, *The UFO Controversy in America*, 31.
13. John A. Keel, "The man who invented flying saucers," *Whole Earth Review*, Fall 1986, 55, 56.

14. Ron Goulart, *Cheap Thrills: An Informal History of the Pulp Magazine* (New Rochelle, N.Y.: Arlington House, 1972), chap. 11.
15. Menzel and Boyd, *The World of the Flying Saucers*, 16, 17.
16. Brian Ash, *Who's Who in Science Fiction* (New York: Taplinger Publishing Co., 1976), 160.
17. Keel, "The man who invented flying saucers," 56.
18. Martin Gardner, *The New Age* (Buffalo: Prometheus Books, 1988), 219
19. Keel, "The man who invented flying saucers," 57.
20. Menzel and Boyd, *The World of the Flying Saucers*, 17, 18.
21. Gardner, *New Age*, 212, 220–222.
22. Richard S. Shaver, "I remember Lemuria!," *Amazing Stories*, March 1945, 12–70.
23. Richard S. Shaver, "Thought records of Lemuria," *Amazing Stories*, June 1945, 22.
24. Shaver, "I remember Lemuria," 28, 29.
25. Shaver, "Thought records of Lemuria," 16–52.
26. Keel, "The man who invented flying saucers," 57.
27. Alfred M. Freedman M.D., Harold I. Kaplan M.D., and Benjamin J. Sadock M.D., *Modern Synopsis of Psychiatry* (Baltimore: Williams and Wilkins Co., 1972), 235, 236, 791.
28. Keel, "The man who invented flying saucers," 57.
29. Menzel and Boyd, *The World of the Flying Saucers*, 19.
30. Keel, "The man who invented flying saucers," 58.
31. Menzel and Boyd, *The World of the Flying Saucers*, 20, 21.
32. Adam B. Ulam, *Expansion and Coexistence* (New York: Holt, Rinehart & Winston, 1974).
33. William Taubman, *Stalin's American Policy* (New York: W. W. Norton, 1982).
34. Walt Andrus, "Air Intelligence Report no. 100-203-79," *MUFON UFO Journal*, July 1985, 10.
35. *Project Blue Book*, Brad Steiger, ed., (New York: Ballantine Books, 1976), 34.

Chapter 2

1. *Project Blue Book*, 26–36.
2. John Spencer and Hilary Evans, eds., *Phenomenon—Forty Years of Flying Saucers* (New York: Avon Books, 1989), 29, 30.
3. Kenneth Arnold and Ray Palmer, *The Coming of the Saucers* (privately printed, 1952), 13, 14.
4. Edward J. Ruppelt, *The Report on Unidentified Flying Objects* (Garden City, N.Y.: Doubleday & Co., 1956), 19. This is actually a revised edition published in 1959 with three additional chapters. It still carried the 1956 copyright date.
5. Spencer and Evans, *Phenomenon*, 30, 31.
6. Ted Bloecher, *The Report on the UFO Wave of 1947* (privately printed, 1967), I-1, I-5, II-1, IV-3.
7. Ruppelt, *Report on Unidentified Flying Objects*, 19, 20.
8. *New York Times*, 4 July 1947, 26.
9. Arnold and Palmer, *Coming of the Saucers*, 16–19.
10. Spencer and Evans, *Phenomenon*, 31–35.
11. *Daily Current—Argus*, 9 July 1947, 2.
12. Ruppelt, *Report on Unidentified Flying Objects*, 21, 22.
13. Bloecher, *Report on UFO Wave of 1947*, III-4, III-5.
14. Ruppelt, *Report on Unidentified Flying Objects*, 22, 23.
15. Arnold and Palmer, *Coming of the Saucers*, 21–23.
16. Ruppelt, *Report on Unidentified Flying Objects*, 22–24.
17. Spencer and Evans, *Phenomenon*, 41.
18. Menzel and Boyd, *The World of the Flying Saucers*, 21, 22.
19. Arnold and Palmer, *Coming of the Saucers*, 25–52.

20. Ruppelt, *Report on Unidentified Flying Objects,* 24–27.

21. Arnold and Palmer, *Coming of the Saucers,* 66, 67.

22. Ruppelt, *Report on Unidentified Flying Objects,* 26, 27. Ruppelt deleted the names from the report and changed the names of Crisman, Dahl, Arnold, Smith and Palmer in his account.

23. Bloecher, *Report on UFO Wave of 1947,* I-16.

24. Edward U. Condon, *Scientific Study of Unidentified Flying Objects* (New York: Bantam Books, 1969), 894, 895.

25. Ruppelt, *Report on Unidentified Flying Objects,* 16, 28.

26. Condon, *Scientific Study of Unidentified Flying Objects,* 896.

27. Jacobs, *The UFO Controversy in America,* 270.

28. Ruppelt, *Report on Unidentified Flying Objects,* 29. The Air Force solutions for the sightings are as follows:

Date	Site/Witness	Solution
April 1947	Richmond VA Weather Bureau	Unidentified
June 24	Kenneth Arnold	Mirage
July 4	Portland, Oregon	Chaff*
July 4	E. J. Smith and the DC-3 Crew	Unidentified
July 8	Muroc Field	Balloons[29]

*A flight of B-29s and a flight of P-80 jet fighters flew over the city just before the sightings. The B-29s dropped the chaff to practice jamming radar.

29. Bloecher, *Report on UFO Wave of 1947,* I-13, III-11, III-16, Section V.

Chapter 3

1. Mantell Accident Report, Project Blue Book Files, National Archives, Case 136.

2. Check-List—Unidentified Flying Object Incident #33g, Project Blue Book Files, National Archives, Case 136.

3. Statement of Capt. Gary W. Carter, Project Blue Book Files, National Archives, Case 136.

4. Mantell Accident Report.

5. Statements by Capt. James F. Duesler Jr., Capt. Gary W. Carter and T/Sgt. Quinton A. Blackwell, Project Blue Book Files, National Archives, Case 136.

6. Mantell Accident Report.

7. Statement of PFC Stanley Oliver, Project Blue Book Files, National Archives, Case 136.

8. Check-List—Unidentified Flying Object Incident #33g.

9. Report of Unusual Incident, Project Blue Book Files, National Archives, Case 136.

10. Ruppelt, *Report on Unidentified Flying Objects,* 31, 33.

11. Mantell Accident Report. The Mantell accident report eliminated any possibility of mechanical failure—there had been no maintenance write-ups while any of the aircraft were at Marietta AFB. Moreover, Mantell's F-51 S/N 44-63869 was virtually a brand-new aircraft. It had been delivered on December 15, 1944, and had only 174 hours 25 minutes of flight time when the crash occurred. The airframe, engine and propeller were not yet due for their first overhaul.

12. Statements by Capt. James F. Duesler Jr. and T/Sgt. Quinton A. Blackwell. For instance, Sergeant Blackwell recalled Mantell saying it was a "metallic object" of tremendous size while Captain Duesler used more general terms—that the object was bright and that it was climbing away from him.

13. Ruppelt, *Report on Unidentified Flying Objects,* 31, 33, 35–38, 60.

14. Supplement to Trip Report to Atlanta 25–28 July Inclusive and Statement of Clarence S. Chiles and John B. Whitted, Project Blue Book Files, National Archives, Case 179.

15. *Atlanta Constitution*, 25 July 1948, Project Blue Book Files, National Archives, Case 179.

16. Descriptions and Drawings on Henry Grady Hotel Stationary, Project Blue Book Files, National Archives, Case 179.

17. Supplement to Trip Report to Atlanta 25–28 July Inclusive. Some newspaper accounts and later books state the DC-3 was rocked by the object's wake turbulence. In several statements to the Air Force both Chiles and Whitted denied this.

18. Newspaper Clippings, Project Blue Book Files, National Archives, Case 179.

19. Ruppelt, *Report on Unidentified Flying Objects*, 40.

20. Menzel and Boyd, *The World of the Flying Saucers*, 91, 111–113.

21. Incident #144—near Montgomery, Alabama, Project Blue Book Files, National Archives, Case 179.

22. Air Intelligence Information Report 102-122-79, Project Blue Book Files, National Archives, Case 179.

23. Ruppelt, *Report on Unidentified Flying Objects*, 30, 40, 41.

24. Gardner, *New Age*, 213, 214.

25. Menzel and Boyd, *The World of the Flying Saucers*, 15, 16.

26. Gardner, *New Age*, 214.

27. Gardner, *Fads and Fallacies*, 61.

28. Keel, "The man who invented flying saucers," 59.

29. Ruppelt, *Report on Unidentified Flying Objects*, 41.

30. Statement of an interview conducted by Maj. Donald C. James and Interrogation Report No. 2, Project Blue Book Files, National Archives, Case 234.

31. A statement by Doctor _____ October 1st at 11:20 P.M., Project Blue Book Files, National Archives, Case 234.

32. Certificate 23 October 1948, Project Blue Book Files, National Archives, Case 234.

33. Ruppelt, *Report on Unidentified Flying Objects*, 41–45.

34. Ibid., 43–46. Ruppelt included accounts of several other "dogfights" between pilots and balloons. They also had similar wild maneuvers.

35. Menzel and Boyd, *The World of the Flying Saucers*, 80–85.

36. Incident a, b, c,—Fargo, North Dakota—1 October 1948, Project Blue Book Files, National Archives, Case 234. A personal experience may shed some light on the balloon's "maneuvers." I was flying in a friend's light airplane when I saw a "metallic object" ahead of the aircraft, traveling right to left. The object flew across the nose of the aircraft, then curved and passed down the left side. The object was metallic and reflected the sun. It was traveling much faster than our speed. The object was clearly visible as it passed within about 100 feet of the aircraft—it was a heart-shaped mylar party balloon. The illusion of high speed was due to the balloon's closeness. The curved flight path was caused by flying past the balloon. If one adds darkness, the lack of altitude references, and the G-forces of a dogfight, it can be seen how the Gorman sighting could have occurred. Recall how the object made repeated head-on passes. This could be explained by the great differences in speed. Gorman also had to keep watching the light, which meant he could only look at his instruments sporadically.

37. Jacobs, *The UFO Controversy in America*, 270.

38. Ruppelt, *Report on Unidentified Flying Objects*, 48, 49.

39. Stephen M. Miller, "The capabilities of the American nuclear deterrent 1945–1950," *Aerospace Historian*, Spring, March 1980, 27–32.

40. Bloecher, *Report on UFO Wave of 1947*, III-19.

41. Ruppelt, *Report on Unidentified Flying Objects*, 50–55.

42. Ibid., 54, 55, 57–60.

43. *Project Blue Book*, 34–36.

44. Ruppelt, *Report on Unidentified Flying Objects*, 17, 18. An incident from the mid-1980s may have a bearing on the Arnold sighting. D was flying in a T-38 over Edwards AFB. Suddenly he saw a bright flash of light in the sky which lasted several seconds—it was a reflection from an F-15's canopy. At the time, the F-15 was well outside visual range. The similarity with Arnold's "flash" is suggestive.

45. Ruppelt, *Report on Unidentified Flying Objects*, 57–60.

46. Jacobs, *The UFO Controversy in America*, 41, 43.

47. *Project Blue Book*, 170–172, 173, 181, 182–184.

48. Condon, *Scientific Study of Unidentified Flying Objects*, 846, 852, 900–903, 904.

49. Michael J. H. Taylor and David Mondey, *Milestones of Flight* (London: Jane's, 1983), 163, 168, 172.

50. William Manchester, *The Glory and the Dream* (New York: Bantam Books, 1974), 490–509.

51. Robert J. Lamphere and Tom Shachtman, *The FBI-KGB War* (New York: Random House, 1988), 36–40, 78–113.

52. Ruppelt, *Report on Unidentified Flying Objects*, 59–61.

53. Arnold and Palmer, *Coming of the Saucers*, chap. 6.

54. Sidney Shalett, "What you can believe about flying saucers, part 1," *Saturday Evening Post*, 30 April 1949, 20, 21, 136–139.

55. Sidney Shalett, "What you can believe about flying saucers, part 2," *Saturday Evening Post*, 7 May 1949, 36, 184–186.

56. Ruppelt, *Report on Unidentified Flying Objects*, 60–64. Although the Air Force had started investigating flying saucer reports in July 1947, Project Sign's official starting date was January 22, 1948. The "reluctance" was probably a reflection of the attitudes of the Project Grudge staff. The Shalett article makes several references to the "silence" about flying saucers and the suspicions this caused.

Chapter 4

1. Donald A. Keyhoe, *The Flying Saucers Are Real* (New York: Fawcett Publications, 1950), 7.

2. Jacobs, *The UFO Controversy in America*, 49.

3. Gordon Creighton, "Obituaries—Major Donald Edward Keyhoe, U.S. Marine Corps, Ret'd," *Flying Saucer Review* 34, no. 2 (June quarter 1989): 9, 10.

4. Goulart, *Cheap Thrills*, 94–96.

5. Philip J. Klass, "The father of UFOlogy, the FOIA and the FBI," *Skeptical Inquirer*, Winter 1982–83.

6. Goulart, *Cheap Thrills*, 182–184.

7. Keyhoe, *Flying Saucers Are Real*, 7, 8, 18–23, 33, 44, 50–52, 73, 74, 82, 84, 86.

8. Ruppelt, *Report on Unidentified Flying Objects*, 65.

9. Keyhoe, *Flying Saucers Are Real*, 135–143.

10. Ruppelt, *Report on Unidentified Flying Objects*, 65–69.

11. Keyhoe, *Flying Saucers Are Real*, 149.

12. Ruppelt, *Report on Unidentified Flying Objects*, 40, 41.

13. Keyhoe, *Flying Saucers Are Real*, 147, 148, 153.

14. Ruppelt, *Report on Unidentified Flying Objects*, 70, 71.

15. Gardner, *Fads and Fallacies*, 63.

16. Jacobs, *The UFO Controversy in America*, 270.

17. Condon, *Scientific Study of Unidentified Flying Objects*, 514.

18. Ruppelt, *Report on Unidentified Flying Objects*, 72, 75–77.

19. Keyhoe, *Flying Saucers Are Real*, 6, 14, 38–45, 62, 63, 90–93, 132–134, 137, 154–159, 164, 173, 174.

20. Ruppelt, *Report on Unidentified Flying Objects*, 69, 88.
21. Lamphere and Shachtman, *The FBI-KGB War*, 110–122.
22. Manchester, *The Glory and the Dream*, 487–489, 509–512.
23. Lamphere and Shachtman, *The FBI-KGB War*, 132–157.
24. "UFO update," *Omni*, September 1988, 81.
25. Keyhoe, *Flying Saucers Are Real*, 139, 165, 166.
26. Ruppelt, *Report on Unidentified Flying Objects*, 83.
27. Jacobs, *The UFO Controversy in America*, 50, 51.
28. Frank Scully, *Behind the Flying Saucers* (New York: Henry Holt & Co., 1950), xi, xii, 4–7, 15, 20–30, 33–41, 106, 108, 127–140, 163, 164, 169.
29. Jacobs, *The UFO Controversy in America*, 51. *Behind the Flying Saucers* is often thought of as being the first book on flying saucers. This is incorrect; Keyhoe's *The Flying Saucers Are Real* came out three months earlier. The first two printings were made in June 1950. Scully's book was the first hardback (Keyhoe's was a paperback).
30. "Saucers flying upward," *Time*, 25 September 1950, 75, 76.
31. *The Film Encyclopedia: Science Fiction*, Phil Hardy, ed., (New York: William Morrow & Co., 1984), 125, 126.
32. Bill Warren, *Keep Watching the Skies! American Science Fiction Movies of the Fifties*, vol. 1, *1950–1957* (Jefferson, N.C.: McFarland, 1982), 6, 7.
33. *The Day the Earth Stood Still* (Twentieth Century Fox, 1951, CBS Fox Video). Klaatu's flying saucer lands on a baseball field on the Ellipse. In several shots, the White House, which is across the street from the Ellipse, can be seen. This is the source of the familiar phrase about a flying saucer "landing on the White House lawn." Klaatu's insistence on seeing the world's political and scientific figures is also the source of the phrase "Take me to your leader."
34. Warren, *Keep Watching the Skies!*, 19–28.
35. *The Thing from Another World* (Winchester Pictures, 1951, The Nostalgia Merchant). *The Thing . . .* is the source of this book's title.
36. Warren, *Keep Watching the Skies!*, 48–53.

Chapter 5

1. Ruppelt, *Report on Unidentified Flying Objects*, 86.
2. Ibid., 83, 86–88, 91–94, 111.
3. Jacobs, *The UFO Controversy in America*, 57, 58.
4. *Project Blue Book*, 394.
5. Ruppelt, *Report on Unidentified Flying Objects*, 6, 114–117, 144. It is sometimes thought Ruppelt "invented" the term UFO. In fact, it had been used in both the Shalett article and the Grudge Report.
6. *Project Blue Book*, 400, 401.
7. Ruppelt, *Report on Unidented Flying Objects*, 34–39.
8. David R. Saunders and R. Roger Harkins, *UFOs? Yes!* (New York: Signet Books, 1968), 64, 65.
9. Condon, *Scientific Study of Unidentified Flying Objects*, 514.
10. Jacobs, *The UFO Controversy in America*, 270.
11. "More saucers," *Time*, 3 March 1952, 92, 94.
12. Jacobs, *The UFO Controversy in America*, 58, 59.
13. Ruppelt, *Report on Unidentified Flying Objects*, 128–130, 140, 143.
14. Jacobs, *The UFO Controversy in America*, 60–62.
15. Ruppelt, *Report on Unidentified Flying Objects*, 132, 133.
16. H. B. Darrach Jr. and Robert Ginna, "Have we visitors from space," *Life*, 7 April 1952, 80–84, 89–96.

17. Ruppelt, *Report on Unidentified Flying Objects*, 129, 131, 132, 136, 137.
18. Condon, *Scientific Study of Unidentified Flying Objects*, 514–516.
19. Ruppelt, *Report on Unidentified Flying Objects*, 136, 137.
20. Condon, *Scientific Study of Unidentified Flying Objects*, 514.
21. Ruppelt, *Report on Unidentified Flying Objects*, 139, 140–144, 147–153.
22. Jacobs, *The UFO Controversy in America*, 63–65.
23. Ruppelt, *Report on Unidentified Flying Objects*, 150, 152, 153, 156, 157.
24. Condon, *Scientific Study of Unidentified Flying Objects*, 862.
25. *Project Blue Book*, 144.
26. Condon, *Scientific Study of Unidentified Flying Objects*, 155, 156.
27. Ruppelt, *Report on Unidentified Flying Objects*, 160.
28. *Project Blue Book*, 145.
29. Condon, *Scientific Study of Unidentified Flying Objects*, 155, 156.
30. *Project Blue Book*, 145, 146.
31. Ruppelt, *Report on Unidentified Flying Objects*, 158–163, 170.
32. Condon, *Scientific Study of Unidentified Flying Objects*, 155.
33. *Project Blue Book*, 147, 148.
34. Ruppelt, *Report on Unidentified Flying Objects*, 165, 166. It appears Ruppelt reversed the order of the two interception attempts. In Major Fournet and Lieutenant Holcombs's account, the first pair of F-94s were vectored to the targets while the second had no strong targets. Ruppelt said the opposite.
35. *Project Blue Book*, 148.
36. Ruppelt, *Report on Unidentified Flying Objects*, 166.
37. Jacobs, *The UFO Controversy in America*, 67–68.
38. Ruppelt, *Report on Unidentified Flying Objects*, 166–170.
39. Jacobs, *The UFO Controversy in America*, 69–71, 270.
40. Menzel and Boyd, *The World of the Flying Saucers*, 158.
41. Condon, *Scientific Study of Unidentified Flying Objects*, 514.
42. Philip J. Klass, "That was no saucer, that was an echo," *Aviation Week*, 20 July 1953, 26–30.
43. Condon, *Scientific Study of Unidentified Flying Objects*, 157, 158, 862–865.
44. Ruppelt, *Report on Unidentified Flying Objects*, 169, 170. Both July 19–20 and 26–27 were dark, clear nights. The Moon was only 2% illuminated on July 20 and did not rise until dawn. On July 26–27 it was 25% (first quarter) and set before the sightings began. Many of the visual sightings were of meteors. The peak of the Delta Aquarids shower was on July 28. (The only planet visible was Jupiter.)
45. J. P. Cahn, "The flying saucers and the mysterious little men," *True*, September 1952, 17–19, 102–112.
46. J. P. Cahn, "Flying saucer swindlers," *True*, August 1956, 36, 37, 69–72.
47. Leonard H. Stringfield, "The UFO crash/retrieval syndrome status report II: New sources, new data. Part II: New support data," *Flying Saucer Review* 28, no. 4 (1983): 9.

Chapter 6

1. Jacobs, *The UFO Controversy in America*, 72, 73, 76, 77.
2. Memorandum For:Deputy Director/Intelligence, Subject: Recent Sighting of Unexplained Objects, 29 July 1952. CIA UFO Files. In the late 1970s, the CIA declassified a total of one memo and two sighting reports from 1949 and 1950. Most of the documents, fewer than 350 classified pages, were from mid-1952 through mid-1953.
3. Memorandum: Deputy Assistant Director / SI Acting Chief, Weapons & Equipment Division "Flying Saucers," 1 August 1952. CIA UFO Files.
4. Philip J. Klass, *UFOs—The Public Deceived* (Buffalo: Prometheus Books, 1983), 16, 25–27.

5. Carrollton Press Declassified Documents Reference System CIA 1979 16A.
6. Lawrence Fawcett and Barry J. Greenwood, *Clear Intent* (Englewood Cliffs, N.J.: Prentice-Hall, 1984), 123–126.
7. Memorandum For: Deputy Director (Intelligence), Subject: Flying Saucers, 13 October 1952. CIA UFO Files.
8. Klass, *UFOs—The Public Deceived*, 27.
9. Thornton L. Page, letter to author, 9 December 1989.
10. Condon, *Scientific Study of Unidentified Flying Objects*, 517.
11. Page, letter to author, 9 December 1989.
12. Condon, *Scientific Study of Unidentified Flying Objects*, 419–424, 906–908.
13. Jacobs, *The UFO Controversy in America*, 80, 81.
14. Fawcett and Greenwood, *Clear Intent*, 126, 127.
15. Condon, *Scientific Study of Unidentified Flying Objects*, 909–917.
16. Page, letter to author, 9 December 1989.
17. Condon, *Scientific Study of Unidentified Flying Objects*, 910, 915, 916, 917.
18. Ruppelt, *Report on Unidentified Flying Objects*, 198, 228, 229.
19. Condon, *Scientific Study of Unidentified Flying Objects*, 913, 914.
20. Jacobs, *The UFO Controversy in America*, 59, 86, 87, 126, 127.
21. *Project Blue Book*, 153–169.
22. Condon, *Scientific Study of Unidentified Flying Objects*, 514.
23. Ruppelt, *Report On Unidentified Flying Objects*, 218, 228–232.
24. Jacobs, *The UFO Controversy in America*, 87, 91, 270.
25. Klass, *UFOs—The Public Deceived*, 31–34.
26. Memorandum To: P. G. Strong, From: F. C. Durant, Subject: Unidentified Flying Objects, 31 March 1953. CIA UFO Files.
27. Memorandum To: Assistant Director, SI, From: Chief, Physics & Electronics Division, SI, Subject: Unidentified Flying Objects, 3 July 1953. CIA UFO Files.
28. Memorandum To: Assistant Director, Scientific Intelligence, From: Chief, Physics & Electronics Division, SI, Subject: Current Status of Unidentified Flying Objects (UFOB) Project, 17 December 1953. CIA UFO Files.
29. Gardner, *Fads and Fallacies*, 65, 66.
30. Arnold and Palmer, *Coming of the Saucers*, 94, 95, 103–121, 156–159.
31. Jacobs, *The UFO Controversy in America*, 88.
32. Donald E. Keyhoe, *Flying Saucers from Outer Space* (New York: Henry Holt & Co., 1953), 70–73.
33. Ruppelt, *Report on Unidentified Flying Objects*, 168. Keyhoe seems to have gone beyond "mind reading" and stylistic problems. On page 38 of the paperback edition of *Flying Saucers from Outer Space*, he quotes two paragraphs from the Project Sign Report. The Condon Report made a careful examination of the Sign Report which "shows that these paragraphs are not contained in it."
34. Keyhoe, *Flying Saucers from Outer Space*, 73–89, 100–104, 122.
35. Jacobs, *The UFO Controversy in America*, 91, 92.
36. Condon, *Scientific Study of Unidentified Flying Objects*, 529–534.
37. Harry L. Helms, *How to Tune the Secret Shortwave Spectrum* (Blue Ridge Summit, Pa.: Tab Books Inc., 1981), 57.
38. Condon, *Scientific Study of Unidentified Flying Objects*, 532, 533.
39. Donald E. Keyhoe, *The Flying Saucer Conspiracy* (New York: Henry Holt & Co., 1955), 7, 13, 24, 25, 31, 32.

Chapter 7

1. Douglas Curran, *In Advance of the Landing* (New York: Abbeville Press, 1985), 43, 44, 71, 72.

2. Desmond Leslie and George Adamski, *Flying Saucers Have Landed* (New York: British Book Center, 1953), 171–177.

3. Eric Herr, "George Adamski: An historical note," *Flying Saucer Review* 34, no. 3 (September quarter 1989): 15.

4. Leslie and Adamski, *Flying Saucers Have Landed*, 177–184, 187–220.

5. Curran, *In Advance of the Landing*, 46.

6. Ruppelt, *Report on Unidentified Flying Objects*, 263–266.

7. Curran, *In Advance of the Landing*, 46, 47. The similarity between Adamski's run-in with the three FBI agents and Bender's supposed encounter, several months later, with the three men in black suits is suggestive.

8. "Special Adamski Expose Issue," *Saucer News*, October 1957. It has provided great sport to believers and skeptics alike to figure out what it was Adamski used for his "scout ship" photos—a light fixture, a Chrysler hubcap, a chicken brooder, or a 1937 cannister vacuum cleaner. Jerrold Baker gave what may be the best possibility: he recalled how Adamski used to wear an old khaki pith helmet. It struck Baker how much the scout ship resembled the pith helmet with its top cut off. There was even a black round object on the rim that corresponded to an eyelet which held the chin strap. The underside could be the top of the helmet glued underneath. The three landing pods could have been ping pong balls.

9. Bryant and Helen Reeve, *Flying Saucer Pilgrimage* (Amherst, Wis.: Amherst Press, 1957), 20.

10. Jacobs, *The UFO Controversy in America*, 98, 99.

11. Spencer and Evans, *Phenomenon*, 124, 125.

12. Daniel Fry, *The White Sands Incident* (Louisville: Best Books, 1966), 12–22, 29, 30, 33–41, 48–50, 59–62, 67, 70, 71, 75, 80. Fry's two books were combined into this edition and reissued. Fry also claimed to have a Ph.D. from St. Andrews College of London. This was a "diploma mill" that granted degrees for a payment and a "learned thesis." The reader may have noticed a tendency for contactees to have questionable doctorates.

13. Reeve and Reeve, *Flying Saucer Pilgrimage*, 103–109.

14. Orefo M. Angelucci, *The Secret of the Saucers* (Amherst, Wis.: Amherst Press, 1955), 1–15, 18, 25, 31, 36, 38–51, 55–57, 84–113.

15. George Adamski, *Inside the Space Ships* (New York: Abelard-Schuman, 1955), 36–40, 45–49, 57–63, 76, 77, 85–92, 113–118, 157–169, 191–210, 226–228.

16. Howard Menger, *From Outer Space to You* (Clarksburg, W.Va.: Saucerian Books, 1959), 26, 30–48, 50–54, 71–73, 98–101, 138–156, 170–180.

17. Jacobs, *The UFO Controversy in America*, 100, 101, 104, 105.

18. Reeve and Reeve, *Flying Saucer Pilgrimage*, 233–267.

19. Jacobs, *The UFO Controversy in America*, 106.

20. Reeve and Reeve, *Flying Saucer Pilgrimage*, 23–28, 123–144.

21. Curran, *In Advance of the Landing*, 63–69.

22. G. W. Van Tassel, *Into This World and Out Again* (Los Angeles: DeVorss & Co., 1956), 4.

23. Reeve and Reeve, *Flying Saucer Pilgrimage*, 90–92, 95.

24. Visit by author to Giant Rock, 18 November 1989.

25. Curran, *In Advance of the Landing*, 79–81.

26. "C," interview with author, 2 December 1989.

27. Stringfield, "The UFO Crash/Retrieval Syndrome Status Report II," 9. "Saucerian" was a term for believers in the 1950s. Frank Scully attended the first Giant Rock Convention and seemed impressed by the contactees. He gathered material for a book titled *This Side of Saucers*. In a 10 June 1954 letter he said he had been "listening now to personal histories of those who have talked with live crews and even flown in their saucers." Scully's book was never published.

28. Ruppelt, *Report on Unidentified Flying Objects*, 131.

29. Robert Sheaffer, *The UFO Verdict: Examining the Evidence* (Buffalo: Prometheus Books, 1981), 147–151.
30. Jacobs, *The UFO Controversy in America,* 108–111.
31. H. Taylor Buckner, "Flying saucers are for people," *Trans-Action,* May/June 1966, 10–13. The contactees also seemed to have a similar background. All had limited educations, were self-taught, and came from manual-labor backgrounds. Their lack of power or influence makes them poor "messengers" for a "mission" as important as they claimed. That the aliens should choose such people is the most basic flaw in the contactee myth. Not until the 1980s would it be claimed that the aliens were "dealing" directly with the government.
32. Jacobs, *The UFO Controversy in America,* 101–105, 112, 113.
33. Van Tassel, *Into This World and Out Again.*
34. Spencer and Evans, *Phenomenon,* 131, 132.
35. Jacobs, *The UFO Controversy in America,* 103, 104.
36. Gray Barker, *They Knew Too Much about Flying Saucers* (New York: University Books, 1956), 92, 93, 114, 128–150.
37. Jerome Clark, "Book Reviews," *International UFO Reporter,* May/June 1991, 18, 19.
38. Vicki Cooper, "Fascist trends spotted in UFO past," *UFO* 7, no.4 (1992): 28. "Dr." George H. Williamson (AKA Michel d'Obrevnic) was reportedly associated with American Nazi leader William Dudley Pelly's Silver Shirts in the 1930s. Pelly wrote on mysticism, and the Silver Shirt membership overlapped that of Guy Ballard's I AM (another mystic group.) These, in turn, can be traced back to Helena Blavatsky's Theosophy Society of the 1870s and its "Ascended Masters" of the "Great White Brotherhood." It was former members of groups like I AM who made up the membership of the contactee groups in the 1950s. Jim Moseley feels that Williamson's influence on the contactees has not been appreciated. He was close to Adamski, and during the 1950s, he wrote four books—*The Saucers Speak, Secret Places of the Lion, Road in the Sky,* and *Other Tongues, Other Flesh.* Williamson's conspiracy theories about "International Bankers" with obviously Jewish names are clearly the forerunners of today's MJ-12/aliens among us/secret treaty stories.
39. Spencer and Evans, *Phenomenon,* 132.
40. Warren, *Keep Watching the Skies!,* 19–28.
41. *It Came from Outer Space,* (Universal International, 1953, Good Times Home Video).
42. Warren, *Keep Watching the Skies!,* 121–130. *It Came from Outer Space* was a classic film in several ways. The original screen treatment was by Ray Bradbury and he gave the film a haunting, poetic quality. The film was the first of a number of science fiction films directed by Jack Arnold. It was also the first science fiction film to use the desert, giving a feel of "sunlit menace." The main character, John Putnam (Richard Carlson), became the pattern for heroes of 1950s science fiction films.

Chapter 8

1. Jacobs, *The UFO Controversy in America,* 117–120, 270.
2. Otto Billig, *Flying Saucers: Magic in the Skies* (Cambridge, Mass.: Schenkman Publishing Co., 1982), 221, 222.
3. Air Force Press Release No. 1053-55, "Air Force Releases Study on Unidentified Aerial Objects," 25 October 1955, Curtis Peebles UFO Files.
4. Jacobs, *The UFO Controversy in America,* 120, 121.
5. Condon, *Scientific Study of Unidentified Flying Objects,* 514.
6. Manchester, *The Glory and the Dream,* 700–716.
7. Jacobs, *The UFO Controversy in America,* 117, 118, 121, 130.
8. Keyhoe, *The Flying Saucer Conspiracy,* 13, 25–28, 38–56, 82, 84, 98, 104, 110, 116, 130, 172.

9. Harold T. Wilkins, *Flying Saucers on the Attack* (New York: Citadel Press, 1954), 139–141, 250.

10. Keyhoe, *The Flying Saucer Conspiracy,* chap. 19. As the Navy accident report was still classified in 1955, Keyhoe must have used the A.P and *Fate* articles.

11. Lawrence David Kusche, *The Bermuda Triangle Mystery—Solved* (New York: Warner Books, 1975), 107–129, 293, 294.

12. Larry Kusche, *The Disappearance of Flight 19* (New York: Barnes & Noble Books, 1981).

13. Barker, *They Knew Too Much about Flying Saucers,* app. 2.

14. Ruppelt, *Report on Unidentified Flying Objects.*

15. *The Film Encyclopedia: Science Fiction,* 155–164. The yearly totals for flying saucer-type films was: 1950, 1; 1951, 4; 1952, 2; 1953, 4; 1954, 2; 1955, 1; 1956, 6; 1957, 3; 1958, 1; and 1959, 5 (3 were low-budget Japanese films and another was *Plan 9 from Outer Space*). They were replaced by the "Big Bug" cycle of films. Starting with the 1953 film *Them!*, the screen was soon overrun with mutant tarantulas, locusts, snails, scorpions, gila monsters, and that full-size Japanese import, Godzilla. They were awakened/created by nuclear testing and/or fallout. The "Big Bug" films thus reflected Cold War fears more directly than the flying saucer movies.

16. Jacobs, *The UFO Controversy in America,* 115. *Earth vs. the Flying Saucers* was "suggested" by Keyhoe's book *Flying Saucers from Outer Space.* Keyhoe later said he had been told the film was to be a documentary. He was angry about it and refused to make personal appearances for the film and tried to have his name removed from the credits.

17. Warren, *Keep Watching the Skies!,* xiv, xv, 188, 189, 257–260, 361, 362. At the end of *Invasion of the Saucer Men,* the Air Force tries to cut into the saucer but it catches fire and explodes. After the team cleans up the debris, one officer turns to another and wonders how many others were also hiding such events. This was the most blatant (and, ironically, effective) use of the cover-up idea in any 1950s saucer movie.

18. "'Towards a broader understanding . . .,' the story of how NICAP began," *The UFO Investigator,* October 1971, 2, 3. Given the anticontactee stance NICAP took under Keyhoe, the involvement of Clara L. John in the group's founding is, to say the least, ironic.

19. Jacobs, *The UFO Controversy in America,* 129, 130.

20. Donald E. Keyhoe, *Flying Saucers: Top Secret* (New York: G. P. Putnam's Sons, 1960), 44–46.

21. Jacobs, *The UFO Controversy in America,* 130–132.

22. "8 point plan offered Air Force," *The UFO Investigator,* July 1957, 2, 5, 25.

23. Ruppelt, *Report on Unidentified Flying Objects,* 252.

24. Jacobs, *The UFO Controversy in America,* 126–128.

25. Keyhoe, *Flying Saucers: Top Secret,* 70–72, 81–96.

26. Manchester, *The Glory and the Dream,* 734–736, 799–810.

27. Curtis Peebles, "A traveller in the night," *Journal of the British Interplanetary Society,* August 1980, 282–286.

Chapter 9

1. Condon, *Scientific Study of Unidentified Flying Objects,* 514.

2. Air Intelligence Information Report AISS-UFOB-386-57, pp. 3–12, Project Blue Book Files, National Archives, Microfilm Roll 29.

3. UFO Sighting, White Sands Proving Grounds, New Mexico 3 November 1957, Project Blue Book Files, National Archives, Microfilm Roll 29.

4. Menzel and Boyd, *The World of the Flying Saucers,* 175, 196.

5. *Tucson Daily Citizen,* Project Blue Book Files, National Archives, Microfilm Roll 29.

6. United Press stories, November 3, 4, Project Blue Book Files, National Archives, Microfilm Roll 29.

7. Levelland Incident—2 November 1957 (unclassified), Project Blue Book Files, National Archives, Microfilm Roll 29.

8. Air Intelligence Information Report AISS-UFOB-438-57, Project Blue Book Files, National Archives, Microfilm Roll 29.

9. Gulf of Mexico, 5 November 1957 Coast Guard Cutter *Sebago*, Project Blue Book Files, National Archives, Microfilm Roll 29.

10. Air Force Press Release No. 1083-58, "Air Force's 10 Year Study of Unidentified Flying Objects," 5 November 1957, Curtis Peebles UFO Files.

11. United Press story November 5, Project Blue Book Files, National Archives, Microfilm Roll 29.

12. Air Intelligence Information Report AISS-UFOB-388-57, pp. 2, 3, Project Blue Book Files, National Archives, Microfilm Roll 29.

13. United Press story November 5, 1957, Project Blue Book Files, National Archives, Microfilm Roll 29.

14. Air Intelligence Information Report AISS-UFOB-388-57, pp. 2–8.

15. United Press story November 5, 1957, Project Blue Book Files, National Archives, Microfilm Roll 29.

16. Reinhold O. Schmidt, "The Kearney incident," *Flying Saucers*, October 1959, 34, 35, Project Blue Book Files, National Archives, Microfilm Roll 29.

17. "The Kearney, Nebraska 'contact' claim," *CSI Newsletter*, Project Blue Book Files, National Archives, Microfilm Roll 29.

18. "Kearney, Nebraska 'Space Ship' Incident, 5 November 1957," Project Blue Book Files, National Archives, Microfilm Roll 29.

19. Air Intelligence Information Report AISS-UFOB-388-57, pp. 2, 7, 8. The "Kearney Incident" also saw a strange coincidence—a farmer was driving his truck about two miles from the site of the "landing," at around the same time, when his engine failed. The Air Force investigators found a broken rotor had been replaced in the truck about ten days before. A piece of the broken rotor had not been removed and it had become wedged between the points, causing the failure.

20. Memorandum, Major Friend to Colonel Wynn, 1 December 1957, Project Blue Book Files, National Archives, Microfilm Roll 29.

21. "The Kearney, Nebraska 'Contact' Claim."

22. Schmidt, "The Kearney Incident," 36–38.

23. Joint Messageform T57-30468 8 November 1957, Project Blue Book Files, National Archives, Microfilm Roll 29.

24. Air Intelligence Information Report AISS-UFOB-386-57.

25. UFO Sighting, White Sands Proving Ground, New Mexico 3 November 1957.

26. Air Intelligence Information Report AISS-UFOB-438-57.

27. Joint Messageform T57-30468 8 November 1957.

28. Air Force Press Release No. 1108-57, 15 November 1957, Curtis Peebles UFO Files.

29. Condon, *Scientific Study of Unidentified Flying Objects*, 514.

30. Peebles, "A traveller in the night," 285, 286.

31. Billig, *Flying Saucers: Magic in the Skies*, 81, 82.

32. "The Unparalleled UFO 'Flap' of November 1957," Project Blue Book Files, National Archives, Microfilm Roll 29. Similar effects on autos had been reported during the 1954 French flap, and the 1944–1945 "Foo Fighters" were believed to have been intended to interfere with aircraft ignition systems. In *The Day the Earth Stood Still*, there were many shots of stalled cars when Klaatu shut off electrical power worldwide. Despite these earlier reports, it is clear the "car stop" stories have their direct origins with the Levelland sightings—or more precisely, the press reports of the Levelland sightings.

Chapter 10

1. *The UFO Investigator,* January 1958.
2. Keyhoe, *Flying Saucers. Top Secret,* 155–165.
3. "CIA evades, then denies charge of attempted UFO censorship," *The UFO Investigator,* June 1958, 4.
4. Klass, *UFOs—The Public Deceived,* 7, 37.
5. "CIA evades, then denies charge of attempted UFO censorship," 4.
6. Jacobs, *The UFO Controversy in America,* 141.
7. Keyhoe, *Flying Saucers: Top Secret,* 189–190.
8. Jacobs, *The UFO Controversy in America,* 141–144, 156.
9. "Policy on contact claims announced," *The UFO Investigator,* July 1957, 19, 28.
10. "Interim report on answers to 'contact' questionnaire," *The UFO Investigator,* August–September 1957, 18, 19.
11. Keyhoe, *Flying Saucers: Top Secret,* 241, 242.
12. Resignations, *The UFO Investigator,* August–September 1958, 3.
13. "Contactees told to return NICAP cards," *The UFO Investigator,* August–September 1958, 2, 4.
14. Jacobs, *The UFO Controversy in America,* 163.
15. *Saucer Smear* 32, no. 1 (10 January 1985): 1, 2.
16. James W. Moseley, lecture, 17 March 1991, at the Clarion Hotel Bar, San Diego, CA. Moseley said nothing about his and Barker's role in the Straith Letter hoax until after Barker's death in December 1984.
17. George Adamski, *Flying Saucers Farewell* (New York: Abelard-Schuman, 1961), 73–110, 121–174, 189, 190.
18. Donald E. Keyhoe, "Director's report to NICAP members," *The UFO Investigator,* August–September 1958, 7, 8.
19. "This is an emergency," *The UFO Investigator,* July–August 1960, 4.
20. "Over $12,000 owed to NICAP," *The UFO Investigator,* October–November 1962, 2.
21. "This is an emergency," 4, 7.
22. Jacobs, *The UFO Controversy in America,* 156–157.
23. "Senator Johnson orders UFO watch," *The UFO Investigator,* July–August 1960, 1.
24. "New Capitol Hill backing for NICAP," *The UFO Investigator,* April–May 1961, 1, 2.
25. Jacobs, *The UFO Controversy in America,* 159, 160.
26. "UFO inquiry behind closed doors," *The UFO Investigator,* July–August, 1961, 1–4.
27. Jacobs, *The UFO Controversy in America,* 162–163
28. Menzel and Boyd, *The World of the Flying Saucers,* 23–24.
29. "The attack on NICAP," *The UFO Investigator,* July–August 1961, 8.
30. "NICAP called smoke screen to hide truth about UFOs," *The UFO Investigator,* June 1958, 5.
31. Menzel and Boyd, *The World of thr Flying Saucer,* 25.
32. Leon Davidson, *Flying Saucers: An Analysis of the Air Force Project Blue Book Special Report No. 14,* 5th ed., December 1976, 145–154, 174–176, Curtis Peebles UFO Files.
33. Donald E. Keyhoe, "Capt. Ruppelt revising his UFO book," *The UFO Investigator,* June 1959, 5.
34. Jacobs, *The UFO Controversy in America,* 111. Ruppelt was writing a second book at the time of his death from a heart attack. The book was never completed.
35. Coral Lorenzen, "UFOLOGY—according to WHOM?," *The APRO Bulletin* 32, no. 7, (1984): 3. An examination of 1958–1959 issues of *The APRO Bulletin* shows few mentions of Air Force cover-up charges. This is unlike *The UFO Investigator* for the same years, in which such claims made up the bulk of the text.
36. Jacobs, *The UFO Controversy in America,* 162.

37. "UFO's cause panic, one death," *The UFO Investigator,* January–February 1962, 1, 2.
38. Jacobs, *The UFO Controversy in America,* 133–134, 163.
39. "Answer to AF release," *The UFO Investigator,* January–February 1962, 4.
40. Study by AFCIN-4E4 Unidentified Flying Objects—Project #5771 (Blue Book) 28 September 1959, Project Blue Book Files, National Archives, Microfilm Roll 86.
41. Letter, Subject: (U) Transfer of USAF Aerial Phenomena Program, Project Blue Book Files, National Archives, Microfilm Roll 86.
42. Letter, Transfer of USAF Aerial Phenomena Program, 5 February 1960, Project Blue Book Files, National Archives, Microfilm Roll 86.
43. Jacobs, *The UFO Controversy in America,* 157–158, 164.
44. Note by Edward Trapnell, Project Blue Book Files, National Archives, Microfilm Roll 86.
45. Trip Report (UFO) Lt. Col. Robert J. Friend, 9 April 1962, Project Blue Book Files, National Archives, Microfilm Roll 86.
46. Letter, Project Blue Book (Unidentified Flying Objects), 20 April 1962, Project Blue Book Files, National Archives, Microfilm Roll 86.
47. Col. Edward H. Wynn, letter to Col. Carlisle, April 1962, Project Blue Book Files, National Archives, Microfilm Roll 86.
48. Jacobs, *The UFO Controversy in America,* 165–166, 270.

Chapter 11

1. Jacobs, *The UFO Controversy in America,* 270.
2. "Board member corrects Menzel," *The UFO Investigator,* January–February 1963, 8.
3. Curran, *In Advance of the Landing,* 47.
4. Lou Zinsstag and Timothy Good, *George Adamski—The Untold Story* (England: Ceti Publishers, 1983), chap. 9.
5. UFO Report 24 April 1964 [FBI Interview with Zamora], Project Blue Book Files, National Archives, Microfilm Roll 50.
6. Information Related to the Socorro Sighting of UFO by Lonnie Zamora, Project Blue Book Files, National Archives, Microfilm Roll 50.
7. W. T. Powers, "The landing at Socorro," *Flying Saucer Review,* September/October 1966, 51.
8. Report on Socorro New Mexico Trip, Project Blue Book Files, National Archives, Microfilm Roll 50.
9. Coral Lorenzen, "UFO occupants in United States reports," *Flying Saucer Review,* November/December 1966, 52.
10. Information Related to the Socorro Sighting of UFO by Lonnie Zamora.
11. Report on Socorro New Mexico Trip. The Socorro file does not indicate why Hynek was so quick to assume the "object" was a secret test aircraft. A possibility presents itself: starting in April 1962, the A-12 reconnaissance aircraft was secretly test flown from Groom Lake, Nevada. Over the next two years, there were a number of sightings of the A-12 by airline pilots. The A-12's existence was declassified in February 1964—two months before the Socorro landing. The A-12 "sightings" may have suggested a similar cause for Socorro. The A-12 was further developed to become the SR-71 Blackbird.
12. J. Allen Hynek, letter to Donald Menzel and Mrs. Lyle Boyd, 29 April 1965, Project Blue Book Files, National Archives, Microfilm Roll 50.
13. "Physical evidence landing reports," *The UFO Investigator,* July–August 1964, 4, 5.
14. Gordon I. R. Lore, Jr., letter to Philip J. Klass, 25 July 1968, Philip J. Klass UFO Files.
15. Coral Lorenzen, "Socorro sequel," *Flying Saucer Review,* January/February 1965, 3–5.
16. Socorro Revisited, Project Blue Book Files, National Archives, Microfilm Roll 50.

17. Report on the Trip to Albuquerque—Socorro, 12–13 March 1965, Project Blue Book Files, National Archives, Microfilm Roll 50. The idea that the Socorro landing was of a secret aircraft was also believed by Lincoln La Paz, of "Green Fireball" fame. Hynek wrote, "La Paz is thoroughly convinced that both the green fireballs and Zamora's sighting were observations of tests of advanced vehicles being produced by some project, even more secret than the Manhattan Project. I am afraid that La Paz is unshakable from this hypothesis." In La Paz's view, Hynek, FTD, and Blue Book were all part of this cover-up.

18. Jacobs, *The UFO Controversy in America*, 169.

19. Report on the Trip to Albuquerque—Socorro, 12–13 March 1965.

20. Philip J. Klass, *UFOs—Identified* (New York: Random House, 1968), chap. 19. The U.S. Surveyor, Viking, and Apollo Lunar Module, and the Soviet manned lunar lander all used symmetrical landing gear with equal-length legs and circular landing pads. The Socorro "object" would have had one leg coming straight down and the others at odd angles.

21. Maj. Donald E. Keyhoe, USMC (Ret.), "U.S. Air Force Censorship of the UFO Sightings," *True*, January 1965, 38, 40, 41, 84–86.

22. "New approach pays off," *The UFO Investigator*, March–April 1965, 2.

23. Jacobs, *The UFO Controversy in America*, 174, 175.

24. *The UFO Investigator*, March–April 1965.

25. Maj. Donald E. Keyhoe USMC (Ret), "A Gemini test orbit," *Flying Saucer Review*, May/June 1965, 14, 15.

26. *Summary Report DOD Support of Project Gemini Jan 1963–Nov 1966*, Department of Defense, 6 March 1967.

27. Gordon Creighton, "Astronauts forced down by UFOs?," *Flying Saucer Review*, May/June 1965, 15, 16.

28. Barton C. Hacker and James M. Grimwood, *On the Shoulders of Titans—A History of Project Gemini* (Washington: NASA, 1977), 245–250.

29. United Press International, *Gemini—America's Historic Walk in Space* (Englewood Cliffs, N.J.: Prentice-Hall, 1965), chap. 4.

30. James E. Oberg, "Astronauts & UFOs—the whole story!," *Space World*, February 1977, 6, 7.

31. James E. Oberg, "Astronauts and UFOs," *Skeptical Inquirer*, Fall 1978 [expanded July 1983].

32. Condon, *Scientific Study of Unidentified Flying Objects*, 205–208.

33. Jim Mesko, *Ground War—Vietnam*, vol. 1, *1945–1965*, (Carrollton, Tex.: Squadron/Signal Publications, 1990), 38–64.

34. Condon, *Scientific Study of Unidentified Flying Objects*, 514.

35. Jerome Clark, "The greatest flap of all?," *Flying Saucer Review*, January/February 1966, 27, 28. The quote about the stars being on the other side of the Earth during the 1–2 August 1965 sightings has been used in several books. Frank Edwards wrote, "The Air Force 'explanation' was a miss—by 12,000 miles. Cynics will conclude that even then it was better than usual for them." (*Flying Saucers—Serious Business*, p. 167.) In fact, Jupiter rose at 3:05 A.M. CDT on 2 August 1965 (Saturn rose at 10:20 P.M. on August 1). As for the stars, Capella rose at 2:30 A.M., Aldebaran at about 4:00 A.M. and Rigel and Betelgese rose at 5:58 A.M. Jupiter, Capella, and Aldebaran would have been prominent objects in the eastern sky in the hours before sunrise. Rigel and Betelgese would have risen at dawn and might have been difficult to see. The "exploding" UFOs sound like meteors—the Alpha Capricornids meteor shower peaks on August 1st. The weak, slow-moving radar targets observed at Wichita sound like false echoes, similar to the Invasion of Washington. The Air Force lists no unidentified sightings on August 1–2.

36. Jacobs, *The UFO Controversy in America*, 172.

37. Condon, *Scientific Study of Unidentified Flying Objects,* 514.

38. Jacobs, *The UFO Controversy in America,* 175, 197, 270.

39. Gary Gerani, "The Invaders," *Starlog,* September 1978, 46–51.

40. Michael J. Wolff, "Schedule for The Invaders," *Starlog,* June 1988, 13–16. *The Invaders* is considered to be one of the better science fiction shows of the 1960s. Produced by Quinn Martin, it combined the "running man" theme of *The Fugitive* with science fiction. The suspense came from not knowing who was the invader—as often as not Vincent's allies proved to be the enemy. *Star Trek* also used a similar theme in one show; the "Assignment: Earth" episode had specially trained humans being sent to Earth in the 1960s by an alien civilization. Given *Star Trek*'s optimistic view of the future, they were not sent to destroy but to help mankind to survive the trials of the late twentieth century.

41. Jacobs, *The UFO Controversy in America,* 196–197.

42. John G. Fuller, *Incident at Exeter* (New York: G. P. Putnam's, 1967): 9–15, 92, 98, 108, 124, 201–210, 220. In the 1970s, skeptic Robert Sheaffer reexamined the sightings and found that several, including Muscarello's two sightings, might have been caused by Jupiter, which was visible in the early morning sky. Another possible cause was Venus, which was visible in the early evening. This included several of the "power line" sightings. One witness noted the UFOs were almost never seen on cloudy nights (which would have obscured planets). Stars and planets were the largest cause of UFO reports in Blue Book files.

43. Jacobs, *The UFO Controversy in America,* 198.

44. Frank Edwards, *Flying Saucers—Serious Business* (New York: Bantam Books, 1966): 117–122.

45. Frank Edwards, *Flying Saucers—Here And Now!* (New York: Bantam Books, 1968): 117, 118, 154–157.

46. Curran, *In Advance of the Landing,* 48.

47. Zinsstag and Good, *George Adamski—The Untold Story,* chap. 17.

48. Fritz Korn as told to B. Ann Slate, "The great UFO 'ride'," *Fate,* 1971, 38–49.

49. John G. Fuller, *The Interrupted Journey* (New York: Dell Publishing Co., 1967), 17–45.

50. Martin Kottmeyer, "Entirely unpredisposed," *Magonia,* January 1990, 8.

51. Fuller, *The Interrupted Journey,* 46–67, 73–77, 330, 331, 342–350.

52. Sheaffer, *The UFO Verdict,* 36.

53. "Sigmund," analysis of *The Interrupted Journey,* Curtis Peebles's UFO Files. "Sigmund" (a licensed California psychotherapist) read the book and provided the analysis. The specific symbols are common ones in dreams. Although trauma can often cause a person to have recurring dreams—even for years afterwards—Sigmund had never heard of one that exactly followed the real events. A man who was shot had dreams of seeing the gun, then the face of a teacher or a childhood enemy, and finally the pain. The real attacker's face was seen only occasionally. When Dr. Simon saw the Hills in 1964, the only explanation for dreams was that of Freud's—that they were repressed fears, wishes, etc. In the 1980s, another theory was developed—that they are random thoughts caused by chemical changes in the brain due to sleep. This debate is academic because, whether dreams have meaning in and of themselves or we impose meaning on them, the outcome is the same.

54. Fuller, *The Interrupted Journey,* 10, 209, 210, 311.

55. Summary of a conversation with Dr. Benjamin Simon by Philip J. Klass 29 October 1966, Philip J. Klass UFO Files.

56. Edwards, *Flying Saucers—Here And Now!,* chap. 7. Edwards made a number of errors: he said Adamski claimed to have met a female crewman (Adamski said he was male with long hair) and that he died in 1963 (it was actually 1965). Still, he reflects a common attitude about contactees during the 1960s.

57. Gordon Creighton, "Even more amazing . . .," pts. 1–4, *Flying Saucer Review,* July/August 1966 through January/February 1967.
58. "Important Discoveries," *Flying Saucer Review,* November/December 1966, 17.
59. Jim Moore, *Conspiracy of One* (Fort Worth: The Summit Group, 1990).
60. Condon, *Scientific Study of Unidentified Flying Objects,* 514.
61. Jacobs, *The UFO Controversy in America,* 270. On a per year total, the rankings are as follows:

Year	No. Reports	No. Unidentifieds
1952	1,501	303
1966	1,112	32
1957	1,006	14
1967	937	19
1965	887	16
1956	670	14

The total for the 28 months between July 1965 and November 1967 is 2,679 reports. This is 21.23% of the 12,618 reports the Air Force received over 22 years.

62. Paul E. McCarthy, "Politicking and Paradigm Shifting: James E. McDonald and the UFO Case Study" (Ph.D. thesis, University of Hawaii, 1975), 89–91, 109, 114, 116.
63. Edwards, *Flying Saucers—Here And Now,* 39–49.
64. Edwards, *Flying Saucers—Serious Business,* 178, 179.

Chapter 12

1. Washtenaw County Sheriff's Department Comp. No. 01058 March 20, 1966, Project Blue Book Files, National Archives, Microfilm Roll 60.
2. Report on the Dexter-Hillsdale, Michigan, UFO Sightings of 20–21 March 1966, Project Blue Book, National Archives, Microfilm Roll 60. One of the Hillsdale witnesses said he first thought the lights were marsh lights until they began to get brighter and rose into the air.
3. Calls of 22 March 1966, Project Blue Book Files, National Archives, Microfilm Roll 60. One of the calls about the Dexter-Hillsdale sightings was from "Phil Donahue WHIO, Dayton."
4. Report on the Dexter-Hillsdale, Michigan UFO Sightings of 20–21 March 1966.
5. Statement on the Dexter-Hillsdale UFO Sightings, by Dr. J. Allen Hynek, Project Blue Book Files, National Archives, Microfilm Roll 60. For all their impact, the Dexter-Hillsdale sightings are a classic example of publicity over substance. After reading over the case file, it is hard to understand why the sightings of dim, distant lights should spark such press interest. When compared to such cases as the Classics, the Invasion of Washington, or the Levelland sightings, it is clear how unimpressive these sightings were.
6. Edwards, *Flying Saucers—Here And Now!,* 15.
7. Jacobs, *The UFO Controversy in America,* 175–179, 181, 182.
8. Ibid., 181, 182.
9. "House of Representatives Armed Services Committee hearing on UFOs," *Flying Saucer Review,* July/August 1966, 4, 5.
10. Condon, *Scientific Study of Unidentified Flying Objects,* 811–815.
11. Jacobs, *The UFO Controversy in America,* 181–183.
12. "House of Representatives Armed Services Committee hearing on UFOs," 4.
13. "James E. McDonald," *Flying Saucer Review,* May/June 1971, 27.
14. McCarthy, "Politicking and Paradigm Shifting," 28–37, 40, 42. The CIA's sensitivity

about the Robertson Report was not due to its contents but to the fact it included the names of intelligence personnel and sections within the CIA. When the text was published in the Condon Report in 1969, these were removed.

15. Jacobs, *The UFO Controversy in America*, 196, 197.
16. McCarthy, "Politicking and Paradigm Shifting," 54, 55, 69, 90, 114, 116.
17. Klass, *UFOs—Identified.* Ironically, the IEEE seminar on UFOs was canceled before being held. By that time, however, Klass was deeply involved with UFOs. By the early 1970s, Klass had abandoned the ball lightning theory.
18. McCarthy, "Politicking and Paradigm Shifting," 65.
19. Jacobs, *The UFO Controversy in America*, 183–185.
20. Memo To: E. James Archer and Thurston E. Manning, From: Robert J. Low, Subject: Some Thoughts on the UFO Project, 9 August 1966, Curtis Peebles UFO Files.
21. David R. Saunders and R. Roger Harkins, *UFOs? Yes!*, chap. 3.
22. *Washington Evening Star*, 20 October 1966, C-14.
23. McCarthy, "Politicking and Paradigm Shifting," 66, 69–72, 75, 84–87.
24. J. Allen Hynek, "Are flying saucers real?," *Saturday Evening Post*, 17 December 1966, 17, 21.
25. McCarthy, "Politicking and Paradigm Shifting," 43, 61, 90, 104, 108, 114.
26. Air Force News Release No. 847-66, "Air Force Selects University of Colorado to Investigate Unidentified Flying Object Reports," October 7, 1966, Curtis Peebles UFO Files.
27. Saunders and Harkins, *UFOs? Yes!*, 50–57, 62–69, 75–80, 92, 103–106, 117. The Condon Study has been likened to a jury. I feel this better describes the Robertson Panel: it was presented with the "best cases" (i.e., evidence) and was asked for a "verdict." The role of the Condon Study was much wider, akin to an independent Blue Book. It conducted its own investigations, analyzed them, then reached a conclusion. Ironically, in the "Labyrinth" episode of *The Invaders*, a staff member of a Condon-like university UFO study was an invader. His job was to misdirect the investigation teams away from promising cases.
28. Philip J. Klass, "NICAP Views on Dr. Edward Condon and the University of Colorado Study" [Notes] 2 May 1968.
29. Maj. Donald E. Keyhoe, USMC Ret., letter to President Lyndon B. Johnson, 30 April 1968, Curtis Peebles UFO Files. Having expressed a belief in UFOs and a cover-up, Saunders should not have been allowed to stay on the project. Ruppelt had a rule that any Blue Book staff member who could no longer objectively investigate UFOs was to be transferred. Three staff members left Blue Book for this reason during Ruppelt's time.
30. McCarthy, "Politicking and Paradigm Shifting," 96.
31. Philip J. Klass, "The Condon UFO study: a trick or a conspiracy?" *Skeptical Inquirer*, Summer 1986, 333.
32. McCarthy, "Politicking and Paradigm Shifting," 101–106.
33. Saunders and Harkins, *UFOs? Yes!*, 110, 114, 120–122.
34. Klass, "The Condon UFO study," 332.
35. Saunders and Harkins, *UFOs? Yes!*, 116–119.
36. Edwards, *Flying Saucers—Here And Now!*, 90–92. On 10 May 1966, CBS telecast a documentary entitled "Flying Saucers: Friend, Foe or Fantasy?" It included footage of the Giant Rock Convention and interviews with George Van Tassel, George Adamski, and other contactees. Frank Edwards described it as "sorely lacking in objectivity." He also quoted an *Oakland Tribune* review as saying "CBS interviewed a collection of quacks and characters who infest the saucer movement. . . . CBS may have felt that there was some entertainment value in displaying these gifted folk, but their relevance to the controversy was questionable, to say the least." NICAP (as usual) accused the CBS program of being "apparently under Air Force guidance, if not control." From this, it is clear how sensitive the believers were on the subject.

37. Saunders and Harkins, *UFOs? Yes!*, 127, 134–141, 135, 151, 152. Low's snub of Charles Bowen (to go to Loch Ness) has been mentioned several times by believers as an example of his negative attitude toward UFOs. A point in Low's defense should be made— *Flying Saucer Review* had long accepted contactee stories and was, at the same time as Low's Loch Ness trip, running a series on the Villas Boas case. Again it was a question of perceptions—to the believers *Flying Saucer Review* was the best UFO magazine in the world, to the skeptics it was just another source of wild stories.

38. McCarthy, "Politicking and Paradigm Shifting," 134–137.

39. Saunders and Harkins, *UFOs? Yes!*, 141, 274.

40. McCarthy, "Politicking and Paradigm Shifting," 138–140.

41. Saunders and Harkins, *UFOs? Yes!*, 143, 144, 146.

42. Philip J. Klass, "NICAP Views on Dr. Edward Condon and the University of Colorado Study" [Notes] 2 May 1968.

43. Saunders and Harkin, *UFOs? Yes!*, 178–180, 249.

44. McCarthy, "Politicking and Paradigm Shifting," 142.

45. Saunders and Harkins, *UFOs? Yes!*, chap. 20 and app. B [McDonald's letter].

46. John G. Fuller, "Flying saucer fiasco," *Look*, 14 May 1968, 58–63.

47. Saunders and Harkins, *UFOs? Yes!*, 201.

48. McCarthy, "Politicking and Paradigm Shifting," 176–185. It was quite a contrast between the futile years Keyhoe spent seeking congressional hearings and McDonald's sudden success. There are several reasons: Keyhoe's efforts took place in the late 1950s/early 1960s when interest in flying saucers was low, McDonald's came at the end of the great Sixties flap. Also, Keyhoe launched attacks on the Air Force, while McDonald stressed the scientific importance of both UFOs and his own stature (while still attacking the Air Force/Condon Report). Most important, Keyhoe was an outsider, McDonald knew how to cultivate and flatter men of power.

49. Jacobs, *The UFO Controversy in America*, 207–211.

50. *Aliens in the Skies*, John G. Fuller, ed. (New York: Berkley Publishing, 1969).

51. McCarthy, "Politicking and Paradigm Shifting," chap. 5.

52. Lou Drendel, *Air War over Southeast Asia*, vol. 2 (Carrollton Tex.: Squadron/Signal Publications, 1983), 18–27.

53. Manchester, *The Glory and the Dream*, 1054–1056, 1128–1134.

54. Jacobs, *The UFO Controversy in America*, 270.

55. Billig, *Flying Saucers: Magic in the Skies*, 6, 7.

56. McCarthy, "Politicking and Paradigm Shifting," 146–158.

57. Condon, *Scientific Study of Unidentified Flying Objects*, 1, 561, 568–577, 579, 580, 585–587. The Zond 4 sighting shows not only the limitations of witnesses, but also of belief. Saunders rejected the meteor solution for the Chiles-Whitted sighting in his book *UFOs? Yes!*, published in December 1968 (before the Condon Report). Several times McDonald said there was no possibility the Invasion of Washington was caused by a temperature inversion. Yet, the Condon Report included a long analysis showing conditions on those two nights did cause the radar returns.

58. Saunders and Harkins, *UFOs? Yes!*, chap. 16.

59. Condon, *Scientific Study of Unidentified Flying Objects*, 176–209, 344, 345.

60. Jacobs, *The UFO Controversy in America*, 213–220.

61. *Aliens in the Skies*, 31.

62. Saunders and Harkins, *UFOs? Yes!*, 74.

63. Condon, *Scientific Study of Unidentified Flying Objects*, 548.

64. "Q," interview with author, 17 November 1991. Low seems to have come out the worst. He soon left the University of Colorado under a cloud due to his handling of the Condon Study. He went to another university but was killed in a plane crash in the mid-1970s.

65. Klass, "The Condon UFO study," 335.

66. Saunders and Harkins, *UFOs? Yes?*, 194, 195.

67. Jacobs, *The UFO Controversy in America*, 226, 227.

68. Air Force Press Release No. 1077-69, "Air Force to Terminate Project 'Blue Book'," 17 December 1969, Curtis Peebles UFO Files.

69. *New York Times*, 18 December 1969: 1.

70. Maj. Donald E. Keyhoe, letter to NICAP Members, 14 August 1967, Curtis Peebles UFO Files.

71. Keyhoe, *Flying Saucers: Top Secret*, 203.

72. Maj. Donald E. Keyhoe, *Aliens from Space* (New York: Signet Books, 1974), 241–251.

73. Maj. Donald E. Keyhoe, letter to NICAP Members, 10 April 1969, Curtis Peebles UFO Files.

74. NICAP Board of Governors, letter to membership, 6 August 1969, Curtis Peebles UFO Files.

75. Maj. Donald E. Keyhoe, "An emergency message from the director," *The UFO Investigator*, September 1969, 8.

76. Memorandum, Philip J. Klass, 18 December 1969, Philip J. Klass UFO Files.

77. Jacobs, *The UFO Controversy in America*, 227, 228.

78. McCarthy, "Politicking and Paradigm Shifting," 75.

79. Philip J. Klass, letter to author, 14 December 1988. The *New York Times* and *Washington Post* included the UFO questions in their articles on McDonald's appearance. Ironically, *Aviation Week & Space Technology* did not. Klass felt they were unfair and had no bearing on his theory. When the magazine's executive editor asked why he had not mentioned the questions, Klass was able to convince him to run the article as written.

80. Mel Horwitch, *Clipped Wings: The American SST Conflict* (Cambridge: MIT Press, 1982), 319, 320, 325.

81. Jacobs, *The UFO Controversy in America*, 232. Conte's cheap shot against McDonald was not the only time he used UFOs to smear an opponent. In 1990, he equated UFO clippings from tabloids to a $12.1 million NASA project to listen for radio signals from possible extraterrestrial civilizations. He attacked the effort by saying, "We shouldn't be spending precious dollars to look for little green men with misshapen heads." The funding was cut, but later restored in committee. Conte's performance left some with the feeling he either did not know, or did not care, about the difference between a serious scientific experiment and the fiction of the tabloids.

82. Philip J. Klass, letter to author, 14 December 1988.

83. "James E. McDonald," 27.

Chapter 13

1. Klass, *UFOs Explained*, 260.

2. D. B. Hanlon and J. F. Vallee, "The truth about Aurora," *Flying Saucer Review*, January/February 1967, 27.

3. Jerome Clark, "UFO crashes, part 1," *Fate*, January 1988, 46. A number of pieces of "saucer debris" were turned into Blue Book over the years but all were hoaxes or terrestrial. Frank Edwards wrote about a piece of a UFO knocked off by gunfire from a Navy jet during the Invasion of Washington. APRO had a piece of "pure" magnesium supposedly from an exploded UFO. The Condon Report examined the Edwards story and found it was not valid. The APRO sample was found to be no purer than commercial magnesium.

4. Bill Case, "Aurora's old-timers 'thinking over' UFO," UFO File, National Air and Space Museum.

5. Bill Case, "Pioneer recalls hearing of crash," UFO File, National Air and Space Museum.

6. Bill Case, "UFO unit wants body exhumed," UFO File, National Air and Space Museum.

7. Bill Case, "Aurora headstone bears 'cigar shape," UFO File, National Air and Space Museum.

8. Bill Case, "More UFO clues sought," UFO File, National Air and Space Museum.

9. Cohen, *Great Airship Mystery,* 115, 117.

10. Bill Case, "Grave believed UFO pilot's at Aurora, entered, robbed," UFO File, National Air and Space Museum.

11. Cohen, *Great Airship Mystery,* 117–121. Bill Case died in December 1974. Etta Pegues, who had investigated the crash in the 1960s, said, "It was all a hoax cooked up by Hayden and a bunch of men sitting around in the general store." She added Hayden was a well-known joker and reiterated that Judge Proctor never had a windmill on his property. There has been some suggestion that Judge Proctor himself was behind the hoax—an old-timer recalled her father saying the judge had outdone himself that time.

12. Clark, "UFO crashes, part 1," 48. In the 1890s, "journalistic hoaxes" were both quite common and acceptable. These were fictional stories published in respectable newspapers. Most times, they were never intended to fool the reader, but rather, to entertain. "Liars clubs" where local people would get together and tell "whoppers" were similar.

13. Frank X. Tolbert, "Tolbert's Texas—'The Honest Brakeman' Never Stole a Box Car," UFO File, National Air and Space Museum. Tolbert wrote several columns on the Aurora "crash," quoting the 1967 *Flying Saucer Review* letter. He also said that he had been told the whole airship flap had been started by a group of railroad telegraphers in Iowa during April 1897. A conductor named Joseph E. "Truthful" Scully was selected as spokesman for the hoax (Scully had a reputation for integrity). Other railroad men joined in the fun.

14. Klass, *UFOs Explained,* 278–280.

15. Jacobs, *The UFO Controversy in America,* 235. There was a flurry of UFO reports from Kansas during the 1972 presidential election. Between January and March 1973, there were reports from Alabama, Rhode Island, Missouri, and Pennsylvania. These "mini-flaps" did not receive the kind of national attention the Georgia flap did in August/September 1973.

16. Klass, *UFOs Explained,* 283.

17. Warren Smith, "The behind-the-headlines story of the Pascagoula UFO kidnap," *SAGA'S 1975 UFO Annual,* 12–15, 80, 81.

18. Klass, *UFOs Explained,* 297–298.

19. Smith, "The behind-the-headlines story of the Pascagoula UFO kidnap," 81.

20. Klass, *UFOs Explained,* 298.

21. Smith, "The behind-the-headlines story of the Pascagoula UFO kidnap," 81.

22. Jacobs, *The UFO Controversy in America,* 262, 263.

23. Klass, *UFOs Explained,* 286–290.

24. Joe Eszterhas, "Claw men from the outer space," *Rolling Stone,* 17 January 1974, 27, 42–47.

25. Klass, *UFOs Explained,* 295, 296, 30–309.

26. Eszterhas, "Claw men from the outer space," 47

27. Jacobs, *The UFO Controversy in America,* 235.

28. Ralph Blum with Judy Blum, *Beyond Earth: Man's Contact With UFOs* (New York: Bantam Books, 1974), "About the Authors."

29. *The National Tattler,* 25 August 1974, 5.

30. *Skeptics UFO Newsletter,* March 1992.

31. Sheaffer, *The UFO Verdict,* 123–126. The *U.S. News & World Report* story was apparently based on a comment by news secretary Jody Powell that the Carter administration had

or would soon release the Blue Book files to the National Archives. In fact, this had been done the year before by the Ford administration.

32. D. Shapley, "UFO's Just Will Not Go Away," *Science* 198 (1977): 1128.

33. Herbert J. Rowe, letter to Sen. Mark O. Hatfield, 3 November 1977, UFO File, NASA History Office.

34. Robert Frosch, letter (draft no. 2) to Frank Press, 1 December 1977, UFO File, NASA History Office.

35. Robert Frosch, letter to Frank Press, 21 December 1977, UFO File, NASA History Office.

36. Sheaffer, *The UFO Verdict*, 172, 173.

37. Kusche, *The Bermuda Triangle Mystery—Solved*, 58–61, 84–91, 100–102, 130, 131, 145–147, 179–186, 193–199, 204–220, 225, 247–263, 287, 288, 292–295. The book gives an example of how differing times respond when presented with a mystery. In January of 1921, the five-masted schooner *Carroll A. Deering* was found abandoned and aground. Several other ships also disappeared at the same time. This was seen as strange because, as the *New York Times* put it, "Ordinarily ships that disappear leave some trace either in the way of boats, wreckage or dead bodies, but it is said that none of the ships . . . left any trace whatever." Rather than blame UFOs or "time warps," the cause was thought to be "pirates or possibly Bolshevist sympathizers." Each age has its own set of demons.

38. James E. Oberg, *UFOs & Outer Space Mysteries* (Norfolk: Donning, 1982), 42, 43.

39. Oberg, "Astronauts & UFOs—the whole story!," 15–18.

40. Oberg, *UFOs & Outer Space Mysteries*, 39–41.

41. Robert Emenegger, *UFOs Past, Present & Future* (New York: Ballantine Books, 1974), 100–106.

42. Oberg, "Astronauts & UFOs—the whole story!," 13, 17, 18.

43. J. Allen Hynek and Jacques Vallee, *The Edge of Reality—A Progress Report on Unidentified Flying Objects* (Chicago: Henry Regnery Co., 1975), 63–65. To give a few examples, the name of the pilot on a "May 30, 1962" X-15 flight was given as "Joe Walton"—the pilot's name was actually "Joe Walker," and no X-15 flight was made on this date; it should be April 30, 1962. The Mercury 8 flight was listed as having taken place in 1963, not 1962, both the Soviet Voskhod 2 and Gemini 4 missions were listed as being flown in 1964, rather than 1965, and the Gemini 7 sighting is listed twice, as Gemini 8 and Apollo 8.

44. Oberg, "Astronauts and UFOs." Oberg's research on the astronaut sightings was published in the Fall and Winter 1977 *Search*, the February 1977 *Space World*, the Fall 1978 *Skeptical Inquirer* and NASA press releases. The first two were from Palmer Publication—owned by Raymond A. Palmer. This partnership between the original believer and the new skeptic was all the more remarkable given their physical differences. Palmer was a hunchback dwarf only 4 feet tall. Oberg is 6 feet 8 inches tall.

45. Carrollton Press DoD 145F 1979.

46. Oberg, "Astronauts & UFOs—the whole story!," 6, 7, 8.

47. James E. Oberg, "Astronauts and UFOs," *Skeptical Inquirer*, Fall 1978) [expanded July 1983].

48. Oberg, "Astronauts & UFOs—the whole story!," 9, 11–13.

49. *Saucer Stews* 24, no. 9 (10 September 1977): 4.

50. *Saucer Crud* 25, no. 1 (10 January 1978): 2.

51. Oberg, *UFOs & Outer Space Mysteries*, chap. 3.

52. Oberg, "Astronauts & UFOs—the whole story!," 12, 14, 17–22, 27.

53. Condon, *Scientific Study of Unidentified Flying Objects*, 198.

54. Oberg, *UFOs & Outer Space Mysteries*, 50–58. Needless to say, there was no nuclear device on Apollo 13 and the oxygen tank explosion was due to heater switches which failed

and caused the tank to overheat and burst. The 1963 Limited Nuclear Test Ban Treaty banned nuclear explosions in space. The 1967 Outer Space Treaty banned even the placement of nuclear weapons in space or on the Moon.

55. Oberg, "Astronauts & UFOs—the whole story!," 18.

Chapter 14

1. Daniel Kagan and Ian Summers, *Mute Evidence* (New York: Bantam Books, 1984), xiii–xvi, 31–35, 39–46. The film *The Thing from Another World* anticipated the mute myth. The Thing carries seeds in the palms of his hands. Dr. Carrington tries to grow the seeds using the base blood supply. The Thing is doing the same in the base greenhouse, using the blood drained from first a dog, then two of the scientists. The stories of a massive Satanic cult were told to police by two prison inmates. Their claims were investigated for several months but could not be substantiated.

2. Summary, College of Veterinary Medicine, Colorado State University, 24 November 1975, Curtis Peebles UFO Files. Rommel asked a noted Santa Fe doctor how he would define "surgical precision." He responded, "Well, it means I try to cut in a straight line."

3. Kagan and Summers, *Mute Evidence*, 44–65.

4. Harry Lebelson, "Death on the range," *Omni*, January 1980, 28, 116, 117.

5. Kagan and Summers, *Mute Evidence*, 58, 59.

6. Howard and Lovola Burgess, "Close encounter at the old corral," *True UFO & Outer Space Quarterly*, Summer 1979, 28–33.

7. Kagan and Summers, *Mute Evidence*, 344, 348, 349, 351–357, 362–368.

8. *The Cattle Report*, December 1977, 1, 7, 8. *The Cattle Report*, published in 1977 by Edward Sanders, was the first mute newsletter. The government conspiracy theory was its centerpiece. It was filled with shrill attacks on "the arrogance of power in the name of clandestine operations on the part of esoteric death technicians and the boys of National Security," "the Boys from Bacteria and the Clems of Chem-war," and "the leaders of the sickie network of night surgeons." It was this kind of rhetoric that did so much to shape the flying saucer myth in the early 1990s. *The Cattle Report* lasted only two issues.

9. Kagan and Summers, *Mute Evidence*, 14–17, 60, 312, 403.

10. Janet Bord, "After Snippy—what next?," *Flying Saucer Review*, November/December 1972, 19.

11. Kagan and Summers, *Mute Evidence*, xvii, 385, 401–403, 487.

12. Howard and Lovola Burgess, "Close encounter at the old corral," *True UFOs & Outer Space Quarterly*, Summer 1979, 28.

13. *Newark Sunday News*, 6 October 1968. When Snippy's bones were examined, two 22-caliber bullet holes were found in its flanks. It was speculated these could have been the source of the infection.

14. Transcript, "A Strange Harvest," KMGH-TV, (1980): 5, 12, 39, update to first broadcast.

15. Kegan and Summers, *Mute Evidence*, 93–95, 117, 118, 124–158, 163, 168, 170–172, 181–183, 208, 214–216, 342, 343, 353, 367–373, 386, 406, 410, 411, 480–481, 494–500. (All Rommel quotes are from this source.) Linda Moulton Howe is understood to have been involved with UFOs since childhood when Kenneth Arnold had been a house guest. Tom Adams was listed as a research consultant for "A Strange Harvest."

16. Moore, *Conspiracy of One*, 95–110, 135–146, 215–217.

17. Kagan and Summers, *Mute Evidence*, 152–154, 481–502. Behind all the smoke of the mutologists' claims and theories, Kagan and Summers felt there were a very few "true" mutes being done by Satanist groups. These amounted to a half dozen per year at most.

18. Thomas R. Adams, "Endangered species: the movie that not everyone is talking about," *Stigmata #19* (4th quarter 1982): 1–9.

19. Coral E. Lorenzen, "Mutilations continue," *The APRO Bulletin*, 32, no. 1 (1984): 7. APRO published few articles on mutes, but said, "No one who had done any on-site investigation of an actual mutilation could accept the natural death" idea and continued to endorse the Snippy case.

20. Linda Moulton Howe, "Strange harvest: thoughts beyond the scenes," *Denver Magazine*, September 1980, 49.

21. Kagan and Summers, *Mute Evidence*, 302, 410. Despite the claims of the mutologists, it was "run-of-the-mill" cows that were reported as mutes. It was also noted that it was small, part-time ranchers that were reporting mutes, not the larger, more experienced and better equipped operations. The professional ranchers were "completely skeptical" about the mutes. Kagan and Summers did not know of a single mute report from a huge cattle-raising operation. One aspect which seems to have been overlooked is the nonsystematic nature of the damage done to the reported mutes. One mute might have its tongue and skin on its lower jaw removed, another would have an ear and eye missing, while still another would be missing an ear and sex organs. One does not see a set pattern, such as would be done as part of a ritual or a scientific sampling operation. Instead, one sees the randomness of nature.

Chapter 15

1. Philip J. Klass, *UFO Abductions: A Dangerous Game* (Buffalo: Prometheus Books, 1989), 14, 15, 18.

2. Sheaffer, *The UFO Verdict*, 41–43.

3. Robert Sheaffer, "The New Hampshire abduction explained," *Official UFO*, August 1976. It is worth noting that this was the first attempt to figure out what the Hills saw on the night of the abduction. It is well worth wondering how the flying saucer myth might have developed had it been known in 1966 that they had actually seen Jupiter. A UFO report similar to Barney Hill's sighting of the aliens in the window appears in *The UFO Handbook* (p. 85). A woman saw Venus and, believing it was a UFO, "saw" the heads of the occupants through the window.

4. Summary of a conversation with Dr. Benjamin Simon by Philip J. Klass, 29 October 1966, Philip J. Klass UFO Files.

5. Dr. Benjamin Simon, letter to Philip J. Klass, 28 October 1975, Philip J. Klass UFO Files.

6. *The UFO Incident* (Universal Pictures, 1975).

7. Transcript, *The Today Show*, 20 October 1975.

8. Dr. Benjamin Simon, letter to Philip J. Klass, 28 October 1975. Simon explained to Klass that he had more limited control over the content of the film than he had over the book. The scenes dealing with the Hills' psychological problems "rang true"—one had the sense these were real people with real problems. Simon's "doubts" lacked this—the scenes were simply dramatic devices stuck in to give a pro-UFO viewpoint.

9. *The UFO Incident* (Universal Pictures, 1975).

10. Klass, *UFOs—The Public Deceived*, 161–173.

11. Jeff Wells, "Profitable nightmare of a very unreal kind," *Skeptical Inquirer*, Summer 1981, 47–50.

12. Klass, *UFOs—The Public Deceived*, 173–179. Dr. Rosenbaum's conclusion that Travis Walton's abduction story was the result of a "mental aberration" is contradicted by the failed lie-detector test. If Travis had believed his story was true, the test results should have been positive. (A lie-detector cannot establish "absolute" truth, but only what the test subject "believes" is true.) From Wells's description of Travis's personality it is clear he was a troubled individual.

13. *National Enquirer*, 16 December 1975, 4.

14. *National Enquirer*, 7 July 1976.

15. Klass, *UFOs—The Public Deceived*, 181.
16. Philip J. Klass, "New evidence that the Travis Walton 'UFO abduction' is a hoax," [White Paper], 20 June 1976, 16. Curtis Peebles UFO Files.
17. Klass, *UFOs—The Public Deceived*, 181–196. Klass was not alone in suspecting a hoax. The local police thought it was a hoax from the start. Soon after Travis's return, he was interviewed by Sheriff Marlin Gillespie. Gillespie later noted several changes in Travis's story compared to his original telling. Klass also noted problems with the lie-detector test of Mrs. Kellett. One of the questions she was asked was, "Have you yourself ever seen a flying saucer?" She answered, "No," and Pfeifer concluded she was truthful. Yet, she had previously said she had seen UFOs on several different occasions. UFOlogists are often suspicious of "repeaters"—people who claim to have seen UFOs several times. The credibility of the case would be improved if she was not a "repeater" and Travis and Duane were not "buffs."
18. Klass, "New evidence that the Travis Walton 'UFO abduction' is a hoax." Some UFOlogists suspected that Travis Walton was off on a "drug trip." Several witnesses reported seeing a fresh puncture mark on Travis's arm soon after his return. Among these was Lester H. Steward, a psychologist who saw Travis some nine hours after his return. Steward noted Travis was dazed and confused—sitting silently with his head in his hands while Duane described what had happened. At first, Steward told Klass, he thought this was due to the experiences aboard the UFO. As time passed, Steward noted, Travis began to emerge from his confused and depressed mental state. This was similar to the behavior of drug users coming off a "high." Steward, who had experience with treatment of drug addicts, suspected Travis had injected LSD, possibly in combination with PCP. Steward subsequently joined GSW's Spaulding in labeling the case a hoax.
19. Klass, *UFOs—The Public Deceived*, 196–198. The State of Arizona had the final word on APRO's slander. In late 1976, the Arizona Polygraph Licensing Board was established to license examiners. Two of the board members were John J. McCarthy and Tom Ezell.
20. Sheaffer, *The UFO Verdict*, 20, 44.
21. Klass, *UFO Abductions: A Dangerous Game*, 41. The Travis Walton abduction is the only one in which the person was reported "missing" while the "abduction" was still underway. All other cases were reported months and even decades later.
22. Allan Hendry, *The UFO Handbook* (Garden City, N.Y.: Doubleday & Co., 1979), 122, 138–143.
23. *Close Encounters of the Third Kind* (RCA/Columbia, 1977/1980). The title is a Hynek-developed term for the sighting of a UFO occupant and/or abduction. A "Close Encounter of the First Kind" is a close UFO sighting, while a "Close Encounter of the Second Kind" is a physical trace case, such as Socorro, where pad prints, debris, radiation, etc. are found.
24. *The Film Encyclopedia: Science Fiction*, 332, 333.
25. Klass *UFO Abductions: A Dangerous Game*, 42–43.
26. Budd Hopkins, *Missing Time* (New York: Ballantine Books, 1988), 9.
27. "CUFOS reports fewer UFO events," *UFO* 7, no. 1 (1992): 15.
28. James E. Oberg, "Anti-matter—UFO update," *Omni*, August 1987, 83. This was one of a series of mass sightings of such "fuel cloud UFOs" in South America. In at least two other instances they generated occupant/abduction reports.
29. Hopkins, *Missing Time*, 11–25, 39–46, 62, 79, 80, 146, 201, 211–215, 223. Hopkins was selective in his accounts. He stressed the consistency of the abduction reports, but ignored elements which did not "fit" his description. To give two examples, the Hills' abductors were described as having hair while in the Pascagoula case, the aliens did not look anything like the Grays.
30. Budd Hopkins, *Intruders* (New York: Ballantine Books, 1988), 40, 77–81, 85, 108,

110–120, 149, 176, 192, 199–201, 231, 232, 260, 267, 269, 273, 274, 277. "Kathie Davis's" medical history makes her an extremely dubious donor for high-quality genetic material to save a dying planet. She is described as being obese since childhood due to hormonal imbalance, having had her gall bladder and appendix removed, and having suffered from hepatitis, legionnaires' disease, fused vertebrae, an asthmatic attack, years of insomnia and paralyzing anxiety, a collapsed lung, heart arrhythmia, hypoglycemia, hyperadrenalism, high blood pressure, chronic allergic reaction to medications, ovarian cysts, and kidney failure.

31. Klass, *UFO Abductions: A Dangerous Game*, 154.
32. Martin Kottmeyer, "Entirely unpredisposed," *Magonia*, January 1990, 3.
33. *The Manchurian Candidate* (MGM/UA Home Video, 1988).
34. Kottmeyer, "Entirely unpredisposed," 4, 5. In addition to the science fiction influences, the shape of the "Grays" have other symbolism. On a cultural level, the Grays resemble television images of starving African children—large heads, spindly arms and legs, malformed bodies, and physically weak. This is symbolic of a dark future for mankind. It is the negative version of the angelic beings described by the contactees. A starving children/Grays symbolism also fits the picture of "alien beings from a dying planet."
35. John Javna, *The Best of Science Fiction TV* (New York: Harmony Books, 1987), 52–55.
36. Kottmeyer, "Entirely unpredisposed," 5.
37. Jan Harold Brunvand, *The Choking Doberman* (New York: W. W. Norton, 1984), 107–112. Brunvand noted that the idea of a living creature (an alien creature) entering the human body is a common one in folklore. These include stories of people drinking water and having a snake, frog, or octopus grow inside their bodies.
38. Marc Scott Zicree, *The Twilight Zone Companion* (New York: Bantam Books, 1983).
39. Kottmeyer, "Entirely unpredisposed," 3–10. Kottmeyer noted a 1930 *Buck Rogers in the 25th Century* comic strip had the same structure as a "real" abduction. Wilma is captured by a giant claw from a spherical spacecraft, examined on a table while in an "electro-hypnotic" trance, confers with a subordinate and then a leader, gazes at the Earth, and is finally returned. Wilma's sister, Sally, is then abducted. Kottmeyer observed that this order of events was dramatically correct—the examination (i.e., peril and conflict) should come first. It is the right way to tell a story—the human way to tell a story, not the alien way. The claw is identical with that described by "Steven Kilburn" in *Missing Time*. It is also worth remembering that Betty Hill's abduction dreams were *not* in chronological order; she had to rearrange them into "proper" order.
40. Alvin H. Lawson, "What can we learn from hypnosis of imaginary abductees," *MUFON Symposium Proceedings 1977*, 107–129. Abductions were not the first time hypnosis was used to prove a pseudoscientific belief. In early 1956, the book *The Search For Bridey Murphy* was published. In it, a Pueblo, Colorado, housewife "remembered" under hypnosis her previous life as a 19th century Irish girl. This sparked a brief-lived reincarnation fad. In June 1956, the *Chicago American* newspaper investigated and discovered that the story was based on fragments of her own childhood, a long-standing interest in Ireland, and stories told her by a neighbor—Bridie Murphy. The implications are obvious: as with "Bridey Murphy," the abductees' stories are a mixture of their own life histories, beliefs, the effects of being under hypnosis, and the prompting of the abductionist.
41. Kagan and Summers, *Mute Evidence*, 314–317. With the exception of Dr. Sprinkle, none of the other abductionists have any formal training in psychology—Hopkins is an artist and Harder is an engineering professor. (The hypnotic sessions for the Lawson study were conducted by a psychologist.) This lack of training is obvious—in several accounts by abductees, they describe the aliens as holding long rods with rounded tips. The implants are described as being a small ball on the tip of a long rod. The abductionists point to these multiple descriptions as being a consistent factor, rather than obvious phallic symbols. More seriously, the lack of psychological training means there is a risk

an abductee with a psychological problem might have his condition made worse by the abductionist's mishandling.

42. Hendry, *The UFO Handbook*, 132–145, 149–159, 166–180.

Chapter 16

1. *The Tampa Tribune*, 16 October 1974. Soon after Carr made his claims, the Air Force gave the press a tour of the two buildings numbered "18" at Wright-Patterson. One was a propulsion laboratory, the other was used for ground maintenance equipment. It was noted that some elements of Carr's story were similar to a 1968 novel called *The Fortec Conspiracy* written by R. N. Garvin and E. G. Addeo. Both Carr and the novel said the bodies were kept on ice at "Hangar 18" at Wright-Patterson AFB.

2. "U.S. Air Force hiding bodies of 12 men from outer space," *The National Tattler*, 5 January 1975.

3. Jerome Clark, "UFO crashes, part 2," *Fate*, February 1988, 93–97.

4. *Dayton Journal Herald*, 31 July 1978.

5. Gordon Creighton, "Close encounters of an unthinkable and inadmissible kind," *Flying Saucer Review*, July/August 1979, 11, 12.

6. Leonard H. Stringfield, "Retrievals of the third kind, part 1," *Flying Saucer Review*, July/August 1979, 13–20. An objection (made by both believers and skeptics) to the crashed saucer stories is the problem in moving the saucer to Wright-Patterson AFB. In the late 1940s–early 1950s, there was no transport plane or helicopter able to carry an object 15 feet (much less 90 feet) in diameter. There are a few vague descriptions of the saucers being loaded on trucks. Moving the UFO in one piece (either horizontal or tipped up on end) would be like moving a house across the country.

7. Leonard H. Stringfield, "Retrievals of the third kind, part 2," *Flying Saucer Review*, September/October 1979, 11, 12.

8. Leonard H. Stringfield, "Retrievals of the third kind, part 1," 15, 16.

9. *Saucer Steer* 27, no. 9 (1 October 1980): 2.

10. *Saucer Rear* 27, no. 10 (25 October 1980): 5, 6.

11. *Saucer Jeer* 28, no. 4 (5 April 1981): 4.

12. *Saucer Leer* 28, no. 5 (30 April 1981): 2. Other flaws in the "Tomato Man" story were a mention of the DEW Line (a network of radar stations in Canada that was not operational until mid-1957) and five people and their equipment fitting in an L-19 light aircraft. The L-19 was similar to a Piper Cub and was only able to hold two people. The prototype L-19 did not fly until December 1949—more than a year after the "crash." Many UFOlogists doubted the photo from the start, suspecting it was of a monkey killed in a V-2 flight from White Sands.

13. *Saucer Ghoul* 27, no. 1 (1 January 1980): 3.

14. Charles Berlitz and William L. Moore, *The Roswell Incident* (New York: Berkley Books, 1988), 23–26, 37, 59–86, 99, 100.

15. *Carlsbad Daily Current-Argus*, 9 July 1947, 2.

16. *Skeptics UFO Newsletter*, May 1991, 1–3. Believers in the Roswell incident have claimed that Brazel was coerced into making this statement and that he was locked up for a time afterward. Phil Klass noted, however, that the Brazel interview was given at about the same time that Ramey was displaying the debris in his office. It would have been difficult for him to find debris which matched the description that Brazel was giving several hundred miles away.

17. Joe Kirk Thomas, "Analyzing the Roswell debris," *MUFON UFO Journal*, January 1991, 9–11.

18. Berlitz and Moore, *The Roswell Incident*, 35–37.

19. *Just Cause*, March 1989, 4.

20. Teletype, FBI Dallas to Director and SAC [Special Agent in Charge] Cincinnati, July 8, 1947, Curtis Peebles UFO Files. Believers have made much of the phrase "telephonic conversation between their office and Wright Field had not borne out this belief." However, the teletype message was sent at 6:17 P.M. on July 8. Wright Field had not yet seen the debris as it was still at Carswell. Naturally, Wright Field could not confirm it was a balloon. Headquarters, 8th Air Force, on the other hand, *had* seen the debris. It has often been claimed that "SAC" in this message stood for Strategic Air Command. As it is an FBI message, it stood for Special Agent in Charge—the agent who runs a field office. "_____" indicates a name removed from the text.

21. Berlitz and Moore, *The Roswell Incident,* 154–156.

22. Philip J. Klass, "Crash of the crashed-saucer claim," *Skeptical Inquirer,* Spring 1986, 239.

23. *Saucer Smear* 39, no. 4 (5 May 1992): 7.

24. Berlitz and Moore, *The Roswell Incident,* chaps. 6, 7. Gerald Light, for instance, wrote a letter to Meade Layne in May 1954 claiming he had spent two days at "Muroc" (Edwards AFB's old name before 1950) and looked at five different captured UFOs. He said he went with journalist Franklin Allen of the Hearst newspapers, financier Edwin Nourse of the Brookings Institute, and Bishop James F. A. McIntyre of Los Angeles.

25. Research File, "Groom Lake (Nevada) 'Area 51' and Project 'Red Light'" (W. L. Moore Publications, compiled 1987).

26. Berlitz and Moore, *The Roswell Incident,* 156, 157. UFOlogists have skated over this denial—implying the Air Force had lied about the documents, rather than acknowledge that the reason the Air Force had no crashed saucer documents was because there were no crashed saucers.

27. Letters, *Flying Saucer Review,* November/December 1979, 29.

28. Doug Richardson, *Stealth* (New York: Orion Books, 1989), 66, 67.

29. *Saucer Rear* 27, no. 10 (25 October 1980): 6.

30. Letters, *Flying Saucer Review* 26, no. 5 (1981): 29.

31. Bill Sweetman and James Goodall, *Lockheed F-117A* (Osceola, Wis.: Motorbooks, 1990), 81, 82.

32. Larry Fawcett, Editorial, *CAUS Bulletin,* no. 5 (September 1986): 1, 2. A "Blue Beret" is a part of the standard uniform of an Air Policeman. This has been true since the early 1960s.

33. Barry Greenwood, "UFOs and Stealth: A Link?," *Just Cause,* September 1986, 1–4.

34. Letters, *Flying Saucer Review* 30, no. 5 (June 1985): iii. I feel that secret military activities have (unintentionally) caused a greater number of UFO reports than generally realized. In one example, in the early 1950s, drop tests were made of the EC-14 H-bomb. The unarmed bomb cases were covered with many multicolored high-wattage lights. The drops were made at 4:00 A.M. from a B-36 flying at 45,000 feet over the Nevada test site. Needless to say, Las Vegas underwent a flap.

35. Letters, *Flying Saucer Review,* November/December 1979, 29, 30.

36. Martin Kottmeyer, "UFOlogy as an evolving system of paranoia," *UFO* 7, no.3 (1992): 28–35.

Chapter 17

1. Jacques Vallee, *Revelations* (New York: Ballantine Books, 1991), 73.

2. William L. Moore, "Text of William L. Moore's MUFON speech, July 1, 1989," *Focus,* 30 June 1989, 5.

3. Thomas R. Adams, "Some aspects of the investigation," *Stigmata #21* (1st half 1984): 9.

4. Moore, "Text of William L. Moore's MUFON speech, July 1, 1989," 4–7.

5. Linda Moulton Howe, letter to Barry Greenwood and Larry Fawcett, 17 October 1987, *CAUS Bulletin,* December 1987, 8.

6. "The MJ-12 fiasco," *Just Cause,* September 1987, 8.

7. "Press confirmation of the Kirtland base affair," *Flying Saucer Review* 30, no. 1 (1984): 5.

8. Moore, "Text of William L. Moore's MUFON speech, July 1, 1989," 7, 8.

9. Adams, "Some aspects of the investigation," 9.

10. Vallee, *Revelations,* 74.

11. Moore, "Text of William L. Moore's MUFON speech, July 1, 1989," 7, 8.

12. AFOSI Complaint Form, "Alleged Sightings of Unidentified Aerial Lights in Restricted Test Range," 9 September 1980, Curtis Peebles UFO Files.

13. Moore, "Text of William L. Moore's MUFON speech, July 1, 1989," 13, 17, 18. The inspiration for the phrase "MJ-12" is not clear. One possibility is *MIJI Quarterly,* a classified Air Force publication. The title stands for "Meaconing, Intrusion, and Jamming Incidents." (Meaconing means "Masking Beacon," the use of a powerful radio beacon to lead aircraft astray.) Others are "KH-11," a photo reconnaissance satellite camera, "MI 5" and "MI 6," the British counterparts to the FBI and CIA, and the 5412 Committee.

14. "More on MJ-12," *Just Cause,* March 1989: 4. *Just Cause* found Moore's decision to use the MJ-12 material in a novel suspicious. The real "Deep Throat" was able to provide solid information that could be checked out and proven. It was noted, "The novel smacked only of a money making deal to cash in on what was then a poorly-developed story." The newsletter continued: "Do we have a situation where we have a fiction novel based on 'fact' which itself is based on fiction, which fiction would later be declared fact based on documents which seem to be based on fiction!!! If any reader can sort this out they are a better editor than I am!"

15. Moore, "Text of William L. Moore's MUFON speech, July 1, 1989," 9.

16. Philip J. Klass, "Did William L. Moore create a counterfeit document—the first to mention MJ-12—or did he knowingly lie to the FBI?," [White Paper], 25 June 1989, Curtis Peebles UFO Files. The FBI questioned Moore on 1 March 1989 about the (supposedly classified) Project Aquarius Document. The FBI report stated that, "Moore declared that he had never had in his possession any classified documents from any government agency." Yet, the Project Aquarius was stamped "Secret," had secret designations within the text, and would not be downgraded (i.e., reduced in classification) until 17 November 2020. The document, if real, had clearly not been properly declassified. If Moore believed it was "real," he had lied to the FBI. If he thought otherwise, yet still passed it around, he was part of a hoax as early as 1981–1982.

17. Barry Greenwood, "Notes on Peter Gersten's meeting with SA Richard Doty, 1/83," *Just Cause,* June 1988, 7.

18. Linda Moulton Howe, *An Alien Harvest* (LMH Productions, 1989), 135, 136, 145–156, 269–271. With the exception of the second crash at Roswell and "Ebe," the "briefing paper" seems to have been drawn from Stringfield's articles published in *Flying Saucer Review*—the description of the EBE's physical form is identical and both refer to the same crashes. The comments about reincarnation seem to have been drawn from the contactee myth. It seems redundant to investigate the claim that the U.S. government has secret research teams on a planet 55 light years away.

19. Timothy Good, *Above Top Secret* (New York: William Morrow & Co., 1988), 364, 365.

20. Adams, "Endangered Species: the movie that not everyone is talking about," 7.

21. E. Edwin Austin, "MDC report," *Stigmata #19* (4th quarter 1982): 14, 15.

22. Loren Coleman, "The occult, MIBs, UFOs and assassinations," *Crux* no. 2/*Stigmata #23* (1986): 1, 7–11. Crisman was the perfect suspect to create a "link" between UFOs, the occult, and the various assassination theories. His testimony was never released and he is now dead. Garrison's investigation was worthless, relying on hearsay, nonexistent "links," and spurious "unanswered questions." Most of the "suspects" were dead by the time Garrison sought indictments. The only man brought to trial, Clay Shaw, was acquitted in short order.

23. George Kalogerakis, "Coincidence? perhaps," *Spy*, July 1990, 50–60.
24. "Lite UFOlogy," *Crux* no. 2/*Stigmata #23* (1986): 3. This is the same issue which carried the conspiracy article. (_____) indicates blanked out segments in the 1986 version.
25. "The Aquarius Documents," *UFO* 7, no. 1 (1992): 8–10.
26. Forgery, Briefing Document: Operation Majestic 12, prepared for President-elect Dwight D. Eisenhower: (Eyes Only), 18 November 1952, Curtis Peebles UFO Files.
27. Forgery, Memorandum for General Twining, 14 July 1954, Curtis Peebles UFO Files. The "Cutler Memo" is generally thought to have been smuggled into the Archives. Even if one could somehow excuse the numerous inconsistencies, it only proves that something called "MJ-12" once existed. The memo said nothing about UFOs or even what MJ-12 deals with. It could equally be about the breaking of a Soviet code system or reports of a Soviet "agent-in-place." Such intelligence matters are closely held, with few details put down on paper.
28. Press Release, 29 May 1987, Curtis Peebles UFO Files.
29. Jo Ann Williamson, "Reference Report on MJ-12," National Archives, 22 July 1987.
30. Philip J. Klass, "The MJ-12 crashed-saucer documents," *Skeptical Inquirer*, Winter 1987–88, 140, 143.
31. Philip J. Klass, "The MJ-12 Hillenkoetter briefing document and William L. Moore's 'unneccessary comma'," [White Paper], 28 September 1987, Curtis Peebles UFO Files.
32. "On dating abnormalities by MJ-12 proponents," *Just Cause*, June 1990, 5–7.
33. Robert G. Todd, "Another 'smoking gun'," *Just Cause*, March 1990, 1–3. CAUS has long specialized in publication of authentic declassified documents on UFOs. As such, they have the most experience of any pro-UFO group with the particularities of government documents. They noted that the very official-looking EXECUTIVE CORRESPONDENCE was nothing more than a clear plastic cover used to transfer and file documents. They also contacted the Truman Library and learned that the Executive Order number listed in the briefing document, #092447, was bogus. The EOs issued in September and October 1947 were #9891-9896 (092447 was the date 09-24-47).
34. Curtis Peebles, "Analysis of Majestic 12 documents," (unpublished). The analysis of errors in the Majestic 12 documents is based on my experience as an aerospace historian since 1977. In that time I have looked at thousands of pages of declassified documents. These range up to Top Secret (Codeword) and go back to the late 1940s.
35. Books, *Strange Magazine* 8, (Fall 1991): 40, 41.
36. *The Central Intelligence Agency: A Photographic History* (Briarcliff Manor, N.Y.: Stein & Day, 1987), 222, 223.
37. *Houston Chronicle*, 7 June 1987.
38. *Saucer Smear* 34, no. 5 (5 July 1987): 4.
39. *Saucer Smear* 36, no. 5 (25 May 1989): 1, 8.
40. Philip J. Klass, "New evidence of MJ-12 hoax," *Skeptical Inquirer*, Winter 1990, 135–140.
41. "FBI opinion on MJ-12," *Just Cause*, March 1989, 3. The FBI also made an investigation of the MJ-12 documents. On 11 October 1988, FBI Special Agent Bill Vinikus met with CAUS director Peter Gersten. He said the FBI had determined they were not genuine classified government documents. The agent found it difficult to believe the documents had been presented to the public as real.
42. Philip J. Klass, "Moore & Shandera's 'high-level intelligence operatives'," December 18, 1988, Curtis Peebles UFO Files.
43. "UFO cover-up live!," *Just Cause*, December 1988, 5.
44. *Skeptics UFO Newsletter*, no. 7 (January 1991): 3–5.
45. Jerome Clark, "UFO crashes, part 4," *Fate*, April 1988, 100.
46. James W. Moseley, "I go to see the MUFON Symposium," *Caveat Emptor*, Fall 1989, 26.
47. Moore, "Text of William L. Moore's MUFON speech, July 1, 1989," 1–10.
48. Moseley, "I go to see the MUFON Symposium," 26.

49. *Saucer Smear* 37, no. 5 (10 July 1990): 6.

50. "Document fakery," *Just Cause,* December 1991, 4.

51. Timothy Good, *Above Top Secret: The Worldwide UFO Cover-Up* (New York: William Morrow & Co., 1988), 388–394, 397, 413. The Smith interview is believed by some to have been the starting point for the MJ-12 forgeries. The "insect-like" aliens able to withstand high-G maneuvers mentioned by Sarbacher are similar to those described by Gerald Heard in his 1951 book *Is Another World Watching?* The strong but light UFO material sounds like the debris described in *The Roswell Incident.*

52. Dennis Stancy, "Doodlebugs & little green men," *MUFON UFO Journal,* September 1985, 3, 16.

53. *The Denver Post,* 9 August 1958 and 9 October 1959.

54. Clark, "UFO crashes, part 2," 90–93. Moore suspected Newton and GeBauer got the idea for the crashed saucer story from a publicity stunt connected with the film *The Flying Saucer.* Mikel Conrad, the director, producer, and star of the film, claimed in August 1949 that the footage of the flying saucer in the film was real and had been provided by the government. Two press agents later resigned and apologized for their unwitting role in the deception. At about the same time, two Death Valley prospectors said they had seen a UFO crash in a sand dune. The two crewmen got out and ran off, with the prospectors in hot pursuit. They said they were unable to catch the aliens, and when they returned to the dune, the saucer, itself, was also gone. Newton used the two stories to develop the tale he told Scully. He had known Scully since 1944, and used him to gain access to Hollywood stars. (Scully bought Conrad's story.) That "witnesses" should come forward to "describe" the Aztec crash, when it can be be shown the whole story was a hoax, is a point against other UFO crash stories. Moore blamed "disinformation" for the Aztec stories—another example of how useful the concept can be.

55. Kevin D. Randle and Donald R. Schmitt, *UFO Crash At Roswell* (New York: Avon Books, 1991).

56. *Skeptics UFO Newsletter #11* (September 1991): 1, 2.

57. *Skeptics UFO Newsletter #12* (November 1991): 3, 4.

58. Frank Kuznik, "Aliens in the basement," *Air & Space,* August/September 1992, 34–39.

59. William B. Scott, "Black projects must balance cost, time savings with public oversight," *Aviation Week & Space Technology,* 18 December 1989, 42, 43.

60. William B. Scott, "Scientists' and engineers' dreams taking to skies as 'black' aircraft," *Aviation Week & Space Technology,* 24 December 1990, 41, 42.

61. Industry Observer, *Aviation Week & Space Technology,* 20 July 1992, 13. "Impulse engine?"

62. *Los Angeles Times,* 17 April 1992, B-1, B-8.

63. Janice Castro, Grapevine, *Time,* 25 May 1992, 15. It has also been claimed for several years that the B-2 bomber is actually powered by an engine removed from a crashed saucer. Ironically, the 20 B-2s are to be assigned to the 509th Bomb Wing, once based at Roswell AAF.

64. "High Government Official," interview with author. This individual also stated that the stories had come from UFO believers. This was confirmed by a private individual who has long researched black aircraft projects.

65. John Lear, "The grand deception: how the gray EBE's tricked MJ-12 into an agreement," *CUFORN Bulletin,* March–April 1989, 2–8.

66. "Lear briefed by Area 51 source," *CUFORN Bulletin,* March–April 1989, 12.

67. "An interview with John Lear—part two," *CUFORN Bulletin,* May–June 1988, 9.

68. Grant R. Cameron, T. Scott Crain, and Chris Rutkowski, "In the land of dreams," *International UFO Reporter,* September/October 1990, 5–7.

69. Don Ecker, "The saucers and the scientist," *UFO* 5, no. 6 (1990): 17.

70. Cameron, Crain, and Rutkowski, "In the land of dreams," 5, 8.

71. Milton William Cooper and John Allen Lear, "Indictment," (1988), Curtis Peebles UFO Files.
72. Milton William Cooper, "The Secret Government: The Origin, Identity, and Purpose of MJ-12," (23 May 1989), Curtis Peebles UFO Files.
73. Book Reviews, *International UFO Reporter,* May/June 1991, 19.
74. Vallee, *Revelations,* 52–58.
75. Vicki Cooper, "The UFO fascists," *UFO* 7, no. 4 (1992): 27–29.
76. Paul W. Blackstock, *Agents of Deception* (Chicago: Quadrangle Books, 1966), chap. 3.
77. *Saucer Smear* 38, no. 10 (1 December 1991): 8.
78. Vallee, *Revelations,* 70. Such "End Days" ideas are a common part of Ultra-Right ideology, along with "Jewish-Communist" conspiracy theories. Historically, UFO believers have been center-right politically. Cooper's "Project Joshua" sounds like the weapon in the film *Earth vs. the Flying Saucers.* "Excalibur" was the code name for an X-ray laser undertaken as part of SDI.
79. Colin Brown, "'The Octopus' revisted," *UFO* 7, no. 2 (1992): 12, 13.
80. Map, *Nevada Aerial Research Group Newsletter,* September 1989, 14.
81. Bill Hamilton, "Aliens in dreamland," *UFO Universe,* July 1990, 11.

Chapter 18

1. Gerry Wills, "The power of the savior," *Time,* 22 June 1992, 41, 42.
2. Matthew Cooper and Greg Ferguson, "The return of the paranoid style in American politics," *U.S. News & World Report,* 12 March 1990, 30, 31.
3. Ruppelt, *Report on Unidentified Flying Objects,* 22.
4. Chuck Hansen, *U.S. Nuclear Weapons: The Secret History* (New York: Orion Books, 1988), 145–148.
5. James Norris Gibson, *The History of the U.S. Nuclear Arsenal* (Greenwich, Conn.: Brompton Books, 1989), 86, 87.
6. Lamphere and Shachtman, *The FBI-KGB War.*
7. Curtis Peebles, *The Moby Dick Project* (Washington: Smithsonian Institution Press, 1991).
8. Chris Pocock, *Dragon Lady* (Shrewsbury, England: Airlife, 1989).
9. Paul F. Crickmore, *Lockheed SR-71 Blackbird* (Osceola, Wis.: Motorbooks, 1986).
10. Curtis Peebles, *Guardians* (Novato, Calif.: Presidio Press, 1987).
11. Philip J. Klass, "The 'Top Secret UFO papers' NSA won't release," *Skeptical Inquirer,* Fall 1989, 65–68. Deuley endorsed withholding the documents, saying the damage to intelligence sources and methods "far outweigh the value of the information under question." Given the NSA's mission of intercepting and decoding foreign communications, it is possible to make guesses about the nature of the withheld documents. A decoded Soviet message from KGB headquarters to the Washington embassy, ordering an investigation of Blue Book, to give one hypothetical example, would tell nothing about the existence of UFOs, but would reveal that all messages sent in that code system were compromised. This would negate the intelligence advantage the U.S. gained from breaking the code system.
12. Billig, *Flying Saucers: Magic in the Skies.*
13. *San Diego Tribune,* September 5, 1991, E-4.
14. Scott Minerbrook, "The politics of cartography," *U.S. News & World Report,* 15 April 1991, 60.
15. James E. Oberg, "Sakhalin: sense and nonsense," *Defence Attaché,* January/February 1985, 37–47. The academics betrayed a stunning lack of technical knowledge. Several of the spy plane stories required the Earth to be flat.
16. John Leo, "A fringe history of the world," *U.S. News & World Report,* 12 November 1990, 25, 26.

17. Bernard Ortiz De Montellano, "Multicultural pseudoscience," *Skeptical Inquirer,* Fall 1991, 49.

18. John Taylor, "Are you politically correct?," *New York,* 21 January 1991, 38–40. One of the Challenger's crew was black, another was Hawaiian, and two were women.

19. *San Diego Union-Tribune,* 16 March 1992, B-1.

20. *Christian Science Monitor,* 6 September 1988, 6.

21. *San Diego Tribune* 26 May 1989, A-28.

22. *Los Angeles Times,* 17 September 1990, A-1.

23. "AIDS related developments," *Stigmata #24* (Spring 1989): 9–11.

24. B. W. L., "AIDS . . . and the UFO connection: a possible plan for genocide?," *Flying Saucer Review* 34, no. 1 (March quarter 1989): 6, 12–14.

25. *San Diego Union-Tribune,* 31 May 1992, B-1.

26. Vicki Cooper, "1992 predictions," *UFO* 7, no. 1 (1992): 25–29.

27. Don Ecker, "Hatonn's world—part I," *UFO* 7, no. 4 (1992): 30, 31.

28. Robert Sheaffer, "Psychic vibrations," *Skeptical Inquirer,* Summer 1990, 360, 361. Historically, extremist groups have often shown a mystic streak. They have a leader possessed by a vision of a messianic mission to transform both society and the nature of man.

29. Kottmeyer, "UFOlogy as an evolving system of paranoia," 28–35.

Index